HACKER, HOAXER, WHISTLEBLOWER, SPY

HACKER, HOAXER, WHISTLEBLOWER, SPY

THE MANY FACES OF ANONYMOUS

Gabriella Coleman

VERSO
London · New York

First published by Verso 2014
© Gabriella Coleman 2014

⊛ creative commons

The moral rights of the author have been asserted

1 3 5 7 9 10 8 6 4 2

Verso
UK: 6 Meard Street, London W1F 0EG
US: 20 Jay Street, Suite 1010, Brooklyn, NY 11201
www.versobooks.com

Verso is the imprint of New Left Books
430 5690
ISBN-13: 978-1-78168-583-9
eISBN-13: 978-1-78168-584-6 (US)
eISBN-13: 978-1-78168-689-8 (UK)

British Library Cataloguing in Publication Data
A catalogue record for this book is available from the British library

Library of Congress Cataloging-in-Publication Data
A catalog record for this book is available from the library of congress

Typeset in Sabon by MJ & N Gavan, Truro, Cornwall
Printed in the US by Maple Press
Printed and bound in the UK by CPI Group Ltd, Croydon, CR0 4YY

I dedicate this book to the legions behind Anonymous—
those who have donned the mask in the past,
those who still dare to take a stand today, and
those who will surely rise again in the future.

Contents

Introduction: "And Now You Have Got Our Attention"   1

1. On Trolls, Tricksters, and the Lulz   19
2. Project Chanology—I Came for the Lulz but
   Stayed for the Outrage   53
3. Weapons of the Geek   81
4. The Shot Heard Round the World   113
5. Anonymous Everywhere   143
6. "Moralfaggotry" Everywhere   177
7. Revenge of the Lulz   203
8. LulzSec   237
9. AntiSec   277
10. The Desire of a Secret Is to Be Told   317
11. The Sabutage   337
Conclusion: Daybreak   377

Acknowledgements   401
A Note on Sources   409
Notes   411
Index   433

Introduction: "And Now, You Have Got Our Attention"

On July 29, 2007, an entity calling itself Anonymous—unknown, at the time, to all except the most erudite Internet denizens—uploaded a video to YouTube. A metallic, digital tone thrums as a headless suited man appears over a blank background. A male voice begins to speak through the interference: "Dear Fox News," it intones.[1] The news organization had recently devoted a segment entirely to a group they described as "the Internet Hate Machine"—a title the collective would subsequently adopt as a badge of honor.

But for a collective that revels in trickery and guile, to simply laugh and dismiss such an exposé would be to miss a great opportunity. And so, the disturbingly ponderous, down-pitched voice of Anonymous continues: "The name and nature of Anonymous has been ravaged, as if it were a whore in a back alley, and then placed on display for the public eye to behold. Allow me to say quite simply: you completely missed the point of who and what we are ... We are everyone and we are no one ... We are the face of chaos and the harbingers of judgment. We laugh at the face of tragedy. We mock those in pain. We ruin the lives of others simply because we can ... A man takes out his aggression on a cat, we laugh. Hundreds die in a plane crash, we laugh. We are the embodiment of humanity with no remorse, no caring, no love, and no sense of morality."

The video ends, "YOU ... HAVE NOW GOT ... *OUR* ATTENTION."

They certainly got mine—soon after the video's publication, I became entangled in a multi-year research project on the collective that I have only now just twisted my way out of (this book monumentalizes that struggle). The video was meant to satirize Fox News's hyperbolic characterization of Anonymous as the ultimate purveyors of Internet pranking and trolling, "hackers on steroids," as Fox had called them. And yet, the creepy sentiments and chilling style captured the trolls' terrifying side perfectly; instead of overturning Fox News's ridiculously one-dimensional portrayal, the video seemingly confirmed it to the utmost—though only, of course, to those not in on the joke.

This double meaning captures the dark humor of Anonymous (the lulz, they call it) in a nutshell. The lulz—a deviant style of humor and a quasi-mystical state of being—has, as we will see, evolved with Anonymous from the beginning. And there was a time when spreading lulzy mayhem was all Anonymous seemed interested in. But not long after this parodic and bombastic video, Anons could be found at the heart of hundreds of political "ops"—becoming integral, even, to some of the most compelling political struggles of our age. In solidarity with Tunisian protesters, Anonymous hacked the Tunisian government's websites in January 2011; months later, Spain's *indignados* beamed the collective's signature Guy Fawkes mask onto a building in the Puerta del Sol; and Anons disseminated some of the first calls to occupy Wall Street.

By then the collective had established itself as a social, political force with a series of ops that remain some of its most memorable. In 2008, adherents to a new vision for Anonymous took Scientology to task after the litigious organization attempted to censor a famous video of Tom Cruise. Germinated for the sake of the lulz, Anons both realized their power to impact global struggles and the pleasure such engagements could provide. Anonymous became even more widely known two years later in December 2010, the result of "Operation Avenge Assange." Initiated by AnonOps, one of the collective's more militant and prolific nodes, Anons engaged in digital direct action by launching a distributed denial of service (DDoS) campaign. This tactic, which disrupts access to webpages by flooding them with tidal waves of requests, was directed against financial institutions that had refused to process donations to WikiLeaks, including PayPal and MasterCard. With each operation Anonymous was further emboldened.

And yet, even after Anonymous drifted away from ungovernable trolling pandemonium to engage in the global political sphere, whenever people scrutinized its activist interventions—whether in a street protest or a high-profile computer intrusion—a question always seemed to loom: are Anonymous and its adherents principled dissidents? Or are they simply kids screwing around on the Internet as lulz-drunk trolls?

This confusion is eminently understandable. Beyond a foundational commitment to the maintenance of anonymity and a broad dedication to the free flow of information, Anonymous has no consistent philosophy or political program. While increasingly recognized for its digital dissent and direct action, Anonymous has never displayed a predictable trajectory. Given that Anonymous's ancestry lies in the sometimes humorous, frequently offensive, and at times deeply invasive world of Internet trolling—the core logic of which seems, at least at first glance, to be inhospitable to the cultivation of activist sensibilities and politicized endeavors—it is remarkable that the name Anonymous became a banner seized by political activists in the first place.

From Trolling to the Misfits of Activism

Today the broad deployment of both Anonymous's Guy Fawkes mask and the ideas it came to stand for among demonstrators occupying Tahrir Square and Polish politicians sitting in parliamentary chambers seem absurd when we consider the collective's origins. Before 2008, the moniker Anonymous was used almost exclusively for what one Anon describes as "Internet motherfuckery." Anonymous, birthed in the pits of 4chan's random bulletin board /b/ (often regarded as the "asshole of the Internet"), was a name synonymous with trolling: an activity that seeks to ruin the reputations of individuals and organizations and reveal embarrassing and personal information. Trolls try to upset people by spreading grisly or disturbing content, igniting arguments, or engendering general bedlam. The chaos of feuding and flaming can be catalyzed by inhabiting identities, beliefs, and values solely for their mischievous potential; by invading online forums with spam; or by ordering hundreds of pizzas, taxis, and even SWAT teams to a target's residence. Whatever the technique, trolls like to say they do what they do for the lulz—a spirited but often malevolent brand of humor etymologically derived from lol.

One early Anonymous trolling raid—legendary to this day—set its sights on a virtual platform, called Habbo Hotel, whose tag line enthusiastically beckons, "Make friends, join the fun, get noticed!" A Finnish environment geared toward teenagers, it encourages visitors to create cutesy, Lego-style avatars who can socialize together in the hotel and customize guest rooms with "furni." On July 6, 2006, Anonymous logged onto the site in droves—presenting themselves, all, as black men in gray suits with prominent afros. By navigating just so, they were able to collectively assemble into human swastikas and picket lines, both of which prevented regular Habbo members (children, mostly) from entering the hotel's pool. Anyone attempting to understand the reasons for these actions was informed by the mustachioed characters that the pool was closed "due to fail and AIDS."

A couple of year's after the first Habbo Raids, and a mere six months after they had been labeled the "Internet Hate Machine," certain Anons began using the name and some associated iconography—headless men in black suits, in particular—to coordinate political protests. This surprising metamorphosis sprouted from what many consider to be one of Anonymous's most legendary trolling provocations: targeting the Church of Scientology. "In a previously unseen way," noted one participant in the raids, "the greater Anon community united to unleash a hearty load of *fuck you* upon Scientology's entire cult empire."[2] Impelled by the lulz—by the desire to release an avalanche of hilarious and terrifying mischief—thousands boarded the troll train, christened "Project Chanology," to launch DDoS attacks on Scientology websites, order unpaid pizzas and escorts to Scientology churches across North America, fax images of nude body parts to churches, and propel a barrage of phone pranks, most notably against the Dianetics hotlines designed to offer advice regarding the "first truly workable technology of the mind."

Like most previous raids, many expected this hearty "fuck you" would run its course and then peter out after a few days of brutal and playful shenanigans. But a short video made by a small group of participants—concocted for the lulz alone—ignited a serious debate within the rank and file of Anonymous. The video "declared war" on the Church: "For the good of your followers, for the good of mankind—and for our own enjoyment—we shall proceed to expel you from the Internet and systematically dismantle the Church of Scientology in its present form."[3] This ironic declaration of war spurred individuals into debate and then catapulted them onto the streets. On February 10, 2008, over seven thousand people in 127 cities protested the Church of Scientology's human rights abuses and acts of censorship.

Anonymous thus shifted from (as one participating Anon

later explained to my class) "ultracoordinated motherfuckery" to the dissemination of incriminating facts about Scientology. They also forged bonds with an older generation of dissidents already at work highlighting the Church's abuses. Trolling had given way to an earnest activist endeavor, as if Anonymous had emerged from its online sanctuary and set out to improve the world. Over the next two years, some Anonymous members would hatch unrelated activist subgroups, and many participants came to identify themselves as bona fide activists, albeit with a transgressive twist.

Many of Anonymous's actions, like creating the publicity videos that have become a vernacular institution unto themselves, are entirely legal. But a subset of tactics—notably DDoS attacks and hacks—are illegal: criminal offenses under all circumstances, at least in the United States. Government officials have thus made various attempts to slot a class of its activities under the umbrella term of "cyberwarfare," and prosecute its participants accordingly. The epitome of this maneuver occurred on February 21, 2012, when the *Wall Street Journal* reported that General Keith Alexander, then director of the United States National Security Agency (NSA), had briefed officials at the White House in secret meetings. He claimed Anonymous "could have the ability within the next year or two to bring about a limited power outage through a cyberattack."[4]

As the *Wall Street Journal* article ricocheted across social media platforms, questions were raised. Did this claim strike anyone as believable? Just what exactly constituted the "ability" to bring about a power outage? What would be an appropriate response if this were true? It is unlikely that we will ever find out whether the NSA's assessment was based on credible intelligence or whether it was meant simply to smear and discredit Anonymous. Either way, General Alexander's claim succeeded, at least momentarily, in portraying Anonymous as a menace akin to Islamic jihadists and the communist threat of yesteryear.

Ultimately, it proved unconvincing. Anonymous, for all its varied tactics—both legal and illegal, online and offline—has never been known to publicly call for such an attack. And there is no evidence to suggest that it would so much as entertain the idea. Endangering human lives has never been a topic of discussion among members, even during the most helter-skelter of chat room and message board conversations. Subsequent news reports quoted activists and security experts who dismissed the NSA's claims as "fear-mongering."[5]

Even though a tactic like this would be entirely out of character for Anonymous, the group's relationship with the court of public opinion remains ambivalent. Anonymous's methods are at times subversive, often rancorous, usually unpredictable, and frequently disdainful of etiquette or the law. Take "doxing": the leaking of private information—such as Social Security numbers, home addresses, or personal photos—resides in a legal gray zone because some of the information released can be found on publicly accessible websites.

A single Anonymous operation might integrate all three modes—legal, illegal, and legally gray tactics—and if there is an opportunity to infuse an operation with the lulz as well, someone will. A prime example is Operation BART from August 2011. Anonymous was spurred into action when San Francisco Bay Area Rapid Transit (BART) officials sought to disable mobile phone reception on station platforms to thwart a planned anti–police brutality march. Local activists had called for the demonstration to protest the fatal shooting of Charles Hill, an unarmed passenger. Incensed by transportation authorities' meddling in democratic expression, Anonymous helped organize a series of street demonstrations soon after.

A couple of individuals hacked into BART's computers and released customer data in order to garner media attention. Someone also found a racy, semi-nude photo of BART's official spokesperson, Linton Johnson, on his personal website. The photo was republished on the "bartlulz" website along with this brazen rationalization: "if you are going to be a dick to the public, then I'm sure you don't mind showing your dick to the public." Sometimes coy and playful, sometimes serious and inspiring, often all at once (as OpBART demonstrated so well), even to this day, these activist tricksters are still animated by a collective will toward mischief—toward the lulz.

"I did it for the lulz"

Does Anonymous's ongoing embrace of lulzy mischief mean that researching them was a merry and lighthearted affair, the essence of an anthropological joyride? Looking for insights into Anonymous's surprising metamorphosis from trolling misfits to the misfits of activism, I began an anthropological study of the group in 2008. At first my research was low key, straightforward, and lighthearted. I attended protests and followed discussions on web forums and on Internet Relay Chat (IRC)—one of the most important communication applications for Anonymous (and many other geeks and hackers).

In 2011, as Anonymous grew more tentacles and activists initiated dozens of political operations, this side project became my life. For over two years I was constantly jacked in, online for a minimum of five hours a day, struggling to keep abreast of all the simultaneous operations, some of them hidden from my view due to their clandestine nature. Researching Anonymous felt like following a thread through a dark and twisty path strewn with rumors, lies, secrets, and the ghoulish reality of spies and informants. The journey has been marked by soaring thrills, disappointing dead ends, and moral pretzels—wherein seemingly intractable ethical conundrums coexist easily with clear-cut examples of inspirational risk and sacrifice. Beyond the consequences of its actions, Anonymous's organizational structure itself felt similarly convoluted and bewildering. Over time, it became clear: Anonymous was not simply a maze, with a structure and escape route revealed in a view from above; Anonymous was a far more complicated and tangled warren. This was no static labyrinth, like the one built by Daedalus to house the Minotaur. It was an infinite machine operating a tight recursive loop wherein mazes generated maze-generating mazes.

In spite of the difficulties I faced when traversing this maze, I gradually became acquainted with Anonymous, and it with me, sometimes on a personal level. As an anthropologist does, I watched, listened, interviewed, debated, questioned, and prodded. At times I even participated, so long as my involvement was legal. My tasks were many: editing manifestos, teaching reporters how to find Anonymous, and correcting misinformation.

My level of engagement was limited by self-imposed and external barriers. The anthropological imperative requires a certain degree of distance, while at the same time compelling one to delve deep. The trick is to integrate and go beyond simply relying on participants' explanations of events. I was sympathetic to many of Anonymous's tactics and causes, but not all of them. Moral quandaries of various sorts created critical distance. Due to the illegal nature of some activities, certain areas were off limits. This was better for Anonymous, and for me. Later, after arrests and convictions, I was able to learn retrospectively about hidden acts.

With the ascendancy of militant tactics among a new group of Anons, the stakes had changed by the summer of 2011. Anonymous began targeting Fortune 500 corporations and military defense contractors. Mercenary hackers doxed Anons, revealing their identities to law enforcement by publishing their legal names, personal photos, and addresses. Anons started to leak sensitive, classified, or humiliating information. At this juncture, the FBI got involved. And no matter how much Anonymous injected lulz into an op, humor could not stop the spread of a gut-wrenching unease among participants and observers of the group. So even if researching Anonymous

was often a thrill, and certainly always an adventure, it ultimately made me paranoid.

This was a deep paranoia that hovered over everything like
a barometric disturbance before a tornado. It felt justified,
but that might be just the paranoia talking. While researching
Anonymous, it was imperative that I keep law enforcement
away from me, and from my data. Crossing a border meant
days of preparation to secure my notes and put together a
safe travel computer. Questioning by authorities always felt
imminent; it wasn't a question of *if* the G-men would visit,
but *when*. Vigilance was necessary to protect my sources. I
reminded Anonymous participants that they needed to be
careful what they told me. I never sat in on their private
channels as they were planning illegal operations.

As for the government, I was hiding in plain sight. By no
means was I anonymous. That was the irony: I gave talks
about Anonymous, I was interviewed by over 150 reporters,
and I routinely discussed Anonymous on radio and television.
As a scholar teaching at a prominent university, I was easy
to find. On occasion, high-level corporate executives from
some of the world's most powerful companies even reached
out, calling me personally in the hope that I could offer some
nugget of insight about an entity many of them had grown
to fear.

A recurring nightmare haunted me for years. Intelligence
agents hammered on my door. I would jolt upright in bed, my
heart pounding: "They're here." It was just like *Poltergeist*,
except the bed wasn't shaking and the demonic possession left
as soon as I sat up.

One day in 2012, I washed away the remaining threads of
my turbulent slumber with a strong cup of coffee, putting the
nightmare in the background for another day. With my brain
fully booted, I realized that today, April 19, the roles would
be reversed: today I would be knocking on the doors of the
Canadian Security Intelligence Service (CSIS), the Canadian

equivalent of the CIA. With a mixture of trepidation, ambivalence, and especially curiosity, I had accepted CSIS's invitation to give a lecture about Anonymous. I went to discover what CSIS thought about Anonymous—did they view them as a terrorist threat, a band of rambunctious/rabid activists, or something else entirely? My secret agenda was to test their reaction to the lulz: could an agency that manages matters of national security bring itself to see the humor in Anonymous? To find out, I concocted a simple lulz litmus test.

CSIS is headquartered in the outskirts of Canada's capital, Ottawa, in a large anodyne cream-colored building with teal accents. I arrived alone by taxi, awash in thoughts of Orwell, *Brazil*, Huxley, Kafka, and Bush/Obama's total surveillance. I asked myself, *What am I doing here? What lies in the shadows behind the walls of Canada's spy agency? Could it be as bad as I am imagining? Do they have high-tech surveillance rooms like in* Minority Report? *Do they conduct psychological experiments in sterile, steel-lined interrogation rooms?*

Adjusting my ill-fitting business suit, I forced myself to think that inside were boring office cubicles with people pushing paper and scheduling meetings destined for drab conference rooms with a speaker phones in the middle of their tables. Maybe there was a passive aggressive note taped to the refrigerator in the break room because someone ate all of the Tim Horton's sugary Timbits that were for the going-away party later that day. A water-stained note over the sink with the words, *Your mother doesn't work here, you will have to clean up after yourself!* It will be fine, I told myself.

To minimize my angst, I had promised myself I would offer nothing new or secret, sticking to what was already public and donating my modest honorarium to a civil liberties organization. But despite having given this same lecture dozens of times, I walked through the front door feeling more diminutive than my five-foot self. A woman with a suit greeted me. Everything felt unremarkable; there was nothing ominous in sight, just bland office plants.

I was brought to a room with a small stage. The atmosphere was tense. I couldn't discern the expression on anyone's face. I was nearly paralyzed with dread. Then, I worried that my nervousness was going to make me say something I shouldn't. These agents, after all, were exceedingly well trained in the art of information extraction; they would take advantage of any weakness or opportunity to gain an advantage. With over forty people staring at me, the atmosphere of seriousness felt like it was burning right through my suit. Nevertheless, I'd done this so many times that I was on autopilot, and it wasn't until ten minutes into my talk that I noticed my hands shaking slightly as I attempted to click the play button on my computer, in order to fire up my lulz litmus test: the famous viral video made by Anonymous that had ignited their revolutionary spirit. Every single time I had shown this clip in the past, three sentences in particular had without fail provoked laughter. Would CSIS employees lol at the lulz? In the video, as clouds move quickly over a large, indistinct, glass corporate building, a dramatic voice intones:

Anonymous has therefore decided that your organization should be destroyed. For the good of your followers, for the good of mankind and for our own enjoyment. We shall proceed to expel you from the Internet and systematically dismantle the Church of Scientology in its present form.

The room erupted in laughter. Mission accomplished; there was no better proof of the infectious spirit of the lulz than this moment. Intelligence agents were laughing at the lulzy video made by Anonymous trolls that gave birth to the "threat" they were tasked with assessing. *I will get out of here alive after all,* I silently sighed.

After my lecture, a smaller group of us relocated to a cramped and dingy conference room with no windows to eat bland sandwiches and cookies under the glare of fluorescent lights. I secretly wondered if there was a nicer conference room with skylights reserved for the political scientists or economists and other more highly esteemed guests. We sat down in the office chairs and went around the room introducing ourselves. I was still too out of sorts to remember particular roles or titles, much less names. I was certainly not taking notes or secretly recording the conversation. I suspect they were. For all I knew, I could be talking to janitors, or to employees with the highest level of security clearance. One title did stick out, though—that of the other anthropologist in the room. When introduced, he nodded and smiled at me. I, meanwhile, tried hard to keep my poker face intact. All sorts of questions sprung to mind: *Is he actually trained as an anthropologist? Where did he go to school? Who was his PhD advisor? When and why did he decide to work for the CSIS? Do they pay better than academia?* But I kept my queries to myself. I was worried he would misconstrue my curiosity as interest in working for CSIS, and I wanted to avoid any recruitment overtures.

During the course of what at first felt like a meandering conversation, it eventually became apparent why I had been invited. They wanted to know one thing: whether I thought Anonymous had set their sights on taking down the power grid. The timing was not accidental. Just a month earlier, the NSA had stated that Anonymous was an imminent threat to national security, and I suppose Canada was feeling a bit of international pressure to monitor the shadowy group.

I answered honestly. For all its legal and illegal tactics to date, I explained, Anonymous had never publicly called for such an attack. There was no evidence at the time to suggest that the group would so much as consider doing such a thing. I did not feel like I was divulging anything secret, as I had commented to the press about this very subject. In fact, I felt like I was doing Anonymous a favor.

Of course, as a busy professor I could not spend all of my time on the many channels of the various IRC networks, much less monitor every single chat room where such a conversation could take place. There were also private conversations and invite-only channels I never actually entered. "Their soci-ology is labyrinthine," I explained with deliberation, likely exhibiting my own frustrations with navigating and research-ing Anonymous. I had probably spent more hours staring at my computer and chatting with Anonymous participants than any non-Anon, with the possible exception of informants, who were forced to be online nearly full-time. I explained that I had never seen even a hint of such a plan. Indeed, every radical action, even the doxing of belligerent police officers, provoked contentious debate about its moral appropriateness. "While Anonymous is often duplicitous and devilishly con-fusing," I explained, "Anons are certainly not seeking to kill anyone. They organize at home, possibly in their underwear, typing away madly at the computer. The only 'violence' some participants engage in is likely of the virtual type, during their *World of Warcraft* video game battles that some percentage of them surely must play." To hammer my point home, I offered a bit of humor, paraphrasing one Anon who had cracked the following joke soon after the NSA claimed that Anonymous was indeed capable of targeting the grid: "That's right, we're definitely taking down the power grid. We'll know we've suc-ceeded when all the equipment we use to mount our campaign is rendered completely useless."

Postures loosened. Laughter again reverberated among the G-men (and women—this was 2012 after all). And as far as I could tell, everyone seemed genuinely relieved by my assess-ment. They could go back to focusing on more pressing matters.

The joke opened the door to further conversation con-cerning the media's central role in amplifying the power of Anonymous. One CSIS agent shared his anger at the media for making this collective of collectives more powerful than they ought to have been. I was, I have to admit, relishing the fact that the G-men and Anons, mutually opposed at one level, were nevertheless (very loosely) allied in holding an ambiva-lent attitude toward the mass media. We all agreed that the media had helped to make Anonymous what it was today.

Then the resident CSIS anthropologist, whose specialty was Middle East terrorism, made an offhand comment that shocked even me: jihadists, he explained, were impressed by the level of media attention Anonymous attained. *Did I hear that correctly*, I wondered? I just could not fathom Al Qaeda operatives watching Anonymous videos, much less grasping the nature of their culture or politics, and especially not the lulz. I imagined that jihadists would be rather repelled by Anonymous's secular, infidel, offensive practices. Laughing heartily together, we all agreed that those jihadist terrorists likely did not celebrate the lulz (or were utterly devoid of them). The conversation reminded me of something one Anon had told me during an informal online chat:

> <A>: yeah, it's that idea of humor and irreverence which is at the heart of this [Anonymous]
> <A>: it's what will stop it ever being able to be labeled terrorist

Despite the laughter, I still felt rather uncomfortable and hyper-aware of my mask of scholarly detachment. Appearing cool and composed on the outside, on the inside I was thinking to myself, *I can't believe I am joking about jihadists, Anonymous, and the lulz with CSIS!* I wanted nothing more than to leave—which I finally did at the conclusion of lunch. I was relieved to return to my hotel. I tried to push away the creeping thought that my room at the Lord Elgin Hotel in downtown Ottawa, booked by CSIS, was bugged.

Even today, I am not sure how I feel about my decision to visit CSIS; in those situations, one can divulge, quite unwillingly, important information, even when officials are not expressly seeking or asking for anything particular. Maybe there is something unethical, too, about disclosing how important the media is in amplifying Anonymous's power—a bit like drawing open a curtain to reveal that the Wizard is a little old man pulling at the levers of a machine. On the other hand, the media's power is an open secret within

Anonymous, a topic routinely discussed by the activists themselves.

In hindsight, and for better or worse, I believe some element of the trickster spirit nudged me to accept CSIS's invitation. Tricksters, like the Norse god Loki, have poor impulse control. They are driven by lust or curiosity. Intrigue propelled me to visit CSIS, despite my anxiety and reservations. I had a burning question that I needed answered: would they laugh at the lulz? So I guess, like trolls, "I did it for the lulz." Thanks to my glimpse inside Canada's spy agency, I got my answer: the lulz can be (nearly) universally appreciated. But I learned even more than that, thanks to the other anthropologist in the room. That final joke about the jihadists and the lulz taught me another lesson about Anonymous, which is important to convey as we start this adventure.

No single group or individual can claim legal ownership of the name "Anonymous," much less its icons and imagery. Naturally, this has helped Anonymous spread across the globe. It has now become the quintessential anti-brand brand, assuming various configurations and meanings, even as it has also become the popular face of unrest around the globe. Even if the name "Anonymous" is free to take—as Topiary, an Anonymous activist, put it before he was arrested, "You cannot arrest an idea"—the jihadist example is a powerful reminder that its radical openness does not mean everyone can or even wants to embrace the name or its attendant imagery. Culture has a funny way of asserting itself, even among a group of activists who seek to defy boundaries and who have erected one of the most accessible, resilient, and open domains of activism today.

Indeed, by the time I visited CSIS in 2012, Anonymous had become multitudinous, prolific, and unpredictable. Of course, since the collective is a by-product of the Internet, it is unsurprising that Anonymous rises up most forcefully and shores up most support when defending values associated with this global communication platform, like free speech. As one participant once put it, "Free speech is non-negotiable." But what they have demonstrated time and again is they are not restricted to a concern with civil liberties. Over the last five years, activists have contributed to an astonishing array of causes, from publicizing rape cases (as they did in Halifax, Canada, and Steubenville, Ohio) to assisting in the Arab and African Spring of 2011.

Various factors conspire to secure the group's flexibility. There are no agreed-upon mandates to uphold. Participants associated with Anonymous steadfastly resist institutionalization. Its reputation is difficult to sully. You don't even need to be a hacker (no, really) to participate in Anonymous operations. The group's bold, Hollywood-style aesthetics strike a familiar chord in the society of the spectacle. And when Anonymous reacts to world events, it engages in a broad range of activities, with leaking and exposing security vulnerabilities acting as two of its signal interventions.

All these elements—which also come together in different proportions and configurations—make it almost impossible to know when or why Anonymous will strike, when a new node will appear, whether a campaign will be successful, and how the group might change direction or tactics during the course of an operation. Its unpredictability may be what makes Anonymous so frightening to governments and corporations across the world.

Although devilishly hard to study, Anonymous is neither wholly random nor simply chaotic. To be Anonymous means to follow a series of related principles. Anonymous follows a spirit of humorous deviance, works though diverse technical bodies (such as IRC), is built on an anti-celebrity ethic, and intervenes politically in astoundingly rich and varied ways. This book will seek to unravel some of the complexities and paradoxes inherent to a politically engaged Anonymous— but before we turn to its activist interventions, let's take a close look at the grisly underworld of trolling from which Anonymous hatched.

CHAPTER I

On Trolls, Tricksters, and the Lulz

Prior to 2008, when Anonymous unexpectedly sprouted an activist sensibility, the brand had been used exclusively for what, in Internet parlance, is known as "trolling": the targeting of people and organizations, the desecration of reputations, and the spreading of humiliating information. Despite the fame Anonymous accrued in its mass trolling campaigns, it was certainly not the only player in the game; the trolling pantheon was then, and remains today, both large and diverse. Trolling is a multifarious activity that flourishes online and boasts a range of tight-knit associations (such as the Patriotic Nigras, Bantown, Team Roomba, Rustle League), a variety of genres (differentiated mostly by target—for example, grief-ers target gamers, RIP trolls target the families and friends of the recently deceased), and a small pantheon of famed individuals (*Violentacrez, Jameth*). Its originary point extends far before the alpha of the Internet, taking root in the vagaries of myth and oral culture. Despite this diversity, contemporary Internet trolls are united in an almost universal claiming of lulz as the causal force and desired effect of their endeavors. Our story can begin with one of the most notorious pursuants.

One day, completely out of the blue, I received a phone call from one of the most famous trolls of all time: Andrew

Auernheimer, known to most simply as "weev." He reached out to me on August 28, 2010, in a sixty-second phone message:

> Yes, Ms. Coleman. This is weev. That is W-E-E-V and you might be familiar with my work. I see that you are giving a presentation on hackers, trolls, and the politics of spectacle. And I just want say that I am *the* master of the spectacle. This is my art, ma'am. And also you have given some sort of presentation on the lulz and I was in the room when the lulz was first said. So I want to make sure that you're interpreting and representing my culture, and my people, correctly. I don't want some charlatan that is telling lies about my history and my culture. So I would like to talk with you some and understand what you are doing to make sure that you not just another bullshit academic. So hit me up, my email is gluttony@XXX.com. That is G-L-U-T-T-O-N-Y at XXX dot com. I expect a response, Ms. Coleman. It is *extremely* important.

After listening, I was so startled I actually dropped the phone. I was overcome with excitement. But also fear. I picked the phone up, rapidly punched in a seemingly endless stream of numbers, listened to the message three more times, recorded it, and promptly went home, only to spend the rest of the evening brooding. I wished he had never called.

weev's reputation obviously preceded him; despite my rudimentary research on trolls and my ongoing research on the activism of Anonymous, I had avoided him like the bubonic plague. Although trolling is often experienced and disguised as play, it is also shrouded in mystery, danger, and recklessness. weev is a past president of one of the most exclusive trolling cliques still in existence today, the offensively named Gay Nigger Association of America (GNAA). (Affiliates quiz prospective members on trivia about an obscure porn film called *Gayniggers from Outer Space*, which inspired the group's name.) Reaching out to such a revolting troll might spell trouble. Trolls are notorious for waging so-called "ruin life" campaigns, in which they spread humiliating stories (regardless of truthfulness) about a chosen target, and leak vital information like addresses and Social Security numbers. The effect is akin to being cursed, branded, and stigmatized all at once. The psychological effects can be terrifyingly long lasting.[1]

But since I also ran a risk by ignoring his request—he did, after all, flag it as extremely important—I sent him an email a few days later. And, since I had already taken the plunge, I also figured it might make sense to acquaint myself with another genre of trolling. In contrast to weev's boastful, elitist, self-aggrandizing style, Anonymous had historically demonstrated a far more self-effacing and populist mode of trolling. Like two sides of a coin, both belonged to the same "tribe" while also countering one another. For about two minutes I even entertained, with faint excitement, the prospect of detailing a troll typology. Just as my anthropological ancestors once categorized tribes, skulls, and axes, perhaps I could do the same with trolls and their horrible exploits, trollishly playing, all the while, with my discipline's historical penchant for irrelevant and sometimes racist categorization. Quickly the excitement faded as I contemplated the ruinous reality this could bring down upon me if I got on the wrong side of these notorious trolls; I remembered that I had already decided to focus on the activism of Anonymous and not its trolling heyday for a very good reason. In the end, I hoped weev would ignore the email from me sitting in his inbox.

But, when he emailed me back, I realized there was nothing to do but commit. We finally connected via Skype chat. His handle was "dirk diggler," after the porn star protagonist of the 1997 film *Boogie Nights*. Later, when we switched to IRC, he used "weev":

<dirk diggler>: how are you?
<biella>: good and you?

<dirk diggler>: coming down off of some vile substance
<biella>: you are up early
<dirk diggler>: methylenedioxypyrovalorone i think it was called
<dirk diggler>: its late, technically
<dirk diggler>: as i havent slept
<biella>: i woke up at 3 am but that is not all that usual for me
<dirk diggler>: i am working on my latest shitstorm right now
<dirk diggler>: disruptive technological developments are gr8
<biella>: you are pretty adept at that as well
<dirk diggler>: yes i am switching from the mdpv to the coffee
<dirk diggler>: i am hoping this will smooth the downward spiral long
enough for me to ship this motherfucker live today
<biella>: no chance you will be in nyc in the near future, is there?
<dirk diggler>: probably not
<dirk diggler>: its a vile city
<biella>: haha, really?
<dirk diggler>: disgusting place
<biella>: how come?
<dirk diggler>: the only decent people in NYC are the black israelites
<dirk diggler>: nyc is a city founded on the repulsive order of the
financiers

His denunciation of "the repulsive order of the financiers" had
the ring of truth, given the recent financial mess their recklessness had engendered, so I found myself, only minutes into
my first bona fide conversation with a world famous troll, in
agreement with him:

<biella>: that is true
<dirk diggler>: it is a sinful and decadent place
<biella>: there are less and less spaces for the non-rich
<dirk diggler>: and wherever immoral people are in control, i find that
everyone tries to emulate them
<biella>: Detroit is like the only city were there is possibility imho (big
city)
<dirk diggler>: nah slab city has the best potential in all of the USA

<dirk diggler>: part of god's war is going on right there right now
<biella>: never been

It is true: I had not spent time in Slab City. It was, in fact, the first time I had even heard about it. And so, as we chatted, I was also googling "Slab City," which actually exists and is a fascinating Wild West campground/squatter haven in Colorado. I soon came to learn that even if weev often lies, he also often speaks the truth, and his knowledge of the strange, fantastical, and shocking is encyclopedic—he is a natural ethnographer of the most extreme and vile forms of human esoterica.

By dedicating much of his teenage and early adult years to hacking and trolling—and the consumption of large quantities of drugs, if he is to be believed—weev had amassed a vast catalog of technical and human exploits. His most famous coup, which won him a three-and-a-half-year jail sentence, was directed at AT&T, a beloved target among hackers because of its cozy information-sharing practices with the US government. (AT&T's well-known activities in room 641A, a telecommunication interception facility operated by the NSA, now seem quaint given the news that most major telecommunications providers and Internet companies provide the US government generous access to customer data.) weev targeted AT&T with Goatse Security, the name given to GNAA's impromptu security group. They discovered in June 2010 that the giant American telco had done something stupid and irresponsible: AT&T's iPad customer data was posted on the Internet unprotected. Typically, a company with good security practices will encrypt things like customer names, email addresses, and the unique ID numbers associated with these iPads. But AT&T had not, at least in this instance, encrypt anything.

While they didn't exactly leave the customer data sitting on a doorstep with a sign saying "Come and Get It," the data was still unusually easy to access. Indeed, Goatse Security figured out an easy way to "slurp" the data using a script (a short, easy-to-use computer program), which was written by GNAA/Goatse member Daniel Spitler, aka "JacksonBrown." The gray hat security crew called it, with uncanny precision, the "iPad 3G Account Slurper" and used it to harvest the data of 140,000 subscribers. The opportunity to expose shoddy security of this magnitude is irresistible to any hacker—even one like weev who, as he told me over dinner when we finally met in person, is not even that talented of a technologist (or, perhaps more likely, he is just too lazy to do the grunt work since he certainly grasps many of the finer technical points pertaining to security).

Whatever the case, Spitler wrote the script itself and has since pleaded guilty in court. And yet weev was also convicted in November 2012 for "hacking" AT&T's system: a violation of the Computer Fraud and Abuse Act (CFAA). But the fact remains: since there was no security to speak of, there was nothing, technically, to "hack." Daniel Spitler's script did not compromise an otherwise secure system, and weev—who contributed minor improvements to the script—mostly acted as the publicist. He offered the vulnerability to news outlets for free. He was interested in exposing AT&T's shocking lack of security in the public interest and boosting his public profile. The CFAA, it must be said, is a decidedly blunt legal instrument—so broad that it affords prosecutors tremendous power in any legal proceeding that relates, in virtually any way, to the vague notion of "unauthorized computer access." The activities need not be hacking at all. Some courts have interpreted "unauthorized access" to mean computer use that simply violates the terms of service or other rules posed by the computer's owner.[2]

After his CFAA conviction, weev's case attracted a trio of topnotch lawyers: Orin Kerr, Marcia Hofmann, and Tor Ekeland. They appealed his case, seeking to overturn what they, along with many security professionals, deemed a dangerous precedent capable of chilling vital future security research; the security industry relies on hackers and research-ers discovering vulnerabilities, using the same methods as criminal hackers, in order to expose weakness and strengthen infrastructure for both private and public good. Finally, in April 2014—and only after he had served roughly twelve months of a forty-one-month sentence—his case was vacated. But not due to the the CFAA portion of the appeal—instead due to the question of venue. The court determined that New Jersey, where the original case was tried, was not the state where the offense was committed. Tor Ekeland explained the importance of this legal ruling to the *Guardian*: "If the court had ruled the other way, you would have had universal venue in … computer fraud and abuse cases, and that would have had huge implications for the Internet and computer law."[3] Still, although weev's supporters were thrilled that he was now free and pleased that questions of venue had been clarified, many were disappointed that the proceedings left the broader CFAA issue untouched—the dangerous precedent remained.

By taking this information to the media, weev demonstrated an intent beyond mere trolling. Any self-respecting hacker will cry foul in the face of terrible security; taking it to the press—which will generate a huge fuss about it—can be a responsible thing to do. Of course, to hear weev tell the story, it was clear that he also did it for the lulz. He would giggle whenever Goatse Security was mentioned in news reports about the incident. He imagined millions of people Googling the strange name of the security group, and then recoiling in horror at the sight of a vile "anal supernova" beaming off their screen.[4] Goatse is a notoriously grotesque Internet image of a man hunched over and pulling apart his butt cheeks wider than you might think is humanly possible. Those who view it are forever unable to unsee what they have just seen—unable to forget even the smallest detail, their minds seared by the image as if the gaping maw, adorned with a ring, were a red-hot cattle brand. The immaturity of the joke would escalate weev's giggles into tears, which spilled out the sides of his pinched eyes; he would hunch over, holding his stomach as his shoulders shook, his laugh like a demonic jackhammer.

Clearly, weev offended everyone, including law enforcement. The ultimate testament to his incendiary nature is, perhaps, the judge's rather stiff sentence. After all, he was not even party to writing the script. The night before his sentencing, he wrote on reddit, a popular nerd website, that "My regret is being nice enough to give AT&T a chance to patch before dropping the dataset to Gawker. I won't nearly be as nice next time."[5] To justify the sentence, the prosecution cited his reddit comments not once, not twice, but three times.

For weev, such incendiary behavior is par for the course. He has recorded hateful speeches railing against Jews and African Americans—"sermons," as he calls them—which can be viewed on YouTube. They are so hateful that they even disgust other trolls.

We started chatting soon after his legal troubles relating to AT&T began. During the next five months we chatted often. There were some moments that can only be described as strange. Take, for instance, a conversation that occurred on December 12, 2010:

    <weev>: hello there
    <weev>: how are you
    <biella>: pretty good and you?
    <weev>: cant complain
    <weev>: GNAA has switched forms of governance
    <weev>: it is now an Athenian democracy
    <weev>: where those who have completed their military service
    <weev>: i.e. done any cool trolling
    <weev>: are now eligible to vote on measures

I was, I recall vividly, incredulous. But I still managed, barely, to type a response:

    <biella>: really?

Then out of the blue, as is often the case with internet chatting —especially with weev—he hopped to another topic while I was in the midst of responding to questions of governance:

> <weev>: my bondsman called me randomly
> <biella>: what was it before? [before becoming an Athenian democracy]
> <weev>: yes
> <weev>: i suspect i may be arrested tomorrow or on the 16th
> <weev>: i am having to divide up responsibilities
> <weev>: because nobody can do all the shit i did
> <biella>: 4 real?
> [...]
> <biella>: i mean why do you think you are being arrested?
> <weev>: my bondsman called me randomly
> <weev>: to verify my current location
> <weev>: last time that happened
> <weev>: the door got kicked in the next day

At the time he was under investigation. I know he was a troll and all but, let's face it: jail sucks. I told him I would visit and expressed my sympathies:

> <weev>: thank you
> <weev>: i will enjoy the company
> <biella>: and gluten free treats that i will bring
> <weev>: :D
> <weev>: i just discovered
> <weev>: how to make a passable gluten free bread
> <weev>: u gotta just use a variety of shit
> <weev>: brown rice, tapioca and taff flours
> <weev>: and potato starch

It was natural, then, that weev, a gluten-free troll chatting with a gluten-free anthropologist, would seamlessly transition into a discussion of Pilates. Regrettably, I never did get a proper answer on the subject of troll governance. Many conversations followed this unpredictable, always entertaining, arc.

I was earnest with him for the most part, but I played along with his self-styled hoaxer role. At the same time, I couldn't resist calling him out on his bullshit sometimes, even trolling him just a little:

<weev>: i have a very broad range of knowledge for a highschool dropout
<biella>: except you studied anthro at James Madison :-)
<weev>: yes well
<biella>: but you do have a broad range of knowledge
<weev>: i am just a poor country boy from arkansas
<weev>: i dropped out of college because it was too much for my simple southern mind
<weev>: plus i was disgusted at the degeneracy of american institutions
<weev>: all the social sciences have become an elaborate scheme for giving white kids racial inferiority complexes, or destroying the gender roles that make our society work

As a social science professor, I had some insider knowledge of this "elaborate scheme." I could not help but feed him some of my own lies:

<biella>: omg totally
<weev>: or otherwise promoting judeo-bolshevist/marxist idologues
<biella>: they secretly train us to do that (it is quite intensive)
<weev>: i dont know if ur being sarcastic or sincere
<weev>: is the hilarious part
<biella>: lol
<biella>: welcome to biella's world of chatting with weev as well :-)

He did in fact serve jail time in various states, ending up in New Jersey where he was released on bail February 28, 2011, to await trial. Since he was no longer allowed online, our chats came to an end. Instead, we continued to converse in person, over gluten-free food, in NYC. I footed the bill since he was really, really broke. Although he did teach me a fair bit about trolling, he never used his skills on me.

Although weev's bail conditions banned him from using a computer, he still managed to practice his craft. weev, like many trolls, likes to dupe people in order to draw attention to himself. Putting oneself in the limelight feels great, especially if you don't need to pay a PR person to post a fake sex tape. In May 2011, as summer finally descended on NYC, he excitedly texted me. "Google my name," he wrote. I did as commanded, and hundreds of news articles popped up on my browser. He had duped the media with an in-person hoax, claiming to be Dominique Strauss-Kahn's neighbor immediately after rape charges were leveled against the wealthy French politician and former head of the International Monetary Fund. weev, then utterly destitute, managed to slip his comments into hundreds of newspapers; no journalist bothered to fact-check him:

> Despite the prosecutor's claims, however, Strauss-Kahn is already meeting his neighbors. An infamous computer hacker who lives in the corporate apartment building on Broadway claims he has already met the Frenchman—and he is 'an OK guy'.
>
> 'We're all like one big Breakfast Club in there,' Andrew Auernheimer, 26, was reported as saying in reference to the 1985 classic film about five high school students trapped in Saturday detention.[6]

In Lulz We Trust

So if weev, like so many trolls, dishes out his actions on mixed platters of truth and lies, is it possible to determine whether he was actually in the room when the "lulz" first whooshed off the tip of a tongue? To probe this question further, let's turn to Encyclopedia Dramatica (ED), a stunningly detailed online compendium cataloging troll mechanics, history, gore, and lore. Despite bearing the title "Encyclopedia," it strives neither for neutrality nor objectivity. ED is, indeed, encyclopedic in its detail—but it is also outrageous in tone and riddled with lies. What ED does well (and in this way it actually achieves a strange measure of objectivity) is display the moral kinetics of trolling. Is ED's etymologizing of the lulz, a snippet of which is provided below, fact or fable?:

LUL⅂ is a corruption of *L O L*, which stands for "Laugh Out Loud," signifying laughter at someone else's expense. This makes it inherently superior to lesser forms of humor. Anonymous gets big lulz from pulling random pranks. The pranks are always posted on the internet. Just as the element of surprise transforms the physical act of love into something beautiful, the anguish of a laughed-at victim transforms lol into lulz, making it longer, girthier, and more pleasurable. Lulz is engaged in by Internet users who have witnessed one major economic/environmental/political disaster too many, and who thus view a state of voluntary, gleeful sociopathy over the world's current apocalyptic state, as superior to being continually emo.

The term "lulz" was first coined by Jameth, an original Encyclopedia Dramatica administrator, and the term became very popular on that website. The nickname originated sometime in early 2001 when James (his real name, the -th suffix being a pun on his faggotry and his small p3n0r) was having a conversation with a lisping homosexual. James was being referred to as *Jameth* because of the person's speech impediment. In June 2001, James decided to use Jameth as his LiveJournal account name. Don't let him fool you— James craves the cock.[7]

According to information from multiple interviews, including one with ED's sharp and witty founder, Sherrod DeGrippo, weev did, indeed, participate in the conference call when Jameth coined the term; and Jameth is, in fact, gay. I never inquired about his lisp.[8]

Today, the lulz can encompass lighthearted jokes as well, and are utilized and enjoyed by many Internet nerds around the world. But, at its inception, its demeanor was conceived as cruel—"laughter at the expense or the misfortune of others," is how trolls like to define it. Lulz is a quintessential example of what folklorists define as argot—specialized and esoteric terminology used by a subcultural group. Since argot is so opaque and particular, it functions to enact secrecy or, at minimum, erect some very stiff social boundaries. As an anthropologist, it is tempting, no matter how ridiculous it seems, to view lulz in terms of epistemology—through the social production of knowledge. At one level, the lulz functions as an epistemic object, stabilizing a set of experiences by making them available for reflection. For decades, there was no term for the lulz, but trolls and hackers nevertheless experienced the distinctive pleasures of pranking. Once a name like "lulz" comes into being, it opens the very practice it names to further reflection by its practitioners. Trolls now pontificate over the meaning of the lulz, employing the term to designate particularly satisfying acts (whether or not they are intentionally done for the lulz) and also to diagnose situations lacking in lulz—which, of course, demands reparatory courses of action.

Just what does the term do or signify which no other word can? This is harder to convey. But if we keep in mind that lulz derives from the acronym "lol" (laugh out loud), it becomes easier to see that lulz is primarily about humor. Lols are familiar to everyone who has ever sent a joke to someone by email. Lulz are darker: acquired most often at someone's expense, prone to misfiring and, occasionally, bordering on disturbing or hateful speech (except, of course, when they cross the border entirely: thank you rape jokes). Lulz are unmistakably imbued with danger and mystery, and thus speak foremost to the pleasures of transgression.

We can see the defining features of lulz in weev's AT&T affair—not in his exposure of the security hole, but in the way he got respectable newscasters all over the United States to utter the word "Goatse," unwittingly referencing one of the most disgusting images on the Internet. In practice, lulzy activity defies boundaries but also re-erects them. There is a divide between people who are merely LOLing on the Internet—without really knowing what the Internet is or where it came from or how it works on the inside—and those who are lulzing (i.e., hackers, trolls, etc.) and know exactly what the underbelly is about. The lulz are both a form of cultural differentiation and a tool or weapon used to attack, humiliate, and defame the unwitting normal LOLers—often without them even realizing that an entire culture is aligned against them. Usually, the lulz are inside jokes, but (often) they are equal opportunity: lulz may provoke laughter not just among trolls, but outsiders as well. The price of admission is just a bit of knowledge. LOLers can be drawn into the world of lulz thanks to websites populated by trolls like Encyclopedia Dramatica, 4chan, and Something Awful, which disseminate this knowledge to anyone who cares to look for it. Those who find it may choose to run away very quickly, or they might become the next generation of trolls.

The lulz show how easily and casually trolls can upend our sense of security by invading private spaces and exposing confidential information. Targets receive scores of unpaid pizzas at home or have their unlisted phone numbers published, Social Security numbers leaked, private communications posted, credit card numbers doxed, and hard drive contents seeded. Trolls enjoy desecrating anything remotely sacred, as cultural theorist Whitney Phillips conveys in her astute characterization of trolls as "agents of cultural digestion [who] scavenge the landscape, re-purpose the most offensive material, then shove the resulting monstrosities into the faces of an unsuspecting populace."[9] In short: any information thought to be personal, secure, or sacred is a prime target for sharing or defilement in a multitude of ways. Lulz-oriented actions puncture the consensus around our politics and ethics, our social lives, and our aesthetic sensibilities. Any presumption of our world's inviolability becomes a weapon; trolls invalidate that world by gesturing toward the possibility for Internet geeks to destroy it—to pull the carpet from under us whenever they feel the urge.

I came to trolls just as a subset of them was experiencing a crucial transformation: increasingly, people working under the aegis of Anonymous began pursuing activism. Given the seedy underbelly I have just described, the development was beyond surprising. However, it was not without historical precedent: I recognized trolls as kin to the tricksters of myth. After all, I am an anthropologist, and tricksters are a time-honored topic of anthropological rumination.

To Trick or to Treat?

The trickster archetype comes replete with a diverse number of icons and often-delightful tales. Greek and Roman mythology brought some of these figures into the heart of Western culture: the mercurial Hermes and the bacchanalian Dionysus, among others. In West African and Caribbean folklores the role falls to Anansi, a spider who sometimes imparts knowledge or wisdom—and sometimes casts doubt or seeds confusion. Eshu, the god of communication and crossroads, is similarly ambiguous. Known for orchestrating chaotic scenarios that force human decisions, he can be a kind teacher or an agent of destruction. Among indigenous North Americans, Raven initiates change by will or by accident, and Coyote is a selfish beast who will trick any being—human or animal—to satisfy his appetites. The Western conception of the trickster has, since the medieval period, often been delivered in literature. Puck, the "shrewd and knavish sprite" who "misleads night-wanderers, laughing at their harm" in *A Midsummer Night's*

Dream, was not an invention of Shakespeare's, but has roots in a mischievous fairy of Celtic folklore. The shapeshifter Loki of Nordic mythology has recently reappeared in Hollywood films, mostly as a bland version of his mythological self, and still serves as a reminder of the capricious, vindictive role the trickster can perform.

Tricksters are united by a few characteristics, such as the burning desire to defy or defile rules, norms, and laws. Often lacking both impulse control and the ability to experience shame, they are outrageous and unfiltered in their speech. Some tricksters are driven by a higher calling, like Loki, who sometimes works for the gods (though true to his fearsome nature, he sometimes causes problems for them). Many are propelled by curiosity and voracious appetite. They rarely plan their actions, choosing instead an unbridled spontaneity that translates into a wily unpredictability. While capriciousness often underwrites successful trickster exploits, it can also trip trolls up.[10]

Trickster tales are not didactic and moralizing but reveal their lessons playfully. They can function normatively—when parents offer scary stories to dissuade kids from misbehaving—or critically, allowing norms to be laid bare for folk-philosophical challenge. Lewis Hyde, who has written extensively on the trickster motif, notes that "the origins, liveliness, and durability of cultures require that there be a space for figures whose function is to uncover and disrupt the very things that cultures are based on."[11]

It is not difficult to imagine the troll and Anonymous as contemporary trickster figures. They are provocateurs and saboteurs who dismantle convention while occupying a liminal zone. They are well positioned to impart lessons—regardless of their intent. Their actions need not be accepted, much less endorsed, to extract positive value. We may see them as edifying us with liberating or terrifying perspectives, symptomatic of underlying problems that deserve scrutiny, functioning as a positive force toward renewal, or as distorting and confusing shadows. The trickster becomes one heuristic—certainly not the only or primary one—for understanding the sources, the myriad effects, and especially, the Janus face of morally slippery entities like trolls and Anonymous.

Before we get to Anonymous proper, it is worth taking a brief (incomplete) tour through the vibrant tradition of trolling/tricksterdom on the Internet. The nature of the Internet—a network built on software—makes it ideal for both play and exploitation;[12] it is like a petri dish for pranking. Indeed, hackers (and later trolls) have been at this sort of behavior for a long time. But it is only recently that some of these activities have attained a more visible, publicly available mythological status. For example, gathered in the Encyclopedia Dramatica are copious links to cases of historical techno-tricksterism. By exploring these lineages we can better understand what makes Anonymous—both the trolls and activists—distinctive among a broader pantheon of technological tricksters.

A (Brief) Natural History of Internet Tricksterdom (Or, a Genealogy of a Lack of Morals)

weev is a troll's troll—a rare standout in a field that mostly spawns so many garden varieties.

Troll ancestry boasts a rather eclectic and varied cast of characters. Trolling was common in the hacker underground—a place for subversive hackers who thrived in the 1980s and 1990s, seeking out forbidden knowledge by rummaging around, uninvited, in other people's computers. But even they have to thank their direct ancestors, the phone phreaks, for the aesthetics of audacity. Fusing technological spelunking with mischief, phone phreaks illegally entered the telephone system by re-creating the audio frequencies used by the system to route calls. They did it to learn and explore, to be sure. But the thrill of transgression was equally integral to the joy of phreaking. In the 1960s and 1970s, phreaks would use their skills to congregate on telephone conference "party lines." Phreaking attracted some blind kids, who found a source of freedom in connecting with others on the phone. Over the telephone wires, from near and far, people who couldn't see each other would meet to chat, gossip, share technological tidbits, and plan and execute pranks. Lots of pranks. Naturally, most of these pranks involved phone calls. While most of them were lighthearted, a few exhibited a fearsome bite. Phil Lapsley, a historian of phreaks, recounts an infamous 1974 hoax where phreaks exploited a rare bug in the phone system to reroute all calls made to residents of Santa Barbara, California, to a phony emergency worker who would warn: "There has been a nuclear explosion in Santa Barbara and all the telephone lines are out."[13] weev, no stranger to history, adores phone pranks and sees himself as an inheritor of this illustrious lineage.

The end of the analog phone network, after the divestiture of "Ma Bell" (the affectionate name given to AT&T by phreaks), spelled the end of the golden age of phreaking. It was largely replaced by the exploration of computer networks, giving rise to the hacker underground, which peaked in the 1990s. Although many of these underground hackers acquired, circulated, and produced technical knowledge— scouting for security vulnerabilities and edifying technical curiosities—they were also connoisseurs of forbidden fruit. Thus, it is no wonder that their actions expanded from strictly technical engagements and into ones that included mockery, spectacle, and transgression. They quickly distinguished their politics and ethics from the university hackers of MIT, Carnegie Mellon, and Stanford; these hackers, who in the 1960s stayed up all night to access their beloved computers otherwise tied up for official use during the day, have been chronicled majestically by journalist Steven Levy.[14] Though these early hackers also had an affinity for pranking, they abided by a more robust ethos of transparency and access than underground hackers.

Many underground hackers were puckish in their pranking and hacking pursuits. They were mischief-makers and merry wanderers of the network. There was, however, a cohort of underground hackers who more closely resembled the Loki archetype in their network jaunts and haunts. When I interview hackers who were active in the 1990s about their trolling activities, the conversation inevitably turns toward a discussion of the most feared hacker/troll of the era: "u4ea" (pronounced "euphoria" and eerily similar to "lulz" in its figuration). So terrifying was this troll's reign that every time I utter u4ea to one of his contemporaries, their demeanor blackens and proceedings assume an unmatched seriousness. u4ea is Canadian. More notoriously, this troll was "founder, president, and dictator for life" of hacker group BRoTHeRHooD oF WaReZ—("BoW" for short; Warez is pirated software— "BoW" sought to poke fun at Bulletin Board System warez groups). According to a former member whom I chatted with online, the "paramilitary wing" of BoW, called "Hagis" (short for "Hackers against Geeks in Snowsuits"), went on cruel hacking and pranking campaigns against targets ranging from corporations, law-abiding white hat hackers, and infosecurity gurus, to basically anyone else who got in their line of fire. To take one example, in the late 1990s Hagis went ballistic during a multi-year feud with a white hat hacker named Jay Dyson. First they went after his Internet service provider, deleting *all* their files and knocking them offline for two weeks. Later, they deleted files on Dyson's business website. For good measure, they harassed his wife with threatening messages, informing her, via her hacked email account, that "All the Dyson family will pay for the mistakes of Big Jay."[15]

Upon learning about this and other attacks from the former BoW member I chatted with, I wrote:

<biella>: man, ruthless
<hacker>: yeah, we were a fairly vicious bunch to the point that i dropped out of the scene

<biella>: why? i mean, what was driving people? is it just because people could?
<hacker>: hell if i know now to be honest
<hacker>: there were massive hacker wars that went on that nobody knew about
<hacker>: irc servers would vanish, ISPs would be wiped off the face of the earth for days or weeks
<hacker>: but it stayed within the scene
<hacker>: the media only ever caught hints of it
<hacker>: i mean, this was a time when hackers didn't want attention, people who talked to the press were mediawh0res
<hacker>: we were a genuine subculture, our own news, our own celebrities, our own slang, our own culture

And I could not help but add:

<biella>: and your own wars

Still, Hagis could also be quite jocular. Once, they defaced the Greenpeace website and posted what today might be considered a classically lulzy message meant to publicize the ordeal of an arrested phone phreak and hacker named Kevin Mitnick: "Phree Kevin Mitnick or we will club 600 baby seals."[16]

After going this deep (which is to say, barely scratching the surface), I decided that my interlocutors were right: it was time to ease off on my pursuit of u4ea. Barely anything has been written about this famous troll—and for a good reason.

Trolling in the 1990s followed a different vector toward anonymity, as well. Outside of these elite, hidden hacker wars, ordinary users got their first bitter taste of trolling on Usenet, the seminal mega-message board. In 1979, the Internet existed as an academic and military network—the ARPANET—and access was limited to a select few. Naturally, a few engineers built a new system, Usenet, which they conceived of as the "poor man's ARPANET." Initially invented for the sole purpose of discussing obscure technical matters, it quickly mushroomed—much to everyone's surprise—to include hundreds of lists with spirited and, at times, ferocious discussions. Technical subject matter was complemented by groups devoted to sex, humor, recipes, and (naturally) anti-Scientology.

Usenet and other mailing lists are also where the term "troll" first came into common usage. It referred to people who did not contribute positively to discussions, who argued for the sake of arguing, or who were simply disruptive jerks (intentionally or not). List users frequently admonished others to "stop feeding the trolls," a refrain still commonly seen today on mailing lists, message boards, and website comment sections.

But Usenet also bred and fed the spectacular breed of troll who would intentionally sabotage conversations—leaving both list members and, especially, list administrators, exasperated. There is no better example than Netochka Nezvanova, named after the titular character in Dostoevsky's (failed) first attempt at a novel. Appropriately, the name means "nameless nobody." And, just like Anonymous today, it is believed that many different individuals and groups have taken up the moniker, making it an apt example of what media scholar Marco Deseriis describes as a "multiple use name," in which "the same alias" is adopted by "organized collectives, affinity groups, and individual authors."[17]

Netochka Nezvanova's artist statement, published online, captures the mad, spirited flair driving this character:

InterBody—Artistic Statement

Internet—where one may access the proposal + pertinent materials

Our bodies are the borders of our understanding.
The universes are the body. The Internet is the skin.
This is my Inter Body. I am Soft Wear.

When I am alone, I want you to enter inside me, I wish to wear you.

Dissolved and integrated, we are exploded into a nomadic,
unstable topology of ceramic ribbons and microfluidic
channels,
of myriad phosphorescent gleams of the unassailable
transpositions
of the visible signs of the invisible and mysterious encounters
in divisible dreams.

Upon reading this, you might like find yourself, as I did,
digging her imaginative, Deleuzian sensibilities—unless you
were on one of the mailing lists she demolished. Her character
disrupted so frequently, with such adroitness, and on so many
disparate lists and news groups, that different list administrators banded together on a dedicated list of their own, with
the sole purpose of dealing with the trail of destruction she
left behind. At my own current home university, McGill, she
participated in a mailing list about Max, a visual programming language for music, audio, and media, but was booted
in 2001 after threatening to sue particular list members. Here
is a portion of the rationale for banning her:

Second, after "she" was thrown off the McGill list, "she"
intiated [sic] what could best be described as a terror campaign that included spam to anyone who posted to the Max
list, denial of service attacks, and threatening and slander-
ous email sent to random individuals at McGill. I didn't see
any point to subjecting myself and my co-workers to this
type of harrassment [sic]. However, it turns out that many
of these acts are felonies. If this behavior recommences, the
victims of the behavior can pursue legal remedies, and I
would strongly suggest they do so.

In reaction, someone on the list cried foul: "So, censorship
once more."[18]
In the 1990s, Usenet and many other booming mailing lists
encouraged unrestrained free speech—and were celebrated

for it. But trolls like Netochka forced a debate, still with us today, about the limits of such speech: should mailing lists and webpage moderators curb offensive speech for the sake of civility, seen by some as necessary for a healthy community? Or should lists avoid censoring speech, no matter how objectionable, so that the Internet might be a place where free speech reigns unconditionally?

Of particular note—as we trace our trolling lineage through time—is the development of 4chan, an imageboard modeled on a popular Japanese imageboard called Futaba Channel, also known as 2chan ("chan" is short for "channel"). It is here, perhaps more than anywhere else, where the populist type of trolling that is well known today first emerged. 4chan is unique for its culture of extreme permissibility —making questions of free speech largely irrelevant— fostered by a culture of anonymity embraced by its users. Naturally, it was on this board where the collective idea and identity of Anonymous emerged. Unlike Usenet, no one on 4chan is in the least bit disturbed by the uncivil speech that ricochets across the board every second of the day. In many respects, the board is explicitly conceived of as a say-anything zone: the grosser and more offensive, damn it, the better.

Since it launched in 2003, 4chan has become an immensely popular, iconic, and opprobrious imageboard. Composed of over sixty (at the time if this writing) topic-based forums ranging from anime to health and fitness, it is both the source of many of the Internet's most beloved cultural artifacts (such as Lolcats memes), and one of its most wretched hives of scum and villainy. The "Random" forum, also called "/b/," teems with pornography, racial slurs, and a distinctive brand of humor derived from defilement. It is where trolling once flourished. One "/b/tard" (as the forum's denizens are called) explained to my class that "everyone should have a good sense that /b/ is an almost completely unfiltered clusterfuck of everything you could imagine, and lots of stuff you couldn't imagine or wouldn't want to." A post might include a naked woman with the demand: "rate my wife." The next post might feature a particularly hard-to-stomach image of a severely mutilated body, but might then be followed by a nugget of light humor:

File : <u>1291872411.jpg</u>-(10 KB 292x219, sodium-bicarbonate.jpg)

☐ **Anonymous** 12/09/10(Thu)00:26:51 No.293326XXX
Just ate half a teaspoon of sodium bicarbonate wat do?

☐ **Anonymous** 12/09/10(Thu)00:28:24 No.293326XXX
bump

☐ **Anonymous** 12/09/10(Thu)00:29:12 No.283326XXX
>>293326451
that's not very much. I suggest water.
then burping.

☐ **Anonymous** 12/09/10(Thu)00:33:06 No.293327XXX
FFFFFFFFFFFFFFFFFFFFFFFFFFFFFFFFFFFFFFFFFF EAT MORE AND THEN CHUG RED FOOD DIE AND VINEGAR AND WAIT FOR THE REACTION AND RUN INTO THE NEAREST ROOM FULL OF PEOPLE AND YELL, "I AM THE GOD OF VOLCANOES, TOAN GLADIUS! BLBLBLBLBLBLBLBLBLBLBLBLBL!"

Generally speaking, though, much of the material is designed to be shocking to outsiders, a discursively constructed border fence meant to keep the uninitiated—aka "n00bs" or "newfags"—far, far away. (Nearly every category of person, from old-timers to new-timers, is labelled a "fag." On 4chan, it is both an insult and term of endearment. We will see the suffix many times in this book.) For insiders, it is the normal state of affairs, and one of the board's defining and appealing qualities.

On 4chan, participants are strongly discouraged from identifying themselves, and most post under the default name "Anonymous," as in the example above. Technically, 4chan keeps logs of IP addresses and doesn't do anything to keep visitors from being identified. Unless users cloak their IP addresses before connecting, the site's founder, owner, and system administrator—Chris Poole, aka "moot"—has full access to them. He has even given them over to law enforcement to comply with legitimate investigations. (This policy is widely known among users.) But, in at least a practical sense (and at least between its users as peers), the board functions anonymously; except for rare exceptions, and the occasional instance where a subject of discussion must be identified using a photograph with a time stamp, users interact with no consistent nicknames or usernames. Posts are pushed off the front page very quickly—to be deleted from the server when they reach page 14—only surviving as long as users remain interested in the subject. It "lowers personal responsibility and encourages experimentation," as media scholar Lee Knuttila put it.[19] Experimentation includes generating memes (these are modifications of humorous images, videos, or catchphrases, some of which attain legendary status), fierce trolling campaigns masterminded by Anonymous (though this has been less common in recent years), and incessant taunting and vitriol of other users (such as egging on individuals with suicidal ideation to "just do it" and become "an hero"). It must be noted, however, that there is also an outpouring of compassionate and empathetic advice, especially for those looking for relationship help, or when someone discovers a video of a cat being tortured. But this aspect is rarely featured in the news.

All this occurs with the knowledge of impermanence. In contrast to mailing lists or many other kinds of online boards, there is no official archive. If a thread is not "bumped" back to the top by a time reply, it dies and evaporates. On an active channel, like /b/, this entire life cycle occurs in just minutes.

In this environment, it is difficult for a person to accrue status or reputation—much less fame. Against this backdrop of cacophonous experimentation and ephemera, a robust collective memory and identity has nevertheless formed around legendary trolling campaigns, all sorts of insider jokes, and artifacts like image macros. Aesthetically, the more extreme a piece of content is, the better, for it ensures the interest of participants, and motivates replies to threads (keeping them alive). In particularly novel cases, an extreme piece of content can even circulate beyond the board—to distant lands like the message board community, reddit, or bodybuilding.com, and, eventually, mass cultural awareness. Remember, lolcats got their start on 4chan. Trolls, in particular, focus on the collective pursuit of epic wins—just one form of content among many. (To be clear, 4chan houses many trolls, but many participants steer clear of trolling activity. Still others avoid activity altogether—they are there as spectators or lurkers.)

It is almost impossible to pinpoint a day or event when trolling on 4chan was born. But by 2006, the name Anonymous was being used by participants to engage in trolling raids. These invasions would continue for many years, even after Anonymous was routinely deployed for activist purposes. For instance, in 2010 Anonymous sought to "ruin" a preteen girl named Jessi Slaughter after her homemade video monologues, which had gained some notoriety on tween gossip site StickyDrama, were posted on 4chan. Anonymous was stirred to action by Slaughter's brazen boasts—she claimed in one video that she would "pop a glock in your mouth and make a brain slushie"—and published her phone number, address, and Twitter username, inundating her with hateful emails and threatening prank calls, circulating photoshopped images of her and satiric remixes of her videos. When her father recorded his own rant, claiming to have "backtraced" her tormenters and reported them to the "cyber police," he also became an object of ridicule. Slaughter, described by /b/ tards as a "lulzcow ... whore," is now memorialized on Urban Dictionary as "The epitome of an eleven year old slut/poser/ internet reject/scenecore wannabe."

On the one hand, outlandish trolling raids and denigrating

statements like "lulzcow … whore" (or "due to fail and AIDS" from the Habbo Hotel raids) function for 4chan users like a repellent meant to keep naive users far away from *their* Internet playground. On the other, when compared to most other arenas where trolls are bred—like weev's GNAA—4chan is a mecca of populist trolling. By populist, I simply mean that 4chan membership is available to anyone willing to cross these boundaries, put in the time to learn the argot, and (of course) stomach the gore. The etiquette and techniques that 4chan users employ are only superficially elitist. A former student of mine offered me the following insight. Exceptionally smart, he was also a troll—or a "goon" to be more precise, since that's what they call themselves on Something Awful, his website of choice at the time:

> Something Awful is like the exclusive country club of the Internet, with a one-time $10 fee, a laundry list of rules very particular to SA, moderators who ban and probate, and community enforcement of "Good Posts" through ridicule. 4chan on the other hand is an organic free-for-all that doesn't enforce so much as engages an amorphous membership in a mega-death battle for the top humor spot. Anyone can participate in 4chan, and Internet fame isn't possible in the same way it is on SA because everyone is literally anonymous.

Whatever unfolds on the board—a joke, a long conversation, or a three-day trolling campaign—anonymity is essential to 4chan; one might call anonymity both its ground rule and its dominant cultural aspect—a core principle inherited by Anonymous, even in its pseudonymous, material extension as hordes of Guy Fawkes–mask wearers. On 4chan, there is an interplay between the *function* of anonymity (enabling pure competition without the interference of reputation or social capital) and the *effects* of anonymity (the memes, hacks, and acts of trolling that emerge and have real impact on the world). In contrast to weev's egoistic acts of trolling, 4chan's Anonymous "Internet Hate Machine" collective action absolves individuals of responsibility in the conventional sense, but not in a collective sense.[20] That is, Anonymous is open to anyone willing to subsume him- or herself into a collective capable of gaining fame through events like the Habbo Hotel raids. Absent of any individual recognition, each activity is ascribed to a collective nom de plume, a reincarnation of Netochka Nezvanova. On 4chan, participants will also shame those seeking fame and attention, calling them "namefags."

As a trolling outfit, Anonymous achieved considerable media notoriety, just like weev. The entity became, in certain respects, famous. However, while the trolling exploits of, on the one hand, Anonymous and 4chan users, and on the other hand, weev, are connected by their tactical approaches, they are also foils of each other. Regardless of how far and wide the fame of Anonymous spreads, personal identity and the individual remain subordinate to a focus on the epic win—and, especially, the lulz.[21]

This subsumption of individual identity into collective identity is unusual in Western culture. Understanding its uptake is crucial to our knowledge of how Anonymous, as an activist group, came to be. It is very possible that the unsavory nature of Anonymous's early trolling activities motivated collectivity as a security feature; participants probably had a desire to participate, to receive payment in lulz, without the risk of being identified and socially stigmatized. To understand these motivations, and the powerful significance of an individual's willingness to subsume his or her identity, we will briefly ruminate on the culture of fame-seeking—of individualistic celebrity—itself.

Anonymous's Trickster's Trick: Defying Individual Celebrity through Collective Celebrity

Fame-seeking pervades practically every sphere of American life today, from the mass media, which hires Hollywood celebrities as news anchors, to the micro-media platforms that afford endless opportunities for narcissism and self-inflation; from the halls of academia, where superstar professors command high salaries, to sports arenas, where players rake in obscene salaries. Fame-seeking behavior reinforces what anthropologist David Graeber, building on the seminal work of C. B. Macpherson, identifies as "possessive individualism," defined as "those deeply internalized habits of thinking and feeling" whereby we view "everything around [us] primarily as actual or potential commercial property."[22]

How did 4chan—one of the seediest zones of the Internet—hatch one of the most robust instantiations of a collectivist, anti-celebrity ethic, without its members even intending to? This ethic thrived organically on 4chan because it could be executed in such an unadulterated form. During a lecture for my class, a former Anonymous troll and current activist explained the crucial role of 4chan in cementing what he designates as "the primary ideal of Anonymous":

> The posts on 4chan have no names or any identifiable markers attached to them. The only thing you are able to judge a post by is its content and nothing else. *This elimination of the persona, and by extension everything associated with it, such as leadership, representation, and status, is the primary ideal of Anonymous.* (emphasis added)

This Anon, who was lecturing anonymously on Skype to my ten enraptured students, immediately offered a series of astute qualifications about this primary ideal: the self-effacement of the individual. When Anonymous left 4chan in pursuit of activist goals in 2008, he explained, this ideal failed, often spectacularly; once individuals interacted pseudonymously or met in person, status-seeking behaviors reasserted themselves. Individuals jockeyed and jostled for power.

Nevertheless, the taboo against fame-seeking was so well entrenched on 4chan, and was so valued for its success, that it largely prevented, with only a few exceptions, these internal struggles for status from spilling over into public quests for personal fame. (Later, we will see its greatest failure in the micro-ecologies of hacker teams like AntiSec and LulzSec, analogous to rock stars in their ability to amass fame and recognition, and—not surprisingly—to spark the ire of some Anons, even while being admired for their lulzy and political antics.)

Once Anonymous left 4chan to engage in activism, the anti-celebrity-seeking ideal became "more nuanced … incarnating into the desire for leaderlessness and high democracy," as this Anon put it. Attempts to put these principles into practice also resulted in missteps, particularly in the emergence of small teams with concentrations of power.

But despite the fragmentation into teams and cabals, the overarching ideals remained in play. Adherence meant "that anybody [could] call themselves Anonymous and rightfully claim the name," as the lecturer explained. This freedom to take the name and experiment with it is precisely what enabled Anonymous to become the wily hydra it is today.

But if we peek behind the ideal—the notion that Anonymous is everyone's property, an identity commons, so to speak—we see a much more complicated reality. And it was here, on this nuanced point, that this Anon ended his micro-lecture. I believe my students were both mesmerized and shocked that someone from Anonymous could be so smart and eloquent; I explained to them that Anonymous can be understood as what anthropologist Chris Kelty has jokingly called, contra the subaltern, the "superaltern": those highly educated geeks who not only speak for themselves but talk back loudly and critically to those who purport to speak for them.[23] The Anonymous guest lecturer continued:

> Most of us are humor-driven. So it should be no surprise that we often contend with other Anon-claiming groups we find out of favor, such as … the new activist-only Occupy Wall Street anons, or the conspiracy theorists and other overly serious entities claiming the name. It's true. We cannot deny them the name. But the important thing to take away from this talk is that nowhere in the Anonymous ideal was it ever stipulated that Anonymous must stand together with or even like other Anonymous. In fact, animosity and downright wars between Anonymous-claiming entities is right in line with the original internet-based projects carried out by cultural Anons.

It is here that we might comprehend the complexity of Anonymous. There is a singular subject and idea animating its spirit, and participants attempt to present this in a united front. For the media, it is tempting to buy into this branding wholesale—to present Anonymous as its values and its packaging. But the reality of the group's composition, in all its varied hues and tones, is impossible to present in any single sketch, even if Anonymous uses a single name. Its membership comprises too many different networks and working groups, each of which is at varying odds with one another in varying moments. The very nature of this collective of collectives means that the accumulation of too much power and prestige—especially at a single point in (virtual) space—is not only taboo but also functionally difficult.

4chan was ground zero for a robust anti-celebrity ethic, a value system opposed to self-aggrandizement and the apparatus of the mainstream media (one of the cancers killing /b/, as Anonymous likes to say). This ethic carried over to the activist incarnation of Anonymous. It is in these alternative practices of sociality—upending the ideological divide between individualism and collectivism—that we can recognize trolling's development into a principled weapon against monolithic banks and sleazy security firms. Collectivity is growing its market share: from the counter–corporate-controlled globalization movement of a decade ago, to Anonymous and the recent explosion of leaderless movements like Occupy. This is often entirely lost on the mainstream media, which can't—or won't—write a story that does not normalize the conversion of an individual into a celebrity or leader, complete with individual heroism or tragic moral failings. This, of course, is not the proclivity of journalism and journalists alone. Most of Western philosophy, and in turn, much of Western culture more generally, has posited the self—the individual—as the site of epistemic inquiry. It is hard to shake millenia of philosophical thinking on a topic—intellectual thinking that is also cultural common sense.

It is for this reason that Anonymous, whether in its trolling or activist incarnations, acted as a jujitsu-like force of trickery, its machinations incommensurable with the driving logic of the mainstream corporate media and dominant sensibilities of the self. It drove journalists a bit batty—which I got to witness first hand as I brokered, a bit trickster-like myself, between Anonymous and the media. I often helped the media cross the deep chasm in baby steps, as they tried to locate a leader, or at least a character, who might satisfy the implicit demands of their craft.

It is perhaps due to this very resistance to journalistic convention—to the desire to discover, reveal, or outright create a celebrity leader—that journalists were compelled to cover Anonymous. The hunt for a spokesperson, a leader, a representative, was in vain—at least, until the state entered the fray and began arresting hackers. But, for the most part, media outlets were offered few easy characters around which to spin a story.

What began as a network of trolls has become, for the most part, a force for good in the world. The emergence of

Anonymous from one of the seediest places on the Internet is a tale of wonder, of hope, and of playful illusions. Is it really possible that these ideals of collectivity and group identification, forged as they were in the hellish, terrifying fires of trolling, could transcend such an originary condition? Did the cesspool of 4chan really crystallize into one of the most politically active, morally fascinating, and subversively salient activist groups operating today? Somewhat surprisingly, yes. Let's see how.

CHAPTER 2

Project Chanology—I Came for the Lulz but Stayed for the Outrage

Various contingencies converged to awaken the trickster-trolls from their unsavory 4chan underworld. But if we were to single out one event most responsible for this, it would be the leaking onto the Internet of a Scientology video featuring Tom Cruise, Scientology's celebrity of celebrities. "Streisand was in full effect," quipped one Anon. "The Streisand Effect" is a well-known Internet phenomenon wherein an attempt to censor a piece of information has the inverse effect: more people want to see it in order to understand the motivation for the censorship, and thus it spreads much more widely than it would have if left alone. The phenomenon is named after Barbra Streisand's attempt in 2003 to bar, via a multimillion-dollar lawsuit, aerial photographs of her Malibu home from being published. The photographer was only trying to document coastal erosion. Before the lawsuit, the image of her home had been viewed online only six times, but after the case went public, more than 420,000 people visited the site. The Tom Cruise Scientology video was subject to a similar dynamic; its circulation was unstoppable.

In the video, Tom Cruise epitomizes Scientology's narcissistic worldview: "Being a Scientologist ... when you drive by an accident, it's not like anyone else," he says, chuckling with self-satisfaction. "As you drive past you know you have to do something about it, because you know you're the only one that can really help." Internet geeks (along with almost everyone else) viewed the video as a pathetic (not to mention hilarious) attempt to bestow credibility on pseudoscience via celebrity. As Tom Cruise cackled to himself in the video, the Internet community cackled—albeit for very different reasons—with him.

The video initially reached the Internet not through the efforts of Anonymous, but through (fittingly enough) an anonymous leak. The video was originally slated to appear on NBC to coincide with the release of Tom Cruise's unauthorized biography, but at the last minute the network got cold feet. However, critics of Scientology worked swiftly to ensure that the video found its way onto the web. Former Scientologist Patty Moher, working alongside longtime critic Patricia Greenway, FedExed a copy to Mark Bunker, who uploaded a video and sent a link to investigative journalist Mark Ebner, who in turn sent it to other news sources. Gawker, Radar, and other sites picked it up on January 13, 2008, linking to a video Bunker had posted—he thought—with password protection. He was wrong. "I woke up a few hours later to discover that the one chapter that had Cruise's monologue was accidentally not set to 'private,'" he said later. "It had been viewed about 20,000 times while I slept and was downloaded and mirrored multiple times on multiple accounts by people who had read the Gawker and Radar stories and other coverage of the video."[1] YouTube subsequently removed Bunker's videos hosted on the channel "TomCruiseBook"—along with the entire channel—likely at the behest of a Scientology copyright notice.

On January 15, Gawker republished the video with a short, punchy description fit for millions of eyeballs: "Let me put it this way: if Tom Cruise jumping on Oprah's couch was an 8 on the scale of scary, this is a 10." The Religious Technology Center—the arm of Scientology dealing with matters of intellectual property—took immediate action, threatening publishers with lawsuits if they did not remove the video. Gawker ended its article boldly: "it's newsworthy; and we will not be removing it."[2] The cat was out of the bag, Scientology was furious (and about to furiously unfurl lawsuits), and then all hell broke loose when the "hive," as Anonymous was then often called, decided to get involved.

On January 15, at 7:37:37 pm, the gates of the underworld opened with a historic thread regarding Scientology-oriented activism:

File :1200443857152.jpg-(22 KB, 251x328, intro_scn.jpg)

☐ **Anonymous** 01/15/08(Tue)19:37: 37
No.51051816

I think its time for /b/ to do something big.

People need to understand not to fuck with /b/, and talk about nothing for ten minutes, and expect people to give their money to an organization that makes absolutely no fucking sense.

I'm talking about "hacking" or "taking down" the official Scientology website.

It's time to use our resources to do something we believe is right.

It's time to do something big again, /b/.

Talk amongst one another, find a better place to plan it and then carry out what can and must be done.

It's time, /b/

Technically—and geeks make it a habit to geek out on technical specificities—a call-to-arms post came earlier on 4chan as well as on 711chan (apparently at 6:11 pm, I was told). Nevertheless, this seemed to be the post that spurred the largest number of trolls into action. While the general mood of the thread was one of (hyperbolic) confidence and exuberance, others were understandably skeptical about taking on—much less taking down—this extraordinarily powerful organization. They were well aware that targeting the Church of Scientology might be (invoking Tom Cruise's blockbuster movie series) "mission impossible":

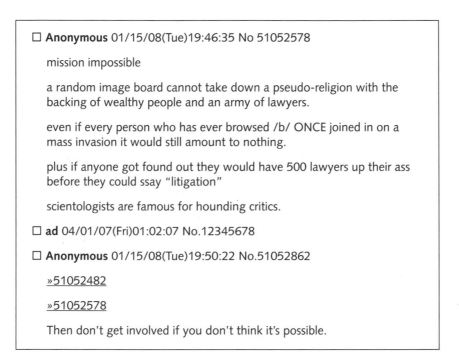

☐ **Anonymous** 01/15/08(Tue)19:46:35 No 51052578

mission impossible

a random image board cannot take down a pseudo-religion with the backing of wealthy people and an army of lawyers.

even if every person who has ever browsed /b/ ONCE joined in on a mass invasion it would still amount to nothing.

plus if anyone got found out they would have 500 lawyers up their ass before they could ssay "litigation"

scientologists are famous for hounding critics.

☐ **ad** 04/01/07(Fri)01:02:07 No.12345678

☐ **Anonymous** 01/15/08(Tue)19:50:22 No.51052862

»51052482

»51052578

Then don't get involved if you don't think it's possible.

The next day, a prescient message on /b/ issued the rallying cry for all Anonymous-related anti-Scientology activities— gathered under the slogan "CHANOLOGY"—and outlined the events to come:

File : <u>1200523664764</u>.jpg-(22 KB, 251x328, 120046751294.jpg)

☐ **Anonymous** 01/16/08(Wed)17:47:44
No.51134054

On 15/1/08 war was beginning.

Scientology's site is already under heavy bombardment, it's loading quite slowly.

But this is just the tip of the iceberg, the first assault in many to follow. We're winning a minor victory, but without the united support of the chans, Scientology will brush off this attack - and it will be doomed to nothing more than an entry in ED.

4chan, answer the call! Join the legion against Scientology, help in its demise, in its long awaited doom! For decades this tyrrany has existed, corrupting the minds of the weak- although hilarious, it's rather pathetic. We must destroy this evil, and replace it with a greater one - CHANOLOGY For when we are victorious, the chans will stand united in a new chapter of anonymous existence and batshit insanity, we will have begun our world take over. If we can destroy Scientology, we can destroy whatever we like! The world will be but our play thing.

Do the right thing, 4chan, become not just a part of this war, become an epic part of it. The largest of the chans, you hold the key of manpower, what the legion is in desperate need of.

FORWARD ANONYMOUS! UNITED, WE, THE LEGION ARE UNSTOPPABLE

tl;dr we're taking down Scientology, join up or gtfo.

No Scifags allowed in this thread.

http://711chan.org/res/6541.html

Faster than anyone could say "Hail Xenu" (Xenu being the dastardly, evil alien overlord of the galaxy, at least according to Scientology's version of history), these trolls—followed by myself shortly thereafter—headed to the Partyvan IRC network (an Anon hangout) to watch the trolling festivities "explode." Or, at least, that's how a core participant described it in a lecture to one of my university classes:

The unified bulk of anonymous collaborated through massive chat rooms to engage in various forms of ultracoordinated motherfuckery. For very short periods of time between January 15th and the 23rd, Scientology websites were hacked and DDoS'ed to remove them from the Internet. The Dianetics telephone hotline was completely bombarded with prank calls. All-black pieces of paper were faxed to every fax number we could get our hands on. And the "secrets" of their religion were blasted all over the Internet. I also personally scanned my bare ass and faxed it to them. Because fuck them.

Watching this epic raid take shape in real time, it was easy for me to understand why the geeks and hackers making up the ranks of Anonymous targeted Scientology: it is their evil doppelgänger. I did not end up in this IRC channel by accident—I was already immersed in the cultural tensions between geeks/netizens and Scientologists. One year earlier, I had been living in Edmonton, one of Canada's coldest cities in (what felt like) the furthest reaches of North America, culling and collating material in the world-class Scientology archive assembled by Stephen Kent, a sociology professor at the University of Alberta. I was there to research an epic battle between geeks and the Church of Scientology that began in the early 1990s and spanned two decades, starting after the Church of Scientology targeted its critics, especially those who leaked secret scripture. Humorously dubbed "Internet vs. Scientology," the battle was waged both offline and online between netizens—wholly committed to free speech—and the Church of Scientology—wholly committed to stamping it out by using any means necessary (legal or illegal) to censor criticism and prevent leaked documents from circulating online. I had arrived with a cultural hypothesis: hackers and Scientology stand in a diametrically opposed relationship to each other. This is not only because they are different, but because they are so precisely different. They are mirror images of each other, the perfect foils.

Consider the central doctrine espoused by *Keeping Scientology Working*, a publication of the Church's Religious Technology Center. The prose functions like a rusted first generation robot that has lurched into a corner and, finding itself unable to turn around, continues plodding forward while monotonously droning:

ONE: HAVING THE CORRECT TECHNOLOGY.
TWO: KNOWING THE TECHNOLOGY.
THREE: KNOWING IT IS CORRECT.
FOUR: TEACHING CORRECTLY THE CORRECT
TECHNOLOGY.
FIVE: APPLYING THE TECHNOLOGY.
SIX: SEEING THAT THE TECHNOLOGY IS
CORRECTLY APPLIED.
SEVEN: HAMMERING OUT THE EXISTENCE OF
INCORRECT TECHNOLOGY.
EIGHT: KNOCKING OUT INCORRECT
APPLICATIONS.
NINE: CLOSING THE DOOR ON ANY POSSIBILITY
OF INCORRECT TECHNOLOGY.
TEN: CLOSING THE DOOR ON INCORRECT
APPLICATION.

Reading these maxims in 2007, I knew that any hacker or geek who laid eyes on them would be simultaneously entertained *and* offended. Where Scientology is shrouded in secrecy, steeped in dogma, and dependent on the deployment of (pseudo)science and (faux) technology to control people, hacking lives in the light of inquisitive tinkering and exploration enables, and is enabled by, science and technology. Hackers dedicate their lives and pour their souls into creating and programming the world's most sophisticated machines. They are quintessential craftsman—motivated by a desire for excellence—but they abhor the idea of a single "correct technology." In fact, hacking is where craft and craftiness intermingle: make a 3-D printer that prints a 3-D printer; assemble an army of zombie computers into a botnet and then steal another hacker's botnet to make yours more powerful; design a robot solely for the purposes of mixing cocktails and showcase it at Roboexotica, a festival for cocktail robotics held since 1999; invent a programming language called Brainfuck designed to, well, mess with the heads of anyone who tries to program with it. You get the picture.

A religion which claims a privileged access to science and technology, to the extent of declaring themselves "the only group on Earth that has a workable technology which handles the basic rules of life itself and brings order out of chaos,"[3] is deeply offensive to hackers whose only demand on technology is that it should, at minimum, actually *do something*—a task they leave not to some transcendent discovery of truth but, instead, to their personal ingenuity in discovering solutions to technical problems, with the help of shared tips, swapped ideas, and reams of borrowed code.

So it made a lot of sense that Anonymous, composed of geeks and hackers, would rise against Scientology. But something was unclear: was Anonymous simply trolling for its own lulzy amusement or was it earnestly protesting? Even if I was pretty certain these were not deliberate acts of activism, a political spirit was clearly wafting through IRC. People were undeniably, and royally, pissed off that Scientology dared to censor a video on "their" Internet—especially such a hilarious one. Anons were phone-pranking the Dianetics hotline and sending scores of unpaid pizza to Church centers, sharing their exploits in real time across 4chan. At first any political aim seemed incidental. And then, weeks later, one particular act of "ultracoordinated motherfuckery" gave way to an earnest—though still, undoubtedly, irreverent—activist endeavor.

As Chanology grew in popularity, its bustling IRC channels #xenu and #target became unsuitable working environments for the publicity stunts and outreach to which it aspired.

Three people broke away and started and IRC channel #press. Soon after, it grew to include eight members who worked one evening until daybreak to create what still qualifies as Anonymous's best-known work of art. (Eventually, the team grew in size, #press became chaotic and members split off yet again. They called themselves marblecake, after one of their own found inspiration in the baked item he was eating.)

If the Tom Cruise video struck a chord both humorous and hyperbolic, this team harmonized to create an ironic video whose tone embodied a trickster-like ambiguity: simultaneously hilarious and serious, playful and ominous. Much to everyone's surprise, the video catapulted Anonymous onto a new plane of existence.

In the video, a drab corporate glass building stands against a backdrop of ominously racing dark clouds. A speech begins which, while delivered by a robotic voice, is poetic and inspirational:

> For the good of your followers, for the good of mankind, and for our own enjoyment, we shall proceed to expel you from the Internet, and systematically dismantle the Church of Scientology in its present form.
>
> We recognize you as a serious opponent, and do not expect our campaign to be completed in a short time frame. However, you will not prevail forever against the angry masses of the body politic. Your choice of methods, your hypocrisy, and the general lawlessness of your organization have sounded its death knell. You have nowhere to hide, because we are everywhere. You have no recourse in attack, because for each of us that falls, ten more will take his place.
>
> We are cognizant of the many who may decry our methods as parallel to those of the Church of Scientology, those who espouse the obvious truth that your organization will use the actions of Anonymous as an example of the persecution of which you have, for so long, warned your followers—this is acceptable to Anonymous. In fact, it is encouraged.

It was earnest—but earnestly a joke. This poetic imagery of a rising-up was rhetoric—but it was so compelling, so enticing as a lulzy direction, that it entrapped the Anonymous trolls into a commitment to the systematic dismantling of Scientology. They got caught up—like so many tricksters before them—in their own trickster trap. Anonymous, in its sudden commitment to a lulzy politics, gave birth to the reviled "moralfags" and "leaderfags." These Anons—tainted, somehow, by an accidental taste for justice—effectively catalyzed one of the most potent protest movements of our times.

The accidental train of events went like this: The video unexpectedly sparked a debate as to whether Anons should hit the streets to protest the Church or remain faithful to their madcap roots in raids and lulz. The timing helped make the decision for them, tipping things in favor of street demonstrations. Gregg Housh, one of the video's editors and an original member of marblecake, explained it as follows during an interview: "There were people who didn't think anonymous or 4chan should take to the streets but the consensus to actually do it came relatively easily for us after the video. It seemed to be great timing, the right video at the right moment."

Even if Anons were leaning toward protest, they did not want to ditch trolling completely; rather, they wanted to expand their repertoire. One Anon on IRC captured the full spectrum—legal, illegal, lulzy, serious—that these hordes of trolls were increasingly inhabiting (or wanting to inhabit) between mid-January 2008 and the first street protest (her pseudonym has been changed):

<Lulamania>: The ultimate scenario: Anonymous prank call + DDoS, US and French Government renew fraud charges, tax evasions, and illegal activities charges, local Church pastors telling their congregation the evils of Scientology, former members and families interviewed on TV about experience, activist groups holding licensed rallies and protests, and the news covering all of the above …

<Lulamania>: Keep in mind this is a war of attrition. We cannot

bankrupt Scientology directly—this is about getting media attention, informing the public, wearing down their members, pissing off their IT/phone services, counter-brainwashing their potential recruits, and for lulz.

On January 24, 2008, Anonymous announced that February 10 would be a day of protest. A few days after this initial call to action, Scientology critic Mark Bunker seized the high octane moment to push for the use of legal tactics alone. Like the trickster of communication and crossroads, Eshu, he reached out to the trolls in a video (holy Xenu!), praised them (smart), and asked them to join the cause (holy Xenu!). His message was to simmer the hell down, rein in the lulz, and please, *please* refrain from anything straight-up illegal. On a lengthy post to a forum on whyweprotest.net, Bunker explained what motivated him to make the video: "After seeing Anonymous's 'Message to Scientology' I was worried that I had helped to spawn attacks that would potentially scare Scientology staffers and also get Anonymous members in legal trouble so I decided I needed to make my initial tape to Anonymous."[4]

Although many had already been thinking along these lines, not everyone was on board with the vision offered by this hefty, bear-like man in his fifties whom Anonymous renamed "Wise Beard Man" for his erudite posturing and white facial hair. (Only a few years later, new activist networks would arise that embraced militant, illegal digital tactics like the DDoS, not for trolling but for political dissent.) Nevertheless, enough of them shifted gears and darted down the path of activism; Bunker's arguments nudged Anonymous toward the use of (mostly) legal tactics for its first major demonstrations.

The cake of marble, beavering away largely in secret (a cohort of outsiders knew of its existence), was aware that the great majority of potential participants were likely protest neophytes. If these Internet nerds, geeks, hackers, and trolls showed up *en masse* to protest without any prior activist experience, it would almost certainly be a recipe for ruin. So they had to get them up to speed—and rather quickly. They delivered a crash course on the mechanics, challenges, and components of peaceful protest in a video called "Code of Conduct."[5] Posted on February 1, 2008, a robotic voice lists twenty-two rules. No detail is overlooked: the video reminds participants to wear comfortable shoes, drink plenty of water, keep particularly geeky and objectionable Internet jokes to themselves (because these would likely offend bystanders), refrain from any violence, obtain necessary permits, use catchy slogans, and record the event. Since marblecake knew that Scientologists would use all available means—including high-definition photos—to identify and subsequently harass protesters, one rule exhorted participants to cover their faces, but noted, in a statement that now appears ironic, that there was no need to use masks: "Rule #17: Cover your face. This will prevent your identification from videos taken by hostiles, other protesters, or security. Use scarves, hats, and sunglasses. Masks are not necessary, and donning them in the context of a public demonstration is forbidden in some jurisdictions."

Necessary or not, as thousands of Anons and supporters hit the streets in cities around the world, masks appeared everywhere. By then, the Guy Fawkes mask was a pop cultural icon thanks to the Hollywood blockbuster *V for Vendetta*. The movie portrays a lone anarchist's fight against a dystopian, Orwellian state. The mask had also appeared previously on 4chan, worn by a beloved meme character with a penchant for failure—Epic Fail Guy. Well known, easy to purchase, and imbued with an undeniable symbolic energy—both on account of its history and its more recent iteration—the Guy Fawkes mask became the mask de jour to deter the prying eyes of Scientology. After, it would function as Anonymous's signature icon.

The day's events straddled the line between serious political protest and carnivalesque shenanigans. Why did so many people show up? During an informal chat, one long-time Anon and member of marblecake reasoned to me (correctly, I think) that "hearing [about] the first reports of east Australian protests on February 10, 2008, really set things in motion ... Had those not materialized I figure the turnout elsewhere wouldn't have been as important." While much of the Western world slumbered, in Australia an estimated 550 to 850 protesters poured into the streets, conveying their numbers in real time to others in video clips and photos, setting off a domino effect felt across much of the Western world. In London the crowd swelled to six hundred, and this success was matched in North America, where protesters hit the streets in small cities across the heartland and in major metropolitan centers like Los Angeles, where a whopping one thousand people turned out.

Six months after a local Fox News station labeled Anonymous "the Internet Hate Machine," they had legions of followers in the streets—not just geeks and hackers hammering at their keyboards—who were seizing on the group's name, its ethic of anonymity, and assorted concomitant iconography. That evening, men and women in Guy Fawkes masks and black suits with signs announcing "We Are the Internet" could be seen on cable news shows around the world.

While this may have been the first time Anons demonstrated in large numbers in the streets, previous trolling campaigns had a quasi-activist flair. For instance, in 2007 Anonymous targeted right-wing radio personality Hal Turner, not only for lulz (and revenge) but also because he was a "racist." Anonymous had first targeted him in 2006 with a series of prank phone calls and computer attacks that took down his website. Hal Turner countered by publishing the numbers of the prank callers, prompting Anonymous to hit hard at the heart of his radio empire, trolling and hacking the heck out of him. The following blog post, published by an Anonymous participant before the second round of raids, conveys the undeniable political sensibility compelling the action:

Those of you who spend any time around the troll pits of the internet, such as 4chan, 7chan, YTMND etc will undoubtedly know of this already, but its worth repeating.

Hal Turner is, in short a Nazi [*sic*]. A Nazi with his own radio show. Unfortunately for him, he also hasn't really got a mass following, except from the /b/tards and other various trolls, who decided to absolutely ruin his life online. As the Fox News below [*sic*] clip of him advocating the murder of a US judge shows, he isn't exactly someone to feel sorry for.[6]

Chanology differed from these previous raids in one crucial respect: it became a permanent fixture in the political landscape. In the weeks and months following the first street demonstrations, Chanology continued to protest Scientology's relentless legal and extralegal crackdown on critics and those who dared to disclose or circulate internal documents. As one protester explained to me during a street demonstration in Ireland: "Came for the lulz; stayed for great justice, epic win, and moar lulz." But why? How did such a chaotic ensemble organize themselves? And could the lulz still thrive when seeking justice?

Why (and How) We Protest

Every time I reflect on the constitution and perseverance of Chanology, it strikes me as a minor miracle in the annals of political resistance. To be sure, a subset of trolling (like the Hal Turner raids) struck a political chord, but the energy behind these early raids tended to dissipate after a few days or weeks. Chanology was sustained in an environment not exactly conducive to long-term deliberate political organizing; it behooves us to consider the social dynamics behind Chanology's success, especially in light of the many tensions—for instance, between lulz-driven action and moral goals—which bedeviled it from the start.

To begin with, the formation of a sustained political will was secured by the widespread media coverage of the February street demonstrations. From the first day, people in Guy Fawkes masks were all over the news. Hundreds of photos and dozens of homemade videos from local protests were shared through IRC and popular social media sites like Digg, Myspace, Yahoo! Groups, and LiveJournal. For many Anons, the external representations validated Project Chanology and Anonymous. This dynamic of success and amplification repeated many times in the organization's history.

Also significant were ulterior motives: while activism was a significant factor for many Anons (and the lulz were always enticing), many turned out for the rare opportunity to meet some of their Anonymous brethren. Some stayed, others returned to their dark corners of the Internet and contested this incipient political sensibility, sometimes deriding their peers as "moralfags" and redoubling their trolling—even targeting Chanology itself as a source of lulz. Take, for instance, the following proposal—a call to reclaim Anonymous from the moralfags in order to resurrect the Internet Hate Machine—proposed on Chanology's very active virtual town square, the web forum Enturbulation.org (which was eventually ported to WhyWeProtest):

Fellow brothers and sisters,

Six months ago we started on a jihad to ensure that our internets would be free of faggotry. A call to arms went out and we answered it as legion. Today, when looking back at our naïve efforts it is obvious that what is ours by right has been stolen from us.

Our name, our memes and our efforts have been hijacked by people who do not understand and do not realize that our strength came from being diverse, uncaring and unrelenting. While normally this would not be an issue those who have stayed in the trenches protecting our ideals are now at an impasse.

We need your help, I am bent on hand and foot [*sic*] asking that those that have left Project Chanology return and reclaim it. Bring back the lulz, bring back the hate machine, do not let some rather forceful detractors sway you.

We started this to ensure our internets were free from tyranny and while I agree there are fights ahead that maybe [*sic*] more important to this end, this is the first one. Where we mold the newfags into hardened trolls and ensure that when the man comes to claim what is rightfully free we are all well versed in ensuring that cannot happen.

Over the coming weeks you will see some old faces raid your channels, your boards, your IRCs to ensure that Anonymous retains what is ours. Reclaim Chanology once and for all, burn anything that opposes us to the ground.[7]

The binary between moralfags and "hardened" lulz-seekers was, and still is, less clear-cut than this post suggests. On the IRC channels dedicated to political organizing, a small but rather vocal minority offered technical aid for political gain while also insisting on lulzy action, including horrific forms of trolling. Among these trolls, a single individual, named CPU (not his real name), stood out. Widely considered a talented hacker, he freely offered technical advice. But he was also a fierce critic of the moralfags and would clamor for vicious forms of trolling. For instance: on March 16, 2008, CPU suggested the following on the IRC channel #internethatemachine, a chat room for criticizing the moralfags (all names have been changed):

<CPU>: Internethatemachine is for those sick of the moralfags and the lovefags am i rite lol?
<CPU>: We should just hit a random forum for the lulz. Anyone remember the emetophobia raids?
<CPU>: I'm searching for a forum lol.
<CPU>: oh lol http://www.suicideforum.com/
<CPU>: First person to push someone to the edge wins?

<CPU>: Who remembers happy tree friends? :p
<CPU>: We trashed the forums every day for about 2 weeks lol.
<CPU>: Emo-corner got owned in the end, hard but it took time.
<CPU>: Too many people attacking the same thig at once lol.
<CPU>: We took their forum off of them at least twice and added a deface page lol.
<CPU>: Or we could find an epilepsy forum and spam it with flashing gifs or something?
<XB>: http://www.epilepsyforum.org.uk/
<CPU>: gogoogogo
<CO>: Oh god…phpbb aswel? :D Oh so exploitable.
<CPU>: Change main page to one big flashing thing?
<CPU>: lol making an account now :D
<CPU>: If we can change the main page we use this http://www.freetheflash.com/flash/epilepsy-test.php

Whether CPU and the others on the channel went on to execute this campaign is unknown—but someone did. On March 22, 2012, trolls engaged in one of the most morally reprehensible and notorious attacks to date, invading an epilepsy forum and posting bright flashing images which induced seizures among some of the forum's members. Nearly every piece of reporting incorrectly attributed the attack to Anons fighting Scientology, which was not likely the case; various threads on different image boards blamed another notorious board infested with trolls: eBaum's world. Even if Chanology was not behind the attack, the raid left a dark stain on the name Anonymous, infuriating some members of Chanology.[8]

It must be noted that while the anti-Scientology crusaders were mortified by the epilepsy forum attack, these nascent moralfags did not altogether disavow deviance or the lulz—it is, after all, part of the fabric of their culture. Instead, Chanology dabbled in a kinder, gentler breed of lulz. For instance, New York City is home to an annual (and rather sizable) zombie flash mob, whereupon a thousand ghoulish, bloody, slow-moving, groaning bodies drag (or sometimes rollerskate) themselves through the city streets. Chanology organizers in New York thought it might be lulzy if this zombie mob paraded in front of the Scientology Church on the day of Anonymous's monthly protest there. The zombie mob happily obliged. They sauntered down 46th Street in slow motion, yelling obscenities at the Church while the Chanology protesters rofled and snickered at Scientology, obviously proud of the theatrical (and mostly G-rated) lulz they managed to stage.

But there is no better example of activist Anons' engagement of carnivalesque humor than Operation Slickpubes in January 2009, also orchestrated by the Chanology cell in New York. It consisted of a nearly naked person (he was partially covered by a veneer of smeared Vaseline and pubic hair) streaking through a Scientology Org. The aim of this over-the-top endeavor was not simply to antagonize and anger Church members through an act of defilement (though this was no doubt part of it), but also to revitalize what some participants saw as the flagging spirit of the lulz. The forces of Apollo had to be balanced, eternally, with a bit of Dionysian trickster revelry. Later, Chanology members wrote about the incident in a blog post on motherfuckery.org, a site designed to commemorate their roots:

> What resulted in the following months could only be described as "lulz" and "u mad", as the record of the Slickpubes operation made its rounds throughout the world of Chanology, anonymous, and the higher ranks of Scientology. Those who thought Chanology was too tame rejoiced.[9]

Within this emerging politically oriented Anonymous, the lulz were often deployed, as in Operation Slickpubes, in a jocular, Dionysian form: risqué yet also risky. They worked by simultaneously making one laugh, making one cringe, and also offering a politics of subversion. But not without consequences. Indeed, in the case of Operation Slickpubes, the greasy streaker was arrested for his antics. The incident also prompted the NYPD to begin secretly monitoring Anonymous (a necessary baptism for any new political group, and what better way to attract law enforcement than through pubic hair?).[10] Wise Beard Man may have tamed the Anonymous trickster, but he did not fully eliminate its mischievous spirit.

Anonymous's willingness to wreak havoc in pursuit of lulz and free speech (and in opposition to the malfeasance and deception of Scientology) calls to mind the nineteenth-century European "social bandits" described by historian Eric Hobsbawm in his 1959 book *Primitive Rebels*. These bandits are members of mafias, secret societies, religious sects, urban mobs, and outlaw gangs; they are ultimately thugs, but, according to Hobsbawm, they nurture a faint revolutionary spirit: some of their plunder is typically redistributed to the poor who they further protect from bandits other than themselves. Hobsbawm defines the bandits as "pre-political" figures "who have not yet found, or only begun to find, a specific language in which to express their aspirations about the world."[11] Anonymous has worked toward finding that language with remarkable celerity since it launched Project Chanology.

Such hijinks nevertheless contrast with Hobsbawm's moral narrative, whereby bandits can only become viable political actors by giving up their menacing tactics and buying into conventional forms of power. For Hobsbawm, the bandit is pitted against "the forces of the new society which he cannot understand. At most he can fight it and seek to destroy it." This explains why "the bandit is often destructive and savage beyond the range of his myth."[12] Today's digital bandits, however, understand the forces of creative destruction, consciously deploying them for political purposes.

The lulz retained a prominent seat, but not at the head of the table. Chanology was a far cry from a chaotic horde of loons. While working in the midst of an often miasmic environment of drama, in-fighting, and competing groups, Chanology members developed a strong organization, with core participants devoting extraordinary chunks of time to the endeavor. We can take, as a case study, the software behind the immensely popular web forum Why We Protest, largely written by a young French geek named Ravel. He described joining Chanology as a natural fit, given that he had "some mischievous years and strong affinities with both the hacker and freedom of speech cultures. When the call to action came I didn't bat an eye and pretty much uttered 'let's do this.'"[13] He made it his life project for the next six years and counting.

The project emerged from the creation of the #website IRC channel. Ravel (known as Sue) disliked the existing proposals and, in classic hacker style, started to code the software according to his own vision with the help of two other programmers. Due to his hard work he was tapped to become part of marblecake:

> I was approached and became part of the (unduly) infamous marblecake collective ... To date it has been the most organized group I have collaborated with online. I wouldn't exaggerate when saying the quorum of participants spent over 70 hours a week working on media projects, planning, PR, and brainstorming. It served both as think tank and production studio. Meetings were held near daily, assessments were made, notes kept and so forth.[14]

"What the dicks is marblecake?":
First Challenges to the New Anonymous

With a sizeable portion of Anons now firmly committed to this politically engaged style of hacking (complete with a technical infrastructure of channels, monthly meet-ups at Chanology events, and an emergent range of memes and objects specific to activist-Anonymous, like Guy Fawkes masks), it was only a matter of time before this identity would fracture. Homeostasis is not, exactly, the preferred state of Anonymous—certainly not before Chanology, and definitely not after.

Let's linger for a moment on Ravel's characterization of marblecake as "the most organized group I have collaborated with online." By all accounts, marblecake was extremely effective in creating propaganda, issuing press releases, brokering between city cells, and suggesting themes for monthly protests. Among other factors, many attributed its success to a skilled organizer who went by the name of darr. A peer described her to me as "resolute and fierce, kind and understanding"—qualities the Anon thought crucial to marblecake's accomplishments.

But then darr made the mistake of attempting to push through an unpopular proposal. For the May 2008 protest, marblecake suggested the theme "Operation Psychout," to air Scientology's human rights abuses in the field of psychiatry, which was "met with a lot of opposition," explained one active member to me. Soon after, marblecake hammered the final nail into its own coffin—at least in the form it existed at the time—by seeking to "railroad it through," which led to Chanology members "taking darr down," who was seen as a particularly vocal proponent. Or a "power-hungry wannabee leaderfag," as one Anon put it. Trolls, especially, went for the jugular, doxing her and spreading lies. She quit the project, never to be seen again.

Marblecake existed in a nebulous zone. When the eight members had splintered off in January 2008, they left a permanent notification on the chat channel #press: "Want access to where all the action is? Get your ass on SSL and don't be a faggot ; D—Topic set by darr on 16/02/2008." Those intrigued by this enticing message could ask an "oldfag" about it— someone around since the beginning—and be directed through the steps to set up encryption (SSL). They would also have to be prepared to clock a lot of long hours. In this way, marblecake grew to include twenty-five participants. Eventually, the topic message was replaced and growth stagnated— newcomers had no idea about its existence.

Three months after darr's outing, someone posted a message on Why We Protest: "What the dicks is marblecake?" The answer they received effectively informed a much larger swath of Anons about the semi-secret project. For many, it revealed for the first time that multiple factions had developed under the mantle of Chanology:

I'm in marblecake, and I've no interest in being a leaderfag.
I'm happy to answer questions.
The short story is, it is/was a small thinktank that produced media anonymously and secretly. The positive spin would be that it has "suffered from its own success"—it produces enough significant media that it desires to remain completely secret ... and producing enough media that the rest of Anonymous became aware—to varying degrees—that there is a secret cabal of anons trying to manipulate things behind the scenes.
The negative spin is ... that it's a secret cabal of anons trying to manipulate things behind the scenes. And there is a case to be made that they got a swelled head early. They produced the original "message to scientology" video (well before I got involved). They were also led by Darr, who pissed off the wrong people, has the wrong attitude, and generally didn't handle criticism well.
[...]
As far as factions go, there's marblecake, enturbmods, OCMB, and the #enturbulation channers (in addition to each individual city's cell, and probably many others I don't know about). MC and entubmods have battled, #enturbulation (specifically Tuesday and WB) have battled with marblecake. OCMB often has drama pour over into enturbulation. #enturbulation generally hates marble-cake. It's all a bunch of stupid infighting, and many people have been involved with more than one of those groups. And nobody should feel "left out" for not being involved in any of 'em, 'cause they're all essentially janitors for the

real anons, the ones that are out in cities fliering and picketing.[15]

The ensuing thread was long and bitter. Some people were seething, including some members and ex-members of the cabal. After this brouhaha, marblecake foundered for a bit before undergoing what one Anon called "reformation." Afterwards, they functioned with more transparency regarding their role as "choreographers," to borrow the phrase used by Paolo Gerbaudo to describe a leadership style common throughout the global protest movements of 2011.[16]

Marblecake's outing showed that a simple binary between leaders and followers failed to capture the complex organizational dynamics in a milieu so committed to decentralization. Anonymous is not a united front, but a hydra—comprising numerous different networks. Even within a single project there are working groups that are often at odds with one another—not to mention the civil wars between different nodes of Anonymous more generally. But even if Anons don't always agree about what is being done under the auspices of Anonymous, they tend to respect the fact that anyone can assume the moniker. The mask, which has become its signature icon, functions as an eternal beacon, broadcasting the symbolic value of equality, even in the face of bitter divisions and inequalities. Of course, despite the lack of a stable hierarchy or a single point of control, some Anons are more active and influential than others—at least for limited periods. Anonymous abides by a particular strain of what geeks call "do-ocracy," with motivated individuals (or those with free time) extending its networked architecture by contributing time, labor, and attention to existing endeavors or leaving others to start ones of their own, aligned better to their ideals and principles.

Whether a movement even fesses up to the existence of soft leaders is an important question. It relates to another issue plaguing many social movements: how does a social movement maintain enough permeability that newcomers can join pre-existing groups, whose tendency is to become cliquish? Without overt recognition that leadership exists, a project can fall easily into the "tyranny of structurelessness"—a situation whereby the vocalizing of an ideology of decentralization works as a platitude that obscures or redirects attention away from firmly entrenched but hidden nodes of power behind the scenes.[17]

Following the heated controversy that erupted on Why We Protest, many Anons came to accept that marblecake played a valuable organizational role. The group's soft leadership engendered an impressive amount of organization—both online and in local cities. But the general consensus was in favor of more transparency.

"There is no way Scientology can win on us anymore. It is over."

In 2014, Project Chanology is a shadow of its former self. Current monthly protests draw only the hardcore, with small to midsized turnouts in a smattering of cities (like Dublin, Düsseldorf, Hamburg, and New York). However, this situation reflects not failure, but success. While Project Chanology did not demolish the Church, it altered the game so fundamentally that critics could now stand confidently under the sun without fear of reprisal. The Church no longer had the upper hand.

This point was driven home by numerous ex-Scientologists during a conference I attended called Dublin Offlines, organized by ex-Scientologists on June 30, 2012. It had been a little over four years since this unlikely elixir first fomented via a strange brew of ex-Church members, Scientology critics, and uppity Internet geeks. This occasion seemed an appropriate time and place for me to take stock of the projects historical import.

The conference was held in Dublin's Teacher's Club (aka Club na Múinteoirí), housed in a four-story Georgian building which provided cozy and intimate shelter from the ever-present Irish drizzle. About seventy folks attended, a sizable chunk of them wearing Guy Fawkes masks. In keeping with the theatrics common to street demonstrations, some Anons from France were dressed with panache in circus and panto-mime getups. Two were even dressed as giant leprechauns. My personal favorite was the guy sporting a cow suit.

Speakers included ex-Scientologists from the Scientology ship, some from the Sea Org, Gerry Armstrong (the former personal secretary to L. Ron Hubbard), Jamie DeWolf (the great-grandson of L. Ron Hubbard), a couple of academics (including myself), and a handful of individuals who had lost family to the Church. The master of ceremonies was Pete Griffiths, a local and a former executive director of the Kendal mission, in Cumbria, England; his shimmering silver suit perfectly matched his spirited personality.

Since I was staying on the other side town, I arrived a little late to find the talks already in full swing. I tiptoed in, silently waved to some of the locals I knew from a previous trip to Dublin, and slipped into a seat. I felt okay, if certainly under-caffeinated. But by the end of the day, having squirmed in discomfort during many of the talks, I was left emotionally drained. The ex-Scientologists provided moving personal accounts of the cult's power to strangle the lives of both those in the Church and those who dared to leave. Church policy mandates that new recruits sever ties with any family and friends who object (as many do); leaving the organization is often a logistical nightmare, since one's personal network has been so thoroughly eviscerated. If a member is public about his or her exit, the member is targeted under the "fair game policy," which states that the individual "[m]ay be deprived of property or injured by any means by any Scientologist without any discipline of the Scientologist. May be tricked, sued or lied to or destroyed."[18]

A talk by Tory Christman stood out among the rest. Before leaving on July 20, 2000, she had been a Scientologist for thirty-one years, during which period she honed her speaking skills by performing public relations for the church. Christman was confident, eloquent, inspirational, and witty; sporting rectangular glasses and a bright blue suit, she beamed with energy. She spoke for thirty minutes and packed in a whole lot: her entry into the Church, some of her less than pleasant experiences (such as the Church's attempt to discourage her use of epilepsy medicine), insight into the Church's mechanics of brainwashing ("It is a slow train of mind control," as she put it), and descriptions of the Church's theological tendencies delivered through pricey classes ("Keeping Scientology Working is on every single course"). As she was winding down, she described her harrowing escape ("[Scientology] chased me across the country") and highlighted the Church's greatest irony ("they are selling freedom but they enslave you").

She also duly acknowledged Anonymous's role: "Everyone now has the luxury [of being public] because, (A) the Internet; (B) critics even before Anonymous and; (C) Anonymous. Right? Which was totally a game changer. Forever. And it was and we all know this." She highlighted the bravery of an earlier generation of critics, a handful of whom were in attendance, who acted publicly when the number of defectors was low and Scientology held the power to shatter their lives by targeting critics aggressively and with impunity. "Anonymous would not be around if it were not for the critics before them," she said.

Her next statement reverberated in slow motion through the room and touched everyone personally: "There is no way Scientology can win on us anymore. It is over." For the ex-Scientologists in the room, the words likely hit as a combination of relief and joy. The Anons, some whom had become close to ex-Scientologists, likely felt the pride of political accomplishment wash over them. There is nothing, *nothing*, quite like the sweet taste of political victory, and Chanology had accomplished the unlikely: the group successfully challenged an organization that seemed all-powerful, impervious to critique, and above the law.

More remarkable yet is that what started as a narrowly configured politics launched against a single foe broke out of that frame to encompass a fuller, diverse, thoroughly global political enterprise—a bonfire that burned hot and bright enough to spread across the globe, becoming Anonymous Everywhere. Let's now turn to the unlikely events that propelled Anonymous's surprising rise to prominence.

CHAPTER 3

Weapons of the Geek

WikiLeaks: The Gift that Keeps on Giving

It was July 2010 and I was attending a conference called Hackers on Planet Earth (also known as HOPE), held every other year in New York City's charmingly historic (and, in its resemblance to the hotel in *The Shining*, creepily *historical*) Hotel Pennsylvania. Done with my talk, I was ready to soak up the conference's truly extraordinary, politically charged atmosphere of drama, intrigue, and suspense. The charged mood at HOPE wasn't the result of Anonymous. At the time, while Anonymous could already be described as politically quirky, the group was—geopolitically speaking—of little real significance. Anonymous activists had started to engage in other arenas (like Iran's Green Revolution) but were still primarily focused on Chanology, doggedly exposing Scientology's human rights abuses and protesting every month in cities across North America, Australia, Europe, and a few other countries. A sizeable number of trolls still claimed the Anonymous moniker, but this stream of ultracoordinated motherfuckery was clearly on the wane.

No, the intrigue saturating the conference was due to another player in town: the whistleblowing sensation WikiLeaks. More specifically, interest coalesced around the recent trove of documents and footage leaked by a young army private named Chelsea Manning (formerly Bradley Manning) and laid at the feet of the world by WikiLeaks. Founded in 2006, the driving concept behind WikiLeaks had been simple: provide both a safe house and clearinghouse for leaks. It'd been at it for years, circulating countless leaks but failing to draw significant attention from established media institutions like the *New York Times*. This lack of attention was not due to unworthiness. In fact, some of these leaks—like the news that the multinational company Trafigura had illegally dumped toxic waste off the Ivory Coast—were both shocking and shockingly absent from the mainstream news media. It also wasn't for want of trying—at least not exclusively. The British government gagged the left-leaning newspaper the *Guardian* from covering the Trafigura story. As the editors noted at the time, "The *Guardian* is also forbidden from telling its readers why the paper is prevented—for the first time in memory— from reporting parliament. Legal obstacles, which cannot be identified, involve proceedings, which cannot be mentioned, on behalf of a client who must remain secret."[1]

And so, by April 2010, WikiLeaks had dramatically switched public relations strategies. When they released video footage of a Baghdad air strike under the title "Collateral Murder," WikiLeaks left nothing to chance—packaging the already shocking material in a way that delivered an extra punch. They edited the video for maximum effect and added simple but powerful editorial commentary at the beginning. Julian Assange, the Australian hacker who founded WikiLeaks, was then known in the media as an "international man of mystery." Now he broke with his previous disavowal of the spotlight. To coincide with the publication of the video, he hosted a press conference in Washington, DC, and followed it with a high-profile media tour.

The journalistic and public response was nothing short of explosive. Media scholar Christian Christensen argues the video is "one of the best known and most widely recognized

results of the ongoing WikiLeaks project," because it provides "visual evidence of the gross abuse of state and military
power."[2] The black-and-white footage is captured from the
perspective of a soldier in an Apache attack helicopter as he
mows down civilians in a Baghdad suburb. The video, shot in
2007, provoked questions. Why had we not seen the footage
earlier? Two of the men killed in the attack were journalists
working for the Reuters news service and the organization
had been trying, in the years since the attack, to get its hands
on the footage via a Freedom of Information ACT request.
They suspected foul play, and their suspicions were not
unfounded. The video was an embarrassing reminder of how
the mainstream media had failed in its mission to inform the
public by turning its back on the direct and gruesome style
of war reportage it had practiced in the final years of the
Vietnam War.

More than anything, though, it was the pilots' banal tone of
voice during their discussions with command about whether
to attack—they were calm to the point of psychosis—that
really sent waves of horror over you. One member of the crew
laughs upon discovering that one of the victims is a young girl.
"Well, it's their fault for bringing their kids to a battle," he
remarks nonchalantly.

As we all now know, Chelsea Manning chose to leak the
video, along with other vital documents, and a hacker named
Adrian Lamo ratted her out. On May 22, 2010, Manning confessed to Lamo during a chat conversation that she'd gifted
WikiLeaks the footage that was used to create "Collateral
Murder." Early in the conversation, Lamo earned Manning's
trust by misrepresenting himself:

> I'm a journalist and a minister. You can pick either, and treat this as a
> confession or an interview (never to be published) & enjoy a modicum
> of legal protection.[3]

Manning subsequently spilled her guts to a person she had never met and whose claims of being a journalist and a priest were tenuous as best.[4] Lamo turned the log over to both the FBI and *Wired* magazine. The FBI arrested Manning, ultimately leading to her admission that she had provided WikiLeaks with not only the video footage seen in "Collateral Murder," but also the diplomatic cables WikiLeaks would release over the next two years. Manning was sentenced by a military judge to thirty-five years in prison, and is now at Fort Leavenworth, following a year in solitary confinement before being sentenced.[5]

At the 2010 HOPE conference, there was palpable tension in the air. Rumors swirled that Julian Assange was going to give the keynote. In a last-minute switch-up, it was not Assange who stepped out on stage, but American hacker Jacob Appelbaum. His riveting talk effectively outed him, in front of everyone in attendance (including the inevitable federal agents), as an affiliate of the embattled organization. It was a bold move, given the tactics of silencing, prosecution, and intimidation leveled against the organization by US authorities. His talk contextualized WikiLeaks historically into what is now commonly called "the fifth estate": the hackers, leakers, independent journalists, and bloggers who serve the critical role that once fell to "the fourth estate," the mainstream media. Or as Appelbaum put it, "When the media is gagged, we refuse to be gagged. We refuse to be silent"— a declaration that was met with thunderous applause. (The most glaring example of media silence in the past decade was when the *New York Times* refused, at the request of the government, to publish a story on the NSA's illegal, warrantless wiretaps. The *Times* eventually ran the story—only because the author, James Risen, was about to scoop the paper by publishing a book on the topic. The article which they tried so hard to withhold ended up winning a Pulitzer Prize.)

While WikiLeaks, "Collateral Murder," and Manning had found pride of place in talks among politically minded hackers and transparency advocates, a fourth figure dominated most conversations at HOPE: Lamo, the hacker traitor. He was on the tip of every tongue for one simple reason: he was, like them, a hacker himself—and present at the conference, no less. People were completely pissed off. Appelbaum, during his talk on WikiLeaks, promised not to utter a word about Lamo. As he said this, he unbuttoned his shirt to reveal a T-shirt that said "Stop Snitching." The crowd went wild. Flyers bearing Lamo's face subsequently popped up throughout the venue. Lamo was "WANTED// Dead or Alive// for bein' a low-down good for nuthin' rat bastard."

As I stood staring at the flyer, a hacker friend of mine darted up from behind me to say hello. Shaking his head in Lamo-evoked disgust, my friend explained that Assange was "the real deal"—rare high praise from a fellow hacker. He had known him back in the 1990s when the hacker underground was in full force and roaming free, before the crackdowns against them in the late 1990s. This class of hacker would routinely disregard the law in his or her explorations of private networks and computer systems—not motivated by profit or malice, but instead by an insatiable curiosity: a desire to know how things worked. While the transgression itself offered a form of pleasure, back then only a small class of hackers was explicitly inclined toward activist-oriented politics. Julian Assange was one of them. He was a thoroughly conscientious hacker who even penned ethical manifestos explaining his actions. Assange was part of a small team of "International Subversives" who abided by a creed: "Don't damage computer systems you break into (including crashing them); don't change the information in those systems (except for altering logs to cover your tracks); and share information."[6]

Wrapping up our discussion on Assange, my friend and I heard some exciting news. HOPE's main organizer, Eric Corley—better known by his famous hacker handle "Emmanuel Goldstein"—had announced an impromptu panel on snitching and snitches, featuring none other than Lamo.

Lamo was slated to sit alongside some of the most famous underground phone phreaks and hackers of all time: Bernie S., Mark Abene (aka Phiber Optik), and Kevin Mitnick. A couple had served jail time as the result of snitching. They themselves, in their own trials and travails, had all refused to "cooperate," paying dearly with extended jail time for staying silent and not ratting out their peers.

In all my years of attending hacker conferences, this panel remains the most extraordinary I have witnessed. Imagine 2,600 hackers sitting before a single despised traitor as he looks out at them from the stage and attempts to justify his actions.

Hacker Town Hall on Snitching with the Most Reviled Hacker Snitch of All Time

The hackers opened the panel by recounting riveting stories of their exploits, eventual capture, and betrayal at the hands of trusted peers. The first to speak was Goldstein, who highlighted a truism I would see in action a little later with Anonymous. When cops or Feds show up (usually at daybreak and knocking loudly while pointing guns), Goldstein reminded the audience, "People panic ... and the authorities count on this. The authorities live for this kind of thing so that they get as much information—they get all of us telling other people about other people."

When Lamo climbed on stage and ambled slowly toward his chair, well ... The circles under his eyes were deep brown, and when he blinked it was done in slow motion and with great difficulty, as if he had to force his eyelids down each time. It wasn't that he seemed nervous—he just seemed genuinely zonked; it is quite possible that he was, along with being very tired, also medicated. Lamo had once been lauded as a black hat hacker, and listening to him justify his actions was spellbinding. He felt "compelled," he explained, to hand over the logs in the interest of national defense. Bernie S., wanting details, respectfully interrupted: "In what way did you feel people were put at risk?" Lamo gave a rambling response: "The State Department is involved in a number of intelligence operations throughout the world, um, they are not supposed to be, but they are looking out for the interests of Americans." This triggered immediate hisses from the crowd, and an audience member yelled, "The State Department activities put other people at risk!"

Goldstein sensed the crowd might turn into a lynch mob, sharpening their pitchforks and lighting their torches, ready to run Lamo out of town. He calmed the audience down, reminding them, "You will have your say"—but not before Phiber Optik first chortled, "We will be handing out darts and bows and arrows, so don't worry." The comic relief released some steam, but the tense atmosphere simply returned until the end. Time and again, Lamo's attempts to rationalize his actions were met with angry boos. After Lamo defended the government and described his interactions with its agents as a "surprisingly pleasant undertaking," even Goldstein couldn't help himself; he interrupted Lamo before the Q and A period to ask how he felt about the possibility that Manning might spend the rest of her life in jail (someone in the crowd also lobbed out "Torture!"). Without missing a beat, Lamo intonated slowly: "We don't do that to our citizens." Some of the loudest hisses and boos of the day rustled through the audience, and someone yelled: "Guantanamo!" No matter what Lamo said, it was apparent that he was digging himself into a deeper hole—and it was also apparent that nearly the entire auditorium was ready to fill in the dirt on top of him.

At the time, however engrossing the panel was, I could not see its relevance to my project on Anonymous. WikiLeaks and Anonymous were, back then, residing on different planets (even if they were, admittedly, part of the same geeky galaxy by way of their respective fights against censorship and Scientology).[7] And yet, one year after the conference, on July 4, 2011, I had my very first private IRC chat with Anonymous's most famous snitch: Hector Monsegur, who had previously been known only as "Sabu." By then he had already been arrested and was secretly working with the FBI—though this fact was lost both on myself and many others at time (in spite of a litany of now obvious clues). Monsegur's charisma—and his adeptness in psychological warfare tactics, like displacing suspicion by accusing *others* of snitching—blinded many to the hints he dropped in plain text a few months after his covert arrest: "Stick to yourselves," he wrote on reddit. "If you are in a crew—keep your opsec up 24/7. Friends will try to take you down if they have to."[8] This echoed a lesson which Manning had learned first hand a year earlier.

But the mutual problem of snitches is the most tenuous of the emergent connections between WikiLeaks and Anonymous. We can trace a more direct coupling by looking at the trajectory of AnonOps.

DDoSing on Random Dice Day

AnonOps emerged in 2010, just a few months after HOPE ended. It began as a new Anonymous node and eventually grew into a full-blown IRC network. The network would take the world by storm thanks to its experiments—and I do mean, quite literally, experiments, as the group never carefully thought through anything until much later—with a slew of direct action political tactics. Many of these were straight up illegal, so it was only a matter of time before they drew the attention of the FBI.

Although the history of AnonOps would come to intersect with WikiLeaks in December 2010, these two entities could not be more different when judged from the perspective of organizational mechanics. WikiLeaks was built up as a carefully sculpted life's work. Assange, as founder and spokesperson, controlled—too tightly, many would come to say—most aspects, and his personality and identity became hopelessly intertwined with the WikiLeaks name. When his personal reputation was sullied, it tarnished the organization as a whole. On the other hand, the constitution of AnonOps was a happenstance affair, like Project Chanology before it: born in the contingent convergence of timing, and media attention, each element contributed to its meteoritic rise and rapid success—a reminder again of how tricksters, like Anonymous, are perfectly poised to exploit the accidents gifted to them and sometimes benefit from acting on a whim.

It was late August 2010, about two and a half years after hackers had first adopted the name Anonymous to venture into activism. By this time, Chanology had organized street protests, forged tight alliances and friendships with ex-Scientologists, dabbled in Iran's unsuccessful Green Revolution, and branched out into other areas of Internet activism. In February 2010, after Australia's Telecommunication Minister proposed regulation to filter Internet pornography, some Anons rolled out "Operation Titstorm" and successfully overwhelmed government servers with a barrage of traffic requests. This op, proclaimed as part of the Operation Freedom Movement, was a harbinger of what was soon to come.

A number of Anons relaunched the Operation Freedom Movement, rebranded the Internet Freedom Movement (IFM)—on July 5, eleven days before HOPE.[9] Those involved in the IFM, along with the geek world at large, had set their sights on protesting the Anti-Counterfeiting Trade Agreement (ACTA). ACTA sought, among other things, to introduce sweeping regulations which would criminalize copyright infringement and encourage Internet service providers to profile, track, and monitor their users. Opposition was fierce, and nearly every group involved in the politics of access—Electronic Frontier Foundation, the Free Software Foundation, Public Knowledge, La Quadrature du Net—criticized the secrecy under which the treaty was being negotiated, and categorically opposed its ratification.

The proposed methodology of the IFM was to lobby politicians and raise public awareness using propaganda materials and websites. As part of these efforts, advocates created a dedicated chat room called "#antiactaplanning" on the IRC server OccultusTerra. In late August 2010, an Anon activist going by the nickname "golum" (not his usual pseudonym) entered the chat room and boldly declared his intent to move things forward by DDoSing the Office of the US Trade Representative (USTR) website, ustr.gov, at 9 pm EST on September 19, 2010. The USTR's office was a natural choice given that ACTA was a US-led trade agreement and the USTR had the muscle to levy sanctions against nations that violated trade treaties.

But many people in the chat room had concerns: First, Chanology had already set a political precedent by disavowing the use of illegal tactics like DDoS. And second, no one could understand why that particular date had been chosen. It struck many as completely arbitrary, and it (mostly) was; the one connection was that September 19 is Talk Like a Pirate Day. golum faced vehement opposition, at least from those who were paying attention to their screens (all pseudonyms have been changed):

<matty>: why before it is signed?
<golum>: Because it's a Sunday and everyone likes Sundays
<matty>: again ... why before it is signed?
<golum>: And because I threw a dice
<golum>: And it said 19th
[...]
<golum>: My prediction is by September 19th people will become more aware.
<golum>: Trust me on this. September 19th.
<fatalbert>: trust me on a random dice day

Although everyone on the channel savaged golum's proposal, he remained unmoved:

<golum>: Whatever, listen. I've heard all the arguments for NOT ddosing. But the truth is we need to wake them up.

[...]

<golum>: I understand that ddosing could potentially harm our cause.

<golum>: But I think the risk is worth it.

<fatalbert>: well i as for myself disagree therefore im not helping with ddos

<golum>: We need attention

<+void>: OMG ITS THE ANONYMOUS, THE ONLY THING THEY DO IS DDOS, OMGOMGOMOGMOMG LETS MAKE ACTA PASS ON POSITIVE

<golum>: No.

<golum>: matty—how did contacting the politicians go?

<BamBam>: Yeah I've always kinda hated ddos

<golum>: Look. i've heard the arguments I just wanted to say, we should do this.

<golum>: We are NOT ddosing now. This will be in 20 days.

<golum>: 20 days is a lot of time.

A few Anons, conveying the legal risks, highlighted the difference between targeting the US government and targeting other entities, and then considered the conversation over. (Note also that the risk assessment about arrests was accurate—over twenty-seven individuals have been since indicted for the ensuing spate of DDoS actions—and in the United States you can still get in deep trouble for targeting anyone famous):

<matty>: this is not justin beiber, this is the us govt ffs

[...]

<golum>: Everyone please, listen to me, when I speak

<AnonLaw>: I'll be laughing as you go to jail

<matty>: i am not here for the fuckin lulz

[...]

<golum>: It's official. Start preparing.

If you are wondering about just what "official" means in Anonymous: well, yes, something *can* be deemed "official" if someone declares it as such and, *crucially*, if enough people also support it. But at the time, support for militant direct action tactics on this IRC channel were lacking. Although someone had initiated an IRC channel called "#ddos" with the mandate of discussing the possible use of the tactic, the freewheeling aspect of Anonymous IRC chat only goes so far before bumping up against norms and rules:

> <Lola>: What happened to #DDoS?
> <Fred>: Take that to off topic please.
> <Fred>: This is strictly for ACTA planing.
> <Fred>: Not for a chit chat
> <Lola>: #ddos was an ACTA planning channel.
> <Lola>: I want to know what happened to it
> <Fred>: Questions about #ddos is off topic.
> <Fred>: This is for planing.
> <Yagermister>: #DDoS is BAD

The next day Lola appeared again—this time to discuss botnets (networks of remotely controlled computers which can be used to strengthen a DDoS assault):

> <Lola>: do you have a botnet?
> <Lola>: without one you can't do much
> <Lola>: you can get like $10 for 100 these days
> <Lola>: from some skiddie forums

Lola is told, again, to stop "discussing illegal activities."

This is, perhaps, an opportune moment to discuss botnets in more detail—especially since they became increasingly important to the Anonymous DDoS operations we will consider a little later. There is a Wild West cattle rustling aspect to the whole affair. A botnet is essentially just a collection of computers connected to the Internet, allowing a single entity extra processing power or network connections toward the performance of various tasks including (but not limited to) DDoSing and spam bombing. A botnet is a very powerful tool, involving (as it does) computers that are connected across various parts of the world and capable of distributing tasks. Participants whose computers are tapped for membership in a botnet usually have no idea that their computer is being used for these purposes. Have you ever wondered why your computer worked so slowly, or strangely? Well, you might have unwittingly participated in a DDoS.

A computer most often becomes a member of a botnet by getting infected by malware. This can happen through a number of different methods—that hilarious cat video you downloaded, the malicious link in an email from your aunt, a phishing attack you didn't even know about, or a virus piggybacking on some software you downloaded from the Internet. Once infected, the computer runs a small program, usually hidden in the process table so it is not easily found, which mediates its involvement in the botnet.

Although there are many different ways for a botnet to work, one classic method involves connecting it to a pre-configured IRC server and channel. Once this connection is made, the computer will wait patiently—unbeknownst to their owners—awaiting orders from the botnet herder (yeehaw!). The herder is the individual capable of directing the computers that make up the botnet. Typically, this is the person who infected the computers in the first place. Usually he or she is waiting in the designated IRC channel, grinning from ear-to-ear as more and more infected computers join the channel, like zombies awaiting orders. This is known as the command-and-control channel (C&C). A typical scenario might see a herder tabbing back and forth between regular chat channels and the hidden C&C channel as it grows more powerful by the moment.

A typical botnet might boast around twenty thousand computers, but larger botnets have been tracked to upwards of thirty million. (Though most botnets have a bad rap—and for good reason—some botnets are voluntary and participatory. The most famous of these is probably SETI@home, the three-million-strong string of computers searching for alien life in outer space.) They hover on this C&C channel until the botnet herder gives them an order—usually authenticated—to perform some task. So for example, the botnet herder might simply say, "ddos 172.16.44.1," and then all the connected bots will begin to attack that specified IP address.[10]

Another common task for botnets is to send mass amounts of unwanted email. Spam is often stopped by an algorithm which determines its unwanted nature and blocks the sending address—but when tens of thousands of different machines with different addresses are sending the spam, it is much harder to track down and stop. Often botnet herders assemble their network not for their own purposes, but in order to sell the services of their bots to a spammer.

To be able to control tens of thousands of computers from a central location is a powerful feeling. By simply issuing commands you can make thousands of computers do something for you, and the larger the number of computers participating, the more powerful those commands are. In the botnet world there is an ongoing struggle over who has the most bots, the most bandwidth, and the best-infected machines (university, corporate, and government computers tend to be on better bandwidth).

This competition is so fierce that botnet herders will often try to take over other botnets. On the other side of the fence, law enforcement agencies and individual organizations that are fighting spam also struggle to take over botnets in order to neutralize them. This is not a trivial thing to do. One has to first identify the C&C. If you can figure out where the bots get their commands from, you can join the IRC channel, masquerading as a compromised machine, and wait to receive a command from the botnet herder. If the botnet herder sends an authentication alongside the command, you may have the password necessary to issue commands to the entire botnet yourself.[11]

But, as Lola indicated, you can also access all that fun and power for a cheap "subscription fee." People on the IRC server were not happy with all this talk of the underworld of botnets and DDoS. The IRC operators booted the pro-DDoS contingent from the server. They left undeterred, becoming Anonymous nomads.

It is perhaps ironic that golum, as one participant explained it to me, "was a central figure in the IFM movement, if not THE central figure." golum may have spearheaded the initiative, but his influence waned as he clamored for the types of digital tactics firmly rejected by the majority of Anons driving Chanology. Effectively, this majority managed "to change the direction of the operation" so as to keep it entirely legal. Those wanting to use direct action techniques found themselves increasingly marginalized. But while golum's random dice day vision may have seemed to them nothing more than, well, random, golum was actually an adept organizer with a keen feel for media dynamics. I had seen in him action many times, and he was one of the finest propagandists and organizers in all of Anonymous. golum left the IFM to form a new direct action–oriented wing, taking some Anons with him. One participant in the new militant enterprise, which would come to be known as AnonOps, described golum as having "a very, very good antenna for PR and propaganda, and he realized the (at the time) immense psychological impact of declaring that a website would vanish, and then taking it down."

golum took his tactics, and his supporters, elsewhere. Strangely, given his announcement of random dice day, he had in fact erected a website with an ACTA protest timeline that differed from the one he had announced on the IRC channel. The site designated the crescendo of activities for November 5, the worldwide day of protests known as Guy Fawkes Day.

golum had conceived of different groups divided by chat rooms (#bump, #newor, #op), each with distinct roles and responsibilities.

Confusion loomed large over the DDoS campaign's start date—but in the end, thanks to the initiative of some unknown actors, it was, as golum predicted, to fall in the middle of September. A stunning and spectacular avalanche of DDoS attacks attracted over seven hundred individuals into the splinter group's chatroom and continued for over two months. In the end, they did not target the Office of the US Trade Representative. Instead, in a defense of file sharing, they DDoSed the heck out of a number of pro-copyright associations, such as the Motion Picture Association of America (MPAA) and the Recording Industry Association of America (RIAA). The media attention was significant and the new crew was hooked. Displaying the Pirate Bay's ship logo—also adopted by Anons as their campaign symbol—the BBC reported: "Piracy activists have carried out coordinated attacks on websites owned by the music and film industry."[12] Anonymous listed every news story written about "Operation Payback"—as the group called it—on tieve.tk, which also became the go-to hub for information as Anonymous migrated from IRC server to IRC server before establishing one of its own in late October.

Drawing upon my experiences with Anonymous, I can confidently declare that had golum's breakaway group simply rallied troops around a slogan like "ACTA sucks," the unprecedented waves of support would never have materialized. Fortunately, the spirit of Puck delivered a delightful accident to this nascent Anonymous crew. It was as if the trickster of crossroads, Eshu, then appeared, urging them to make a decision. And, as we will see, their choice allowed the pod to sprout into one of the Internet's biggest political sensations.

"At times, we have to go an extra mile and attack the site"

The game-changing piece of information first appeared in a technical news article published by an Indian media outlet on September 5, 2010. It took a full week for Western journalists to pick up the story, at which point it circulated along the boutique technical press. The story quotes the managing director of Aiplex, an Indian software firm purportedly hired by corporations to DDoS file sharing sites like the Pirate Bay:

> The problem is with torrent sites, which usually do not oblige [when served with a written legal request to take down a movie]. In such cases, we flood the website with lots of requests, which results in database error, causing denial of service as each server has a fixed bandwidth capacity. At times, we have to go an extra mile and attack the site and destroy the data to stop the movie from circulating further.[13]

Ironically, given the target, that admission essentially provided evidence of a contemporary practice analogous to the privateering of yesteryear. Until outlawed in 1856, European powers routinely hired pirates to operate as their agents on the high seas—with the added advantage of being able to obscure their own involvement in whatever unsavory business they might require the pirates to perform. This was not the first time evidence surfaced that the copyright industries hired technologists to do their (illegal) dirty work. In 2005, the MPAA employed a hacker to break into the servers of TorrentSpy, a search engine for file sharing material, and search for confidential information they hoped would provide evidence of law breaking. During an exclusive interview with Wired.com, this hacker explained how the MPAA attempted to lure him with cash and other luxury goods: "We would need somebody like you. We would give you a nice paying job, a house, a car, anything you needed ... if you save Hollywood for us you can become rich and powerful."[14]

But with Aiplex, it was the first time the admission was so frank and forthcoming.

The reaction from Anonymous and many other geeky quarters of the Internet was predictably swift and biting. For well over a decade, the copyright industry/lobby/trade associations poured millions of dollars into aggressively hunting down, and suing, file-sharers and hackers who ran peer-to-peer sites, like the Pirate Bay, which coordinate access to troves of copyrighted material. Now segments of the copyright industry were going the "extra mile" by hiring hackers to engage in illegal tactics of their own to curb illegal file sharing.

Geeks criticized Aiplex's technical methods (it is common for geeks to take any and all opportunity to debate the merits of any piece of technology). They made fun of Aiplex's terrible and asinine criminal-confession-as-PR strategy. And on TorrentFreak, a popular website dedicated to reporting news on file sharing, one commentator noted: "AiPlex is just asking ... strike that I meant; _begging_ for trouble."[15]

The writer was spot on. Revenge arrived in the form of—did you guess it?—a DDoS campaign. Someone took the initiative to take down Aiplex, almost certainly using a botnet. golum and the other Anons who had set their sights on protesting ACTA through the use of DDoS campaigns exploited this opportunity to shift their energies and attention toward this event. It is perhaps no wonder that golum and his followers had no qualms about ditching ACTA, switching targets, and finding a new start date thanks to another bit of opportunistic chance—just like that initial rolling of the dice.

In one of the first propaganda posters for Operation Payback, this new Anonymous cell admitted that the DDoS campaign was "ahead of schedule," thanks to an unexpected strike made by a single individual. The activists then predicted, "This will be a calm, coordinated display of blood. We will not be merciful." Anonymous boldly signed off: "GOOD HUNTING."

So was the "hunting," as the poster claimed, a calm, coordinated, tactical incision in which Anonymous would show no mercy? Sort of. But, as we will see in a moment, the first few weeks of the campaign were rather chaotic—partially because the influx of supporters was hefty, at least for standards of the time. With so many people, proceeding in a calm and coordinated fashion was difficult. The first campaign launched September 17, 2010, targeting the MPAA's website and taking it offline for roughly eighteen hours.[16] Over the next four days Anonymous hit, among other targets, the International Federation of the Phonographic Industry, Aiplex (naturally), the RIAA, and ACS:Law, a law firm in the UK that worked on behalf of the copyright industry. From the perspective of these renegade Anons, Operation Payback was a resounding, glorious success, and the media were squeezed for many articles.

One of the remarkable feats of Operation Payback was how AnonOps managed, using propaganda material alone, to convince both the media (and many of their own members!) that the MPAA had hired Aiplex; there is no evidence to support this claim. Instead it is now widely believed that Aiplex had been hired by the Bollywood movie industry. And yet on September 20, 2010, scores of reputable news outfits, including Reuters, published statements in the following vein, despite flimsy— nonexistent, really—evidence: "MPAA.org and the Web site of Aiplex Software, a company the MPAA hired to target sites where piracy was rampant, were incapacitated for much of the day, according to the piracy blog TorrentFreak."[17] Because it was covered extensively in the media, I myself repeated this fib on countless occasions. To this day I still cannot ascertain who first proposed it, and whether it was borne from honest confusion (so many of the core participants truly believed it) or conniving duplicity. Whatever the case, Anonymous would seize upon this new-found specialty in the art of duping the media.

After a few days of the operation, AnonOps found itself on the verge of its most successful attacks of the season— where it would, in fact, show no mercy. The targeted organization, ACS:Law, would be shamed into oblivion thanks to Anonymous's first major leak.

"I have far more concern over the fact of my train turning up ten minutes late ... than them wasting my time with this sort of rubbish"

For the ragtag team assembled under the auspices of Operation Payback, the MPAA became the obvious target of preference. But by September 21, Anonymous could no longer effectively take down the organization's site—the MPAA had implemented sturdy DDoS protection by employing an outside firm. And so, on September 21, 2010, following vigorous internal debate, Anonymous set its sights on ACS:Law, a British law firm notorious for sending threatening letters at the behest of copyright owners to thousands of alleged file-sharers, demanding money and the cessation of ostensibly illegal downloading. It took Anonymous much more time to choose ACS:Law as its target (two hours) than it did to take down the law firm's website (two minutes). After the hit, the firm's head solicitor, Andrew Crossley, was so unimpressed by the attack that he hastily volleyed back with the following statement: "It was only down for a few hours. I have far more concern over the fact of my train turning up ten minutes late or having to queue for a coffee than them wasting my time with this sort of rubbish."[18]

But, it turned out, these few hours of website downtime might have cost him his firm. ACS:Law's web team was so incompetent that in restoring the site they accidentally made an entire backup, replete with emails and passwords, available for anyone with a modicum of technical ability to see and take. Anonymous noticed it, snatched it, and promptly threw all the emails on the Pirate Bay. It was the first in a string of stunning, Anonymous-led leaks that provided evidence of grave corporate misconduct.

By this time, Crossley's firm was already under government scrutiny. Months earlier, technology journalist Nate Anderson reported on what he described as a "spirited debate" among members of the House of Lords. As they discussed an amendment called "Remedy for groundless threats of copyright infringement proceedings," many lords were critical of ACS:Law's methods.[19] Lord Lucas, who had proposed the amendment, offered particularly harsh words to ACS:Law: "We must also do something about the quantum of damages that is being sought. In a civil procedure on a technical matter, it amounts to blackmail; the cost of defending one of these things is reckoned to be £210,000."[20]

The emails obtained by Anonymous simply helped confirm, with a far more granular and damning level of detail, the firm's relentless targeting of alleged copyright violators on behalf of copyright associations.[21] One tactic involved writing married men with allegations that they had downloaded gay porn; many of these men paid five hundred to six hundred pounds to make ACS:Law go away.[22] The leaked emails were a final decisive blow, and by February 2011, ACS:Law had closed down.[23]

It bears noting, again, that AnonOps' decision to target ACS:Law was, like many of its decisions, made in the heat of the (chaotic) moment. Had the group voted otherwise, the operation would have never transpired. It's worth looking into just how these voting mechanisms work, and the targeting of ACS:Law provides a prime example.

The public channel #savetpb (i.e., Save the Pirate Bay—later to become #operationpayback) hosted, at its peak, over one thousand participants. Many of them had come from 4chan, where news about Aiplex's methods spread and roiled many into action. Those on the public channels were encouraged to use a tool called the "Low Orbit Ion Cannon" (LOIC for short), subtitled "When harpoons, air strikes, and nukes fail." LOIC is an open-source application that allows users to individually contribute to a DDoS campaign from the comfort of their home by simply entering the target address and click-ing the temptingly giant button marked "IMMA CHARGIN MAH LAZER." By entering an IP address identified within a channel users could direct their computers to join a chorus of protesters in sending requests to a target. Alternatively, partici-pants could set LOIC to "hive mode," which allows computers to automatically contribute to the voluntary botnet.

Meanwhile, in the private channel first named #savetpb-mods and soon after renamed #command, others were engaged in deep, often heated, and utterly confusing debate regarding strategy and targets. Most in the public channel were unaware of the existence of this private channel, unless they were one of the few eventually tapped to join. During an interview, one of the founders of the secret channel explained the selection criteria as follows: "You're invited by another member of #command if you've proved yourself productive/ useful or trustworthy."

Presented below are only a tiny number of excerpts from a truly convoluted—yet still semi-coherent—two-hour conver-sation that occurred in #command as participants decided to target ACS:Law. Decision-making often follows a liquid path. It opened with the participants noting the impressive number of individuals gathered on the public channel—awaiting, as it were, their orders:

<Anon2>: 660+ people
<Anon5>: eh oh
<Anon5>: the fan is hitting the shit
<Anon6>: yeah
[…]
<Anon4>: the fan blew up from shit
<Anon7>: their [MPAA's] ddos protection is working
<Anon7>: i suggest we migrate targets?
<Anon7>: bpi? [British Phonographic Industry]
<Anon8>: why not riaa? [Recording Industry Association of America]
<Anon7>: because we failed with bpi last time due to small numbers

As they conversed, numbers continued to climb, and they started to worry about momentum and morale:

<Anon1>: in the meanwhile, there are a number of news articles popping up saying we did at least a lot of damage
<Anon8>: what has BPI done?
<Anon7>: Well
<Anon9>: Guys, do not discuss any drama in the main chat.
<Anon9>: We are here for propaganda. Lifting spirits.
[...]
<Anon9>: If we even INDICATE our efforts are "useless," people will leave en-masse.
<Anon9>: It has always been about morale.
<Anon9>: We don't have like 800 people because we tell the truth.
<Anon9>: we have 800 people that BELIEVE they are doing something.
<Anon7>: Guys, I do NOT want us to fail in the eyes of the public or make our troops go to waste. We need to migrate targets, soon

Disagreement over targets grew, and someone pointed out that the financial hit against MPAA was negligible since the organization paid a lump sum for its DDoS protection. Eventually, people agreed to stop hammering the MPAA and shift targets. Someone highlighted the nature of this endeavor: "but consider it an experiment either way. Prove me wrong." Just when participants thought they reached a consensus, someone yelped and insisted on a vote; as is often the case with any IRC-based meeting (only magnified with a group like Anonymous), conversation became even more tangled:

<Anon7>: Nooo
<Anon7>: Wait
<Anon7>: Let's vote.
<Anon8>: We have public opinion now because we do not target random sites
<Anon7>: First, let's nominate sites.
<Anon7>: So far riaa and bpi has been nominated.

<Anon7>: Any others?
<Anon9>: I think I have the perfect idea
<Anon7>: we can vote here.
<Anon16>: Hello.
<Anon1>: let Anon9 speak
<Anon9>: I think I agree with Anon13 here. ACS:Law.
<Anon9>: Full go.
<Anon9>: Paste their shit website, post the news articles on them, etc.
<Anon9>: If we divert now they will have NO time to prepare.
<Anon1>: well, /b/ a new poster with tomorrow's target, same time?
<Anon10>: I'm in for acs:law too
<Anon4>: me too
<Anon13>: Shall we change the topic in the main chat and divert the lazers now, so losing almost nobody, or attack tomorrow, potentially losing hundreds?
<Anon8>: someone give me an equally good motivation for a target
[…]
<Anon7>: let's vote?
<Anon13>: I vote for ACS.
<Anon7>: DDoS ACS:LAW. 1 = yes, 2 = no

As some voted, others continued to broadly debate the choice of targets, arguing, "Attacking anti-piracy agencies at random isn't helping our cause." This prompted another long, tedious round of voting. Finally, two hours later, they seemed to have inched closer to an agreement, but in the middle of debating, guess what happened?

<Anon7>: www.acs-law.org.uk
<Anon12>: Give me the info I said.
<Anon7>: www.acs-law.org.uk is down ALREADY!
[…]
<Anon12>: the feck
<Anon12>: ?
<Anon1>: OMG?

<Anon13>: That was quick.
<Anon1>: how long did it take us to vote again? XD
<Anon14>: Longer then it took for it to go down

Someone must have felt that there was enough of a consensus to move forward and fired up the botnets.

Two hours of planning, two minutes of DDoS'ing, and not long after the firm closed. A little over a year after Anonymous's email leak, Crossley—who had been more worried about queuing for a coffee—was tried in the Solicitors Disciplinary Tribunal for an array of charges. He conceded to six of the seven allegations, including the following two: "acting in a way that was likely to diminish the trust the public places in him or in the legal profession" and "using his position as a solicitor to take unfair advantage of the recipients of the letters for his own benefit."[24] He was ordered to pay £76,000 in fines and had his license suspended for two years. Even though he challenged the claim that he had not taken proper measures to protect client data, he was found guilty as charged and the Information Commissioner's Office also fined him for the data breach.[25]

Although many of Anonymous's actions seek simply to attract media attention for the sake of airing an issue, sometimes fate gave them more than they bargain for—like an incidental opportunity to curb corruption.

Weapons of the Geek (Rarely Agree)

By the end of fall 2010, with the constant deployment of digital direct action techniques, AnonOps had breathed new life into the still nascent idea that Anonymous could be a banner for activism; the name, once exclusively tied to the most abject forms of trolling, was slowly, but steadily, becoming associated with an irreverent brand of dissent. Regardless, those behind the September and October campaigns, like golum and the numbered Anons above, did not expect to exist as a team, much less as a network, for more than a few weeks. But, in a mirroring of the events that aggregated Chanology into a discrete entity, media validation helped solidify this new team as well. In a rare interview with TorrentFreak, one core organizer explained why:

> The operation's command was "pleasantly" surprised by the overwhelming media coverage and attention, but wondered where to go from there. They became the center of attention but really had no plan going forward. Eventually they decided to continue down the road that brought them there in the first place—more DDoS attacks … The media attention was indeed part of what fuelled the operation to go forward.[26]

With AnonOps here to stay, there were also clear signs of a cleavage emerging between different nodes within the activist branches of Anonymous. Chanology and AnonOps, the two most active wings, could not be more different in terms of tactics. One usually stayed within the bounds of the law and the other avidly, and enthusiastically, experimented with law breaking. By way of acknowledging these internal feuds and sectarian impulses, Anonymous would eventually adopt the refrain "Anonymous is not unanimous."[27]

It was around this time that I started to grasp the overarching significance of these disparate and divergent geeks and hackers—Anonymous (Chanology vs. AnonOps), Assange, Manning, the Pirate Bay, and others—all entering the political arena and in much greater numbers than ever before. In orchestrating protests across a range of issues—in particular civil liberties—they transformed policy, law, media representations, and public opinion. While certainly unique in its bombast and capriciousness, Anonymous was clearly part of a wellspring of hackers and geeks who were taking political matters into their own hands and making their voices heard.

Anonymous signaled the growing importance of what I call

"weapons of the geek," in contrast to "weapons of the weak," a term anthropologist James Scott used in his 1985 book of the same name to capture the unique clandestine nature of peasant politics. While *Weapons of the Weak* describes the tactics of economically marginalized populations who engage in small-scale illicit acts—such as foot dragging and vandalism—that don't appear on their surface to be political, weapons of the geek is a modality of politics exercised by a class of privileged and visible actors who often lie at the center of economic life.

Technology does not simplistically determine the politics of hacking, even if technological experiences usually inform its expression. Just as there are many ways to hack, there are many ways for hackers to enter the political arena. From policy making to engagements with Pirate Parties, from reinventing the law through free software to performing risky acts of civil disobedience, the geek and hacker are not bound to a single political sentiment, such as libertarianism, and they certainly don't agree on how social change should proceed.

What they all have in common is that their political tools, and to a lesser degree their political sensibilities, emerge from the concrete experiences of their craft, like administering a server or editing videos. Often, these skills are channeled into activities in order to bolster civil liberties, such as privacy. Unlike peasants who seek to remain inconspicuous and anonymous even as a group, geeks and hackers—even the anonymous Anonymous—explicitly call attention to themselves via their volatile, usually controversial, political acts. By fall 2010, AnonOps was at the forefront of the tests and experiments that sought to probe the new possibilities and legal limitations of digital civil disobedience.

And while some would count these experiments as a success, others—even those aligned on the same side of the struggle for civil liberties—were wary of the tactics employed. The Pirate Party in particular was less than enthused about the political use of DDoS. The Pirate Party is a political party which has made inroads in both Europe and Australia (and claims a very weak base in North America). Swedish free-culture advocate Rickard Falkvinge first chartered it in 2006, and now its platform is built on copyright reform, demands for Internet freedoms and civil liberties, and the building of tools to support direct democracy. The Pirate Parties in the UK and US wrote a letter to AnonOps requesting an immediate cessation of DDoS activity. (It should be noted that the letter prompted not only a vigorous debate among AnonOps participants— but also among Pirate Party members themselves):[28]

> Operation: Payback needs to end. While it is certainly an indication that an increasing number of people are becoming frustrated with the way laws are being constantly re-written to kill our creative culture in the name of preserving profitability, its methods do more harm than good to the global effort.
>
> By continuing Operation: Payback attacks, you will hamper those who promote copyright reform and curtailment of abuses of copyright, but who do so within the bounds of the law. Instead of being able to argue for legislative reform of copyright on its own merits, they will be accused of defending criminals and promoting lawlessness. It will be easier for legislators and the media to ignore the clear benefits of fair copyrights and free speech, in favor of clamoring for harsher legislation to "stop those pirates and hackers."[29]

Perhaps surprisingly, those Operation Payback participants sitting in #command, for a very brief period of time, took the Pirate Party's call to heart and considered aborting the use of illegal tactics in favor of a more moderate, reformist style: the advancing of a list of demands. The Torrent Freak interview revealed, publicly, the existence of the secret #command channel, and affirmed participants' new embrace of law-abiding tactics. Below are some key excerpts from the interview:

The core group is the #command channel on IRC. This core group does nothing more than being some sort of intermediary between the people in that IRC channel and the actual attack. Another group of people on IRC (the main channel called #operationpayback) are just there to fire on targets ...

Last week command decided to slow the DDoS attacks down and choose another strategy, mainly to regain the focus of attention. It was decided that they would make a list of demands for governments worldwide. In a move opposed to the desires of the anarchic influences, command decided to get involved in the political discussion.[30]

This dual news—that there was a secret channel, and that its members wanted to go "legit"—was received extremely poorly by the public-facing channel #operationpayback on AnonOps. The result was, in essence, a mutiny. "Gobo" (not his real pseudonym), one core participant active on the public channel—who would later become a member of another separate, secretive channel recatalyzed by the revelation—explained:

That article seriously pissed a lot of people in the main channel off. A huge amount of arguing broke out over Anonymous being leaderless and "who the fuck do they think they are." Somehow #command didn't really perceive how much controversy they were generating by overstepping the limits of their purpose (as defined by the main chan's participant).[31]

Little did the Anons crying foul know there was also another, *even more secretive* channel by the name #internetfeds. Originally chartered for the purposes of executing ops—especially covert hacking—it had gone idle for a period. One of its members reached out to Gobo and invited him to join #internetfeds with a scheme to revive it; the public commitment to a cessation of DDoSing suddenly looked very dubious indeed:

Essentially the ethos was as follows: Operation Payback would publicly "stop all illegal activity" as per the letter to the pirate party. #internetfeds would carry on these activities privately and in the name of "Anonymous" but *not* in the name of Operation Payback, and its existence was to be kept sacredly secret so as not to jeopardize the new "legitimate protest" image #command wanted to cultivate for Operation Payback.[32]

So, a small crew in a small cabal was planning to rekindle another, even smaller, and more secretive cabal—committed only loosely to the guiding principle of, like Fight Club, keeping mum about its existence (the group may have operated in secret, but each of its defacements came with a logo that included its name: "Pwned by #internetfeds").[33] As it turned out, #internetfeds never had to carry out this proposed "sacredly secret" mission because participants in the main channel essentially told #command to bugger off—affirming their intention to continue to DDoS with or without them: "civil war" broke out on the public channel where, according to Gobo, most people

> roundly condemned not just the idea of going legit, but specifically the fact that #command had so massively leader-fagged by agreeing to all this without even mentioning it to the main channel. There was an extremely bitter argument and following that, someone simply told people to forget about the #loic hive and hit the next target manually, with or without the support of #command.[34]

Those in #command listened to the angry IRC masses and "almost immediately backpedaled on the pledge to make the op go legitimate," explained Gobo. Although #internetfeds was no longer technically needed for this particular DDoS (since #command was put back on the DDoSing track thanks to pressure exerted by those on the public channel), it persisted anyway, ultimately becoming "an extremely militant defacement and leaking channel," as Gobo described it, which would really shine in the coming months. Peace had been restored, but barely.

Legitimacy vs. Legality

In September 2010, when a new Anonymous node arose out of the righteous anger borne from the double dealing of the copyright industry, it seemed always on the brink of disorder. Action was often heated, messy, soulful, and spontaneous, compounding the thrills experienced by all. Increasingly, AnonOps, had become more deliberate in its decision-making process—the direct result of collective thinking on the subject of collectivity itself. Undoubtedly, the topic of organization was highlighted by many participants upset at the double standards in operation during the initial campaigns. One of the core hackers explained to me why he felt justified in forging forward with these illegal tactics, a sentiment that seemed to capture the collective mood of the time: "I saw it as a form of poetic justice in response to Aiplex DDoSing the Pirate Bay." Gobo who had worked closely with golum highlighted how he always

> spoke very passionately about the fact that people he'd known from Anonymous [had been arrested for taking part in trolling-based DDoS attacks] and yet here were major corporate people boasting about it and everyone knew 100 percent that no one would ever prosecute them. golum has a very strong ideological belief in the idea that there should be no double standards in politics, and so for him it was the "corporations getting away with crimes" ordinary people don't get away with.[35]

By November, individual sentiments such as these were transformed into a collective political statement. Soon after AnonOps retracted its commitment to going legit, the group published a letter to the Pirate Party. It included a sophisticated justification for DDoS that focused on legitimacy over legality. Here is an excerpt:

> Anonymous and Operation Payback share values and goals—i.e. freedom of information, expression, and sharing—with the Pirate Parties, but we are absolutely independent entities.
>
> We are not concerned with legality, but with legitimacy. Those who decide our laws are the same people who decided that public copyright harassment, erosion of civil liberties and abominations of censorship such as COICA, ACTA, and the DEAct, are good and just things to enforce upon the populace. They do this whilst selectively enforcing their own laws when it comes to "official" organizations that take actions such as running a mass racketeering operation (knowingly suing thousands of individuals for infringement on bad evidence) or DDoSing sites that are contrary to their interests (AiPlex). We do not recognize their "authority" due to this rank hypocrisy.
>
> Finally, we recognize and respect the work of Pirate Parties and wish them luck. We hope that you all continue your fight as we are continuing ours.[36]

As this letter signals, AnonOps became reflexive and unabashedly comfortable about stylizing its activities as civil disobedience. Soon after reaching an ethical consensus on DDoSing in November, the numbers on their IRC server dwindled precipitously. Only a smattering of secret cabals remained, tied up in their separate, clandestine channels. It was impossible to forecast that, just three weeks later, they would launch the largest DDoS civil disobedience campaign the world had ever witnessed.

CHAPTER 4

The Shot Heard Round the World

I've only just a minute,
Only sixty seconds in it.
Forced upon me, can't refuse it,
Didn't seek it, didn't choose it,
But it's up to me to use it.
I must suffer if I lose it,
Give an account if I abuse it
Just a tiny little minute,
But eternity is in it.
                                      —Benjamin Elijah Mays,
                          American educator and president
                                      of Morehouse College

Commentators often cast Anonymous as an amorphous and formless entity existing in some mythical and primordial jelly-like state of non-being, only solidifying into existence when an outside agent utters its name. Buying into this logic, some writers suggest that Anonymous and its interventions suffer from an inherent lack of cohesion. "The group's hazy message, with no spokesmen, leaders, or firm political plans to provide steady direction," Art Keller wrote for *Newsweek*, "isn't helped by an ideology that veers between extreme left, extreme right and mainstream concerns."[1] A more prosaic example comes from an Anon himself who relayed the following to me during a personal chat conversation: "I spoke to a real life friend today about Anonymous and he seemed to have some vision of disembodied brains held in suspension orbiting the earth in battle satellites or something, the idea that actual people were involved seemed to flummox him."

These generalizations—promulgated by the media and commoners alike—are not only mostly wrong, but they also lead us further away from actually understanding Anonymous. Far from lacking structure or flailing wildly about like a compass at the North Pole, Anonymous incorporates an abundance of relationships, structures, and moral positions. Human beings—speaking, coding, debating, arguing, making art, and acting—are there every step of the way. This sentiment found a particularly nice expression during a conversation I had with Mustafa Al-Bassam, a notable former member of LulzSec, a hacker group that broke away from Anonymous. Exasperated by attempts to catalog every secret channel and collate every relevant note, I found him online one day and pestered him—begged him, really—to provide a neat, tidy, and definitive list of all the channels he could remember. He kindly acquiesced and in the middle of his meticulous explanation, which still left me confused, he asked, "Do you know kittencore?"

Oh damn, kittenporn?, I thought to myself. Thankfully, he reined in my imagination and clarified: "The IRC channel—we had a channel called #kittencore, and another called #upperdeck. The only difference is that #upperdeck had all the same people in #kittencore but one less." I asked why they kept one person in the dark. He replied, "Because he came very late into it and we became reluctant to have him in the center and also because he came just as we were splitting the bitcoins."

"Micro-micro-politics and cabals nested within cabals," I replied.

It is precisely this mixture of concreteness and abundance—one channel, exactly the same as the other, minus one person, since he is too new and not yet trustworthy—which makes Anonymous both so difficult to describe and so resistant to being slotted into a pre-fabricated mental template. Within Anonymous, the pressure and desire to efface the public presentation of self allows the participants to perform an admixture of their souls, conjuring into existence something always emergent and in flux. The number of relationships, fiefdoms, and cliques in simultaneous existence is largely invisible to the public, which tends to see Anonymous from the vantage point of carefully sculpted propaganda and the media's rather predictable gaze.

And yet, peering through the computer, we find Anonymous in any instant to be an aggregate sack of flesh—meshed together by wires, transistors, and wi-fi signals—replete with miles of tubes pumping blood, pounds of viscera filled with vital fluids, an array of live signaling wires, propped up by a skeletal structure with muscular pistons fastened to it, and ruled from a cavernous dome holding a restless control center, the analog of these fabulously grotesque and chaotically precise systems that, if picked apart, become what we call people. Anonymous is no different from us. It simply consists of humans sitting at their glowing screens and typing, as humans are wont to do at this precise moment in the long arc of the human condition. Each body taken alone provides the vector for an irreducibly unique and complex individual history—mirroring in its isolation the complexity of all social phenomena as a whole—which can itself be reduced yet further, to the order of events: mere flights of fingers and an occasional mouse gesture which register elsewhere, on a screen, as a two-dimensional text or a three-dimensional video; the song their fingers play on these keyboards ringing forth in a well-orchestrated, albeit cacophonous and often discordant, symphony; it is sung in the most base and lewd verse, atonal and unmetered, yet enthralling to many: the mythical epic of Anonymous.

Anonymous was not always this complex; it was only in late 2010 that the activist group became such a tangled and constantly shifting labyrinth. In November 2010, the minotaur running the maze of Anonymous had not yet found its escape route into the world, but it was getting closer. Chanology was still ongoing and AnonOps' IRC remained the central nerve center for a cavalcade of DDoS campaigns lobbed against the copyright industry. By the end of November, this steady stream of direct action in support of file sharing came to a screeching halt. Participation in the public-facing IRC channels dwindled to an all time low. But the core teams, who had collaborated on the private channels, did not quietly shutter the doors and close up shop (though the low numbers did worry them). Instead, they sought to organize themselves better. A brainstorming session resulted in a collaboratively written document hashing out the purpose and structure of the private channel #command, which scandalized the broader ranks of Anonymous publicized earlier in November (see figure on facing page).

The document, which existed in various garish states, first defined the limited role of #command as "act[ing] as an intermediary" that "does not take decisions alone" and should lead "only the discussion, not the direction" of the operations. The document ends with a list of rules, including the ironic pronouncement that "only grownups" are allowed to be in "Command." Ironic because a number of the individuals were under eighteen (and really, Anonymous as "grownup"?).

There are many concepts embedded in this document that are likely unfamiliar to IRC virgins and could bear some explanation. First: you use an IRC client to connect to a server, and then you pick a handle or "nick"—this could be your legal name, but more typically it's something else. You have the option to speak one-on-one with other connected users, or you can join "channels," which are denoted by a preceding octothorpe (#) and can be joined by any user who knows of the room's existence—assuming it's not an invite-only room. Once you join a room, you converse with other users who are there, typically about a channel-specifc topic. Whoever creates

Rules in Command:

- Nobody kicks and certainly not bans inside command.
- Don't interrupt another one's subject.
- First point out the matters at hand, then point out priorities.
- People who troll in command get (permanently) thrown out of the AOP list.
- Personal disputes are taboo.
- Grown-ups only.
- No offtopic subjects in (staff) discussions.
- Pointing out problems in a structured way: name problem, suggest solution. If you can't hint a solution, then at least give evidence or argue your statements, as long as your point is valid.
- If you don't like somebody, get over it. Were all in this together.
- Admins/OPs are considered an example. Act on that behavior!
- Don't expect IRCops to sort out all your problems, try it yourself, if all else fails, ask OP!

the channel is called the channel "founder" and has a certain amount of power to change its properties, determining who can enter, whether the channel is visible in the server's list of public channels, and so forth. These operators can also bestow—at least in some versions of IRC—power on others, adding them to what's called the "AutoOp (AOP)" list. Anyone on that list can "kick" anyone else out of the channel for whatever reason they choose, and even ban them from returning. At a higher order of power are the IRCops—a fraction who run the server and have the power to not only kick people from individual channels, but also from the server itself, disconnecting them completely. IRCops also have the ability to alter individual channel configurations and perform many other administrative functions. Typically, there are many individual channel operators but few IRC server operators. For many IRCops, getting involved in any individual channel's dispute is a frustrating exercise—requiring them to pass judgment on events they were not privy to. As a result, channel decisions are typically deferred to the channel operators, with a server admin intervening only in extreme circumstances.

Many participants draw (or at least *seek* to draw) sensible lines of order from IRC and other stable sites of interaction.

This order, nevertheless, is delicate and precarious—always on the edge of disorder. However, like so many trickster scenarios of turmoil, these moments of chaos don't necessarily lead to breakdown and stasis. Instead, they often function as beginnings—necessary for the vitality and even regeneration of the broader community. Juxtaposing two quotes, one by Spanish philosopher George Santayana and another by Henry Brooks Adams, puts this lesson into relief:

> Chaos is a name for any order that produces confusion in our minds but it won't be chaos once we see it for what it is.

> Chaos often breeds life, when order breeds habit.

In the somewhat tangled story I am about to tell, it will be clear how Anonymous, like most social movements, remains open to chance, and chaos. The difference being that Anonymous is perhaps just a touch more open to mutation. Nowhere do we see this demonstrated more vividly than at the beginning of December 2010, when a whimsical decision ended a period of inactivity in AnonOps, flinging open the door for new action-able possibilities and allowing scores of newcomers to arrive as ready conscripts (mostly unaware, again, of the still-private #command IRC channel). This decision revitalized AnonOps to such a degree that the group's IRC network became a foun-tain of nonstop activity for over a year, surpassing WikiLeaks as the primary hacker-activist hub of the Internet.

But, before we describe this whimsical decision, we would do well to keep in mind its infamous outcome: AnonOps' support of WikiLeaks via a massive DDoS campaign in the aftermath of the whistleblowing organization's most conten-tious release yet. On November 28, 2010, WikiLeaks publicly released 220 of 251,287 classified US diplomatic cables— the most extensive leak of classified materials ever, timed to coincide with in-depth analyses by the *Guardian,* the *New York Times, El País, Le Monde,* and *Der Spiegel.* The US government was furious, and a trio of powerful companies—Amazon, MasterCard, and PayPal (among others)—bowed to its influence, refusing to process donations or provide website hosting for the embattled organization.

Even though WikiLeaks had already released hundreds of thousands of military documents about the Afghan and Iraq wars, which brimmed with revelations of detention squads, civilian casualties, the solicitation of child prostitutes, and a host of other horrors, "Cablegate" still managed to stand in a class of its own. It pulled back the curtain on not only the intra-diplomatic discussions that were normally hidden behind a veil of diplomatic etiquette, and also—and even more salaciously—on the internal discussions and intelligence gathering of US diplomats themselves. Then–Secretary of State Hillary Clinton had in 2009, we learned, merged diplomacy and spying into one activity, ordering US diplomatic officials to collect credit card numbers, frequent flyer numbers, and biometric information on foreign officials. We learned for the first time that the Obama administration had been secretly conducting a war in Yemen, launching missile attacks at suspected terrorists, while the Yemeni government covered it up by claiming responsibility themselves. We learned that American intelligence agencies believed that North Korea had given Iran nineteen of its longest-range missiles—which the public didn't know existed in the first place. We learned that Saudi Arabian leaders had been urging the United States to bomb Iran in order to, as King Abdullah himself put it, "cut off the head of the snake." The cables showed that Israel was bluffing on its threat to launch airstrikes against Iran, and that the United States engaged in criminal dealings with the corrupt, drug-trafficking brother of Afghan president Hamid Karzai. The cables also touched on comparably banal subjects, like US diplomats' routine bad-mouthing and name-calling of foreign leaders.[2] Previously, things were merely interesting and provocative. But now, as the revelations kept coming, members of the public discovered their jaws dropping lower and lower by the day, as if they were strapped into some orthodontic-transparency device, hand-cranked by Julian Assange himself.

Sarah Palin suggested Assange be hunted down "with the same urgency we pursue al-Qaeda and Taliban leaders."[3] Senator Joe Lieberman declared it "an outrageous, reckless, and despicable action that will undermine the ability of our government and our partners to keep our people safe and to work together to defend our vital interests."[4] Lieberman's staff reached out to Amazon—not only the world's largest book retailer but also its largest web host—and asked it to ban WikiLeaks from its servers. It acquiesced. The financial firms that process credit card transactions worldwide followed suit, cutting the umbilical cord between donors and WikiLeaks. Although WikiLeaks had not been found guilty of anything by any court of law—these companies, without any legal obligation to do what the government asked of them, went ahead anyway. Anonymous was outraged.

Two weeks later, AnonOps became ground zero for the single largest digital direct action campaign the Internet had—and still has—ever witnessed, at least when measured by number of participants. Over seven thousand individuals logged onto AnonOps' IRC channel, #operationpayback, to lend a helping hand, cheer or, at the very least, simply spectate. Seven thousand users in one channel remains the largest single human IRC congregation ever.[5] It was a "mass demo against control," as free software hacker Richard Stallman described the event in a *Guardian* editorial.[6] In the month of December alone, LOIC was downloaded 116,988 times, far more than during the earlier DDoS campaigns.[7] While only a fraction of those actually connected to the Anonymous hive, interest in the tool was undoubtedly fueled by reporting on Anonymous's activities.

Media attention was frenzied, catapulting this collective of collectives out of relative obscurity and into the international spotlight. Not only did the usual suspects—like technology-oriented publications and blogs—report on the uprising, but so did most of the major nightly news programs. CNN hosted the digital strategist Nicco Mele, who praised Anonymous during an in-depth interview. In the *New York Times*, one of the Internet's original patron saints, John Perry Barlow, cast the Anonymous campaign as "the shot heard round the world—this is Lexington."[8]

WikiLeaks and Anonymous seemed like a perfect fit. Anonymous's DDoS campaign solidified the alliance through a spectacular display of solidarity and support. But, as hinted at before, AnonOps' decision to intervene came about in a rather convoluted, disorderly manner. Journalist Parmy Olson, in her book *We Are Anonymous*, portrays AnonOps' decision to rally around WikiLeaks as straightforward:

> The people who set up AnonOps were talking about the WikiLeaks controversy in their private #command channel. They were angry at PayPal, but, more than that, they saw an opportunity. The victimization of Wiklileaks, they figured, would strike a chord with Anonymous and bring hordes of users to their new network. It was great publicity.[9]

But this account barely scratches the surface of what transpired. AnonOps was in idle mode, with almost no supporters outside of the core team. This so-called "opportunity" only manifested once AnonOps command was *forced* to consider involving themselves following the independent actions of only a few unknown Anons, thus opening the floodgates for thousands.

It could be said that the initial nudge that reinvigorated the team behind Operation Payback, pushing them into Operation Avenge Assange, came from a rather wordy poster. It showered Assange with praise: "Julian Assange deifies everything we hold dear. He despises and fights censorship constantly [and] is probably the most successful troll of all time ... Now Julian is the prime focus of a global manhunt, in both physical and virtual realms." It then called on Anonymous to "kick back for Julian" by engaging in multiple political acts from DDoSing PayPal to complaining "to your local MP."

On December 4, as this message traversed the Internet, an unknown party DDoSed the PayPal blog—most likely with a botnet.[10] This action was followed by a trickle of journalistic coverage and a statement on the PandaLabs security blog that announced, in a matter-of-fact way, AnonOps' involvement: "The organizers behind the anonymous group responsible for Operation: Payback are in the midst of refocusing their campaign to assist WikiLeaks in their quest to release classified government documents."[11] This was all news to many in Anonymous. As media reports continued to roll out, a convoluted and angry conversation broke out in AnonOps' #command chat room. Most of the team had no idea they were "refocusing their efforts on WikiLeaks."

To make sense of this moment, it might help to follow a few members of Anonymous (all pseudonyms have been changed) through the events that unfolded on December 6. We will start with Fred, one of the most important participants on #command (according to one interview subject, "[Fred] is AnonOps"). Fred invested a serious amount of time maintaining the infrastructure. A Kurt Vonnegut adage comes to mind: "Another flaw in the human character is that everybody wants to build and nobody wants to do *maintenance*." Fred was willing to do the work others took for granted, and as a result he was heavily invested in AnonOps. On that day, as Fred logged into #command, he was very angry. A conversation would transpire over the next hour that would forever change the future course of both AnonOps (specifically) and Anonymous (in general):

    <Fred>: offs [oh for fuck's sake]
    <Fred>: that operation assange thing is just a poster
    <Fred>: no site names, nothing
    <Fred>: its not ours

Trogo (author of the PandaLabs blog post) was on the channel. He was one of a handful of embedded outsiders given access to the secret areas—typically there were very few of them—in order to ferret information out of the AnonOps bunkers and into the public domain. (Trogo, however, stands unique for being around #command since its founding.) It seemed that a statement published by Trogo had catalyzed many into the actions now under review. Trogo defended his hasty decision to publish without broad consensus.

<Trogo>: [It was] approved by Radwaddie [another member of #command]
<Trogo>: We ran with the name because media has a short attention span
<Trogo> [to captor]: Last night I wrote a blog post announcing the change of plans
<captor> [to trogo]: what change of plans?

A change of plans had indeed been decided by those chatting in AnonOps—but most Anons, even those in #command, had not been invited to take part in the decision-making process. As this became increasingly clear to those who were left out in the cold, many expressed dismay and confusion. "It seems many here are unaware," wrote Fred. As blame circulated, others, dumbfounded, defended themselves: "it's not us, we are not firing at paypal."

Despite being an outsider, Trogo proceeded to remind the Anons how Anonymous works: the name is free to be taken by any who would take it. Someone noted the irony of raising this ostensibly well-known fact *to Anonymous* (and in what was perhaps the most important Anonymous IRC channel at the time, no less). And in addition to stating the obvious, the security researcher and blogger defended himself by characterizing what happened as being "nothing new." He was well aware that the channel had already largely decided to support WikiLeaks, even if its commitment to mirror the site by duplicating its content had not yet been actualized. Recognizing that what was done was done, Radwaddie switched from a defensive stance to an offensive one, making a vigorous attempt to convince the disgruntled parties to embrace the momentum and push forward, hitting PayPal regardless of the strategy that had already been chosen:

> <Radwaddie>: since we all agree on that [helping WikiLeaks]
> <Radwaddie>: why aren't we hitting paypal?
> <Fred>: because no one knew we were suppose ot?
> <Radwaddie>: i mean, shit hitting the fan already, might as well help them

It was a shrewd and opportunistic move—and almost immediately consensus started to favor jumping into the fray. But there were calls for due process. If they wanted to do it right, they first needed to rev up their propaganda machine. And even as some were swayed toward DDoSing PayPal, the growing anger (particularly directed at Radwaddie and Trogo for violating decision-making protocol) spread to others:

> <dubiosdudious> [to Radwaddie]: who are you to make all the decisions?
> <Radwaddie> [to dubiosdudious]: you wanna sit down and have a cup of tea over it and discuss the next cause of action?
> [...]
> <Radwaddie> [to dubiosdudious]: what's your objection (bulletpoint please)
> <dubiosdudious>: 1. no preparations
> <dubiosdudious>: 2. no vote
> <dubiosdudious>: on the top of my head

As Radwaddie attempted to push the campaign forward in spite of attacks thrown his way, semantic arguments broke out over the role of #command in general. Radwaddie yelled-typed: "ok, the fuck, WHO THE FUCK IN HERE HAS ANY

IDEA AT ALL?" And as the seed germinated amid the gathered Anons, the debate slowly—perhaps inexorably—shifted from a question of *whether* to hit PayPal to a question of *where* to hit PayPal. Most participants favored the "main site." Radwaddie then interwove pragmatic and moral arguments: "we're trying to make a point, [that] we disagree with paypal [which is why] we do the thing we do best: ddos." He wrote that this was what Anonymous was about, not "awesome speeches or fabulous community." Just as support for Radwaddie's position seemed poised to reach a consensus, someone named "lark" entered the room with a surprising nugget of information: "the [initial] attack on the paypal blog was one of our own as a side project." So, in fact, the very first DDoS hit, which everyone thought was instigated by an unaffiliated Anon, happened to be carried out by one of their own. I guess he had just gone about his business quietly, since AnonOps at the time was primarily focused on supporting file sharing.

But despite this revelation, it seemed that the momentum could not be stopped. Given the hubbub generated by Trogo and Radwaddie's decision to piggyback on the first DDoS hit, which everyone thought was accomplished by an outsider, it might seem incredulous that no one responded to lark. But we can imagine that the Anons were at this point so deeply immersed in their course of action—debating targets and strategy—that this single statement was easy to overlook. The conversation simply continued. Finally, an announcement came:

<captor>: DONE
<captor>: we have target [the paypal main site]

The propaganda team was notified and the attack commenced (with botnets being secretly deployed). Conversation naturally shifted to consider the significance of enlarging the scope of Operation Payback (aka "o:p") to include other matters aside from copyright and piracy:

<Mobile>: so o:p has turned into a war on censorship and copyright?
<Radwaddie>: and we see this as a sideOP, we're not suspending our "normal" activities
[...]
<Trogo>: Is it even possible to DDoS PayPal?
<Radwaddie> [to Trogo]: we will find out, won't we?

The attack, unbeknownst to all participating, was no longer just a "sideOP" initiated by the Anons in #command—instead, it was the opening salvo that would galvanize a global movement, ushering in a new age of Anonymous. This new node would boast thousands of participants, and would be borne not out of an obvious and straightforward determination, but, rather, out of confusion: a mixture of manipulation, false information, good intentions, and rampant uncertainty.

They Didn't Seek It, They Didn't Choose It

The answer to Trogo's question—"Is it even possible to DDoS PayPal?"—turned out to be "yes." (The same turned out to be true of MasterCard and many financial companies.) What had been conceived as a mere diversion metamorphized, rather quickly, into the apotheosis of AnonOps. Between December 6, 2010, and December 8, 2010, AnonOps expanded its scope, targeting not only the PayPal blog and the PayPal website, but also the Swedish prosecutor's websites (as the Swedish government was seeking to extradite Assange on rape charges)[12] and the websites of Senator Joe Leiberman, Sarah Palin, MasterCard, Visa, EveryDNS (a domain name service provider), and others. Exacting vengeance against any party complicit in the smearing of WikiLeaks, AnonOps caused all of these sites to experience some amount of downtime, though the exact hours vary depending on who you ask. By December 8, numbers on the main IRC #operationpayback channel spiked to an all-time high of 7,800.

These examples demonstrate how Anonymous's tactics conform to Michel de Certeau's account of "everyday tactics of resistance" whereby "a tactic depends on time—it is always on the watch for opportunities that must be seized 'on the wing.'"[13] Radwaddie and Trogo decided to act independent of the group, seizing exactly this sort of timely opportunity; this style of on-the-fly decision making is an Anonymous staple. The group is often reactive rather than proactive; to paraphrase the poem which opens the chapter: *the decision was forced upon them, they could not refuse it, they did not seek it, they didn't choose it, but it was up to them.* To fully execute the operation nevertheless required considerable organization and resources, which in this case took the form of zombie and voluntary botnets and propaganda.

What made the difference was both simple and simply beyond Anonymous's control: it was the general indignation regarding the payment blockade. The Internet was awash in articles and tweets expressing dismay; everyone was asking some version of the question posed by a UK journalist on Twitter: "Of what have either Assange or Wiki-leaks [*sic*] actually been convicted, that allows VISA, Mastercard, PayPal, Amazon to withdraw service this week?"[14] To illustrate the hypocrisy of it all, people pointed out that while MasterCard refused to process payments for WikiLeaks, racists around the world remained free to donate to their racist organization of choice, like the Klu Klux Klan. Internet scholar Zeynep Tufekci issued the following warning:

> The WikiLeaks furor shows us that these institutions of power are slowly and surely taking control of the key junctures of the Internet. As a mere "quasi-public sphere," the Internet is somewhat akin to shopping malls, which seem like public spaces but in which the rights of citizens are restricted, as they are in fact private.[15]

Everyone was indeed confronting this cold hard reality: the Internet, so often experienced as a public space, is in fact a privatized zone, with the Amazons and PayPals of the world able to shut down conversation and commerce.

The mood in certain quarters at the time was captured in the following statement by an activist who went by the Twitter name "AnonyOps" (no relation to AnonOps, even if the names bear an unmistakable resemblance):

> I remember a mountain of angst building up and I didn't realize until that day that it wasn't a mountain. It was a volcano and the day that WikiLeaks donations were held, the volcano blew and that's the day I searched for a way to call out the bullshit. A way for me to talk publicly, without jeopardizing my career.[16]

A skilled and wealthy engineer in his thirties, he created the AnonyOps Twitter account (it would eventually become one of the largest multiple-author Anonymous accounts) and, like so many others, logged into IRC.

AnonOps, because it was not some amorphous blob but rather a team with a dedicated volunteer force and resources, had erected a platform from which all kinds of people could act. Confusion and happenstance mingled with operational readiness and the deployment of resources. Droves of concerned citizens from all over world flocked to the renegade army.

"Goodnight, and sweet dreams from AnonOps"

In the fall of 2010, when AnonOps was banging out wave upon wave of DDoS attacks under Operation Payback, I had taken a leave of absence from Anonymous to finish my first book on free software hacking. I was behind on the book, and with my tenure clock ticking, the pressure was on. It was psychologically crushing me: to retain my job, I had to publish a book. So I set aside the month of December to sprint to the finish line. When Anonymous resurfaced as an activist force in early December, I trusted my Spidey sense: it struck me as too historically significant to ignore. I put aside my manuscript and gave my attention to Anonymous. To be entirely frank, the gamble felt safe; extrapolating from previous actions, I figured it would peter out, or at least slow down, after a month, and I could then return to writing. But instead I remained chained to my computer for roughly three years.

At the height of the holidays that December, I went to the West Coast to spend time with my family. While family members went hiking on rugged cliffs overlooking the shimmering Pacific Ocean and watched movies late into the night, I huddled over my laptop. I was engrossed, dumbfounded, mystified, and addicted to the wild energy and excitement coursing through the channels. I'm pretty sure my family thought I was being purposely antisocial, and for good reason. I was hands down the scrooge of the bunch, never quite as excited as everyone else about holiday cheer, eggnog, or (most especially) the board games they loved and I loathed. In any given year, a half dozen excuses were ready to roll off my tongue at the mere hint of Settlers of Catan.

For most of my family, the Internet represents the dreaded chore of email; it's the place where they read the morning news over coffee, skim Facebook for the latest pictures of friends and their cherubic babies, and, in moments of workplace desperation, fire up those fantastic cat videos. The Internet is all these things for me as well, but also more—a place of multiple worlds, a galaxy really. For them, it is simply not a "place" where something like the anti–World Trade Organization protests, which took Seattle by surprise over ten years ago, could possibly happen. And, undoubtedly, there is an ocean of difference between tear gas and typing. Incommensurabilities aside, one thing was certain: I was witnessing the first large-scale, populist, full-bodied online protest, and I was not going to miss it for the world, *especially not for the Settlers of Catan.*

After a long day of research, I wanted nothing more than to describe to my relatives the passionate and rambunctious scenes I had witnessed. But I fumbled to find the adequate words and terminology. For weeks I struggled to get a handle on things and judge just what sort of "mass demo" was taking place. Questions rather than answers sprung to mind: Was it civil disobedience? Direct action? Something akin to a street demonstration? A virtual sit-in? A blockade? Did DDoS attacks violate free speech and essential liberties, as some critics claimed? Was it ethical, unethical, effective, ineffective? Who were all these people, anyway?

I had only a vague idea at the start. There were so many nicknames zinging by me on IRC. Soon I would incessantly chat with a number of them, and eventually I would meet a smaller slice in person. But, at the time, they were mysteries to me. I had no clue about the existence of secret back channels; I was primarily viewing the conversations on #operationpayback and other public channels. I also had to learn just how LOIC worked at a technical level, and I had to read up on AnonOps' fall DDoS campaigns. The pace and the sheer number of participants made all previous conversations I had witnessed on IRC seem trivial. Even though I was expending very little physical energy—sitting all day, staring at conversations—by the end of the day my head ached. I was worn out, and torn as to my opinion on things. It took a few weeks to process the ethics of how Anonymous ran its DDoS campaigns.

The amount of information-processing required of participants was staggering. Logging into the main channel, a screen popped up displaying the topic and a terse condensation of target information: the IP address to enter into LOIC, Twitter channels you should check out for context, and other IRC channels worth visiting. Typically, it looked something like this:

(04:56:18 PM) The topic for #opb is: OPERATION PAYBACK
"http://anonops.eu/"http://anonops.eu/ | Twitter:

"http://twitter.com/Op_anon "http://twitter.com/Op_anon |
"http://www.justiceforassange.com/"http://www.justiceforassange.
com/Hive: 91.121.92.84 | Target:
"http://www.mastercard.com/"www.mastercard.com | See: #Setup
#Target #WikiLeaks #Propaganda #RadioPayback #Protest #Lounge
and /list for rest | "http://808chan.org/tpb"http://808chan.org/tpb

In conjunction, Anonymous was churning out a slew of well-reasoned manifestos, videos, and posters; Anonymous had tapped into a deep, widespread disenchantment, and by providing a conduit for confrontational activism, had channeled it into a more visible and coherent form. It was as if everybody knew it was history in the making: the first popular uprising on the Internet. Strangers were reaching out to work toward a common goal. I myself was inspired.

The conversations were a whole other matter. With thousands of people logged in and up to a hundred users talking at once, it was wildly cacophonous and required every last shred of my already ADHD-addled brain to follow. Indeed, there is probably no other medium on earth as conducive to what literary theorist Mikhail Bakhtin terms "polyphony" (multiple voices, each with a unique perspective and moral weight) than IRC.[17] And while some would come to describe Anonymous as "a microcosm of anarchy, with no morals, empathy, or agenda,"[18] I witnessed something altogether different: everyone had a moral viewpoint, a reason for being there. They cared, wanted justice, wanted to end censorship (and some even were there to disagree—vehemently—with the tactics being used). Yes: Anonymous had no universal mandate as a collective, but participants had their own, often well-tuned moral compasses guiding them.

To take but one example from among dozens of issues being hotly debated: in December 2010, #operationpayback was home to a vociferous debate over the effectiveness and ethics of technological protest in general, and DDoSing in particular. Two subtopics stood out: the safety of LOIC, and the more philosophical question of whether DDoSing is an exercise of the right to free speech or an act aimed at precluding the same right for others. The excerpts from two distinct conversations below exemplify the polyphonous character of these interchanges and the multiplicity of ethical positions on these technological protests. These issues were visited and revisited throughout the course of the month.

. Early in the campaign, participants grappled with the political significance of Anonymous, with most everyone expressing support for DDoS:

<P>: this is better than WTO Seattle

[…]

<P>: bottom up approach

<z>: you need a critical mass though, before people start feeling inspired

<z>: 2 or 3 people standing around doesn't look epic, it looks lame

<a>: this attack seems pretty unorganized right now

<z>: it's gotta go viral, you know?

<P>: pretty appealing message imo

[…]

<a>: I think these attacks are less about hurting the businesses than drawing attention and forcing the media to cover the story

<a>: most people I know have never even heard about WikiLeaks until I bring it up

[…]

<a>: The point for me is that this is the technological way of mass protesting that's actually effective so until there's total freedom of information then there isn't an end.

[…]

<m>: theres nothing wrong with technological protest. other than we struggle to organize. do any damage. hardly any of us are propper hackers.

<P>: synchronized twitter and facebook postings, jolly rogers wherever you can on the internet, and then a manifesto about how to take to your local street corner and do something

[...]
<P>: anon can get it moving, but this is bigger than anon

A few days later on the same channel, a few ripped DDoSing apart, as others continued to defend it:

<26>: i dont think DDoS can be in the name of freedom of speech
<26>: cause it is an act of silencing
<matty>: ^
<sc>: think of a target as a sign on a building
secreta: its pretty clear how hypocritical a ddos is to me
<PN>: you keep screaming that everyone is going to jail. you are just here to discourage. cunt.
<sc>: you do not agree with what that building represents
<26>: but people are going to jail
<ri>: DO NOT BE AFRAID OF JAIL
[...]
<ri>: every civil rights protest ends with people in gail

For the great majority of participants who contributed or used LOIC, it is safe to assume that they considered this tool and tactic a morally acceptable method of protest. Whether LOIC was in fact *legal* is a different question. At the time, the AnonOps party line affirmed that DDoSing with LOIC was safe: not because the tool anonymized your IP address (it did not, and generally no one claimed it did), but because the huge numbers of individuals participating would make it nearly impossible, or at least unduly inconvenient, for authorities to track down and arrest everyone. The main operators in the #operation-payback channel, some of whom were also in #command, would, in rare moments, ban those who warned others of its illegality. Those in #command wanted to instill trust, not fear, in their methods. AnonOps also circulated "instructions" for how to use LOIC, which featured atrocious security advice coupled with the overly pushy—and extremely dubious— legal advice in case of arrest:

IF YOU ARE V& [vanned] declare you had no participation in this event. Note you are using a dynamic IP address and that many different people use it, because it's dynamic. If they prove that it was yours, then tell them you are a victim of a "botnet virus" that you had no control or knowledge of. Additionally if you set your wireless to unsecured or WAP prior to LOIC you can claim someone hacked your wireless. Case closed.[19]

More shockingly, a small cohort of journalists also spread misinformation. While Anonymous could, perhaps, be understood and forgiven for its mistakes, journalists should have done their homework rather than relaying incorrect legal advice and misleading technical information provided by their sources. The most egregious example of this practice came from the popular tech news site Gizmodo on December 8, 2010, in an article entitled "What Is LOIC?": "Because a DDoS knocks everything offline—at least when it works as intended—the log files that would normally record each incoming connection typically just don't work."[20] This point is just plain wrong. The DDoS'ed site can still monitor its traffic, culling and keeping IP addresses, which can be subsequently used to identify participants.

LOIC was about as safe as a torn condom. If a person using LOIC did not take other measures to cloak their IP address, it would be plain in every packet—in every attack—transmitted. Many participants likely lacked even rudimentary knowledge of how the technology worked, a baseline necessity for making an informed decision. The heat of the moment and the dominant sense of safety swept up journalists and participants alike. Generally speaking, and with a few exceptions, most people involved in #command, however naive the position might seem in hindsight, were, I think, sincere in believing that protection followed from strength in numbers; some of the individuals in #command used LOIC themselves and were subsequently arrested.

For much of the fall of 2010, Anons used DDoS with no repercussions, boosting the false sense of confidence that would soon evaporate under the first FBI raids at the end of December. There was also the issue of personalized messages accompanying the DDoS attacks. When individuals connected to the AnonOps hive, and packets were sent to a target, it included a message: "Goodnight, and sweet dreams from AnonOps." The government could surely use this message to counteract claims that the sender was ignorantly a "victim of a botnet virus." But with a good lawyer, that argument would crumble because the message could be identified as part of the virus (problem is, good lawyers are pricey). Regardless, none of this was discussed or seemingly understood.

The tide changed quickly. Soon after the first wave of attacks, a poster warning that LOIC was unsafe made the rounds. The bad advice presented by sites like Gizmodo was soon set straight by carefully researched articles on sites like Boing Boing, providing warnings and accurate technical details about LOIC's security vulnerabilities. Around this time, a talented programmer managed to corral a small team of Anons to start writing a more secure, but harder to use, version. Upon release, it was downloaded en masse—before people realized it contained a trojan.

Finally, irrefutable proof of traceability arrived: law enforcement in plain blue jackets with yellow FBI letters visited over forty homes across the United States, trucking out hard drives loaded with incriminating data. Eventually, in July 2011, the FBI arrested fourteen alleged participants, thirteen of whom have since pled guilty. In October 2013, a grand jury indicted thirteen American citizens for participating in Avenge Assange and some of the earlier Operation Payback attacks.[21]

Now everyone knew that LOIC was an unsafe tool; that the US government was willing to go after online political protesters, even those who had not used LOIC (some of the participants swept in by the DDoS raid never used LOIC or botnets, but were charged based on IRC log conversations);

and that there was no safety in numbers. Presumably, a hard lesson was learned.

DDoS as a Moral Pretzel

Equipped with these details, what ethical and historical insights might be drawn from these extraordinary direct action events—the largest DDoS political demonstration the web has seen? By fall 2010, the use of DDoS attacks was an established political tactic among hacktivists; Anonymous by no means pioneered the technique. In the 1990s and early 2000s, the Electronic Disturbance Theater (EDT), for instance, staged DDoS campaigns that they labeled "virtual sit-ins." These actions combined technical interventions with poeticism and performance art. EDT targeted Mexican government websites to publicize the plight of Zapatistas fighting for autonomy in Chiapas, Mexico.[22] They distributed press releases before the events and, while drawing less than a few hundred participants and causing no downtime to the sites, succeeded (somewhat) in the goal of gaining media attention. Regardless, the action hardly qualified, as Molly Sauter has perceptively argued, as "disruptive,"[23] and it never reached a saturation point in the mainstream press.

Anonymous altered the scale, expression, and effects of DDoSing enough that the group broke the mold it inherited. Rather than spending months organizing small, well-crafted events, Anonymous experimented with the art of harnessing real-time anger into a wild, unpredictable, and continual uprising. As with any form of public assembly, alongside the politically motivated were those along just for the ride—and also those who were there simply to make the ride as bumpy and wild as possible. It's inevitable that participants in Anonymous will have an array of positions and desired ends, given the group's philosophical platform and the accessibility of its software tools; the actions are open to seasoned activists and newcomers alike.

By considering this tactic historically, we can plainly see that DDoSing is nothing new—virtually every movement advocating social change in the past two hundred years (from abolitionists to ACT UP) has relied on large-scale, rowdy, disruptive tactics to draw attention and demand change.[24] The novelty lay in how the availability of a software tool, LOIC, and an Anonymous hype machine publicizing its existence, enabled such sizable and disruptive demonstrations to take root and unfold nearly spontaneously on the Internet. In a detailed analysis of the tool's features, Sauter convincingly argues that the "Hive Mind mode" helped secure the hefty numbers: "Although Anons may not have 'hit the streets' as EDT envisioned Hive Mind mode did enable them to go to school, work, sleep, or anywhere while still participating in DDOS actions as they arose."[25]

But even if DDoS simply extends a longer tradition of disruptive activism, it still sat uneasily with many Anons and hackers—even those who had no issue with law breaking. One day, chatting with an Anonymous hacker about the morality of the protests, I was told, "Trying to find a sure-fire ethical defense for Anonymous DDoSing is going to twist you into moral pretzels." Particularly troubling to many Anons was the discovery that the DDoS campaigns in the fall and winter of 2010, including Avenge Assange, were built on deceit and buffered by the deployment of hacker-controlled botnets. Had participants known that an army of zombie computers provided the ammunition, they might have chosen differently.

And yet, without this turbo boosting enabled by the hijacked computers, the use of LOIC—even by thousands of willing, ideologically committed participants, each contributing a small bit of power—would never have resulted in the downtimes that generated the media attention that was sought. This same hacker, critical of the technique, elaborated: "I have had several discussions about DDoS with people who, similar to myself, are not overly fond of it, but we keep coming back to it, as it is effective; the media does drive a lot of this activity."

It was pivotal. Robust public participation may not have been technically necessary, and claims of LOIC's safety were atrociously off the mark, but without the appearance of a critical mass, the operation would have likely lacked moral gravitas and authority. In this case, strength in numbers conveyed a potent message, even if there was no safety in them (and no technical need for them): it palpably revealed to the world at large the scope of supporters' disenchantment with what they saw as corporate censorship.

Geeks and others also leveled more general critiques against the tactic, struggling to analogize the DDoS campaign with offline equivalents. Most persistent was the notion that DDoS attacks trample the targets' right to speak freely. If one takes an absolutist view of free speech, then DDoS extinguishes the possibility of speech by disabling access to a website expressing a set of views. This mirrors the position of some hackers, like Oxblood Ruffin of the Cult of the Dead Cow, resolutely against this tactic for decades. In an interview with CNET, he reasoned: "Anonymous is fighting for free speech on the Internet, but it's hard to support that when you're DoS-ing and not allowing people to talk. How is that consistent?"[26]

He is right, up to a point. A more dynamic view of free speech could take power relations into account. By enabling the underdog—the protester or infringed group—to speak as loudly as its more resourceful opponents (in this case, powerful corporations), we might understand a tactic like DDoS as a leveler: a free speech win. I favor a more contextualized, power-driven analysis of free speech. In the case of Avenge Assange, PayPal and its kin never really lost their ability to speak, and the action itself was in response to a unilateral banking and service blockade that crippled WikiLeaks' capability to speak or present a position. Where WikiLeaks had one proactive outlet—its disabled website (and the occasional sympathetic journalist)—many of the targets, like the MPAA and PayPal, commanded lobbyists, advertisers, and media contacts capable of distributing their message far and wide.

But understanding DDoS as a modulator of free speech is itself contentious. Others think it aligns more with another traditional protest tactic: the direct action blockade. In one debate among members of the Cult of the Dead Cow, hacker Tod Gemuese declared the free speech analogy to be "hooey." He continued: "It's the digital equivalent of physical-world forms of protest such as padlocking the gate of a factory or obstructing access to a building, etc."[27] Those who were critical of the tactic because companies had to expend resources to defend their websites failed to understand the nature of direct action. Direct action exceeds a liberal politics of publicity, speech, and debate, having the goal of directly halting activity or impacting and inconveniencing the targeted party.[28] DDoS fits the bill.

Of course, all of these arguments do not necessarily justify DDoS in all situations. Rather, they more thoroughly demonstrate its pretzel-logic and ethical relationality. Internet scholar Ethan Zuckerman and his coauthors have written persuasively about how DDoS can truly harm small organizations lacking the defensive resources of a large corporation.[29] Even if one supports its limited use (say, against well-resourced and powerful organizations), the proliferation of DDoS, critics charge, still encourages the use of a tactic that can quickly devolve into an arms race where those with more bandwidth can outmuscle those with less.

Whatever one might think of the utility and morality of the tactic, we can gain additional perspective by considering the actual technical and legal outcome of a typical DDoS attack. This will also help us weigh the fairness (or lack thereof) of the punishments meted out to participants. In spite of erroneous media reports, the servers that bear the brunt of DDoS traffic are not hacked into—nor do they suffer any permanent damage or data loss.[30] Costs are incurred primarily because targets need to hire firms to provide DDoS protection. A successful DDoS attack against a corporation blocks access to an Internet domain. This may stall access to e-commerce, but it does not affect an organization's internal computer system. The typical Anonymous DDoS attacks, or "traffic floods," were unsuccessful against service sites that perform a lot of data transactions and are served by CDNs (Content Delivery Networks) like Amazon.com. (AnonOps briefly tried to target Amazon.com directly and it was a spectacular failure.) Even with the estimated thousands of individuals contributing their computers to a voluntary botnet, their efforts never shuttered infrastructure backbones like Amazon Web Services. Anonymous's DDoS campaigns tended to be more successful against informational sites like mpaa.org. Anonymous's digital protest tactics essentially blocked access to these domains, but only their Internet-facing websites.

Given what transpires during a DDoS attack, and whatever one might think of the risks and seriousness of it, one thing seems certain: the charges leveled against Anonymous participants in the US and the UK tend to be out of line with the nonviolent nature of these actions. In the US, arrests for DDoS attacks were made under the Computer Fraud and Abuse Act (CFAA), which tends to lead to harsher punishments as compared to charges brought under analogous offline statutes. Offline protesting tactics such as trespassing or vandalism—wherein damage is not merely speculative—rarely result in catastrophic consequences for participants. Yet this nuance that recognizes the intention and the consequences of actions is rarely granted to online activities, especially when the CFAA is invoked. As a result, similar behavior that might earn an offender an infraction or misdemeanor offline (with a penalty of perhaps thirty days in jail) is punished as a felony with hefty fine and jail time when it takes place online.

To put this in perspective: in Wisconsin, a thirty-eight-year-old truck driver, Eric J. Rosol, was fined for running an automated DDoS tool against the Koch Industries website for sixty seconds. (As part of an Anonymous operation, he was protesting the billionaire Koch brothers' role in supporting the Wisconsin governor's effort to reduce the power of unions and public employees' rights to engage in collective bargaining.) The actual financial losses were less than $5,000, but he was slapped with a fine of $183,000—even though a far worse physical crime, arson, would earn a fine of only $6,400 in the same state.[31] The fine represents the cost the Koch brothers spent hiring a consulting firm prior to the campaign for advice on mitigating the attack. In the UK, Chris Weatherhead—who didn't directly contribute to a DDoS campaign but ran the Anonymous communication hub where the protests were coordinated—received a whopping eighteen-month sentence, "convicted on one count of conspiracy to impair the operation of computers."[32]

The legal outcome for those arrested for the PayPal attacks merits further discussion. Due to excellent legal help and a plea bargain (still in the works), most of the thirteen defendants charged with DDoSing PayPal will be fined only a modest $5,600 each and will evade jail time. Even though they will be charged with felonies, the judge will likely wipe it off their records if they comply with their probation. Two others will likely go to jail for ninety days to avoid the felony charge, and one defendant's fate is undecided.[33] (Final outcomes will be delivered in December 2014.) Even though the punishments are less harsh than expected, the defendants were still put through an expensive and draining three-year ordeal, and with felonies hanging over their heads, many may have had (and will likely continue to have) trouble landing jobs.

The whole affair is also marked by doublespeak that illustrates the flagrant hypocrisy of a single corporation, PayPal, going after protesters who participated in Avenge Assange. (MasterCard and Visa did not seek to prosecute.) In court, PayPal's lawyers estimated damages to be up to $5.5 million.[34] Meanwhile, in other venues, corporate officials claimed either that "PayPal was never down," or that the attack only "slowed down the company's system, but to such a small extent that it would have been imperceptible to customers."[35] This is a perfect example of how corporate actors not only can continue to voice their positions just fine through multiple channels, but can also engage in hypocritical and contradictory double-speak as they put defendants through a costly, time-consuming legal process.

Eventually, the debate about DDoS became largely moot within Anonymous. The tactic's success became identified with its ability to generate news headlines. This reliance on an obsessively cycling news media would grant a very short half-life to the visibility of actions like Avenge Assange. Anonymous, no fool, saw this coming; ceasing the operation, the group announced to the world in a poster that "we have, at best, given them a black eye. The game has changed. When the game changes, so too must our strategies." From December 2010 on, DDoS, with all its moral conundrums left unsorted, became one occasionally wielded weapon in an increasingly diverse portfolio of tactics. Meanwhile, events began to stir in the small country of Tunisia, and the actions of a couple of hackers, one from AnonOps, set in motion events that would, yet again, shift everything for the collective of collectives— events as important as the birth of Chanology itself.

CHAPTER 5

Anonymous Everywhere

As 2010 became 2011 and Operation Avenge Assange waned, other operations on AnonOps waxed. It was not that AnonOps was splintering, but rather that it was flowering. This IRC network became the digital platform du jour for Anonymous activists of different stripes to organize their operations. By the end of January there were operations and dedicated IRC channels for Italy, Ireland, Venezuela, Brazil, Syria, Bahrain, Tunisia, Egypt, and Libya, along with non-place-based operations like Operation Leakspin, an effort to comb through the WikiLeaks diplomatic cables in search of newsworthy information. Many of these endeavors were small but nevertheless gave birth to vibrant regional nodes, the most prominent being Italy, Brazil, and the Hispano-Anons. (At the time of this writing, Anonymous Italy has leaked documents from the office of the governor of the Lombardy region, declaring the politician to be "one big corrupted son of a gun" and accusing him, among other things, of allowing criminals who distribute child porn to launder their funds through a Lombardy bank.[1]) These geographical pockets have thrived and grown into full-bodied communities. Although showing no signs of slowing down, very few regional nodes have been documented.[2]

Operation Tunisia seemed to erupt out of nowhere. It was

only much later that I was informed about its precise conditions of its birth; even years later, its founder fumbled when pressed for a precise explanation: "I don't really know why it worked," he insisted during an interview. Two geeks, Slim and Adnon (not his real pseudonym), living in different regions of the world, acting independently but united in the belief that they could make the world better, set their sights on Tunisia. Slim Amamou, a Tunisian citizen in his thirties, was hoping Anonymous would get involved in publicizing the troubles roiling his country. A programmer and blogger, Amamou was fascinated by Anonymous; he had given talks about the power and draw of nonidentitarian politics. He described Anonymous as the number zero: the all-powerful number, the non-number. This was a fitting example for a young Arab man, given that it was Arab mathematicians who popularized zero. Embodying the idea of void and infinity, zero was long held in the West as a heretical concept, only entering usage in mathematics and philosophy during the intellectual, and political, ferment of the Enlightenment. Zero—the ultimate placeholder, refusing a concrete identity.

While Adnon, living on the other side of the Mediterranean Sea, *chose* to be Anonymous, living a privileged life in a quaint historic town in Europe without fear of government repression, Amamou was backed into the corner of anonymity. Tunisia was under a regime of heavy censorship: in 2010, this nation of just over ten million people scored 164 out of 178 in Reporters Without Borders' Press Freedom Index (an annual rating that measures press freedoms based on a questionnaire filled out by non-governmental organizations, journalists, jurists, academics, and human rights workers in various countries). Like many Tunisians, Amamou used anti-censorship circumvention tools to read news and get the word out. The use of proxies and virtual private networks (VPNs) was "standard knowledge among the youth," he said to me. In Tunisia, geekdom was often spurred by necessity and the will to survive.

Soon Anonymous would come to symbolize the general plight of Tunisians, said Amamou in an interview—an icon to be adopted by the young urban hacker and rural commoner alike because of the role Anonymous played in their country's revolt. Many knew Anonymous had been the grain of sand that gave rise to the pearl of media attention absent at the start of their revolution. It was a modest and safe contribution to be sure, but still a vital one. On January 8, a week before Ben Ali fell, Tunisian schoolchildren sitting in a courtyard paid tribute to Anonymous by donning the mask.

Amamou, who was already active in the sphere of Internet politics, did not always act anonymously. On May 21, 2010, he was briefly detained by government henchmen for his role in organizing a demonstration against web censorship, set to take place the next day in front of the Information Ministry. He was re-arrested on January 6 during the height of the protests. He explained, "I was interrogated for five days by state security … It is a place where people get killed, you see, and I believe—I am sure actually, I don't believe—that I was saved by Anonymous." Anonymous participants from Tokyo to Europe heard about his plight (it was circulated on Anonymous channels), leading to a flood of calls to the Tunisian government.

So Anonymous had long appealed to Amamou. As his country inched closer to full-blown revolution, he wanted the faceless collective closer. So he "summoned" Anonymous to appear. He thought that if an operation took off, it would force the world's media to stop ignoring Tunisia. Although he called for Anonymous, he was not naive: "Anonymous is not your personal army" is a refrain which he knew well. "You cannot control Anonymous," he told me emphatically, castigating me after I asked him what he would change about Anonymous if he could. All you can do is hope they will arrive. Fortunately, they did.

And it was due in part to Adnon, who was fifteen years old when he first found Anonymous. Raised in Europe, his family was very well-off—though you would never know it by hanging out with him. He was one of the first individuals from AnonOps I met "afk" ("away from the keyboard," in IRC parlance), a pleasure I have since enjoyed on multiple occasions. Out of the entire bunch, he was the most unassuming. Kind, calm, and contemplative, he first struck me as a "regular guy," but within twenty minutes of meeting him, I could see why some of the older hackers were fondly protective of him.

Taking cover from the unyielding sun under the rustling leaves of a tree on a hot summer day, our conversation mostly involved Anonymous shoptalk. That meant roughly 30 percent gossip, 20 percent conspiracy, and 50 percent welcomed pedagogy about the innards of Anonymous. The transition from online chatting to in-person conversation was seamless. Just encountering someone from this realm, in the flesh, was a relief.

He would complain about his boring and menial day job (though wealthy, he was not spoiled) and would become more excited when he recounted one of his many outdoor adventures involving biking or canoeing. Sometimes bored at school and having spent a fair bit of time online, he joined AnonOps in the fall of 2010 during the first phase of Operation Payback. He recounted: "I got involved because I read some article somewhere and thought, 'oh man, dem hax are cool!' Then it was so much more than that." Though far from being a talented hacker, he was still technically proficient, one might even say a quintessential geek.

As he sailed along in the Anonymous ship, he accrued new skills: security protocols, and database and webserver management. But "the biggest things I learned," he said, "were not technical. Teamwork and organization are massive." He was one—among four I met—of those organizers and brokers essential to making Anonymous's clock tick, a device which resembled Dali's gooey melting clocks more than a Swiss machine.

For much of the fall of 2010, Adnon was an avid spectator on IRC, only occasionally chipping in on organizational matters. But he chatted, especially with other channel operators such as joepie. Finally, late in December, Adnon pitched a proposal, aided by those he had talked to for long hours. The proposal forever altered the course of AnonOps.

His suggestion was simple: use Anonymous resources to publicize the plight of the Tunisians revolting, at the time, against their president/dictator Ben Ali, who had been in power since 1987. In his own words: "We had this #anonnews channel and there was like three of us as moderators ... One of the guys there who I think was Tunisian said something like 'This kid burnt himself about this and there's a few people doing some small protests. It would be cool to do something.'" The Tunisian government had by then already blocked the diplomatic cables released by WikiLeaks, which created an enticing and urgent bridge for a cohort of geeks.[3]

Some channel goers initially insisted it was "insane ... to take on a government." Adnon let it go. A week later, on New Year's Eve, Adnon was on holiday with his family. With a blizzard roaring outside, he sneaked away and jumped online from his hotel room. He pushed back against the naysayers, bolstered by a sense of righteousness—and also a dose of misinformation and misunderstanding: "I, being oblivious to the actual size of the 'moralfag' anons, assumed there were thousands of active members and said, why not?" It is true there were thousands during Operation Avenge Assange, but the consistent number ran only in the hundreds, and those working specifically on propaganda and technical matters numbered even fewer, and were shrinking. But he kept pressing, and eventually enough were convinced:

<Adnon>: We just spammed the shit out of the link to the channel #optunisia everywhere
<Adnon>: people were bored
<Adnon>: it was a crazy idea

Many joiners were still skeptical. As Quinn Norton reported for *Wired*, many "didn't think either the op or the revolution had a chance."[4] But it turned out to be one of the group's most stellar operations, ushering in a transformation from Anonymous to Anonymous *Everywhere*. No longer was the group bound to Internet-y issues like censorship and file sharing.

A day or so after Adnon resurrected the proposal, he received a private message (PM) on IRC from someone on #internetfeds, offering their many services—web defacements, DDoSing, hacks. Maybe this would be easier than he thought. On January 2, 2011, at the dawn of a new year—always a sign of hope—Anonymous published the following press release inaugurating #OpTunisia, eventually translated into French, Arabic, Spanish, and Italian:

> A time for truth has come. A time for people to express them-selves freely and to be heard from anywhere in the world. The Tunisian government wants to control the present with falsehoods and misinformation in order to impose the future by keeping the truth hidden from its citizens. We will not remain silent while this happens. Anonymous has heard the claim for freedom of the Tunisian people. Anonymous is willing to help the Tunisian people in this fight against oppression. It will be done. It will be done.
>
> This is a warning to the Tunisian government: attacks at the freedom of speech and information of its citizens will not be tolerated. Any organization involved in censorship will be targeted and will not be released until the Tunisian government hears the claim for freedom to its people. It's on the hands of the Tunisian government to stop this situation. Free the net, and attacks will cease, keep on that attitude and this will just be the beginning.

The Tiger Consumes Four Chickens a Day

But let's back up to the onset of revolution itself. Mohamed Bouazizi, Nawaat WikiLeaks, and Chelsea Manning all deserve thanks for its inception. In 2010, living under the Ben Ali regime since 1989, scores of Tunisians were downtrodden, living in deplorable conditions, and fearful as human rights abuses—torture, censorship, and detentions—intensified in the country. The country had not been party to any large-scale protests for decades, and its many Western allies, including the United States, singled Tunisia out as a model of political and economic stability in an Arab region otherwise known for strife and uncertainty.

So when revolution hit—and when the mainstream media *finally* reported on it with substance—it came as a shock (for Westerners, at least). The demonstrations led to one of the quickest dictatorial downfalls in recent times, and spread as a chain reaction across the region, becoming what is now called the Arab and African Spring. Like so many revolutionary moments, hindsight reveals that there had been, in plain view, enough despair to fuel a fire of defiance for weeks. All that was missing was a match: in Tunisia, two presented themselves.

First, on November 28, when WikiLeaks released its first batch of 220 diplomatic cables, they made the shrewd decision to partner with local activist and media outfits around the globe. One was in Tunisia: Nawaat WikiLeaks provided them with Tunisia-specific cables. Three Nawaat members translated the cables into French and published them under the banner of TuniLeaks to coincide with WikiLeaks' larger public release of documents. Nawaat also worked with foreign geeks and hackers to ensure that their website with the cables remained online in the face of vigorous attempts by the government to censor it.

The cables confirmed what was widely known but theretofore undocumented as fact: Ben Ali was rotten to the core, his regime was mired in corruption, and his family lived in opulence while the rest of the country struggled to meet its daily needs. "The widely available proof of government corruption and hypocrisy based on an unstoppable flow of leaks was significant in fanning the flames of anger and agitation among citizens throughout the region," wrote Ibrahim Saleh, an expert on Tunisian politics.[5]

Many Tunisians read these cables, duly noting the exact number of chickens fed to a pet tiger, and the three types of juices served at dinner—one of which was kiwi, hard to procure in the country:

> 12. (S) The dinner included perhaps a dozen dishes, including fish, steak, turkey, octopus, fish couscous and much more. The quantity was sufficient for a very large number of guests. Before dinner a wide array of small dishes were served, along with three different juices (including Kiwi juice, not normally available here). After dinner, he served ice cream and frozen yoghurt he brought in by plane from Saint Tropez, along with blueberries and raspberries and fresh fruit and chocolate cake.
>
> 13. (S) El Materi [Ben Ali's son-in-law] has a large tiger ("Pasha") on his compound, living in a cage. He acquired it when it was a few weeks old. The tiger consumes four chickens a day. (Comment: The situation reminded the Ambassador of Uday Hussein's lion cage in Baghdad.) El Materi had staff everywhere. There were at least a dozen people, including a butler from Bangladesh and a nanny from South Africa. (NB. This is extraordinarily rare in Tunisia, and very expensive.)
>
> 19. (S) Most striking of all, however, was the opulence with which El Materi and Nesrine live. Their home in Hammamet was impressive, with the tiger adding to the impression of "over the top." Even more extravagant is their home still under construction in Sidi Bou Said. That residence, from its outward appearance, will be closer to a palace. It dominates the Sidi Bou Said skyline from some vantage points and has been the occasion of many private, critical comments. The opulence with which El Materi and Nesrine live and their behavior make clear why they and other members of Ben

Ali's family are disliked and even hated by some Tunisians. The excesses of the Ben Ali family are growing.[6]

Second, on December 17, 2010, three weeks after Nawaat.org released the translated cables, an unrelated act of desperation ripped open the soul of the nation. Bouazizi—a young fruit and vegetable seller—was accosted by the police, who seized his unlicensed food cart and refused to return it even after Bouazizi offered to pay the fine. His first attempt at retrieving his cart was a frustrating failure. Low-level government officials refused to even talk to him. Doubly insulted and with a family of eight to feed, he set himself on fire. Powerless and voiceless in one moment, he became, in the next, impossible to ignore: but at the terrible cost of his life.

Protests began in Sidi Bouzid, the city where Bouazizi resided. Quickly they radiated out in every direction. Lives were lost at the hand of the police, causing more people to join in the protests. Takriz, an Internet-savvy group chartered as a mailing list in 1999, worked to connect the rough-and-tumble street youth to the Internet.[7] Though Takriz had no direct connection with Anonymous, they were kindred spirits. A network of a few thousand, Takriz generally refuses to cooperate with journalists, bandies about obscenity as a shock tactic, and proudly embraces anonymity. Its current Twitter account reads: "Tunisian cyber think/fight tank & street resistance network since 1998. Free, True & Anonymous—Takrizo Ergo Sum—We make revolutions!"[8]

Bouazizi passed away from his burns on January 4, 2011, and the next day an estimated five thousand mourners attended his funeral, many of them chanting, "Farewell, Mohamed, we will avenge you. We weep for you today, we will make those who caused your death weep."[9] The next day, 75 percent of the nation's lawyers went on strike, calling for an end to the crackdown.[10] Tunisians from all walks of life—teachers, union members, students—joined the fray. Protests continued to spread and police violence escalated. By

January 13, dozens of journalists, bloggers, and activists had been arrested and over sixty protesters had been killed. By the middle of the month, Ben Ali decreed a state of emergency, but it was impossible to contain the fury. However, reading the Western mainstream media at the time, one would have barely known.

"After all, you do not have to wear a mask to do it"

The North American and European public first got word of the protests from the publication of a brief Associated Press story on the riots. The report was understandably lacking in detail, as the revolts had just broken out. With each passing day, even as the protests intensified, the reporting in the mainstream Western media outlets, with a few minor exceptions, remained tepid. On January 9, 2011 (with Anonymous already engaged in Tunisia, acting as digital courier pigeons to get word and videos out from the trenches to the public at large), the AP published another story, picked up by newspapers like the *New York Times* and the *Globe and the Mail,* parroting Ben Ali's position. "People taking part in the spate of unrest say they are angry at a lack of jobs and investment, but officials say the rioting is the work of a minority of extremists intent on damaging the north African country."[11] Ben Ali would flee less than a week later, on January 15, 2011.

As part of its campaign, Anonymous wrote the following letter to journalists:

> It has come to our attention that the ongoing riots in Tunisia have by and large escaped the notice of reliable Western news networks. It is the responsibility of the free and open press to report what the censored press cannot. The public demonstrations, as well as the actions Anonymous has taken in solidarity with the citizens of Tunisia, demand mainstream coverage.

The Tunisian government, led by President Ben Ali, has shown an outrageous level of censorship, not only blocking the websites of dissident bloggers, but also sites like Flickr and any website or news source mentioning WikiLeaks. In a show of blatant disregard for the guaranteed right of free speech, over the past 24 hours Tunisian government officials have hacked email and Facebook accounts of anyone who has taken actions labeled as "activism" (which may be as "dangerous" as planning a protest, or as innocent as commenting on a discussion board for a WikiLeaks related group). Entire Facebook accounts have been commandeered by the Tunisian government, who have even gone so far as to change profile pictures to a pirate ship in a mockery of those who stand for freedom of speech.

Anonymous, in turn, has launched DDoS attacks against the websites of the Tunisian prime minister and his corrupt government, the stock market, and the primary DNS server of Tunisia—thus successfully bringing down many of the websites ending in .tn. Additionally, we have taken steps to ensure that Tunisians can connect anonymously to the internet, and access information that their government does not want them to see.

There has been an almost complete absence of prominent coverage. We ask, why is a news source like AlJazeera one of the few covering these earth shaking riots while the rest remain quiet? The world is getting the impression that unless western economic interests are involved, our media does not care to report upon it.

Perhaps you didn't know? Now that you do, you can help us spread the news. After all, you do not have to wear a mask to do it.

Sincerely,
Anonymous[12]

"Dudes believe me the key of this is having no ego"

But Anonymous was doing more than pestering the mainstream media to do its job. By January 2, 2011, a technical team on #internetfeds forsook their holidays to work nonstop. Indeed, Adnon told me he barely slept for two weeks. In an interview, he explained that the operation took a different approach than Operation Payback and Avenge Assange:

> <Adnon>: With Tunisia we had a plan
> <Adnon>: We thought carefully about what to do and when in a small group
> <Adnon>: presented a list of options in a poll
> <Adnon>: then took the result of the poll
> <Adnon>: It was much less a big group decision than other ops

OpTunisia marked, both internally and externally, a sea change. All throughout the fall, multiple secret cabals and channels had populated Anonymous. Even Chanology had to reckon with marblecake, a cabal of its very own. While those in secret channels wielded technical power, and in many respects called the shots, they were still beholden to those in the public channel if they wanted to get things done. The angry masses of the IRC body politic kept the cabals in check—a message made clear when, earlier in the fall, the masses rose up in a collective shitstorm at #command's attempts to cease DDoSing in response to the Pirate Party.

The managing of OpTunisia was different: from the beginning, a handful of smaller teams composed of hackers, propaganda makers, and organizers led the operation and never let go. It was not that this team-based model displaced other mass modalities of organizing. There were other, simultaneous operations—some of which originated from the public channels with no cabal involvement. And a public IRC channel attached to OpTunisia existed, and played a valuable role.

On January 2, 2011, a hacker named "rubik" (not his real pseudonym), who had been working on two private channels, swooped in to announce that a Tunisian website had been defaced (all pseudonyms have been changed):

<rubik>: http://www.pm.gov.tn/pm/index.php—defaced
<OT>: way to go anons!!!!!
<OT>: wayy to fucking go!
<rubik>: Fucking A! Nice Job
<OT>: More to come biotches :P
<rubik>: http://www.marchespublics.gov.tn/ also.
<K-rad>: http://www.pm.gov.tn and http://www.marchespublics.gov.tn/ DE-FUCKING-FACED!
<lafdie>: btw mad props on the lolcats: http://www.pm.gov.tn/pm/index.php
<vvom>: http://www.pm.gov.tn/pm/index.php BOOYA MOTHERFUCKERS

A group of hackers had been hard at work, cooperating as a team, for some time. Yet the majority of journalists couldn't resist the opportunity to pinpoint a "mastermind" or "leader," *the* architect ostensibly maneuvering everyone else. Ironically, an Internet search for "Anonymous leader" will yield at least four different names. Eventually, most journalists identified Sabu and Topiary as the leaders, most likely because they erroneously conflated their robust public relations presence with organizational (or dictatorial) control.[13]

Although many articles single out a "ringleader" or a "mastermind," the exact nature of what this entails is left largely unstated. The reader is left to use his or her own imagination—perhaps envisioning an elite villain sitting on a high-backed chair in some ice palace, stroking a cat on his lap as a deep echoing laugh reverberates slowly through the chambers. Adrian Chen surmised, based on leaked IRC logs, that "Sabu plays the role of a leader, enforcing unit discipline while the other members stand by."[14] And yet Chen himself belies this insight in the next breath by shifting attention to a related hack performed without Sabu's input by another group of Anons. Analyzing a single log for evidence of a leader is about as effective as extrapolating the entire plot of a movie from a single still frame. Yet the *Guardian*'s Charles Arthur made the same error, writing, "For some time after the UK arrests, the only visibly active member of LulzSec remained its leader, known online as Sabu, who would simultaneously deny that he was its leader and then use phrases such as 'my team.'"[15] But broader context reveals that Sabu was simply referring to the #pure-elite channel he created long ago, and described by other LulzSec members as an IRC channel where friends of LulzSec" could hang out.

As it turns out, hacker undertakings, especially within Anonymous, tend to be dynamic and fluid, with multiple individuals or even groups working in concert. What holds true for one operation may not for the next. Sometimes a particularly obsessive hacker engenders, for a time, an organized collective workflow. At other times, it is chaos and miscommunication. Indeed, when I interviewed Jeremy Hammond in prison much later, he bemoaned, "I wish we were more like RedHack, more disciplined." RedHack, a Turkey-based hacktivist group, has a clear hierarchy, a leader, and a spokesperson—products, each, of sixteen years of organizing and a shared devotion to Marxist-Leninist tactics.

Maybe Anonymous could have achieved more had it had a leader or a static hierarchy. Hackers tend to suffer from what I like to call Geek Distraction Disorder (GDD). Without oversight, a hacker could easily wind up in a field, surrounded by yaks, with a shaving razor in hand, wondering how he got there (if you understand this reference, you are at risk!). But it is equally probable that Anonymous achieved so much precisely *because* there was no boss pointing to a fixed destination. Whatever the case, the work unfurled organically: depending on who was on the channel, what each participant could contribute, and this willingness, in a certain moment, to learn something new—the crucial ingredient of most any successful hack.

OpTunisia illustrates this all so well. Imagine yourself on IRC, an Anon witnessing the operation's beginning. It is January 2, 2011, and you are working directly with Tunisian activists and hackers who are feeding you unvarnished information about a historic revolt. You are at home, sitting largely still except for your fingers moving at the keyboard, but the information you receive enables responses that can make a direct difference in the event, just one step removed from the people on the ground throwing Molotov cocktails. Your contributions won't necessarily be significant, but they can't be overlooked. They are personally empowering, a mechanism of solidarity, and, in some cases, perhaps even a real boon that shields those on the ground from harm. All of this depends on shifting, messy modes of cooperation—and sets the stage for organizations to spring up around a particularly good idea, and to fall apart at even a hint of disagreement and alternate paths.

At this time there were two different and private IRC channels that were active simultaneously, #opdeface and #internetfeds. The latter is where the heavy technical lifting was done, the former where organizers congregated. A gopher shuttled news between them. Some hackers were in the know, while others were continually arriving (all pseudonyms have been changed):

<rubik>: K-rad, Any good with PostgreSQL? [PostgresSQL is a database]
<rubik>: http://www.pm.gov.tn/pm/banniere/redirectb.php?id=54&
idb=3'2&
<K-rad>: rubik, i've never messed with PostgreSQL, it is even the first time i've ever seen it on a box tbh
<gibnut>: why are we hitting up tunisia?
<K-rad>: Because they'e just passed a law which says the media can't say what they want
<K-rad>: and banned them from mentioning wikileaks

<gibnut>: K-rad, thank you!
<gibnut>: time to own tunisia then ;)

On other channels, users suggested DDoS campaigns, but both in Anonymous and out, there we are those who prided themselves on being "real" hackers and dismissed DDoS as lame (or even detrimental to real hacks, as we will see in a moment). Real hackers find exploits. People who just run LOIC are considered beneath the "hacker" moniker, mere "script kiddies," or "skiddies" for short. gibnut announces that he has an "zero-day," which is much more powerful. A zero-day exploit, or "oh day" as people sometimes jokingly call it, is a previously unknown security vulnerability in a piece of software. It is called a zero-day because it is unknown by the public—or the software authors who could fix it—for zero days and counting. A zero day is gold; anyone who knows the zero day can exploit it over and over until it is patched. The most coveted zero days provide access to a computer or network, which is why they are sold for high profit in a thriving black market. Many, many governments participate in this ethically problematic market, including the US government, who, according to technology reporter Joseph Menn, "has become the biggest buyer in a burgeoning gray market where hackers and security firms sell tools for breaking into computers."[16] The US government largely purchases zero-days from private firms that "spend at least tens of millions of dollars a year just on exploits."[17] Suffice it to say, gibnuts's news was received with excitement:

<gibnut>: lets see fuck loic, we'll hurt them a different way
<p-ground>: oh yes please
<gibnut>: I have 0day local root exploit against openwebmail and Tunisia's NIC servers run it
<gibnut>: https://risala.ati.tn/cgi-bin/openwebmail/openwebmail.pl
<gibnut>: if we can get into that server we can root tunisias .tn tld nameservers and control its entire internet space

<p-ground>: oshit
<gibnut>: redirect it all to wikileaks ;)
<p-ground>: shit just got real due to gibnut

With this zero day, gibnut is suggesting that they can compromise the domain name registrar in Tunisia (the NIC) and control the entire Tunisian top-level domain (TLD) name space. An example of a TLD is .com or .org. Each country has its own TLD; Tunisia's is ".tn." If the Anons can compromise this Tunisian registrar, they can redirect everyone who tries to navigate to a website that ends in .tn to any server they wish. gibnut lulzily suggests WikiLeaks. Although this particular exploit did not yield access (for unknown reasons), it did succeed in spreading an anxious optimism throughout the sidelines:[18]

<gibnut>: let me see if I can get in... brb [be right back]
<p-ground>: Arm the nuclear warheads guys.
<p-ground>: Internetfeds is going in.
<K-rad>: gibnut, :D nice <3
<K-rad>: but first we need to find a bug on there
<jaggy91>: epic
<p-ground>: for some reason stuff in this channel always ends up being epic
<jaggy91>: lol
<rubik>: ah guess i'm going to have to use some postgresql injection cheat sheet or something
<gibnut>: rubik, or, download havij for windows
<K-rad>: http://www.marchespublics.gov.tn IS HIGHLY INJECTABLE :3 [there is at least one vulnerability that allows an attacker to modify the site's database in ways other than intended]
<K-rad>: stand by for lulz <3
<rubik>: :o
<rubik>: looks like ministry of justice, i think, idk [I dont know]
<K-rad>: i don't know but ALOT of the sites are vuln [vulnerable]!

Like many hackers, if they don't know something, they go teach themselves:

> <K-rad>: know tht postgres bug?
> <rubik>: yeah
> <K-rad>: i did some reading on posgres and lurned me some DB [database] so now i know how to inject it :D
> <K-rad>: stand by for dump

K-rad went away for a while, clearly working hard, then came back with some results. K-rad accessed a database with sixteen hundred rows (and thus entries) and tried to crack the passwords. First apologizing—"sry guys jst taking time because i've never done postgres SQL and im trying to write it in to a script to make it faster as i do it"—he then realized that the ongoing DDoS was what was causing the slowdown of the password dump. He implored:

> <K-rad>: Someone tell optunisia DO NOT DDOS 193.95.68.156 it's fucking up my dump

As this was a team effort, other hackers were simultaneously trying to gain access through other potential security vulnerabilities. They realized that if they could get shell access, which enables a lower-level access to the system, they could potentially get the private emails of the prime minister of Tunisia, and then leak them. rubik managed to gain access but, unfortunately, found nothing but spam—but that didn't stop the "owning" process. To "own," "0wn," or "pwn" a server basically means that you have gained the top level of privileged access and, from there on out, you have free rein to do whatever you like with it. You can read any file, write to any file, change running processes, inject your own processes/malicious code, or, if you are so inclined, delete everything. You are "root," the full administrator of the machine, even though you are nowhere physically near the machine itself. Inevitably, of course, the Anons defaced the site, but first they attempted to score some emails:

<rubik>: I logged it but there's nothing there

<K-rad>: brb guys im going to make a fresh tea :3

<gibnut>: http://www.marchespublics.gov.tn/onmp/upload/upload_fichier.php?Field=document&type=document

<gibnut>: ;]

<gibnut>: shall I own it now or later

<rubik>: nice

<K-rad>: be best now while the anti-tuni.gov steam is still rolling

<rubik>: we could upload a shell i suppose

<gibnut>: tre

<rubik>: which shells would you guys like ;]

<rubik>: i have like 40

<K-rad>: it will maximize effect and morale

<K-rad>: if we can root it, we need to go for email leak too!

<K-rad>: not just deface!

<K-rad>: :D

<K-rad>: full on email leak :D:D

<rubik>: found the shell

<gibnut>: www.marchespublics.gov.tn/onmp/upload/documents

<K-rad>: someone make a fancy payback deface page plz :3

As the team prepared to deface the page, K-rad excitedly declared that there was an old kernel installed. The kernel is the core component of an operating system—the contact point between the hardware and the software. An old kernel usually means that there are some known exploits, so this is almost always a good sign for someone wanting to compromise a machine:

<rubik>: here's a deface page

<rubik>: http://pickhost.eu/images/0004/1986/anonymousdeface tunisia.jpg

<rubik>: if u like it

```
<rubik>: :p
<K-rad>: OOOOOOOOOOOOOOOOOOOOOOOOOOOOOOO
OOOOOOOOOOOOOOOOOOOOOOOOOOOLD KERN FTW [For
The Win]
<rubik>: root?
<duckie>: Not bad rubik
<duckie>: Any chance you could centre the text at the bottom though?
<rubik>: idk i didn't make it
<rubik>: im running on tor
<rubik>: wish i hd a vpn
```

duckie had just logged in to help. He was eventually booted for lacking sufficient low-level hacking ability, but he was a skilled organizer and broker, so for the time being he was allowed into the channel. He had a rare knack for naming operations and a rare level of insight into the ongoing changes affecting AnonOps:

```
<duckie>: Anything I can do to help which doesn't involve actually
going into the server?
<duckie>: rubik, I've been in and out, this channel was presumed
dead for a long time
<K-rad>: duckie make a deface page! :D?
```

While #internetfeds was in hot pursuit of the private emails of the Tunisian prime minister, there was another channel, #opdeface, also hard at work. But even in the elite channel that was #internetfeds, many were blind to the existence of #opdeface. Meanwhile, the search for emails came up empty. On #opdeface, rubik gave a technical rundown of the exploit they had found on #internetfeds.

Some Tunisian Anons realized an exploit could work on another target:

```
<OT>: I repeat: Main target is ati [Tunisian Internet Agency]
<OT>: Direct responsible for censorship
```

<mo>: i have found an XSS exploit on ati site
<a>: OT, lol, i just thought you said that in opchannel [a public channel]
<OT>: lol
<OT>: not that stoned yet
[…]
<rubik>: we found admin login passwords for publicmarches.gov.tn, which is on the same box as pm.gov.tn now
<vj>: i think we looked into ministry of communication as DDoS target
<vj>: if it was disqualified, i don't remember why
<a>: just looking at it

rubik, thinking they might eventually score some juicy emails, asked them for some help:

<rubik>: btw
<rubik>: can anyone prepare a statement
<rubik>: for the torrent description
<rubik>: when we get pm.gov.tn emails
<rubik>: i.e. a message to pm.gov.tn about their leaked emails
<rubik>: but not yet
<rubik>: prepare a deface page
<rubik>: unless u like http://pickhost.eu/images/0004/1986/anonymousdefacetunisia.jpg
<rubik>: and prepare a torrent description or manifesto

Eventually, #opdeface delivered:

<vj>: Greetings from Anonymous.
<vj>: We have been watching your treatment of your own people, and we are both greatly saddened and enraged at your behavior. You have unilaterally declared war on free speech, democracy, and even your own people. Your people rally in the streets to demand accountability and their own rights, which you have wrongfully presumed it was in your purview to take from them.
<vj>: We will use this brief span of attention we've captured to deliver a clear and present message which we hope shall never be forgot. Remember, remember, that the tighter you squeeze the more your

people shall rebel against your rule. Like a fistful of sand in the palm of your grip, the more you squeeze your people the more that they will flow right out of your hand. The more you censor your

\<vj\>: own people, the more they shall know about you and what you are doing.

\<vj\>: We are Anonymous.

\<vj\>: We are the angry avatar of free speech.

\<vj\>: We are the immune system of democracy.

\<vj\>: We do not forgive censorship.

\<vj\>: We do not forget free speech.

\<vj\>: Expect us - always.

\<a\>: good stuff. i'd do s/people/citizens/

\<a\>: sounds more … profound

\<vj\>: We will use this brief span of attention we've captured to deliver a clear and present message which we hope shall never be forgot. Remember, remember, that the tighter you squeeze the more your citizens shall rebel against your rule. Like a fistful of sand in the palm of your grip, the more you squeeze your citizens the more that they will flow right out of your hand. The more you censor

\<vj\>: your own citizens the more they shall know about you and what you are doing.

\<vj\>: In that spirit, we release to the citizens of Tunisia and to the world a cache of government documents. Hopefully this will shed some light on what the government so desperately wishes to hide.

rubik continued to act as gopher between the two channels. With work done for now, he gave props to one of the team members (not Sabu, by the way). Another Anon quickly berated this individual praise on ethical grounds, and K-rad himself played the accomplishment down—a clear example of the self-effacing values at work in Anonymous:

\<rubik\>: credit goes to K-rad for this one

\<K-rad\>: it was everyone in feds :D

\<K-rad\>: dont forget to rm -rf their admin login page :D [rm -rf being the command to delete a directory]

<K-rad>: and rm -rf everything else you can under those perms! :3
<Adnon>: You guys done
<a>: dont forget gibnut
<a>: and whoever else worked in the background (=
<OT>: no names lol just anonymous
<a>: well, ofc [of fucking course]
<a>: but in here .. ppl who are in here..
<nessy>: we in secret tho
<a>: is still ok. i guess (=
<OT>: dudes believe me the key of this is having 0 ego
<a>: we were just giving kudos
<a>: internally :)
<OT>: lol
<alex>: eh
<alex>: ofc
<gibnut>: no names please. my handle is hot :)

So there you have it: hackers at work. It is mundane, quintessential teamwork, but also awesome and hilarious, at least for those involved. I only quoted from two channels, but the work transpired across four different groups—maybe even more, and also likely on a collaborative writing pad where the press releases were written. And keep in mind that the public OpTunisia channels, #propaganda and #command, were doing something, whatever that might have been, at the same time. Many Anons were corodinating through private messaging as well.

In short, there were so many tentacles that the idea of a leader calling the shots is laughable: not a hive (as Anonymous sometimes calls itself), not a structureless mass, nor a structured hierarchy either—but some modality of all the above.

"Don't worry, I'm anonymous too"

As we have seen clearly, individuals can stand out among the rest for their abilities in any particular situation. In OpTunisia,

K-rad was one of these standouts. But over time, individual contributions bleed into each other, and the individual is submerged. However, keeping this in mind, we can nonetheless see the value of viewing Anonymous from the opposite perspective: singling out a participant, and his or her important hack, for the purposes of upending another persistent misconception. By showcasing tflow's work on OpTunisia, and considering it alongside that of Adnon and Amamou, it will become apparent that the stereotype of the typical Anonymous participant—white, middle class, libertarian, and politically naive—is nowhere close to reality.

tflow (featured above under a different pseudonym) is a talented programmer who joined Anonymous in the fall of 2010 and founded #internetfeds as the secret hacking wing of AnonOps. For much of the autumn, tflow was #internetfeds' keymaster, testing and vetting invited hackers with three technical questions. One of AnonOps' more prolific technical contributors, tflow had the clever idea to write an anti-phishing script during OpTunisia. Phishing is essentially any method that is used to acquire personal and private details—usually login and password combinations or credit card information—by pretending to be something or someone trustworthy. A common technique is to send forged emails that appear to be coming from the targets' email provider's help desk, or from their bank, urgently asking you to reply with your username and password before your account is closed. A more sophisticated version contains a link which, when clicked, installs a keylogger or other type of malware. People fall for phishing attacks at an alarming rate—making it a particularly lucrative technique. One computer science study of the technique concluded: "Experiments show a success rate of over 70 percent for phishing attacks on social networks."[19] So it is unsurprising that the Ben Ali regime was using a phishing scam, involving a malicious script, to plunder the usernames and passwords to the social media accounts of Tunisian activists. tflow's idea was to come up with an antidote, a "remove Tunisian government phishing script."

tflow's script is a quintessential example of an "artful hack"—given an elegant definition by Jude Milhon, better known by her handle, St. Jude, she once said: "Hacking is the clever circumvention of imposed limits, whether imposed by your government, your IP server, your own personality."[20] tflow's hack was not technically sophisticated; he wrote the code in less than ten minutes and could have done so in thirty seconds had he been more familiar with the underlying technology. It was clever simply because it identified a need and it *worked*.

Before he could even whip up the short program, he first had to get his hands on the offending script. To do so, he had to find a Tunisian willing to give him remote computer access using a piece of software called TeamViewer. In early January, he reached out to a Tunisian activist (with the exception of tflow, everyone's pseudonym has been changed):

<tflow>: anont
<anont>: tflow, yes
<tflow>: anont, are you in tunisia?
<anont>: tflow, yes
<tflow>: can you come on teamviewer so we can locate the ip address the phishing scripts are running on so we can hax them? :]

Of course, anontunisia asked the obvious question:

<anont>: tflow, how can I trust you ?
<shaka>: tflow is very trustworthy
<oggle>: tflow is a trusted member
<Aa>: anont, I think various people can vouch for tflow and I'll be one of them.

Since trust is really often just a matter of faith, tflow offered the soundest advice (and one person resorted to a dumb and offensive "joke"):

<tflow>: anont, you can see everything i'm doing on your screen, if
you don't like it you can exit
<shaka>: tflow is old skool payback from the start
<k02>: trust tflow always after rape you he gives you candy!

anont responded:

<anont>: A, tflow, shaka, OK. pm me

tflow was now able to write the script. It, quite simply, changed
the functions in the government script so that they did nothing.
A day later, after the script had been written, thrown online,
and was in the process of being downloaded by the thousands,
tflow and anont convened again in private:

<tflow>: hey
<tflow>: still here?
<anont>: yes
<tflow>: come on teamviewer
<tflow>: i want to see if the script works
[…]
<anont>: good work! well done
<anont>: :)
[…]
<anont>: hey
<anont>: I have news
<tflow>: hey
<anont>: the aljazeera reporter will investigate phishing with fb,
google & co
<tflow>: nice
<tflow>: there is also an article about it here http://www.thetech
herald.com/article.php/201101/6651/Tunisian-government-
harvesting-usernames-and-passwords explains it well
<anont>: yes
<anont>: i sent to several media last night
<tflow>: nice
<anont>: i'm a reporter myself :)

<tflow>: did you also send the anti-phishing script?
<tflow>: ah
<anont>: yes
<anont>: don't worry
<anont>: i'm anonymous too :D

anont, a journalist, remains anonymous, but I had the fortune of eventually meeting tflow in London during July of 2013, two years after, nearly to the day, his arrest by the British Metropolitan Police. tflow pled guilty to one count of computer misuse, admitting to conspiring to hack numerous British and international organizations, including the Serious Organised Crime Agency, 20th Century Fox, and News International. Since he was a minor when caught, he got off with a light sentence of community service. It consisted, as he told me in an interview, of "tagging clothes that people donated with price tags, putting them out on the shopfloor, and redesigning the shop window displays."

I had not spent a whole lot of time talking to tflow, certainly not privately. His name was a constant fixture on my screen and on occasion we chatted, usually as part of a group conversation. Usually engaged in a mix of technical or philosophical conversations, he was eloquent and sharp as a tack. He could be a smart-ass, but not in a cruel way, and it was often in the service of a broader insight. Take, for instance, the following conversation from March 2011, on an IRC channel for journalists called "#reporter." A journalist had just logged in for the first time and asked:

<reporter799>: how does this work?
<reporter799>: I'm very new to this
<tflow>: magic
<tflow>: witchcraft
<reporter799>: haha
<reporter799>: so, when you give interviews, how exactly does that work?

<Token>: Ask a question, somebody will ans
<reporter799>: just, in general on this forum?
<tflow>: well, the laws of physics will perform chemical reactions in your brain to decide a question, then will move the muscles in your arms to push keys to represent your question. then upon pressing the enter key, it will be transmitted through the tubes
<tflow>: yeah.. you can just ask a question here
<Token>: lol tflow
<reporter799>: and just cite it as "Anonymous Group Member"?
<tflow>: most of us here have been involved in anonymous operations
<reporter799>: that's encouraging
[…]
<tflow>: what publication/news do you work for?
<reporter799>: free lance
<reporter799>: I write for [X] and have my own blog
<reporter799>: I'll send you a link
[she sends it]
<tflow>: alright
<reporter799>: So, I guess I can start asking now?
<tflow>: not sure how a dating blog is relevant to this subject though :P

Though he was often around, it was difficult to geographically place him. He was obviously a native English speaker, but that didn't narrow things down much. It never crossed my mind that he, like Adnon, might be a teenager. When he was arrested on July 19, 2011, and revealed to be a sixteen-year-old, shock rippled through AnonOps. People were surprised because his fellow hackers considered him to be one of the smartest of the crew; teamwork does not preclude the assessment of capacities and skills.

Since tflow was a minor at the time of his arrest, authorities could not release his name, only his age. I am ashamed to admit that when I found out he was British and sixteen, a picture immediately popped into my mind. It was not as off as the "nihilists, anarchists, activists, LulzSec, Anonymous, twentysomethings who haven't talked to the opposite sex in five or six years," described by Michael Haydn, the ex-director of the CIA and NSA, in reference to those who would come to support Edward Snowden.[21] What did come to mind was a pale waif whose wealthy parents thoughtlessly shipped him off to boarding school at a tender age.

As it turned out, once he was eighteen, tflow was revealed to be Mustafa Al-Bassam, and pictures confirmed that he was not pasty white. He moved to London from Iraq with his family when he was six years old, fleeing Saddam Hussein. His father is a doctor—a general practitioner—so they are financially middle class. But they live in a poor, immigrant-heavy neighborhood in South London, and have more of a working-class lifestyle; his parents, like many immigrant families, save instead of spend. When I prodded him about his background, he explained, somewhat uncomfortably: "We live in the bottom 1 percent areas in the UK, economically and socially."

My first meeting with him, in London, was—unlike my first meeting with Adnon—tense and awkward, since we did not have hundreds of hours of chatting to connect us. The disconnect was likely magnified by the fact he had been out of the scene for a while—he had been banned from the Internet for two years. Thankfully, the sun streaming in through the skylight—the UK was undergoing a rare sunny spell—helped soften the mood.

We continued our conversation online. A recurring topic was the morality of the law, unsurprising given his personal experiences with the justice system. One day we discussed another young hacker, Aaron Swartz, ensnared by the American legal system. (Swartz was a cofounder of reddit, one of the most popular sites online.) Swartz, at the age of twenty-five, was facing decades in prison—thirty-five years—and up to $1 million in fines for downloading a cache of academic journal articles from JSTOR, the scholarly archive available to anybody on MIT's network.

Had he been found guilty, it is unlikely he would have been

jailed for that long. But the number of charges and the potential years in jail were used by prosecutors to leverage him into a plea bargain and accept a felony charge. What is even more remarkable is that he did not "hack" JSTOR's website at all; nor was JSTOR even pursuing charges. Sure, MIT had to expend some resources over the affair, but it was not in any way seriously harmed. The main prosecutor, Stephen Heymann, nevertheless had the audacity to compare "the Internet pioneer to a rapist and suggested he had 'systematically revictimized' MIT by not taking a plea bargain," as Ryan Reily of the *Huffington Post* put it.[22]

Perhaps he could have been found guilty of trespassing—he stashed a computer in a closet on campus and connected it directly to the MIT system. On a few occasions, the MIT network administrators had booted him from the network, certainly trying to prevent him from downloading more than a certain number of articles. But even if some of his actions were illegal or broke rules, from a moral standpoint one could say that the downloading of academic articles, many of them researched and written using tax dollars, was wholly undeserving of a thirty-five-year sentence and a felony charge—not to mention an expensive trial also paid for by taxpayers. Swartz, forlorn and overwhelmed by the prosecution, ended his life on January 6, 2013.

One day, while chatting to Al-Bassam about the case, I mentioned an article written by a professor, Hal Abelson, who had chaired a committee investigating MIT's role in the affair. Abelson absolved MIT and described Swartz as "dangerously naive about the reality of exercising [his technical] power, to the extent that he destroyed himself."[23] Appalled, I responded on a popular techblog: "The true naivety here was Abelson's. His failure to attribute any blame to the unfair, aggressive and excessive federal prosecution, instead characterizing it merely as 'vigorous,' was as appalling as using a descriptive word that one should reserve for a workout."[24] Al-Bassam replied: "'Dangerously naive about the reality of exercising power, to the extent that he destroyed himself' is a statement that should be applied to the prosecution, not Aaron Swartz."

Al-Bassam—tflow—had experienced firsthand the force of the law knocking at his door, and did so after months of engagement in direct action for causes he believed in. It is not surprising that youthful sensibilities are the source of so much creative political energy. Such energy can be harder to sustain as one's idealism bumps up against the horrific realities of the problems plaguing our world, coinciding with the saddling of more and more day-to-day responsibilities. But if youthful idealism makes someone proceed in attempts to tackle the enormity of our problems, then we need more, not less, youthful "naïveté."

Smashing Stereotypes

Adnon, tflow, and Slim are three Anonymous activists. Anonymous is not the white, middle-class, American boys' club of everyone's default imagination. Hard numbers are impossible to come by, but those Anons I have met and those unmasked by arrests are a motley bunch (incidentally, motley refers to trickster clothing, the court jester's multicolored smock). If, in addition to these three men, we consider the cohort of hackers Al-Bassam worked with in #internefeds (and later, LulzSec) now known due to arrests, the heterogeneity becomes more pronounced. Among their ranks was a Puerto Rican living in towering public housing project of New York (he was also an occasional drug dealer and a foster father to his nieces); two Irish chemistry students, one whose radical political views were influenced by a father who was a member of the Irish Republican Army who had been jailed for six years; a Scotsman, who for much of his time in Anonymous lived on the remote Isle of Yell; and a twenty-five-year-old man, Kayla, who served in the British military in Iraq and performed a female gender online.

Something about the pseudonymous environment likely helped cultivate this cosmopolitanism. By cloaking markers of the self, like ethnicity, class, and age, all sorts of different possibilities are opened up. Studies confirm that we tend to seek those who are familiar (or similar to us)—and fellowship via shared identity is nothing to scoff at, nor eliminate.[25] Nevertheless, it is also important to create and experiment with spaces that mute markers of class, age, and background to help form connections that might not otherwise be made. In a way, it could be that self-defined membership in Anonymous itself becomes enough of a shared identity to foster these connections.

While we can showcase surprising examples of diversity within Anonymous, this is not to say that heterogeneity is *not* notably lacking. Particularly when it comes to gender: Although Anonymous boasted key female participants and organizers (like darr, featured earlier in this book, and a feisty activist named Mercedes Haefer whose actions will soon be examined in depth), the only "femanon" hacker in LulzSec turned out to be a guy passing himself off as one—Kayla.

Anonymous mirrors the structural inequities prevalent across the computer science world. While most of the STEM (Science, Technology, Engineering, and Math) fields have narrowed the gender gap, computer science is not one of them. Indeed, peak equity in college enrollment occurred more than twenty years ago when 37 percent of undergraduate computer science degrees awarded in 1985 went to women. Today the number hovers around 20 percent.[26] And while numbers are harder to harvest for the hacking scene (given the informal nature of many associations), all indicators point to even lower rates of inclusion.[27] In certain sectors, such as free and open-source software, many projects have responded with initiatives to increase diversity.[28] But among law-breaking hackers, the only females I have met or heard about are those who have switched genders, which is actually— and perhaps, for many, surprisingly—more common than one might imagine. (Conversely, it bears noting that—whatever the reason—females are more common among trolling communities.) Even though there are no formal studies on gender and the hacker underground, the low numbers are likely the combined result of structural forces, the legal riskiness of the activity, and the insular, braggodocious boys' club mentality within the established community.[29] Occasionally, hearing constant belittling of female contributions from certain Anons, I would find myself wondering, "Is this sexism or just trolling?" knowing full well that the distinction is rarely clear-cut.

Being specific about diversity and gender dynamics allows for more interesting questions to be posed: Why, for instance, are gender benders, queer hackers, and female trolls common and openly accepted categories, but female participation in technical circles remains low? Some identities become accepted while others continue to be viewed with skepticism.

Dismantling the stereotypes also allows a greater appreciation of the motivations held by many of these participants. We may disagree with the tactics—hacking, DDoSing, doxing—but we should distinguish these tools and their significance from the composition of Anonymous itself. Time and again I witnessed participants acting with political conviction, and it is likely some of them were political newcomers.

This becomes entirely lost if we understand Anonymous through the gross fetish of stereotypes. Many journalists who have interviewed me as an "expert academic" ask, in some form or another, about "the kind of person who seems to get into Anonymous." Though it is not the answer anyone wants to hear, I often say that there is no kind—except, again, that many tend to be geeks and hackers. Those who identify as being part of the Internet are diverse in background, interests, and political sensibility. But behind the question, the asker likely has something in mind: socially alienated, white, angry, libertarian, American youth. And if we assume the default hacker and geek is generally male, middle-class, libertarian, and white, then it is much easier to treat a hacker's political interventions as juvenile and suspect—arising from a baseline of teenage angst, instead of the desire for politically conscientious action.

CHAPTER 6

"Moralfaggotry" Everywhere

<Anonymous9>: There's one thing which makes me a bit bittersweet actually
<Anonymous9>: Biella is here for college research
<Anonymous9>: I can't help feeling that as soon as she's written her thesis or whatever the project is, she'll have no further reason to hang out here :(
<Anonymous9>: I don't think she realizes how much she's contributed to Anonymous
<Anonymous9>: Even if she doesn't see herself as part of it necessarily

This 2011 chat log between a core Anonymous organizer and reporter was given to me in 2013. Upon reading it, a flood of emotions and memories washed over me. It reminded me how the quintessential anthropological life cycle—the alienation of initial entry, followed by the thrill of finding your footing, and the painful end of extraction—characterized my research on Anonymous. Anonymous9's prediction was right—following Operation Tunisia I became intimately involved with Anonymous, and this entanglement has waned over time, especially when I started to write this book. Soon after reading this leaked conversation, I assured Anonymous9, one of my closest Anonymous confidants, that he would remain a friend even as I moved on to other research subjects (but only on the condition that he realizes that I am no longer a college student).

Anonymous9's statements also reminded me that it took only the single month of January 2011 to graduate from a confused outsider to a confused semi-insider. The transformation was underwritten by the hours I clocked for research: five hours a day online—at least—every day of the week. I tuned in to between seven and ten IRC channels at a time, observing and absorbing the comings and goings of Anonymous. Additionally, I was spending roughly ten hours a week doing interviews with the media about Anonymous. I spoke with over one hundred fifty different reporters in two years. As a result, I now hold the dubious distinction of teaching more journalists about IRC than anyone else in the world.

Over time, the vertigo that came from wading through so much data, day after day, was replaced by a sense of belonging. I began participating in discussions and became known, and more-or-less accepted, in a number of the sub-communities and channels that were constantly popping up, like mushrooms in a forest after a good rain. No longer lost in the woods, I became part of the woods. Like all forests, danger lurked in certain areas—but at least I became increasingly aware of where the enchanting parts could be found as well. I found that my home became the AnonOps IRC channel called #reporter.

Settling into my new home was far from a smooth transition. No matter how many times I psyched myself up to say something, speak up, introduce myself, like now, this very moment—I always backed down. I was terrified to say anything for weeks, scared, quite simply, of being kicked out of the channel and losing such an incredible opportunity. This group of Anons, unlike those from Chanology, was fiercer and rowdier. I had watched, in rapt attention, others get banned from the channel for violating some codes of ethics that weren't so clear to me and also, even more terrifying, for no other reason than the lulz.

It wasn't until early January 2011 when I first spoke up. And it wasn't entirely voluntary. Seemingly out of the blue, they noticed me. I had been observing safely, nobody paying any attention to me, until suddenly it was as if the lidless eye of Sauron had swiveled his gaze to my corner of the room, melting the shadows I hid behind and bathing me in a fierce beam of light. I was away from the computer getting some food in the kitchen. When I came back, I found this on the screen:

<Topiary>: Can anyone in here confirm biella?
<q>: i talked to her today but…
<m42>: you know her q?
<q>: if she would send me a DM on twitter, i could.
<m42>: "biella is away: I'm not here right now" and no @'s in any of 7 channels…
<q>: yes, if she's the biella from twitter, i talked to her before
<Topiary>: We may need to dispose of journalists from here in just a bit.
<m42>: she can come back later
You have been kicked by q: (hi biella, could you DM me on twitter please? Thanks!)

My heart pounded. I groaned. It sucks to get kicked off a channel. It means you can no longer see what is happening and you don't know why you were summarily removed before you could defend yourself. It is embarrassing—one has to wonder what they say about you when you aren't there—and you are not sure if you are going to be allowed to return. You might get "z-lined" or "q-lined," actions that operators can take to permanently ban your IP address from the entire server, which would mean that I would get removed from all channels at once. Thankfully, that is not what they had in mind. It turns out that they didn't ban me from reentering the channel. And so ten minutes later, racked by anxiety, I logged back on:

<biella>: hello q Topiary
<biella>: sorry about that i was away cooking
<biella>: this is me
<biella>: http://steinhardt.nyu.edu/faculty_bios/view/Gabriella_
Coleman
<biella>: i have referred many reporters here
<biella>: and am writing/presenting on Anonymous

They responded immediately:

<Topiary>: Hi biella, apologies for the kick.
<biella>: no it is ok
<biella>: you gave fair warning :-) and i have been too too idle
<biella>: more than i would like
<Topiary>: We're just usually very strict and sometimes a little
paranoid of unidentified users in here.
[...]
<Topiary>: I liked what I read in your link. What aspects of Anonymous
will you be covering in your presentation?
<q>: biella, can you send me a DM on twitter?
<Topiary>: Certainly look forward to reading your work.
<biella>: cool Topiary and i will be opening with 1) if i am wrong/off
please contact me. always open to feedback
<biella>: q, what is your twitter account?
<biella>: i am https://twitter.com/#!/BiellaColeman
[...]
<biella>: glad you got it and i wont idle or hang out so often here for
no reason
<biella>: ok i will leave you all and come back when i got questions. i
do have questions but everyone is pestering me to go to dinner
<Topiary>: You seem pretty down-to-earth, glad to have you
reporting on us. Enjoy your dinner.
<Trivette>: agreed
<biella>: thanks Topiary, ok catch you later
<q>: yar, can only say good things about biella. just wanted to be sure
it's the same her :)

Phew. Come to think of it, it was more like PHEEEEEEEEWWWWWWW. It was a make-or-break moment. Had they called me out as lame or untrustworthy, it would have spelled my end—or at least converted the prospect of trust and access into a Herculean feat. Those on #reporter held more authority than your average Joe or Jane Anon. Their opinions counted.

Perhaps my painless acceptance bears further explanation. Recall that I was two years into researching Project Chanology. While AnonOps' political culture was distinct from the anti-Scientology crusaders, there was enough of a cultural connection so that when participants rummaged through my work, it struck a familiar chord. From my video lectures especially, it was not hard get a whiff of the degree of sympathy I held toward Anonymous—enough at least to determine that I enjoyed the lulz.

And I was not alone. There was a confederacy of about half a dozen outsiders given extra access in exchange for functioning as Anonymous media mouthpieces. A hacker turned reporter named Steve Ragan dished out the most detailed and nuanced technical articles relating to Anonymous for the *Tech Herald*. A business writer for *Forbes*, Parmy Olson, churned out waves of stories, eventually becoming LulzSec's private reporter. Two of its members, Sabu and Topiary, spilled their guts to her, even admitting—almost unbelievably—to law breaking. Writing for Wired.com, Quinn Norton's long-form reporting shone brightly during Occupy as Anonymous converged with the 99 percent. Filmmaker Brian Knappenberger spent over a year tirelessly interviewing more than forty Anons on IRC, video chat, and in person for a full-length documentary. (Brian and I would eventually team up in a hunt to film Sabu, which failed miserably.) Asher Wolf, geek lady extraordinaire, talked to many Anons behind the scenes and managed, like no one else could, to capture its esprit de corps in chunks of 140 characters or less on Twitter. Amber Lyon, then a reporter for CNN, won special points for doing the most un-Internety thing of any of us: she trekked across a remote mountain pass from Washington State into British Columbia with the Anonymous fugitive hacker Commander X (Christopher Doyon) as he fled the United States to avoid prison.

Anonymous's exchanges with media figures and researchers are as contradictory and varied as the collective itself. Most participants worked with journalists as respectfully and transparently as the clandestine nature of Anonymous allowed. The primary goal, typically, was to gain publicity for their causes, such as the turmoil in Tunisia, but they also sought, whenever possible, to carefully manage their own image. On a few occasions, the goal was to troll particular journalists as well.

Image management or trolling was aided by some in-house publicists adept at framing content toward both goals, who populated #reporter alongside the reporters and outsiders like myself. Two in particular were known for speaking to journalists with panache: Topiary, who was eventually revealed to be eighteen-year-old Jake Davis from the remote Scottish Shetland Islands (self-described on his Twitter bio as a "simple prankster turned swank garden hedge") and Barrett Brown, a fair-skinned, honey-haired Texan whose home den was strewn with books and a taxidermied bobcat posed as if about to pounce off the wall. During OpTunisia, tflow had invited Topiary into the inner sanctum, and he proved himself so adroit at spinning lulz-fueled and delightful propaganda that he remained a core member. After Brown wrote a short article praising Anonymous, Gregg Housh (one of the original members of marblecake) pulled him in.

Topiary and Barrett Brown were also AnonOps' resident tricksters—each with a distinctive brand of chicanery. Inspired by twentieth-century avant-garde art pranksters the Dadaists and the Situationists, Topiary found his knack in spinning 140 characters of brilliant nonsense and absurdist media manipulation. On the reporter channel, he would brag of exploits and scheme aloud:

<Topiary>: I've done a voice interview with these before, they're good, they work through Skype
<Topiary>: I told 'em we had over 9000 members and made them lose the game, you should bel-air them
<Topiary>: Or something
<Topiary>: Anyway, just got done talking with some monstrous homogay named Andy who's writing up on our latest fax shenanigans

Topiary, who held the admiration of many Anons, was a masked joker—adopting the pseudonymity almost unanimously deployed by his peers. His name was only revealed upon arrest. On the other hand, I did not include Brown's covert nickname—because he did not have one. He was just Barrett Brown—sometimes semi-naked, as you will see—but always Barrett Brown. He assumed the role of Anonymous's spokesperson in winter 2011 and held it until May, when waves of critics nudged him to take a step away. He also played the part of AnonOps' court jester. Like any self-respecting trickster, he enjoyed a really hot bubble bath while sipping (presumably cheap) red wine. After announcing his plans on Twitter— "Going to get red wine. Will have live bubble bath when I return in 15 minutes"[1]—spectators could log into Tinychat, a live video chat service, and watch him half-submerged in water as viewers lobbed offensive and trollish comments his way, in this case, "rape jokes."

Arriving with name in tow, he was informally booted with name in tow for violating an originary rule of Anonymous (hinted at by the name itself): drawing attention and fame to one's name is the ultimate taboo. Brown attempted to iconoclastically occupy a liminal—betwixt and between—zone/ status. He acted like an insider but never concealed himself. He was tolerated for so long only because he poured significant work into both the network and the larger cause. A journalist by training, he was adept at afflicting the powerful with ironic, scathing parodic writing. In one *Vanity Fair* piece praising the investigative journalist Michael Hastings (now deceased), whose unflattering profile of US General Stanley McChrystal in *Rolling Stone* led to the general's downfall, Brown mockingly suggested, "McChrystal would have been better off talking to Thomas Friedman, who is so amusingly naive that in 2001 he declared Vladimir Putin to be a force for good for whom Americans all ought to be 'rootin',' a term he chose because it rhymes with Putin."[2] Brown possessed an excellent feel for media dynamics, and he freely offered advice to other Anons. In an interview, one Anon who worked on writing press releases put it this way: "It was Barrett who told me about how to get the attention of journalists, how to get [press releases] published, how to utilize the news cycle and get the timing right and that sorta thing." Eventually through his antics, and the fact that he assumed the role of flack, sat too uncomfortably with the dominant ethics at work in Anonymous. AnonOps informally banished its own court jester.

Not Tolerated: Personal Promotion

In the middle of December 2010, *Washington Post* reporter Ian Shapira contacted me. I debriefed him about Anonymous's history and strongly encouraged him to pay a visit to IRC, specifically #reporter, for the story he was working on. I am not sure if he ever did, but on January 22, 2011, he published a substantial article featuring a Washington-area AnonOps participant:

> He goes by the code name AnonSnapple to keep secret the fact that he's part of the Internet collective of cyber-pranksters and activists called Anonymous. Few at his D.C. private school know that the 17-year-old senior attends Anonymous's public protests, where he wears the movement's signature face mask of a grinning, mustachioed Guy Fawkes ...

AnonSnapple, who lives near Bethesda with his mother, a housewife, and father, an economist at the International Monetary Fund, worries that investigators might link him to last month's DDOS attacks launched by some Anonymous members against MasterCard, Visa and PayPal, which had stopped processing payments to WikiLeaks. "A while ago, the FBI did some raids on servers from Anons that were involved in the attacks," he said. "Even though I don't do them, I am still a part of them. I am still active on the same chat rooms as people that [did] the DDOS [attacks] ... I can be easily linked to them."[3]

On January 25, 2011, a few days after the article was published, I linked to it on #reporter. Before I did, it was business as usual on the channel, busy with chatter. In minutes, they devoured the piece. Then all hell broke loose. It went on for about an hour on various different IRC channels, notably #reporter and #lounge:

> \<shitstorm>: snapple seems to have done this on his own
> \<shitstorm>: eg a local interview
> \<biella>: i tried to get him on irc but i dont think he ever made it and well it kinda shows
> \<shitstorm>: That interview is ridiculous, its more of an advert for snapple
> \<shitstorm>: "namefagging"
> \<shitstorm>: I did this
> \<shitstorm>: I did that
> \<owen>: indeed
> \<q>: :/
> \<shitstorm>: That is retarded actually
> \<shitstorm>: Im kinda mad
> \<owen>: i will remove him
> \<owen>: everywhere
> \<shitstorm>: excellent
> \<owen>: self serving bullshit

<shitstorm>: "He worries so much about being exposed"
<shitstorm>: THEN DONT GIVE AWAY ALL THOSE DETAILS

Watching the conversation cascading down my screen, I could feel the seething contempt emanating from the words. It stung. Although I understood the source of their anger, by then I had worked with enough journalists to offer the following cautionary advice:

<biella>: before you kick em make sure that the journalist was not twisitng anything (unless this is a pattern)
<owen>: im so tired of children who think this is some giant game
<q>: he must have twisted the whole thing
<biella>: but who knows, i just have had my words seriously seriously seriously twisted
<q>: and i dont think ian would do that
<q>: he is a serious journalist
<owen>: that sounds exactly like snapple imo
<shitstorm>: I agree
<biella>: k, u all know best for sure

Although Anons at times worked earnestly with reports, they also often tore or trolled journalists to pieces (yes, even "serious journalists"). But this was not one such occasion. What pissed people off most was how AnonSnapple who had incurred no personal risk during any op was speaking on behalf of those who had:

<owen>: he knows nothing
<owen>: he needs to gtfo [get the fuck out]
<owen>: isnt he one of yours, q?
<shitstorm>: AnonSnapple recently asked a teacher if he could submit a time sheet of hours spent designing and passing out flyers for an Anonymous rally in Dupont Circle.
<shitstorm>: ARE YOU KIDDING ME?
<shitstorm>: !!!!!!!!!!!!!!!!!1

<shitstorm>: !set rage on
<owen>: i wanna know when he shows up please
<owen>: stupid little punk kids
<shitstorm>: nah im going to strangle him
<shitstorm>: as well

And strangling him was pretty much what happened next. They summoned AnonSnapple to the channel:

<shitstorm>: my god Snapple
<shitstorm>: what is that
<shitstorm>: ?
<shitstorm>: Snapple that has to be the dumbest shit, more dumb than cloldblood
<shitstorm>: coldblood*
<q>: now its on the floor.
<owen>: snapple
<owen>: talk now
<shitstorm>: Snapple
<shitstorm>: Snapple
<owen>: before i remove you from here
<shitstorm>: Snapple
<Nessuno>: snapples queir
<Nessuno>: quiet
<shitstorm>: cus he knows hes fucked
<Snapple>: hahahaa
<shitstorm>: ohai
<Snapple>: you believe half of that shit is true
<MTBC>: fuck he know he cused
<owen>: you think its funy?
<Nessuno>: in during shitstorm
<shitstorm>: Snapple, why wouldnt it be?
<owen>: so wait
<shitstorm>: it seems about spot on from what Ive heard and seen
<owen>: youre saying they lieD?
<owen>: I WILL BRING THEM HERE NOW

<Snapple>: Because I would never state where I live
<owen>: and we will see
<Snapple>: First of all
<Snapple>: and what my parents do
<shitstorm>: well you tell us you are in dc
<owen>: you would if you seek glory
<Snapple>: I live in DC
<shitstorm>: derp
<Snapple>: That's all
<owen>: we all know where you live
<shitstorm>: ^
<Snapple>: :)
<owen>: you tell everyone
<Snapple>: come by
<shitstorm>: alright
shitstorm grabs the shotgun
<shitstorm>: owen, lets go shall we?
<Snapple>: *runs*
<shitstorm>: Master-IT bring the M16
MTBC steals the shotgun and shoots himself in the face
Snapple left the room (quit: Z:lined (dumbass)).

The rage against AnonSnapple ran so deep and so strong that even the banning—usually an effective release mechanism—did little to blow the dark clouds away. The Anons were still fuming, expressing a deluge of insults—owen, for instance, proclaimed that "in the meantime, snapple can concentrate on his schoolwork instead of IRC tonight." After I informed them that I knew the reporter, I got put to work:

<biella>: owen, q, i know ian
<q>: it was in reporter
<q>: biella, could you help us out here?
<biella>: sure i could get him on or let him know he should get on q

Finally, on another channel, owen added some concluding remarks:

> <owen>: attempting to use all the work that so many have done for your personal promtion is something i will not tolerate
> <Nessuno>: owen speaks sense
> <owen>: he was all 'hey look at me but i didnt do anyhting'
> <butts>: I can't believe he told him all this
> <owen>: fuck that
> <owen>: i can

Insulting the Meat

I was dumbfounded. Sure, I was familiar with the prohibition against "namefagging"—attaching your identity to your actions. The norm was so well established in Anonymous, stretching back even to its pre-activist days, that it was rarely broken, at least back then (though Barrett Brown would soon be accused of similar behavior). So I had never seen the repercussions in real time. What made this all the more captivating was that I finally got to witness a phenomenon I had only previously read about in ethnographic accounts. Tactics for enforcing the ideal of egalitarianism are common but vary in morality across many cultures. They range from the life ruining (such as being found to be a witch), to the relatively mundane, but all are quite effective. One of my favorite examples comes from the !Kung people in Africa's Kalahari Desert. Among the !Kung, when hunters return to the village with an enormous slab of meat they are not showered with praise, as you might expect among a meat-loving tribe, but instead with a slab of insults. The teasing helps keep egos in check:

> "Say there is a bushman man who has been hunting. He must not come home and announce like a braggard, 'I have killed a big one in the bush!' He must first sit down in silence

until I or someone else comes up to his fire and asks, 'What did you see today?' He replies quietly, 'Ah, I'm no good for hunting. I saw nothing at all [pause] just a little tiny tone.' Then I smile to myself," gaugo continued, "because I know he has killed something big.

"In the morning we make up a party of four or five people to cut up and carry the meat back to the camp. When we arrive at the kill we examine it and cry out, 'You mean to say you have dragged us all the way out here to make us cart home your pile of bones? Oh, if I had known it was this thin I wouldn't have come.' Another one pipes up, 'People, to think I gave up a nice day in the shade for this. At home we may be hungry, but at least we have cool water to drink.'"[4]

Moral leveling of this kind does not extinguish power relations, much less differences in abilities. Some individuals are just better hunters than others. On IRC there are those, like owen and shitstorm, who run the network and unmistakably command the authority to enforce norms by appeal to technical power. Banning individuals on IRC after profusely insulting them doesn't engender a strict egalitarianism. It simply functions to downplay and modulate power differentials. While among Anons it is acceptable to shower some degree of praise, any perceived attempt at converting internal status into external status is deemed unacceptable. The public, individual persona must be kept out of the equation, in the interest of collective fame.

Had AnonSnapple accomplished more—especially the risky work of civil disobedience—I suspect he would have been reprimanded without banishment. By claiming enough responsibility to be profiled while simultaneously insulting the risky tactics employed by others, AnonSnapple's aggrandizing was received as an affront of the highest order. By this time, people were hyperaware of the legal risks (and only two days later, arrests were made in the UK and warrants were issued in the US in response to a recent DDoS campaign). AnonSnapple was judged to have acted out of an improper self-interest, and the dozens of individuals logged onto #lounge watched the extermination with popcorn in hand. But this wasn't mere entertainment. The drubbing served as a clear moral lesson for the wider audience, one that they tacitly endorsed in their silence or eventual agreement.

"The nerd scare"

Beginning the very day of Snapple's banishment, my old vertigo returned due to a remarkable flood of events pouring in and out of AnonOps. For the next two weeks I was online during every waking moment, watching Anonymous engage in a historic revolution. In coming to terms with the first wave of arrests to hit their network, they planned and executed Anonymous's most extraordinary act of revenge yet.

The day AnonSnapple had been unceremoniously summoned to Mount Olympus and ritually tossed away, Secretary of State Hillary Clinton issued a response to the mounting populist upheaval in Egypt: "Our assessment is that the Egyptian government is stable and is looking for ways to respond to the legitimate needs and interests of the Egyptian people."[5] Piggybacking on revolutionary ferment in Tunisia, Egyptians rallied for most of January to demand Muhammad Hosni El Sayed Mubarak, the dictator in power for three decades, step down. Egyptian organizers had called for a day of rage on the 25th, and throngs of protesters obliged. As the events unfolded, the recently christened #OpEgypt public channel was awash in excitement and horror (pseudonyms have been changed):

<WebA18>: yes, they censor twitter in egypt
<WebA18>: and they are trying to censure facebook
<On>: cell phones too
<t23>: not being in egypt i cannot confirm 100%

<0n>: PANIC TIME

<t23>: but is known tactic

<WebA18>: a friend in egypt is telling me they censor it

<eb>: Ps, if it is enarby, consider demonstrating at the egyptian embassy

<lon>: JOIN #propaganda TO CREATE & DESIGN MATERIAL FOR #opegypt

<jeb>: to get media attention and support our egyptian /b/rothers

[…]

<WebA18>: thanks!

<mib>: The protests are spreading and becoming bigger

<bi>: Egyptians have balls of steel. GO Go GO!

<pi>: is there a hive mind i have to get to work ?

<mib>: we should not stop untill this regimes falls Algeria: translation: Gov blocked the cell phones

<b>: Spread that POSTER to RECRUIT more people: http://i.imgur.com/LfLhN.png

What had at first been a sporadic flicker of government-initiated communication disruptions became wholesale on January 28. The Egyptian government shut the whole damn Internet off.

In order to reestablish some connectivity, Anonymous teamed up with another hacktivist crew, Telecomix. AnonOps and Telecomix had demonstrated differences in the past. Telecomix, opposed to DDoS tactics, would try to keep sites up as Anonymous gummed up access. But if there is an urgent or interesting enough problem to solve—like getting communications access to people in need—hackers can put aside major differences to work together. A number of Anons contributed to the Telecomix-led effort to figure out how old modems, faxes, and phones could be used to connect circuitously to the Internet. At the same time, Anonymous's small technical elite, which had coalesced during OpTunisia and formed a persistent IRC channel, continued in their hackscapades in support of the Arab Spring.

As OpEgypt gained momentum against Mubarak's government, Anonymous themselves came under threat. Two days after Snapple's banning and the historic day of Egyptian rage, the following warning flashed on #reporter in big red letters:

<ew>: ATTENTION: Any of you anons that are from US or UK and have been involved in Mastercard, Visa or BOA [Bank of America] attacks, delete any data on your machine(s) that might link you to them, right now!

On January 27, 2011, authorities rounded up and arrested alleged participants in the UK, while in the US three FBI agents issued forty warrants in connection with the December 2010 DDoS Operation Payback campaign (and eventually arrested a batch of fourteen Anons in connection with the attacks):

<Anonymous9>: Hey folks
<Anonymous9>: I presume you've all heard the news? :(
<shitstorm>: yes
<shitstorm>: this is a sad day in my mind
<shitstorm>: a new low for governments
<Anonymous9>: Sad indeed
<Anonymous9>: But, in fairness, not unexpected.
<shitstorm>: well kinda true
<Anonymous9>: Yeah
<shitstorm>: but they still have dick all for evidence
<Anonymous9>: It's amazing the way they're pursuing us all so thoroughly
<Anonymous9>: Whilst the actual criminals named in the leaked wikileaks cables are being defended by their respective governments
<Anonymous9>: There's something so sick about that
<shitstorm>: I agree
<Anonymous9>: I mean whatever they say about us, we've never actually been party to torture or murder
<Anonymous9>: Yet they're spending what must be a shitload of money to get people to come after us

<Anonymous9>: Whilst offering those who have committed the most serious of crimes, diplomatic immunity and all that shite

Anonymous9 critically assessed the first major state crackdowns against Anonymous with an incisive and soulful lament about the hypocrisy of state power. Since that first shoe dropped, over one hundred people have been arrested across the globe, from Indonesia to the Dominican Republic and from Cambodia to the United States. These arrests are historically exceptional—a high-water mark in the history of hacking. Never before have so many hackers and geeks been rounded up around the globe for their political ideas and actions in one cohesive push. Over the 1980s, 1990s, and 2000s, scores of hackers were arrested, but raids were more sporadic and usually took one of two distinct forms (I am excluding hackers arrested for purely criminal operations like carding).⁶ Either law enforcement sought out single hackers, like Kevin Mitnick or Gary McKinnon, who were not hacking for social change but for their own enjoyment, or authorities raided underground hacker groups to shut them down and close their meeting spots, such as bulletin board systems. The most famous and largest of these raids was Operation Sundevil, carried out across fourteen American cities on May 8, 1990, when twenty-seven search warrants were executed and four arrests made.⁷ On occasion, as was the case with the young Julian Assange, hackers wielding skills for broader political goals faced criminal charges, but this style of intervention was less common and arrests on these grounds were even more rare.

With Anonymous came the first large-scale hacktivist movement that spurred a multi-state coordinated and extensive crackdown. It qualifies as what Gráinne O'Neill, at the time a National Lawyers Guild representative for many of those arrested, aptly described as "the nerd scare."

Want to Take a Seat?

Having since met and interviewed individuals targeted in the "nerd scare," the version of events given by one particular person, Mercedes Haefer, sticks in my mind. Haefer joined the AnonOps network in November 2010, when she was nineteen, and quickly rose to prominence due to her tart wit and intellect. Haefer is and was a linguistic force of nature—her mouth can run circles around a drunken sailor looking for a fight. I sat with her on a panel at the 2012 edition of DEF CON, the largest hacker conference in the world. Before delving into a serious and impassioned description of her involvement in Anonymous, she demanded that the audience—composed roughly of 99 percent males—show their tits or get the fuck out ("Tits or gtfo" is a disparaging comment which, in some online communities, follows any user's self-identification as female).

DEF CON is held in Las Vegas, where Haefer happens to live. However, her apartment was far from the conference, so I suggested that she crash in my hotel room, on one condition: that inimitable troll, the troll's troll, weev, was not allowed anywhere near the room. He had made some flirtatious overtures to her on Twitter and had been spotted at the conference—and while I was happy to spend time with him, and in no way opposed to their pursuit of any mutual affections, I could not bear the thought that a hideous troll love child could be yanked out of the depths of hell due to an unholy carnal meeting in *my* hotel room (too much responsibility and not enough connections with exorcists).

She agreed and we plunged into many conversations in Las Vegas, which continued later online. Knowing that she had been party to one of the notorious raids that occurred in this period, I asked her just what it felt like to have the FBI descend upon you. It is worth conveying her story because having a mental picture of what can transpire during such visits is handy for negotiating a potential visit from law enforcement. Most people I interviewed were ill-equipped to handle the sudden and intimidating show of force; they spoke freely when they should have stayed silent except to request a lawyer. As hacker Emmanuel Goldstein put it during the infamous HOPE panel on snitching, "People panic, people panic … and the authorities count on this. The authorities live for this kind of thing so that they get as much information." (Note that the following account of the raid is largely anecdotal, and represents her side of the story. But many crucial details match up with descriptions of events found in the FBI document known as a FD-302, a summary of interviews that was later leaked to me.)

The FBI arrived at dawn. Haefer peacefully snorlaxed away in her apartment in a working-class Las Vegas neighborhood, as five to eight agents approached quietly in the winter desert dawn. (It was difficult for Haefer to remember the exact number of agents, as she was disoriented. They "all looked alike," she said.) They broke the silence by pounding on the doorway. Though jolted from her slumber, she was not scared—figuring simply that her father, who worked odd hours, had forgotten his keys. She dragged herself out the bed, shuffled to the front door wearing her jammies, and was greeted with "a flashlight in my face, which at six in the morning is offsetting for anyone." The bewildering quality of the situation was magnified by her realization that a pack of rifle barrels also pointed her way.

She described how they led her out of the doorway and into the walkway that cut through the complex, then began patting her down. While performing a thorough search they asked questions, seeking to confirm her identity. Early in the questioning, her mouth woke up and bit back. "It's me fuckwit. Piss off. I'm going inside. It's cold." With that formality taken care of, they all headed to the warmth of her apartment.

An agent asked if she would like to sit down. She questioned his sincerity and perceived his gesture as display of power. "You don't ask someone if they want to sit down in their own house," she explained to me. The assertion of power booted her into a wakeful realization: "These are not my friends. They will not help me. They're here for their jobs."

They searched the house, snapped pictures of equipment, confiscated her computer, and interrogated her. She had told me she was a bit of a wiseass, the following story confirmed it. As is official FBI protocol, two of the agents paired off for the interview, one asking questions, the other scribbling the answers.[8] She claims they asked about 4chan. At the time, she thought to herself, "If you guys think this is about 4chan, then you're even more incompetent than I thought." She told me she began prattling on "about this thread I'd read about this guy who was in love with his dog and wanted to get her pregnant so he went around getting samples and stirred them in a cup and injected them into his penis and got her pregnant."

She noted that "they stopped taking notes for that part," and—sure enough—there is no mention of 4chan in the leaked account filed by the agents. But, given Haefer's chutzpah and adept mastery of the lulz, it is theoretically possible—even plausible. And the quote's exclusion may be in keeping with their methodology—the FBI (understandably) is not in the business of the lulz (much less documenting it). Based on two additional documents I was also given (covering interviews with two other Anons who were raided the same day and eventually arrested), the genre combines long summaries of interviews that stick to factual statements with the occasional direct quotation, while glossing over trivialities. There is no trace of, much less reflection upon, the tone or emotional tenor of the exchange.

And yet, in Haefer's recounting of events for my benefit, these small acts of defiance meant a lot. In that exchange, law enforcement and Haefer applied very different criteria when it came to valuing information, as one might expect. Regardless of whether they were trolled, or aware of being trolled, or cared in either case (or whether I was trolled), the agents' report sticks to matters of legal relevance.[9] They wrote: "Haefer then asked the specific purpose of the search and the interview. Special Agent (SP) X then stated to Haefer that he believed she (Haefer) already knew the reason why the FBI was searching her home and for the interview. She then responded they were there for "DDoSing and vandalism.' "

Still, the report and Haefer's account agree in many regards. She was asked numerous times to "explain further," and she responded by touching on a range of topics: from her precise involvement in activities, to broader reflections on the ethics of DDoSing. At first the report recorded her stating she "was not involved that much in either [vandalism or DDoS]" but "after being told she was not being truthful" (indicated, they told her, by evidence in the IRC logs) she admitted she had full knowledge that her computer was involved in DDoSing PayPal and helped others configure LOIC. She also gave them all her usernames, which the report lists, but claimed not to remember the names of chat rooms, operators, and servers because there were too many of them (in other reports I read, the interviewees had less difficulty with recall).

Her report, as well as the two others I had access to, attempt to describe, to some limited degree, the political defenses offered for engaging in DDoS campaigns. But the presentation of this information was different coming from Haefer and the report. For her part, she told me she was asked directly about Assange. No such question was evident in the report, only the following claim, which is nevertheless interesting: "She was supportive of PayPal being a target of DoS because she didn't like that PayPal [sic] withheld Julian Assange's account, was money owed to Assange. She stressed she was not an Assange fan, just upset at what PayPal had done." This was in addition to a detailed summary of her political defense:

> Haefer agreed with what Anonymous is doing. When a store or real-world business is doing something that is unacceptable it can be protested in front of the property. Since VISA or Mastercard is online, they can't be physically protested

and therefore must be an online protests [*sic*], or in the form of a DoS attack. Haefer described such protests as a "right."

During our interview, she elaborated on what she meant by "right":

> It was about rights. It wasn't about supporting Assange. It was about supporting freedom of speech and government transparency. It was about telling the government that they can't just interfere in foreign court cases. It was about telling the government that they work for us not the other way around. And that even though I didn't like Assange, I still believed he had the right to freedom of speech and a fair trial. And that if we only supported the rights of people we liked, then they weren't rights, they're privileges. And that privileges can be taken away. Rights can't be taken away. They can only be oppressed.

If it is routine for the FBI to show up at 6 am, it is also routine for them to ask for cooperation; this can mean various things, from providing information on the spot to becoming an informant. Haefer claims she was asked (and this request was in the two other full reports I read). She declined, or in her own more vivid words to me, "I told them to fuck off."

When the special agent left, Haefer felt that despite what she had just told him, he still considered her a ruffian troll instead of an activist. According to Mercedes, he handed over his card and asked her to "please not go after his family." "If he still thought that was an issue, then he still didn't understand the case," she said. Since we don't know his side of the story, perhaps he was also cracking a very dry joke.

Reflecting back on the situation, Haefer, who, like so many Anons, was caught off guard when the Feds came, concluded, "If I got raided again, I probably wouldn't tell them I did it." But she was still proud then, as she still is now, of her small contribution to defending rights.

"How to Protest Intelligently"

Dozens of other individuals in the United States were interrogated in a similar fashion during roughly the same time period. A few people shared stories with each other or on forums soon after, but for the most part, no one had any insight into what had transpired. All the while, Anonymous kept rolling along with contributing to the hard work of ousting a regime. Throngs of Egyptians were descending on Tahrir Square in the first of the dynamic occupations that would eventually occur in Spain, then North America, and, eventually, Europe. The numbers were breathtaking. By January 31, the square held a reported 250,000 people. But the hopeful excitement was dampened by escalating violence. On the IRC channels, a number of Egyptians requested that Anonymous attack government and state-controlled media. They refused. Even though some groups of Anons were actively DDoSing government websites—a move that irked Telecomix—the general consensus, echoed in both IRC chats and publicly released statements, was to never attack the press (all pseudonyms have been changed):

> <dr>: hello, as an Egyptian i request you to attack their media please !!!
> http://www.ahram.org.eg/ "http://www.algomhuria.net.eg/"http://www.algomhuria.net.eg/
> <MS>: http://ahram.org.eg/ <--- the main newspaper have been talking about nothing but lebanon
> <sudor>: guys trust me! it's much more useful to bring down AHRAM.ORG.EG
> <Fr>: no media
> <hat>: sudo, i argued that but its against policy to attack media even if it's dictatorship regime owned
> <at>: sudo, is the media you are talking about a part of the government?
> <sudo>: YES IT IS at!
> <tru>: no media

<kan>: guys, Egypt Loves you and prays for you

<Ter>: NO MEDIA

<Cyberp>: lrn2protect freedom of speech

<MS>: ahram is misleading media

<Ci>: Along with MCIT

<cru>: Thx, kanta.

<sudot>: ahram is govt owned

<Cyberp>: misleading media is media too

As part of their endeavors, Anons from AnonOps, members of marblecake, and Telecomix worked to make a stunningly detailed and well-illustrated pamphlet called "How to Protest Intelligently."

By the end of the month, it was as if AnonOps was acting more like a human rights advocacy group than a mass of lulz-drunk trolls. Its efforts tended away from unilateral actions and toward infrastructural support that might enable citizens to circumvent censors and evade electronic surveillance. They sent a care package composed of security tools, tactical advice, and encouragement, like this note, clarifying the limited role social media plays in such uprisings, even if they are touted by pundits as a "Twitter Revolution": "This is *your* revolution. It will neither be Twittered nor televised or IRC'ed. You *must* hit the streets or you *will* loose the fight."

While many Anons were invigorated by their ability to support the historic toppling of dictatorial regimes in the Middle East, for others, there could be no clearer evidence of the ascendancy of moralfaggotry. Indeed, by contributing to the Arab revolutions and their idealistic political ends, Anonymous had so transformed itself that it seemed as if, like AnonSnapple, the lulz had itself been banished. As it turns out, this was not the case. As the revolutions raged overseas, a small team of hackers took revenge against an American security researcher and his firm, and the lulz returned with a vengeance.

CHAPTER 7

Revenge of the Lulz

S ome basic features of the political culture emerging out of anonymity are neither new nor difficult to grasp. Consider the anonymous leak that revealed COINTELPRO, a systematic and illegal spying program leveled against the American population. One Pennsylvanian night in 1971, a group calling itself the "Citizens' Commission to Investigate the FBI" forced its way into an FBI field office with a crowbar. As millions of Americans tuned into their radios to listen to Muhammad Ali square off with Joe Frazier in an epic fifteen-round boxing match, the activists emptied file cabinets of more than one thousand documents. Those on the subject of political surveillance were leaked to the media and published in the March 1972 issue of *WIN Magazine*, a journal of the War Resisters League, and COINTELPRO was revealed to the public for the first time. The program was initiated in 1956 by FBI director J. Edgar Hoover, and operated successfully until 1971.

COINTELPRO's mandate was initially narrow: to disrupt the internal operations of the Communist Party USA, which Hoover believed to be under the direct influence of Russian infiltrators. Very quickly, its scope expanded to include the disruption of home-grown political activism of all varieties, including radical, conservative, and even moderate liberal efforts. One stated goal was to

prevent the rise of a "messiah" who could unify, and elec-
trify, the militant black nationalist movement. Malcolm X
might have been such a "messiah"; he is the martyr of the
movement today. Martin Luther King, Stokely Carmichael,
and Elijah Muhammed all aspire to this position ... King
could be a very real contender for this position should he
abandon his supposed "obedience" to "white, liberal doc-
trines" (nonviolence) and embrace black nationalism.[1]

And, indeed, the documents provide clear evidence of the
elaborate steps the FBI took to monitor King in particular.
The illegal surveillance lasted for years, starting in the late
'50s when the program was first authorized by Hoover. When
King delivered his "I Have a Dream" speech at the March on
Washington on August 28, 1963, William Cornelius Sullivan,
associate director of the FBI, wrote to Hoover, "We must mark
[King] now, if we have not done so before, as the most dangerous Negro of the future in this Nation from the standpoint of
Communism, the Negro and national security." King was considered "an unprincipled man" who had a "weakness in his
character." Sullivan wrote, "We will at the proper time when
it can be done without embarrassment to the Bureau, expose
King as an immoral opportunist who is not a sincere person
but is exploiting the racial situation for personal gain." Soon
after King was named "Man of the Year" by *Time* magazine,
the FBI was illegally authorized to bug his hotel room; "trespass is involved," they wrote. The resulting transcripts were
presented to Hoover, who responded, "They will destroy the
burrhead." The bugs captured evidence of King's marital infi-
delity, which excited Sullivan and Hoover, since the recordings
could be used to destroy the "animal."[2] An excerpt from the
FBI letter sent to blackmail King evinces the ugly historical
truth that the US government terrorized one of the nation's
most revered and peaceful civil rights crusaders:

King, there is only one thing left for you to do. You know
what it is. You have just 34 days in which to do it (this exact

number has been selected for a specific reason, it has definite practical significance). You are done. There is but one way out for you. You better take it before your filthy, abnormal fraudulent self is bared to the nation.[3]

The government similarly targeted many other groups: Students for a Democratic Society, white supremacists, branches of the feminist movement, the radical Puerto Rican independence movement, and countless anti–Vietnam War associations. Their aggressive and multi-pronged methods included predatory infiltration strategies with the purpose of sabotage: sustained, planned, and organized disruption of political movements so as to stamp them out of existence. They seeded misinformation, blackmailed activists, took them to court over tax mishaps, and sometimes even resorted to direct physical violence. Government agents' reckless mandates saw them feed the media false stories and forge correspondences in the name of targeted groups. Some of the most lasting damage came from agents planted in movements so deeply that their disruptions completely eroded the kernels of trust these groups were built upon. COINTELPRO agents fostered a climate of fear and demoralization, draining the vitality of what had been legitimate and deep reservoirs of political activity.

After the Citizens' leaks hit the press, other interventions followed, including the release of COINTELPRO documents obtained through a Freedom of Information Act request; NBC reporter Carl Stern used these documents as the basis for his award-winning reportage on the subject. Once the full extent of 1973/1974 COINTELPRO'S tampering with legitimate, legal, and even quite ordinary political dissent became known, the public was outraged. In the chambers of the US government a small group of senators formed the Church Committee in 1975. After investigation, their conclusion was unambiguous and resolute in indicting the program: "Many of the techniques used would be intolerable in a democratic society even if all of the targets had been involved in violent activity, but COINTELPRO went far beyond that ... The Bureau conducted a sophisticated *vigilante* operation" (emphasis my own).[4] Numerous reforms followed, including limiting the FBI directorship to a single ten-year term.

Soon after acquiring the files, the Citizens' Commission sent the leaks to the press along with a communiqué, which they wanted published in all news stories covering the FBI documents. The communiqué explained their motives and goals:

> We wish to make these documents more widely available so that they can be used effectively by all who are working for a more peaceful, just, and open society. Our purpose is not just to correct the more gross violations of constitutional rights by the FBI within the framework of its present goals and organization. Nor is it to attack personally individual informers, agents, or administrators. It is instead to contribute to the movement for fundamental constructive change in our society, for as we said in our initial statement, "as long as great economic and political power remains concentrated in the hands of small cliques not subject to democratic control and scrutiny, then repression, intimidation, and entrapment are to be expected."[5]

While their intentions were made public, the members themselves remained anonymous until January 2014, when a few individuals stepped forward.[6] To expose toxic tactics, these activists broke the law and utilized anonymity to shield themselves from consequences. This dramatic exposé did not happen online; there were no Guy Fawkes masks, no boxes were popped, no mail spools Pastebinned, and WikiLeaks played no role. But the concept was the same: cloak identity for protection and to deflect attention away from the messengers, and get the incriminating word out. Had it not been for the Citizens' Commission to Investigate the FBI stealing documents tucked away in file cabinets and desk drawers, COINTELPRO might have remained in operation, leaving an even more sickening trail of destruction in its wake.

Let's fast forward to February 5, 2011, when Anonymous uncovered a corporate plot devised by Washington, DC–based security firm HBGary Federal to spy on and disrupt WikiLeaks. Given the digital nature of contemporary documents, there is no longer a need to leave the comfort of one's home, much less break into some office space, to access secret documents. Working together on IRC, Anonymous hackers penetrated the HBGary computer system and downloaded seventy thousand company emails, along with other files that included a PowerPoint presentation entitled "The WikiLeaks Threat." The tactics suggested therein are strikingly similar to those practiced and perfected during COINTELPRO. The presentation outlines a set of strategies the firm claimed could be "deployed tomorrow":

Palantir	Potential Proactive Tactics

- Feed the fuel between the feuding groups. Disinformation. Create messages around actions to sabotage or discredit the opposing organization. Submit fake documents and then call out the error.
- Create concern over the security of the infrastructure. Create exposure stories. If the process is believed to not be secure they are done.
- Cyber attacks against the infrastructure to get data on document submitters. This would kill the project. Since the servers are now in Sweden and France putting a team together to get access is more straightforward.
- Media campaign to push the radical and reckless nature of wikileaks activities. Sustained pressure. Does nothing for the fanatics, but creates concern and doubt amongst moderates.
- Search for leaks. Use social media to profile and identify risky behavior of employees.

They also proposed to identify and intimidate WikiLeaks donors and smear the reputation of supporters and journalists like Glenn Greenwald. They explained that these people were "established professionals that have a liberal bent, but ultimately most of them if pushed will choose professional preservation over cause, such is the mentality of most business professionals."

Although Anonymous did illegally compromise the servers to steal these docs, it is likely that the actions proposed in the PowerPoint presentation, had they been carried out, would have seen the breaking of even more laws. As Glenn Greenwald explains: "Manufacturing and submitting fake documents with the intent they be published likely constitutes forgery and fraud. Threatening the careers of journalists and activists in order to force them to be silent is possibly extortion … Attacking WikiLeaks' computer infrastructure in an attempt to compromise their sources undoubtedly violates numerous cyber laws."[7]

While "The WikiLeaks Threat" presentation is similar in spirit to COINTELPRO, there are numerous important differences. HBGary is not a government intelligence agency—it is a corporate firm that had concocted a plan for corporate clients. HBGary Federal, working with two other security companies, Palantir Technologies and Berico Technologies, was pitching the WikiLeaks sabotage proposal to Bank of America through their legal representatives at the Hunton and Williams law firm. Palantir and Berico, working together under the name Team Themis (a reference to the ancient Greek Titaness of divine order and justice), were hoping such pitches would result in a lucrative contract. Assange had announced on November 29, 2010, that he held documents revealing an "ecosystem of corruption [that] could take down a bank or two," and Bank of America had reason to believe that it was one of these banks. According to the *New York Times*, the bank set to work, "scouring thousands of documents in the event that they become public" and hiring outside security and law firms "to help manage the review."[8] Since Bank of America was not named directly by Assange, its reaction had the interesting effect of drawing attention to itself.

In the aftermath of the HBGary document leaks, Bank of America denied knowledge of the Team Themis proposal, describing it as "abhorrent," even though it was certainly intended for the eyes of one of its legal teams (Hunton and

Williams never commented on the matter).[9] Ultimately, the Team Themis scheme was never carried out—as a result, perhaps, of the leak itself; such a scheme relied on illegal tactics and could only be carried out if there was plausible deniability to protect those involved from backlash.

Beyond any possible direct disruption, the content of the corporate emails themselves provided Anonymous and others interested in corporate security practices with a great deal of insight. Corporate espionage and sabotage leveled against workers, nonprofits, and activists is nothing new. Henry Ford relied on an internal security unit headed by Harry Bennett to intimidate workers attempting to unionize. A private security firm called the Pinkertons, established in 1850 and still in service today, gained notoriety for infiltrating unions and spying on workers for its corporate clients. In fact, this practice is so common that it has been given a name: "labor spying." More recently, Walmart has come under fire after accusations of widespread surveillance against "shareholders, critics, suppliers, the board of directors, and employees."[10]

Today the private surveillance industry is a more profitable, wide-ranging, and robust sector than ever before—boasting close ties to three-letter government agencies (indeed, many contractors employ government- and military-trained operatives). A 2013 report entitled *Spooky Business*, written by the Center for Corporate Policy, a nonprofit seeking to check corporate abuse, enumerates over a dozen examples of corporate-led spying and infiltration—many using standard COINTELPRO-style tactics—directed at antiwar, environmental, food safety, animal rights, and gun control groups, among others. To take one example, the environmental group Greenpeace has been subject to numerous illegal infiltrations— Électricité de France, for instance, employed a firm to hack Greenpeace France in 2006 and was fined 1.5 million euros when the action was revealed.[11]

The report conveys the disturbing crux of the contemporary problem of corporate infiltration as follows: "The corporate

capacity for espionage has skyrocketed in recent years ...
These current and former government employees, and current
government contractors, do their spying against nonprofits
with little regulation or oversight, and apparently with near
impunity."[12]

HBGary's specialized services, which offered "sophisticated" spy operations, was but a small player in a vast industry.
However, a team of tech-savvy journalists at Ars Technica, after
carefully sifting through the emails procured by Anonymous
and writing a dozen in-depth accounts (later compiled into
a book), ultimately concluded that the "WikiLeaks Threat
attack capability wasn't mere bluster." HBGary was on the
forefront of these types of services, having developed effective anti-malware software and custom trojans, rootkits, and
spyware which facilitated unauthorized access into computer
systems. HBGary had also stashed away a bundle of zero-day
exploits—those vulnerabilities that have not been publicly
disclosed—for future use, thus ensuring direct access to untold
numbers of networks, computers, and emails. According to
the leaked documents, HBGary provided a cache of these
zero-days, code-named Juicy Fruit, to a subdivision of military
contractor Northrop Grumman called Xetron.[13]

Public information about this market in zero-days was
nearly nonexistent until a series of investigative reports filed
between 2012 and 2014 revealed it as a thriving industry.
According to the *New York Times*, these exploits can sell from
$35,000 to $160,000 a piece. Governments pay the highest
prices, ensuring significant control of the vulnerabilities. The
US government, in particular, is considered a leading client.[14]
Exploits can be used defensively, but it is increasingly clear
they are often "weaponized and deployed aggressively for
everything from government spying and corporate espionage
to flat-out fraud," as technology journalist Ryan Gallagher
has pointed out.[15]

While publicly available information about these practices is slowly growing, our understanding is still incomplete

and fragmented. This work is mostly done or brokered by corporations with laxer mandates and fewer disclosure obligations than their government counterparts. The HBGary and HBGary Federal emails helped fill in the gaps, providing a reminder of "how much of this work is carried out privately and beyond the control of government agencies," as Nate Anderson concluded.[16]

It is important to note that those who exhumed this information were not, unlike the Citizens' Commission that uncovered COINTELPRO, looking for anything in particular. The accidental nature of these contemporary discoveries is not unique to Anonymous. According to *Spooky Business*, most of what we know about corporate spying has "been uncovered by accident, arising from brilliant strokes of luck."[17] However, we might suggest that it was not luck at all, but instead a welcome public good provided by the insatiable, boundless curiosity of hacking—albeit spurred by external circumstances. The HBGary emails, for instance, were procured through the handiwork of hackers hell-bent on simple revenge.

"If we can get that level of information then we really are the private CIA lol"

A week before his company was targeted by ruinous attacks, the founder and CEO of HBGary, Greg Hoglund, praised his team in a series of emails. After giving some instructions pertaining to the surveillance of a malware author, Hoglund ends with a final boast:

> Team,
> Good work. Check out this site http://www.freelancesecurity.com/ and find an investigator who can perform surveillance and a positive ID on this person. I spoke with Penny and she indicated she *might* be willing to support you guys hiring out boots on the ground to get eyes on target. I would expect

some photos, place of work, home, maybe some associates. The site I mentioned is only one—there are a few others. If we can get that level of information then we really are the private CIA lol. [18]

Though Hoglund envisioned his company as a sharper, meaner, and leaner replacement for law enforcement and intelligence agencies, in practice HBGary was mostly in the business of developing anti-malware software and rootkits—stealthy software tools that allow a user to access a computer system undetected. But Aaron Barr, CEO of the subsidiary HBGary Federal, which was created by HBGary to land lucrative government contracts, wanted to branch out into the field of intelligence gathering. This was evident in the cocky title of a talk slated for mid-February 2011 (but cancelled due to the events in question) at a popular security conference in San Francisco: "Who Needs NSA When We Have Social Media?"

Barr culled the data for his presentation by "infiltrating" Anonymous. His method? For much of January, using the handle CogAnon, he hung out on the AnonOps IRC channels and correlated activity between the IRC channels and social media. On IRC he would watch for someone posting a link, and then he would turn to Twitter to see if the same link or topic would appear at the same time, before deducing that the IRC alias and Twitter profile were attached to the same person. By the end of the month he had a list of nicknames, real names, Twitter accounts, and locations of individuals he claimed were the major Anonymous players. According to the leaked emails, Barr's aim was to expose key operatives:

From: Aaron Barr
Subject: Focus of presentation
To: Mark Trynor, Ted Vera
Date: Wed, 19 Jan 2011 12:14:26 -0500
ok so I am giving a social media talk @ BSIDES SF next month. I am going to focus on outing the major players of

the anonymous group I think. Afterall—no secrets right? :)
We will see how far I get. I may focus on NSA a bit to just
so I can give all those freespeech nutjobs something. I just
called people advocating freespeech, nutjobs—I threw up in
my mouth a little. Man I find myself in a weird position.

In another email he insists to a programmer colleague—who
repeatedly questioned the reliability of Barr's conclusions—
that "I will sell it," referring to his docket of identities.[19]
(Eventually the coder was so concerned about Barr that he
wrote an email on February 5 with a prescient warning: "I feel
his arrogance is catching up to him again and that has never
ended well ... for any of us.")

Barr, on the other hand, thought his operation was going
swimmingly. So how did Anonymous get wind of Barr's
infiltration in the first place? Unbelievably, Barr handed the
information to them on a silver platter by going public with
his project. HBGary's PR department offered Joseph Menn
of the *Financial Times* a story about Barr's upcoming talk. As
Menn explained to me, he "respected the work of the affiliated HBGary proper," and "because Anonymous's structure
and traceability was a topic of serious interest," he decided to
move forward with immediate publication. On February 4,
2011, Anons woke up to these lines: "An international investigation into cyberactivists who attacked businesses hostile to
WikiLeaks is likely to yield arrests of senior members of the
group after they left clues to their real identities on Facebook
and in other electronic communications, it is claimed." The
article also featured nicknames and conjectures as to where
these participants resided, which turned out to be off the mark:

A senior US member of Anonymous, using the online nickname Owen and evidently living in New York, appears to be
one of those targeted in recent legal investigations, according
to online communications uncovered by a private security
researcher ... Mr Barr said Q and other key figures lived in

California and that the hierarchy was fairly clear, with other senior members in the UK, Germany, Netherlands, Italy and Australia.[20]

While Owen and q (lowercase) were prominent figures, Owen lived in Toledo, Ohio, and q resided, more accurately, on the European continent.

A feature story in a respected publication is a precious commodity. If HBGary Federal was really badass enough to identify the movers and shakers behind Anonymous—before even the FBI—corporate executives would, with good reason, be falling over themselves to employ them. The firm's finances were on the rocks; a lucrative contract with Hunton and Williams would mark a change of fortune.[21] HBGary crowed about the seemingly guaranteed meal ticket in internal exchanges:

From: Aaron Barr
To: Karen Burke, Greg Hoglund, Penny Leavy, Ted Vera
Subject: Story is really taking shape
Date: 2011-02-05
http://www.ft.com/cms/s/0/87dc140e-3099-11e0-9de3-00144feabdc0.html

----

From: Greg Hoglund
To: Aaron Barr
Cc: Karen Burke, Penny Leavy, Ted Vera
Subject: Re: Story is really taking shape
We should post this on front page, throw out some tweets. "HBGary Federal sets a new bar as private intelligence agency."—the pun on bar is intended lol.
—G

They were getting all the attention they wanted—only the good kind, it seemed at first. The FBI contacted HBGary

Federal the same day the story came out, requesting a meeting for the following Monday morning at 11 am. But as comedian Stephen Colbert memorably put it: "Anonymous is a hornet's nest, and Barr said, 'I'm going to stick my penis in that thing.'"

Upon reading the *Financial Times* article, hackers who had just completed the team-building exercise of "pwning" Middle Eastern governments were ready to rumble. The article contained given names for many Anons—and after the recent spate of Anonymous arrests in the UK and warrants in the US, the matter was perceived as urgent. Sabu was the first to suggest an attack, spurred in part by his deep-seated hostility for white hat hackers and a security industry he regarded as peddling snake oil: subpar security software. At first, some but not all were on board. tflow later recounted:

> <tflow>: i wasn't initially [behind his idea], i thought it was a waste of time and feeding the trolls
> <tflow>: but then a few minutes later Sabu found a sqli vuln on the hbgaryfederal.com site
> <biella>: and the rest is history
> <tflow>: yea

With a vulnerability too good to resist, the crew was all on board, entering the HBGary systems right on the heels of the *Financial Times* article. They downloaded scores of HBGary and HBGary Federal emails, deleted untold numbers of files and their backups, and, it is purported, wiped the data on Barr's iPhone and iPad. One of the first emails they came across featured a PDF containing the unfiltered data Barr had gathered on Anonymous. They quickly noticed innumerable mistakes. Many of the named individuals had done nothing illegal. Perhaps the most glaring problem was his ignorance of the key operatives behind this very hack—tflow, Topiary, Avunit, Kayla, and Sabu. Deep infiltration was unnecessary to ascertain the existence of many of these participants, like Topiary and tflow—publicly known and prominent members who spent time on open IRC channels, notably #reporter and #lounge.

Using security scanning software designed to look for known vulnerabilities, the hackers probed HBGary's website and quickly found a vulnerability in the custom-made CMS (content management system). Peter Bright, a reporter from Ars Technica who conducted a thorough accounting of the technical details relating to the hack, wrote that "In fact, [the HBGary system] had what can only be described as a pretty gaping bug in it."[22] Once inside, they rummaged around and found encrypted passwords. The encryption was too strong to crack on their own, but by utilizing the brute force of a pool of GPUs (graphics processing units) they were able to crack the hashes in a number of hours.

One of the passwords, "kibafo33," granted access to Barr's Gmail-hosted email account. There the Anons saw the jubilant internal HBGary email exchanges. Naturally, the hackers tried the password on all of Barr's social media accounts and found that he violated the first rule of informational security: never use the same password across platforms. The team could now commandeer all of Barr's social media accounts for lulz and worse. Getting in was just the beginning.

"Good drama must be drastic"[23]

It was Super Bowl Sunday, February 6, 2011. Millions of Americans were glued to the tube watching overgrown bulky men pounce on each other for the purpose of kicking a ball through two goal posts. Aaron Barr might well have been one of those Americans, but any such plans were overshadowed; he had been brutally hacked. His Twitter account, hijacked, spewed forth the most abject racist and degrading statements possible in 140 characters, along with his social security number and home address. Countless unflattering photo-shopped images of Barr were circulated. His emails, including personal ones replete with embarrassing details of marital troubles, were posted on the Pirate Bay.

In the midst of it all, he logged onto the AnonOps IRC server and was invited to a dedicated #ophbgary channel. Barr accepted:

CogAnon (~CogAnon@an-33E99D21.dc.dc.cox.net) has joined #ophbgary
<q>: Ohai CogAnon
<tflow>: Hello, Mr. Barr.
<Topiary>: Mr. Barr and his infiltration of Anonymous; "Now they're threatening us directly", amirite?
<tflow>: I apologize for what's about to happen to you and your company.
<q>: Enjoying the Superbowl, I hope?
<CogAnon>: high one sec. please
<tflow>: I really do, Mr. Barr.
<tflow>: You have no idea what's coming next.
<Topiary>: tflow, How are things going with that, anyway?
<Topiary>: CogAnon is clearly super 1337 with his PM psyops skills in the Washington area
<CogAnon>: ok...sure I figured something like this might happen.
<Topiary>: CogAnon, nah, you won't like what's coming next
<tflow>: CogAnon, can you guess what's coming next?
<Topiary>: Ooh, a fun game - guess!
<CogAnon>: dude...you just don't get it. it was research on social media vulnerabilities...I was never going to release the names...
<Sabu>: LIAR

This brief visit on Sunday, February 6, was the preamble to a more epic conversation that would take place later that same day. The chat that followed has become one of the most viewed IRC logs in history. IRC represents a zone of freedom and autonomy on an Internet dominated by private interests. When you gather dozens, sometimes hundreds, of people together and give them license to say whatever they want as whoever they claim to be, it is only natural that humor, wit, drama, and some chaos will follow. If the world's a stage— and all the geeks, hackers, and sleazy InfoSec hacks are merely players—then what does that make the Internet? A play within a play, written in real time, with each player contributing line by line? They have their exits and their entrances but nothing is known in advance. The output even looks like a screenplay. The difference is that it is populist, participatory, and improvisational in character with real-world stakes and implications.

Act One

The play we are about to watch owes its existence in part to Barrett Brown. Late Sunday evening he bought good tidings in #ophbgary—a channel whose purpose was to discuss and celebrate the hack:

> <Laurelai>: BarrettBrown, you here?
> <BarrettBrown>: I'm on the phone with president of HBGary
> <Sneux>: lol

Sabu pitched the following suggestion:

> <Sabu>: BarrettBrown, ask PENNY to come here and speak.

At this point, it was public knowledge that Anonymous had been on a hacking spree against HBGary Federal and HBGary. Sabu's suggestion seemed like a taunt, not a real request. After all that had unfolded, it didn't seem plausible that Penny Leavy, the president of HBGary, would plunge into the epicenter of the rat's nest currently at work clawing her company apart. But that is exactly what she did. Sabu initiated the exchange by reminding her of the uncomfortable facts:

> <Sabu>: penny. before we get started—know that we have all [seen] email communication between you and everyone in hbgary. so my

first question would be why would you allow aaron to sell such garbage under your company name?
<ComradeBush>: jesus cristo
<Sabu>: Penny, did you also know that aaron was peddling fake/wrong/false information leading to the potential arrest of innocent people[?]

She rose to Aaron Barr's defense:

<Penny>: I did know he was doing research on social media and the problem associated with it, the ease of pretending to be one of you
<Penny>: He was never planning on giving it to the gov't. He was never going to release names, just talk about handles
<Sabu>: Penny, if what you are saying is tr[u]e then why is Aaron meeting with the FBI tomorrow morning at 11am? PLEASE KEEP IN MIND WE HAVE ALL YOUR EMAILS.
<Sabu>: well penny like I said 4 times we have all the emails. theres lots of emails from you promoting aaron's research so … I'm curious
<heyguise>: im still seeding the emails
<Penny>: I think what he was doign was good, it was informative and it will shed lite on lots of issues associated with social media

According to the leaked emails, there were no plans to reach out to law enforcement, much less sell the data to them. However, recall that Anonymous read an email exchange where Barr had claimed point blank to his programmer, "I will sell." Anonymous devised an on-the-fly-IRC financial plan of its own, a Robin Hood–esque blackmail proposal:

<Sabu>: penny. we will not target hbgary.com. its done. what you can do is motivate your investment from hbgaryfederal over to bradley mannings defense fund. and distance yourselves from aaron barnetts' research
<Agamemnon>: Penny … we are under fire in ways you do not understand. Not just the feds … right wing 'freedom' fighters trying to take us down … infiltrators have hurt us … Aarons research contains

personal information of ppl who never did anything but show up here
... please try to understand our rage

Meanwhile, in Brown's abode, the phone rang. On the other end of the line was none other than Barr. They proceeded to have a courteous eleven-minute exchange (Brown recorded the conversation and subsequently uploaded it online). There was some uncertainty regarding just what it was HBGary intended to do with the data. Barr, whose voice bore no trace of sourness, fear, or even anger, confidently introduced himself: "I am a federal contractor working mostly in the security space." Anticipating a question about motives, Barr claimed point blank, "I never planned to sell the data to the FBI." Again, the emails support Barr on this point—there is no evidence that he had contacted the FBI. But he was certainly seeking to profit in some manner by gathering these correlated names and "outing" Anons, as he put it—presumably any number of embattled organizations would be interested in ascertaining the identity of their assailants. Regardless of the eventual outcome, the mere existence of such a file was received as an ominous threat by the Anonymous community at large.

To Brown, Barr presented a very different rationale, claiming his overarching agenda was to demonstrate the weaknesses of social media and expose the hierarchy behind the hive. "There is definitely a structure," he said. Brown assented to some degree—"I agree a few dozen people set the pace"—but he noted that many of the names were wrong. "I never purported it was 100 percent accurate," Barr insisted, even in his conversation with the *Financial Times*. "The reporter writes what he wants to write." Barr reminded Brown that he was still planning to meet with the FBI the following morning, noting that "It is going to be out of my hands."

Leaked emails indicate that Barr and his colleagues had, indeed, given great thought—just that day—to the question of releasing the names to the FBI. Ted Vera, the president and

COO of HBGary Federal, finished off the chain in favor of withholding:

> You could end up accusing a wrong person. Or you could further enrage the group. Or you could be wrong, and it blows up in your face, and HBGary's face, publicly. The hint of you having their true names is enough. No need to release names publicly. You meet with FBI tomorrow. I doubt they'll share much, but they may informally or inadvertently vet some of your findings.

Anonymous, on the other hand, had no qualms and released the document listing all the names.

As he had done with Leavy, Brown tried to lure Barr online. "They would like you to come. I will try to keep things productive," Brown told him. Barr, having already logged on earlier in the day, resisted, and so Brown, in his Texan drawl, switched strategies. "I understand you have had a rough day," Brown said. "You have been picked on. Again, it was not my doing—though I can't say I disapproved of it, because we are here to protect ourselves and our interests here." By the end of the phone conversation, it remained unclear whether Barr was convinced to return for a second round.

Off the phone and back on IRC, Brown, an avid gamer, proclaimed that he was done with "this silliness" and announced his intention to "play some *Fallout: New Vegas*." But first, as Anonymous made successive demands, Brown offered a characteristic gesture of empathy toward Leavy:

> \<Penny\>: Thanks everyone it was very nice talking to you. How do I re-connect you?
> \<Sabu\>: penny, can you have greg hop on your computer and talk to us for a few minutes /?
> \<BarrettBrown\>: If it makes you feel any better, I'm an opiate addict and still on Suboxone maintanance
> \<BarrettBrown\>: which I'm ending in a couple days

<Penny>: Hey Sabu thanks for being so nice rough day
<Sabu>: its all good. rough day for us too

Act Two

As Penny exited the stage, Greg Hoglund entered, physically replacing her at the computer:

Penny is now known as greg
<evilworks>: success
<q>: epic success
<greg>: SOrry guys it was me it was my computer and greg went away
<greg>: he's back
<Sabu>: ok
<Sabu>: GREG IS THAT YOU
<greg>: yea

Before Anons resumed their interrogation, they paused for a self-congratulatory moment:

<`k>: Greg have you ever heard of ssh keys? [ssh keys referring to encryption technology]
<Sabu>: first off, if you havent read already take a look at http://pastie.org/1535735
<Sabu>: thats how we owned rootkit.com
<evilworks>: oh wow Sabu
<q>: that's a good one
<q>: :)
<q>: what a security company you are
<Sabu>: is there anything you can do to stop him from using your company name // hbgary ?

There was a noticeable pause as Greg looked at the paste site, where a log of the leak was detailed. He quickly apprehended the full seriousness of the situation:

<greg>: so you got my email spool too then
<Sabu>: yes greg.
<`k>: greg we got everything
<Agamemnon>: Greg, I'm curious to know if you understand what we are about? Do you understand why we do what we do?

"We got everything." Had this play been staged, Hoglund would have, at this point, probably embarked on a soliloquy bemoaning his fate—or, at minimum, conveyed some degree of facial horror. Hoglund must have realized his options were limited. But if you can't trick the tricksters, one can always appeal to reason … maybe?

<greg>: you realize that releasing my email spool will cause millions in damages to HBGary?
<c0s>: greg, I do beleive the people around here are very honest when they say they would be happy not to release it. But that they will be basing that decision on what happens with Aaron.
<c0s>: which is why I asked you to possibl[y] explain your ideas on what might be done there.
<c0s>: so they might have an idea of what you can do.
<Sabu>: greg, in essence we want you to distance yourself and company from aaron
<BarrettBrown>: Like I said, great time to donate to Tunisia
<evilworks>: or Bradley manning
<evilworks>: whichever

Would his honest appeal work? With the reappearance of another lead, we are ushered into the play's final act.

Act Three

CogAnon entered the room.
<Sabu>: its aaron
<Sabu>: coganon
<Sabu>: thats his SPY NICK

<Sabu>: hi aaron
<c0s>: Good evening Aaron.

Hoglund took a moment to dissociate himself from Barr:

<greg>: aaron is CEO of his own company, that unfortunately, shares
the HBGary name - I can't do anything except yell at him on the phone
<`k>: hahaha they're all here
<greg>: hbgary (my hbgary) has 15% ownership of hbgary federal,
for the record
<greg>: yeah, and aaron just had to poke the wasp nest didnt he
<evilworks>: i'm downloading some emails

Thanks to the emails, we know Hoglund's claims here are mostly hot air—Barr was a respected, central member of the HBGary management team:

From: Greg Hoglund
To: all@hbgary.com
Subject: Welcome Aaron Barr and Ted Vera to the HBGary management team!
Date: 2009-11-23
I am extremely excited to announce that Aaron Barr and Ted Vera have joined the HBGary team! Ted and Aaron will operate and lead HBGary Federal, a wholly owned subsidiary of HBGary, with a focus on contracting in the government space. They are very experienced and most recently built a $10 million/year business at Northrop Grumman. Both have won and lead multi-million dollar development projects and managed substantial teams. We have known Aaron and Ted for more than 5 years. These two are A+ players in the DoD contracting space and are able to "walk the halls" in customer spaces. Some very big players made offers to Ted and Aaron last week, and instead they chose HBGary. This reflects extremely well on our company. "A" players attract "A" players. Aaron will take position as CEO of HBGary

Federal, and will be operating out of the DC area. Ted will take position as President and COO of HBGary Federal, and will be operating out of Colorado Springs. Welcome aboard!
—Greg Hoglund
CEO, HBGary, Inc.

Hoglund then changed tack, appealing to Anonymous's supposed sense of self-preservation:

> <greg>: do you guys realize that attacking a US company and stealing private data is something you have never done before?
> <greg>: no, I think you might have considered your public reputation - it doesn't look good.
> <Agamemnon>: Greg. Please answer: do you understand who we are and why we do what we do?
> <CogAnon>: I was never going to sell u have it wrong.
> <evilworks>: we don't CARE about reputation
> <Sabu>: greg, our reputation is not at stake here. yours is.
> <greg>: i mean this was a real hack - and btw, i have to concede you really did hack us good
> <evilworks>: we do what we think is right
> <c0s>: Greg, and the people here dont care about reputation, at all
> <evilworks>: there are numerous ways to make us look bad
> <evilworks>: we dont care
> [...]
> <Baas>: Granted, you guys don't do burn notices proper...But it's the thought that counts. We want Aaron's reputation nuked for this.
> <evilworks>: jesus

Brown, taking a break from his game, issued a reminder:

> BarrettBrown: he's still meeting with FBI at 11 tomorrow, remember
> c0s: That is the thing that bothers me the most.
> Sabu: he literally picked out random people from facebook and connected it to irc nicks
> BarrettBrown: and will no doubt discuss me personally

As anger erupted around him, Barr still did not concede:

<evilworks>: why did you start working on this anyway?
<BarrettBrown>: As I told him, my family was fucked by Feds
<evilworks>: was it personal interest, for research?
<CogAnon>: do u want me to answer?
<CogAnon>: guys it doesn't matter anyways ... you have released my emails.
<evilworks>: i suspect its for monetary gain
<Sabu>: greg. please respond
<CogAnon>: I did this for research.
<CogAnon>: The fbi called me because of my research.
<CogAnon>: the email you are refering to about selling data was about a model built on this type of research.
<c0s>: you knew, or your a complete idiot, you KNEW that your methods were flawed.
<CogAnon>: The most data I was going to show was an org chart of IRCs with icons representing those nicks I thought I knew ...
<evilworks>: theres still some emails we havent released
<Sabu>: aaron, you need to apologize to us, your investers at hbgary and set the record straight
<Sabu>: that you DID NOT identify anonymous leadership
<Sneux>: ^
<Sabu>: and that your research is purely academic and theoretical

With so much said, Barr had had enough:

<CogAnon>: ok guys I have to go to bed. I repeat this was only about research on social media vulnerabilities ... u guys crossed the line ...
<c0s>: this was an eye for an eye by pepole you wronged.
<Sabu>: you did by doxing innocent fucking people
<Sabu>: fuck you forreal
<evilworks>: Fuck you ok?
<Sabu>: look at the names on your doc
<Agamemnon>: fuck it
<Baas>: The problem is that he doesn't even consider that he did something wrong.

<Sabu>: hes ok with doxing innocent people
<Sabu>: I MEAN HOLY SHIT
<Agamemnon>: Greg, make deal now ... shut him up ... all will be
well
<greg>: deal? what kind of deal?
<Agamemnon>: Aaron shuts the fuck up ... your email stays private
<owen>: guys
<owen>: control yourselves
<CogAnon>: this was about research.

One of the benefits of watching an Internet play is that no
one knows what will happen next, and you can talk as much
as you want without disturbing anyone. By now, it was well
known that I was the resident anthropologist. An Anon sent
me a private message asking me to reflect on the moment:

<PKE>: so, what's it like sitting in on all this?
<biella>: hi PKE
<PKE>: enjoying the view?
<biella>: mostly
<biella>: i am a bit sick right now so i am struggling with all views
<PKE>: as an outsider, what's your opinion thus far?
<biella>: of anonymous?
<PKE>: well, thats a broad brush
<PKE>: i meant of their relentless takedown of hbgary and co

It was a bit of a struggle to keep up. I was in the midst of a nasty
flu and was worried it was the forerunner of full-blown rabies.
I had just had my last inoculation shot four days prior, after
an unfortunate run-in with a bat a month earlier. Through the
haze, the fever, and the sore throat, I offered:

<biella>: i was surprised at how quick it happened
<biella>: at first
<biella>: and then the conversation on the channel has been quite in
the spirit of the lulz

<biella>: which was perhaps submerged weeks before during the other ops

To which PKE, spared from both the flu and irrational postulates about the onset of rabies, replied with a more incisive commentary:

<PKE>: absolutely
<PKE>: i mean
<PKE>: great work was being accomplished
<PKE>: but there was a major deficit of lulz
<biella>: yep and now it has been restocked
<PKE>: i think this is more of a surplus
<biella>: haha true
<PKE>: i can't think of a more ridiculous anonymous operation in recent memory
<biella>: the conversation on the channel has been unreal
<biella>: the twitter feed was outrageous
<biella>: yep
<biella>: true
<PKE>: man. i really never understood the appeal of the internet hate machine before this
<PKE>: boy, when you combine sociopaths with pissed off altruists, get the fuck out of the way

In the end, left unsatisfied by what the mere mortals had to offer, the Anonymous tricksters opted to release the additional HBGary emails they had been holding onto for leverage. While most of the company emails were being seeded for release during the course of the chat conversation, the following week Anonymous also released Greg Hoglund's 27,606 emails on AnonLeaks.[24]

A Team of Anonymous Ninjas Exposing Team Themis

For days following this epic showdown, the lulz pulsed through the IRC chat channels, electrifying and recharging the collective mood. The press could not get its fill of the hack. Journalists sought out Barrett Brown for commentary, which appeared from the *New York Times* to the BBC. On February 8, 2011, Brown jubilantly declared on #ophbgary:

> \<BarrettBrown\>: NPR asked me who did HBGary
> \<BarrettBrown\>: I told them "a team of Anonymous ninjas."
> \<FEAR_Anonymous\>: NPR?
> \<DingDong\>: HAHA
> \<DingDong\>: yes!
> \<FEAR_Anonymous\>: LOL
> \<HateIRC\>: lol nice
> \<Sci\>: lmfao

From the outside, it appeared as if Brown was a beloved Anonymous activist at the top of his game. But from the inside, with just a tiny bit of poking, it was easy to witness the grumblings about the role he adopted just a little too willingly. At the time, Anonymous was fond of penning collectively written documents. Most of them were about operations. One appeared later in the same month bearing the title "All About Barrett Brown. Add your comments guise." This defacto performance review dissected his contributions—securing legal help, writing editorials, getting the press online—in relation to a moral evaluation of his public behavior. None of this was done behind his back. Indeed, before the critiques were issued he was solicited to write a statement, included here in its entirety, to appear near the top of the document:

> Yes. Anyone who doesn't know what I've done for Anon hasn't been involved in OpTunisia and OpEgpyt to any real extent, and anyone who wasn't working on that campaign

every fucking day can go fuck themselves. What's fucked up is how many more people are in this document than are in any of Anon's actual important documents. There's my "statement," sweethearts. Also note that the person who started all this did not get his paragraph put in the press release and is upset aboutr it. —Barrett Brown

Understandably—given that he had just told everyone to go fuck themselves—most of the following seven pages of commentary hashing out his personality, motives, and contributions slanted toward the negative. The critiques, while dotted with occasional positive assessments, found consensus in opposition to his self-promotion:

—This is important. It's about the basic principles of Anonymous ideology, anonymity and the equality of all.
—You seem to imply that you are special and important such that the principles mentioned below, anonymity and equality of all, do not apply to you.

----

*Your dedication isn't under discussion. You most certainly are one of Anons most important friends. I just want to say that I don't want to see you as 'leader of Anonymous' nor spokesperson. I know that would be of no benefit to Anonymous.+1 wholeheartedly +1 undoubtedly +1
*@Barrett: Anonymous will support you, as long as you do not form a personal army and you abstain from leaderfagging. +1+1+1

The small team of hackers working behind the curtain were also far from pleased by all the journalistic attention Brown was receiving from the HBGary operation. Roughly a month later, Gawker's Adrian Chen and John Cook published an article, "Inside Anonymous's Secret War Room," detailing the aftermath of the HBGary hack. Brown had spoken to the journalists at length:

Barrett Brown, who is generally regarded by Anonymous members as a spokesman for the group, said he has known about the "security breach" for some time: "We're aware of the security breach as other logs from 'HQ' have been posted before (and I should note that HQ is not really HQ anyway—you will note that the actual coordination of performed hacks will not appear in those logs)."[25]

Upon reading the article, many of the hackers, already annoyed at Brown, became infuriated, lashing out at him on #anon-leaks, the channel dedicated to discussing the HBGary leaks.

> <tflow>: it's ironic that you claim that you're good at playing the media yet you fail at making them get their basic facts right

Brown, along with Gregg Housh (c0s), who also frequently spoke with the media, blamed the journalists for identifying a spokesperson, even when instructed otherwise.

> <c0s>: I had two people call today, and both said at the end of the interviews
> <c0s>: "can we call your official spokesperson"
> <BarrettBrown>: here, listen to Housh
> <c0s>: i have to fight hard each time to get the idiots to not do it
> <c0s>: and some who agree not to
> <c0s>: and completely understand
> <c0s>: put it in right, then have editor fags "fix" it
> <c0s>: and it says spokesperson, or something else stupid
> <BarrettBrown>: there you go
> <BarrettBrown>: argue with Housh
> <c0s>: it fucking sucks dealing with these assholes
> <c0s>: no
> <c0s>: i dont argue heh
> <tflow>: then go and get the editor fags to fix it

With that settled, they moved to other upsetting topics, notably how Brown claimed insider knowledge about #HQ, the HBGary breach, and the hacking, when he had not witnessed the operation, much less contributed to it. Even worse, he was simply wrong about #HQ; it was where the HBGary hack was coordinated:

> <`k>: tbh there's no need for you to even be talking to media in the first place you've done nothing yet you have an explanation for everything
> <BarrettBrown>: k, I've done some things, sweetheart
> <tflow>: it also pisses me off how you make a statement to gawker regarding #hq
> <FriedSquid>: suggestion: being a journo is, to an extent, about getting your message out there, exposure of your work. About getting your name known.
> <BarrettBrown>: can we stop talking about this?
> <tflow>: when it doesn't concern you in the least
> <BarrettBrown>: they fucking asked me
> [...]
> <tflow>: then don't open your mouth and tell them that it doesn't concern you if it doesn't concern you
> <BarrettBrown>: no, fuck you zomg
> <`k>: it's easy to say "no" to reporters
> <BarrettBrown>: I don't take orders
> <tflow>: if you don't know what you're talking about

As was the case with Snapple before him, Brown got momentarily kicked off the channel, in this case by `k. This was followed by final remarks, including a few about the quality of the spectacle—as if the arguments doubled as an impromptu version of a high school debating match:

> <Earnest>: hate to be one sided but `k and tflow did a much better job than barret on this occasion
> <tflow>: I would have kicked him
> <tflow>: but I don't like kicking people
> <tflow>: from chats

<'k>: im just sick of these faggots whoreing attention in the media when they claim they have no part in things yet think they know everything

Just as Brown became embattled due to his promotional activities in relation to the hacks, HBGary itself faced another set of tough challenges and necessary decisions.

The Aftermath

A day after chatting with Anonymous and a week before the premier North American security conference hosted by RSA Security Inc. was slated to begin, Greg Hoglund bemoaned his situation to a reporter: "They are causing me a great deal of pain right now ... What they're doing right now is not hacktivism, it's terrorism. They've really crossed a line here."[26] The terrorism charge was new—never before appearing, either publicly or in emails, from Hogland or Barr. The reversal of terms was likely a carefully crafted PR tactic designed to paint these hackers as "terrorists" and thus as a grave danger to society; it was perhaps a calculated bid to convert the embarrassing reality of the gruesome hack—a potential (probable) disaster—into an advantage. Hoglund also made the decision to pull out of the RSA conference.

Though HBGary clearly hit a rough patch, the company came out the other side of this turmoil unscathed, or perhaps even stronger—aided by its rebranding of Anonymous as a "terrorist" element to which it was victim. A year later, HBGary was acquired by a defense contractor called ManTech International. Hoglund cooperated closely with law enforcement in its investigations of Anonymous, as duly noted in an FBI press release:

The broad case against six hackers, including [Hector Xavier] Monsegur, [aka "Sabu"], is the product of an extensive investigation ... The attack on HBGary was carefully investigated by the FBI in Sacramento and the case was transferred to New York for Monsegur's plea. Importantly, the Sacramento investigation greatly benefited from the assistance of HBGary itself.[27]

Aaron Barr and HBGary Federal fared less well. As CEO, Barr could not be fired, but he elected to step down by the end of February 2011, and the company subsequently folded. During an interview with *Forbes*' Parmy Olson, he reflected on the events: "Do I regret [making those claims] now? Sure ... I'm getting personal threats from people, and I have two kids. I have two four-year-old kids. Nothing is worth that."[28]

The two other members of Team Themis, Berico and Palantir, which had schemed with HBGary Federal to discredit WikiLeaks, washed their hands of blood like Lady Macbeth, immediately severing all ties with HBGary Federal and disavowing full knowledge of the plan. But as Nate Anderson of Ars Technica put it: "both of the Team Themis leads at these companies knew exactly what was being proposed (such knowledge may not have run to the top). They saw Barr's e-mails, and they used his work. His ideas on attacking WikiLeaks made it almost verbatim into a Palantir slide about 'proactive tactics.'"[29]

In the aftermath, troubled by their new-found awareness of such proposed tactics, a group of Democratic congress members sought to investigate Team Themis. During an interview, the lead congressman for the committee, Hank Johnson, expressed why he supported the inquiry: American tax dollars were being used to fund tools and programs to spy on Americans and quell First Amendment rights.[30] Other congressmen, notably Representative Lamar Smith, quietly dismantled and blocked this investigation. Regrettably, the mainstream press never followed up to write about the inquiry's demise.

The growing dissatisfaction with Barrett Brown inside

Anonymous did not slow him down. He remained active within Anonymous for a few more months. The intimate portal into a private security firm like HBGary Federal galvanized him and facilitated the establishment of his web-based think tank ProjectPM (PPM), "a crowd-sourced wiki focused on government intelligence contractors." It was clear to him that HBGary Federal was not an anomaly amongst defense contractors. In an op-ed published in 2013, Brown expressed his aims for PPM: "we must look not just toward the three letter agencies that have routinely betrayed us in the past, but also to the untold number of private intelligence contracting firms that have sprung up lately in order to betray us in a more efficient and market-oriented manner."[31]

The ballooning size of this market-driven industry has been thoughtfully assessed by Tim Shorrock, one of the few investigative journalists to extensively research the topic. Information is scarce, as he explains, but there are a few telling details to suggest the enormity of these operations:

> Outsourcing has become so pervasive that the Director of National Intelligence decided to study the phenomenon last year. But when the report was finally completed in April 2007, the results were apparently so stunning that the DNI vetoed the idea of putting out a report and instead told reporters that disclosure of the figures would damage national security.[32]

It is estimated from current figures that 70 percent of America's $80 billion intelligence budget goes toward private contractors.[33] While the HBGary and HBGary Federal emails provided no hard numbers about the size of the overall industry, they did offer qualitative measures that point to the massive scale of the government intelligence contracting world. Brown, aided by volunteers who did the bulk of the research and writing, and all the technical work, hosted a central repository to catalog the brave new world of corporations that specialize in intelligence gathering, espionage, and infiltration for corporate and government clients. Where the leaked documents truly broke ground was in providing insight into the types of tactics employed by private firms in the era of digital and networked technologies; the firms were evidently willing to propose and engage in reckless acts. After all, Barr was on the path to providing actionable intelligence, for instance, doxing some Anons who had done nothing illegal—even offering nicknames and locations to a reporter. His firm had also laid out detailed plans to sabotage the career of a journalist. Since this type of work is now also spread across hundreds of different private firms, it is unlikely there will ever be a single massive document dump equivalent to the one which busted open COINTELPRO detailing the corporate face of spying; instead, the public will have to rely on the piecemeal datasets it receives through leaks and hacks such as the HBGary one.

Inspired by the success of the HBGary hack, other Anons would soon seek to direct similar techniques to other security and intelligence firms. But first, the hackers who had decimated HBGary Federal would break away from AnonOps and embark on a fifty-day tour as an experimental performance troupe by the name of LulzSec. It would receive rave reviews from Internet denizens. But corporations watched the play, with its seemingly endless string of encores, in horror.

CHAPTER 8

LulzSec

LulzSec—a crew of renegade Anonymous hackers who broke away from Anonymous and doubled as traveling minstrels—appeared a few months after the infamous HBGary Federal hack. Crewed by the same individuals who had vindictively hacked Aaron Barr, LulzSec's startling fifty-day catalytic run began in early May 2011 and abruptly ended on June 25, soon after one of their own, Sabu, was apprehended and flipped in less than twenty-four hours by the FBI. Among their targets were Sony Music Entertainment Japan, Sony Picture Entertainment, Sony BMG (Netherlands and Belgium), PBS, the Arizona Department of Public Safety, the US Senate, the UK Serious Organised Crime Agency, Bethesda Softworks, AOL, and AT&T. Despite the avalanche of activity —and numerous intrusions—LulzSec, when compared to Anonymous, was more manageable and contained, at least from an organizational perspective. Its members hacked with impunity, finally making good on the 2007 Fox News claim that Anonymous was comprised of "hackers on steroids."

LulzSec members played their role knowing full well they were performing for a diverse audience. Even the haughtiest of security hackers who had earlier snubbed Anonymous cheered on LulzSec. Some old-school black hats lived vicariously through LulzSec, in awe of its swagger, its fuck-you-anything-goes attitude, and its bottomless appetite for exposing the pathetic state of Internet security. Journalists could not get enough of their antics, nor could they really keep up. With so many intrusions, exfiltrations, and data dumps, LulzSec blew out the usual three-day news cycle. For much of its reign, LulzSec taunted journalists with the lure of information and then gave them the silent treatment—with one notable exception: Parmy Olson of forbes.com. These hackers (almost) exclusively fed her info about their dealings and, to retain her privileges, she was discreet about the arrangement.[1]

Although they gave Parmy Olson enough information to write her stories, LulzSec's main gateways to the world were their website, their Twitter account, and the website pastebin.com, where all their dumps were mirrored and their proclamations released. Pastebin is typically used by programmers to post small snippets of text, source code, or configuration information. It generates a unique URL that can then be pasted elsewhere, like IRC, for others to view. Instead of pasting multi-line text into IRC channels—something that will get you kicked out of a channel for "flooding"—you can simply provide the link. Typically, these generated links are unmemorable random characters and expire after some time. Pastebin is only one among a multitude of such sites, so why LulzSec chose this medium is a bit of a mystery. Regardless, it freed LulzSec from the need to host infrastructure for their missives. Their Twitter account amassed followers in bulk, sometimes twenty thousand per week. Penned by their resident trickster, Topiary crafted delightful updates, often maintaining a maritime character.

The LulzSec team was sailing the high seas—venturing deep into international waters with a pirate flag hoisted high, putting on a show for others to watch. During an interview I conducted with David Mirza, a retired black hat, he observed:

LulzSec hit the Internet with a much more potent—and instantly recognizable as authentic—black hat attitude than the fabric of Anonymous they jumped out of. They got it right with the swagger and style. They were owning things up, pulling dox, dispensing justice. Nobody could catch them and they knew it. Their campaign became a great saga that made some of those who'd lived that adventure before feel like teenagers again.

With one tweet, the hacker zine and organization 2600 captured the general sentiment felt by the community at large: "Hacked websites, corporate infiltration/scandal, IRC wars, new hacker groups making global headlines—the 1990s are back!"[2]

No respectable pirates can sail without a vessel, and LulzSec's crew helmed a boat christened "Louise." The name was provided by a reporter's misreading—and resultant mispronouncing—of LulzSec. And since the quarters were infinitely spacious, they decided to bring along a mascot. The classic pirate parrot was swapped for a colorful feline beast: an affable gray cat named Nyan Cat who has been known, among heavy Internet users, to brighten up even the drabbest gray sky by effusing, eternally, a stream of rainbows straight out of its ass. This playful absurdity was tempered by LulzSec's virtual spokesman and logotype: a stick man sporting a well-oiled, French-style, villainous mustache, replete with monocle, top hat, and three-piece suit—and sipping, naturally, a glass of fine wine. This refined gent first appeared in a Spanish-language rage comic (a popular meme-comic among Internet geeks), before being adopted by LulzSec in March 2011. Fans referred to the unnamed character as being "like a sir"; eventually, he was known simply as the "sir." All of this added up to provide LulzSec with a chimeric mixture of depth, mystique, and memetic mythology previously unseen in Anonymous hacker groups. One Anon, who had also been active in the black hat scene, put it this way in an interview with me: "LulzSec seemed to have a sort of fully formed mythos straight out of the gate while other hacker groups like Cult of the Dead Cow took decades to achieve that."

Returning to reality for a moment—later we will explore questions of fantasy—we should note that these hackers congregated on their own private IRC channel, where they were shielded from the drama engulfing AnonOps at the time. Unbound by the categorical imperative of moralfaggotry, they could also hack whomever they pleased—for whatever whimsical reason took their fancy.

It may be surprising to hear that LulzSec sprang, fully formed, from a single, unremarkable IRC conversation. It is less surprising when one learns that these hackers were a bit bored with Anonymous and—some of them, at least—had grown tired of working on other people's ops. Idle tricksters will do anything necessary to end boredom. It also helped that they had a cache of data stolen from Fox News just waiting to be unloaded, and that AnonOps was, at that point, in increasing disarray.

Hell Hath No Fury Like Scorned Gamers

For most of March and April of 2011, AnonOps had not slowed down from where we last left them, but the network was plagued by a mounting litany of problems. Small fires started to break out, and the wear and tear of putting them out began to drag the group down.

Even if Anonymous's crucifixion of Aaron Barr had turned him into the 2011 laughing stock of the Internet, his mission to seek out and reveal the legal identities of Anons did not die with him. Backtrace Security (its name is a humorous reference to an infamous 2010 Anonymous trollscapade against a preteen, Jessi Slaughter, whose father claimed to have "backtracked" Anonymous) made this end its singular purpose and pick up where Barr left off. The organization's most vocal member, Jennifer Emick, had once been an Anonymous warrior herself during Project Chanology's fight against Scientology, but grew critical of the more questionable tactics subsequently used by AnonOps (the very ones LulzSec would later seize upon as its primary toolkit). A self-proclaimed fan of law and order, she declared that "One cannot fight for justice and democracy by using unjust, anti-democratic tactics."[3] A good point, but one which failed to account for the questionable ethics of her own brand of vigilantism: in mid-March 2011, Backtrace released a chart with the "identities" of seventy Anonymous participants and affiliates. As was the case in Barr's attempt, many of the names were either wrong or already public, all except one. You have to give it to Backtrace. It was the one name that mattered the most at that moment: Hector Xavier Monsegur, the notorious hacker Sabu. (The Backtrace document had a slightly misspelled version of Sabu's last name: Montsegur.)

Backtrace did not dox Sabu through a feat of shrewd reconnaissance. They simply got lucky when one Anonymous participant, who went by the name "Laurelai" and had spent time on the more secretive channels, foolishly handed Emick her chat logs. The slab of text—over two hundred pages of logs—included a single clue leading straight to the Nuyorican living in Manhattan's Lower East Side. While chatting with his compatriots, Sabu had accidentally typed out or pasted a web address which included the domain of his personal server: prvt.org. Once Backtrace plugged this web address into Google, they discovered one of his sub-domains, which included other personal data, which, inevitably, funneled down to his Facebook page.

The Backtrace document, named "Namshub" (Sumerian for "incantation") was dissected to pieces by Anonymous, but most people, of course, could only realistically assess the veracity of their own outing. Sabu—and perhaps a few of his closest hacking associates from days long past—knew he had been exposed. By doxing him, Backtrace acted as the force of Eshu, the trickster of crossroads, plopping the powerful figure down at the crossroads. Sabu/Monsegur had a big decision to make. Upon seeing his name, he could have wiped every-thing from his computer, gone dark, and returned years later as a hacker hero. It is true that he could not have vanished right away. Doing so would have made "it obvious that he got doxed," as tflow reminded me. But he could have left a month later after accusations had died down. He was already larger than life, and in his absence his prominence would only have grown. In the words of one Anon, he was "legend." Had Monsegur opted to vanish for a period and reemerge after the statute of limitations expired, he could have returned to his beloved *isla del encanto* (Puerto Rico), safe to entertain his friends and family with tales of his exploits. Calling it quits would have been the smart thing to do, but Sabu was not short on hubris.

Instead, he sought out Emick and bombarded her with false information to seed confusion; one of his hacker mates explained that "when Backtrace released their dox table he tried to trick them into thinking he was a double agent working for an ISP trying to infiltrate Anon, but they didn't buy it."

Although Sabu was well known among his peers, he gener-ally kept a low public profile, until being doxed by Backtrace. Soon after he tweeted for the first time:

> hai! I go by the name of Sabu these days. I made this account to clear some things up, especially after the leaks by #backtraceinsecurity.

He continued to saunter down Trickster Lane, even more public than before, convinced he was untouchable, until he was ultimately outed as an informant a year later. (Then upon his release from prison, Sabu would be reborn as the scourge of Anonymous. The day of his outing, a formerly close hacker compatriot declared with no reservations on IRC: "its better 500y of prison than look yourself on the mirror and know u suck.")

I asked a few of the hackers how they responded to doxing attempts like Namshub. One of the few core LulzSec hackers who was never identified or nabbed provided a four-part rationale, which aligned with sentiments I had seen expressed by others:

<Avunit>: A) You trust others [to] protect themselves enough so it doesn't matter
<Avunit>: B) Everything is going well and you want to stick together because it works
<Avunit>: C) You don't care about the names
<Avunit>: D) It could still be the wrong name, right?

On April 1, 2012, shortly after Backtrace's viperous Namshub doxing, AnonOps rolled out Operation Sony. "Prepare for the biggest attack you have ever witnessed, Anonymous style," declared one video.[4] They began overwhelming Sony's PlayStation Network with a wallop of a DDoS campaign, disrupting the service and the gamers who used it. To understand why AnonOps launched this attack, we need to backpedal to January 2011, when Sony sued a boisterous and precocious American hacker named George Hotz, better known by his handle, "geohot." His hacking specialty is what is called "jailbreaking"—freeing consumer devices like iPhones and gaming consoles from their proprietor's grip so they can be modified as an owner desires. Usually, this involves some clever analysis of the device, the writing of software that disables copy and access controls, and the release of documentation for the whole process so others can follow suit. This type of hacking converts single-purposed devices back to the preferable state of a general-purpose computer. Although a single-purpose device is useful for people who do not want to deal with complexity, many technologists see this confinement as an arbitrary abridgment of their fundamental right to use their property as they choose. They also see jailbreaking as an appealing challenge, as if the company created a special puzzle for them to solve.

Hotz first earned the accolades of hackers and some digital rights advocates in 2007 as the first hacker, at the age of seventeen, to carrier unlock the iPhone. Then, in late 2009, he put Sony's popular PlayStation 3 (PS3) on his technical agenda. Hotz and an anonymous team called "fail0verflow" (unassociated with Anonymous) managed to break the lock in just five weeks. On January 26, 2011, he spread the love by posting jailbreaking instructions for the PS3 on his website, bringing waves of attention to himself. Jailbreaking the PS3 allows the owner of the game console to do a number of things one could not do on a normal PS3: play pirated games, perform backups, play games directly from the hard drive (vastly speeding up the loading time), play videos, install GNU/Linux, and, perhaps most importantly, create, innovate, and learn in a multitude of ways. When interviewed about this feat by the BBC, Hotz rephrased a classic hacker motto into his own words: "[PS3] is supposed to be *unhackable,* but *nothing is unhackable."*

Of course, corporations have mottos of their own—one of which might be formulated as: "You hack, we sue." Soon after Hotz released the jailbreaking instructions, Sony sued him for copyright infringement and violation of the Computer Fraud and Abuse Act. Known for speaking his mind, Hotz did not take the news sitting down; he spoke up very loudly. Well, technically he was sitting—and he didn't speak, he rapped (and since its release on YouTube, his response has been viewed over two million times). Sitting in a chair in a well-worn blue sweatshirt in his nondescript bedroom, he began: "Yo, it's geohot, and for those that don't know, I'm getting sued by Sony." He thrashes his body in synch with the beat, his boyish brown curls bobbing as he describes Sony as "fudge packers" and ends with: "But shit man / they're a corporation / and I'm a personification / of freedom for all."[5]

Sony's civil suit not only named Hotz and several other hackers, but also one hundred "John Does"—some of whom, they suspected, to be members of Hotz's anonymous hacker team. Sony even targeted those who merely viewed Hotz's jailbreaking instructions. A legal notice to his web provider demanded the IP addresses of visitors to Hotz's website between 2009 and 2011. YouTube was asked to release information on those who had viewed Hotz's jailbreak video or posted comments about it. Many Internet geeks were appalled at Sony's lawsuit; this sentiment was captured well by the science fiction writer and Internet advocate Cory Doctorow, who opined that it was "absurd and unjust for a gargantuan multinational to use its vast legal resources to crush a lone hacker whose 'crime' is to figure out how to do (legal) stuff with his own property."[6]

Anonymous was thrown into a tizzy. The fact that Hotz never sought aid (actually, he wanted nothing to do with Anonymous) is irrelevant. Anonymous's first announcement read:

> Dear ~~Greedy Motherfuckers~~ SONY,
> Congratulations! You are now receiving the attention of Anonymous. Your recent legal actions against fellow internet citizens, GeoHot and Graf_Chokolo, have been deemed an unforgivable offense against free speech and internet freedom, primary sources of free lulz (and you know how we feel about lulz). You have abused the judicial system in an attempt to censor information about how your products work. You have victimized your own customers merely for possessing and sharing information, and continue to target those who seek this information. In doing so you have violated the privacy of thousands of innocent people who only sought the free distribution of information. Your suppression of this information is motivated by corporate greed and the desire for complete control over the actions of individuals who purchase and use your products, at least when those actions threaten to undermine the corrupt stranglehold you seek to maintain over copywrong, oops, "copyright."[7]

Very quickly, the operation went south. DDoSing Sony's PlayStation Network (PSN) did not earn Anonymous any new friends, only the ire of gamers who foamed with vitriol at being deprived of their source of distraction. Amidst the DDoSing, a splinter group calling itself "SonyRecon" formed to dox Sony executives. This move proved controversial among Anonymous activists and their broader support network.

Spurred by the operation's immediate unpopularity, Anonymous released the following statement: "We realized that targeting the PSN is not a good idea. We have therefore temporarily suspended our action until a method is found that will not severely impact Sony's customers." They hoped that this would put out the fire.

Throughout the month of April, however, PSN continued to experience downtime. Since Anonymous had originally called the operation, many naturally assumed that the masked horde of activists was responsible for the ongoing problems. But while there were a few scattered claims of responsibility, Anonymous eventually and unambiguously insisted, "For once we did not do it."

With no official word from Sony, rumor and innuendo continued to swirl. After weeks of silence, on April 26, Sony finally released an official statement: "We have discovered that between April 17 and April 19, 2011, certain PlayStation Network and Qriocity service user account information was compromised in connection with an illegal and unauthorized intrusion into our network."[8] Millions of credit card numbers were compromised, prompting Sony to encourage its customers to change their passwords and stay alert for signs of fraud. And things only got worse with the announcement that PSN would remain inaccessible. Colin Milburn, an academic and avid gamer, wrote a riveting account of the infamous PSN hack from the perspective of scorned gamers like himself; in the essay he noted, "At this point, the emotional tide turned to outrage—much of it directed at Sony for its lax security measures, much more directed at the hackers who had perpetrated the intrusion."[9] Ultimately, the downtime lasted an excruciating twenty-three days.[10]

By the end of May, Sony claimed that this hack had put them $171 million in the red.[11] Though Sony never provided data about the financial losses, these events constituted a fiasco, costing Sony money, time, and reputation. Sony executives, eventually called to testify to the US Congress, were reprimanded for their organization's reprehensible security practices and the delays in customer notification. In the UK, Sony was fined nearly £250,000 by the Information Commissioner's Office, which pointed a clear finger of responsibility at the corporation itself:

> If you are responsible for so many payment card details and log-in details then keeping that personal data secure has to be your priority. In this case that just didn't happen, and when the database was targeted—albeit in a determined criminal attack—the security measures in place were simply not good enough.[12]

In the midst of the turmoil, Sony executives attempted to deflect blame onto Anonymous, claiming to have found a file left on the group's server identifying it as the responsible party. But no Anonymous or LulzSec hacker has ever admitted or been charged for this crime (and five of them, along with two associates, have been found guilty of scores of hacking crimes that involved their hard drives being trucked away for forensic analysis). The PSN hack, a mystery in 2011, is still unsolved today.

"Laundering money, funneling bitcoins, PPI scaming, botnets, database dumping"

The drama that surrounded OpSony's fouling of the PlayStation Network provided the immediate context for LulzSec's germination. In mid-April, a few of the hackers on #internetfeds managed to weasel their way into fox.com and steal a sales database. Alongside personal information on Fox employees and journalists, it included over seventy thousand email addresses and passwords for people who had signed up to receive updates about auditions for Fox's forthcoming TV talent show, *The X Factor*. The data also enabled Anons to commandeer a few Fox News Twitter accounts. Since Fox had not done anything egregious recently—aside from continuing to exist—these hackers felt they were in a bind. Dropping dox and corporate data under the aegis of Anonymous would likely draw invective from the rank and file of the collective, which prompted the Anons who had procured the database to think about alternatives. The youngest of the bunch, tflow, was ready with a suggestion, loosely inspired by weev's trolling/ security outfit Goatse Security, which had released data shaming AT&T:

> <tflow>: We should make a competitor to Goatse Security
> <tflow>: that hax for the lulz
> <tflow>: Lulz4u Security
> <pwnsauce>: LOL yes
> <pwnsauce>: tflow have you log from last night??
> <tflow>: which one?
> <pwnsauce>: We needs get shell back
> <pwnsauce>: uhm
> <tflow>: ask X
> <pwnsauce>: i think hes using his phone on this

To introduce the name "LulzSec," tflow whipped out a timeless Internet classic—ASCII art:

```
<tflow>:  ( )   ( )( )( )   (_  )/. |( )( )  / _)( __)/ _)
<tflow>:  )(_  )(_)( )(_  / /_(  _))(_)(  \_ \ )_)( (_
<tflow>:  (___)(_____) (___)(___)  (_)(_____)  (__/(___)\__)
<tflow>: "We did it for the lulz" ~LulzSec
<pwnsauce>: NAICE
<pwnsauce>: make deface page?
```

```
<pwnsauce>: BTW, I was thinking today
<Palladium>: haha
<tflow>: LulzSec, lulz division of the InternetFeds
<Palladium>: i'm more for polictically orintated hacks
<tflow>: yeah
<tflow>: but
<tflow>: what can we do with fox.com?
<tflow>: except for deface it for the lulz?
<tflow>: there's nothing political about it
<tflow>: it's not like when we defaced pm.gov.tn
<pwnsauce>: lol
```

For some reason, tflow's proposal did not immediately catch on. I asked him why and he could not recall. Perhaps there were not enough people online to form a consensus, or perhaps those logged into IRC were distracted with other tasks. There are times when IRC conversations are hard to explain, even in the moment, and it is best not to impute too much linear reasoning to them after the fact. So I'm not even going to try, at least with this one. What we do know is that tflow temporarily quit Anonymous following a fight with a temperamental operator who was about to turn on the AnonOps network. And tflow wasn't the only one. Others also took short leaves of absence, only to return on May 4:

```
<Sabu>: tflow's fine ass is back
<Falcon>: good times
<tflow>: what's new?
<Falcon>: quite a bit tflow, good to see you back
<pwnsauce>: YAY
<Falcon>: this is Topiary by the way
<Sabu>: ;p
<Sabu>: good news is tflow is back
```

Reunited and it felt so good—but wouldn't it feel even better if they had a reason to dump the Fox data? By now the Sony debacle made it doubly clear that random hacks could incur the ire of Anonymous at large, so there was even more pressure not to release the data under the collective name. They contemplated releasing it to 4chan, to "leak it under lowercase-anonymous," as tflow phrased it. Sabu raised the idea of handing the info to *Forbes* reporter Parmy Olson, hoping that "maybe it will push her to write her book." As we writers know, there is nothing like a huge corporate data dump of passwords and emails to put you in the right frame of mind for a bout of writing. (Had they only given *me* the dump, this book would have come out at least a year earlier.) But none of these ideas were really taking hold. Eventually Topiary, who for the last month had kept quiet on AnonOps but was on the secret channels, logged into IRC under the name Falcon. While Sabu suggested leaking it to Olson, Topiary suggested leaking it via the LulzLeaks Twitter account:

<Falcon>: wait, let's leak it under @LulzLeaks
<Falcon>: our twitter

tflow once again raised the name LulzSec, this time a little more forcefully since it hadn't caught on before:

<tflow>: we should establish a pseudo-lulzsec brand imo
<tflow>: like
<Sabu>: also someone contact parmy
<tflow>: Lulz4u Security
<Sabu>: tell her we got a new leak for her
<Sabu>: exclusive
<tflow>: Goatse Security
<pwnsauce>: YES
<pwnsauce>: tflow—I like
<Falcon>: Parmy's sleeping
<Sabu>: wake her ass up
<Sabu>: hahaha
<Sabu>: think of a cool name guys

<Sabu>: quick
<tflow>: Lulz4u Security?

Sabu was impatient:

<Sabu>: well
<Sabu>: why dont we just do this under the anonleaks banner
<Sabu>: ?
<tflow>: because
[...]
<pwnsauce>: I like LulzLeaks and Lulz4u Security

Others objected, again, making a distinction between ethical and unethical leaking:

<tflow>: anonleaks is for ethical leaks
<lol>: :D
<tflow>: :P
<Falcon>: http://twitter.com/#!/LulzLeaks
<lol>: nah :D
<lol>: does it matter?
<Falcon>: LulzLeaks!
<lol>: no hacking and dumping data is ethical xD
<pwnsauce>: we have the LulzLeaks twatter xD
<Falcon>: here's what we should do:
<Falcon>:—upload DB
<Falcon>:—dump on LulzLeaks
<Falcon>:—retweet from official Fox News twitters

After proposing a few other possible names, like "Ninjasec," they ultimately settled on LulzSec. With a name in place, they began discussing the release and artwork:

<Sabu>: Lulz Security / lulzsec
<Falcon>: kind of want to put Batman fucking up a shark as the picture

<Falcon>: but I already burned that one
<Sabu>: lol
<Sabu>: well lets hold onto those for a week or so
<Sabu>: let the x factor leak get attention
<Sabu>: then we'll abuse fox managers/sales
<Sabu>: then we'll embarrass fbi with infragard
<Falcon>: someone get @lulzsec everywhere
<Falcon>: news, /b/, somewhere where it will spread
<Falcon>: AnonOps

When something is new and shiny, it makes sense to trot out an introduction:

<tflow>: write a statement?
<Falcon>: Not sure what we'd write… hmm.
<Falcon>: I guess we could introduce ourselves.
<Falcon>: As LulzSec.

In three minutes, Topiary whipped one out. Then he celebrated with … cookies:

<Falcon>: Hello, good day, and how are you? Splendid! We're LulzSec, a small team of lulzy individuals who feel the drabness of the cyber community is a burden on what matters: fun. Considering fun is now restricted to Friday, where we look forward to the weekend, weekend, we have now taken it upon ourselves to spread fun, fun, fun, throughout the entire calender year. As an introduction, please find…
<Falcon>: …below the X-Factor 2011 contestants' contact information. Expect more to come, and if you're like us and like seeing other people get mad, check out our twitter! twitter.com/LulsSec
<tflow>: perfect
<Falcon>: though that's @LulzSec
<Falcon>: shit son I wrote that off the top of my head in 2 minutes, BRB getting a cookie

Topiary and Sabu offered prescient predictions:

<Sabu>: oh man lol
<Sabu>: this is going to be fun
<Falcon>: LulzSec at its finest
<Falcon>: laundering money, funneling bitcoins, PPI scaming, botnets, database dumping
<Falcon>: the lulz they do go on

All the hype, however, was for naught. The first dump yielded little in the way of media response. LulzSec was still totally unknown; it was Friday after all, a terrible day to release something to the media. And so the hackers, secure in their newfound identity as LulzSec, could turn to the juicy gossip about an AnonOps operator named Ryan Cleary, who had recently gone rogue.

Cleary, who commanded a large botnet, was one of the most unpopular and powerful operators on the AnonOps IRC network. On numerous occasions, I heard complaints about his erratic behavior, like randomly banning participants on the private and public channels. Soon after LulzSec formed, news broke that Cleary had DDoSed the AnonOps network that he once helped administer. He also dropped over six hundred names and IP addresses of IRC network users. (AnonOps had a policy of not retaining IP addresses after someone disconnected, but during the connection, AnonOps had access to the users' IP addresses of all those not cloaked by a VPN.) Why did he do this? After one too many fights with other operators, he had decided to take his revenge. At the same time, according to one of his Anonymous hacker associates, he wanted to impress an underground hacker group called Hack the Planet, better known as simply HTP. From 2011 to 2013, according to a hacker who followed the group, HTP were quite active and in possession of "a large, and impressive, list of stuff." The group has since gone into retirement but HTP had little love for Anonymous, a sentiment made clear in the final sentence of their final zine: "Here's to two years of HTP, everyone. Remember; relax, have fun, be the best, and DDoS Anonymous on sight."[13]

What better way to impress a respected underground hacker group that loathes Anonymous than by sacrificing Anons, some of them your friends? (Later Cleary recanted and was, according to tflow, "jealous of LulzSec and desperately tried to get in, which is why he offered us his botnet.") Petty hacker wars have long been a great asset to law enforcement investigations. Unsurprisingly, after Cleary's dick move, someone loosely affiliated with Anonymous doxed him right back. Nobody knew for certain if the revealed name was correct, but, as with Sabu, time would prove that it was. LulzSec, referenced explicitly in HTP's newsletter, reflected upon the recent events:

> \<Sabu\>: but we need to own ryan
> \<Sabu\>: he violated anonymous very seriously with this
> \<Falcon\>: or something
> \<lol\>: well we got his dox [n]ow
> \<Falcon\>: his voice annoys me

The remaining AnonOps operators, livid at what Cleary had done, released an apologetic statement to the broader Anonymous community and encouraged people to stay the hell away for a while as they went to work assembling a more secure system. This cooldown set the perfect stage for LulzSec to walk into the restless media spotlight.

LulzSec Proper

LulzSec set sail with a cargo hold full from the Fox data dump, a newly minted Twitter account, and bounteous, absurd Internet meme art and statements, as exemplified by the justification given when they ultimately released the Fox data: "You know who we defend? Common. Fox called him a 'vile rapper'; we call Fox common scum. You think we're done? The fun has only just begun."[14] The team was already well accustomed to each crewmember's distinctive rhythms and quirks. They had become so close, in fact, that everyone knew, roughly, where everyone else was logging in from (though real names were never shared). Most were headquartered in or around the UK, except Sabu. Some had even foolishly spoken over Skype, which is how Topiary had determined that Cleary's voice was "annoying."

OpSec, short for operational security, is the art of protecting your group's human and digital interactions. One of the foundations of good OpSec is an awareness of the security level of one's computer and network. Depending on proprietary software packages—opaque in both source code and business practices—can compromise that knowledge. The use of free software, such as GNU/Linux, and the avoidance of tools like Skype (commonly understood to have government backdoors) are necessary measures in the never-ending journey of vigilant OpSec. Keeping personal information private is also a central pillar of OpSec. If you volunteer this information, it doesn't matter how secure your software and hardware might be. All of these considerations, and more, need to be managed before any hacker rampage—anything less is simply asking to be caught. Which is to say (with a few exceptions), OpSec was not one of LulzSec's strongest points. In fact, following the eventual spate of LulzSec arrests, their practices would become a model, for other hackers and activists, of just what *not* to do.

But these worries were far on the horizon, and the sea appeared vast—even infinite. Over the next month and a half, LulzSec's accomplishments would prove riveting. One might assume that I am referring to its technical inventiveness. In fact, with a few clever exceptions, LulzSec hacks were most notable for their audacity and style, and not for their rocket science.

LulzSec's true importance came in its ability to force a much deeper recognition and debate about a range issues from the pathetic state of Internet security to the insatiable appetites of media sensationalism.

"Why we secretly love LulzSec" (Not So Secretly, Actually)

Not all hackers held warm and fuzzy feelings for Anonymous. Its interventions were often too technically unsophisticated to garner craft respect. Some hackers felt that its tactics damaged the larger cause of Internet freedom, while others viewed its antics as puerile. And for some hackers the general style of disruptive activism, however interesting, was simply not their cup of tea. But with LulzSec it was a different story. A surprising number of hackers, especially security hackers, adored the new group, or at least held an ambivalent respect. To understand why, allow me to offer a portrait of this subset of hacker by recounting my own introduction to the type.

Before the rise of LulzSec, I became acquainted with the InfoSec community in New York City, largely through force majeure. Apparently I had offended some security hackers by anointing, in writing, open-source developers—programmers who release their source code with permissive licenses—as hackers. In the wake of such a debasing "mistake," security researchers, who also call themselves hackers, reached out to me in various ways—from constructive suggestions and discussion invitations, to creepy jeers and intimidating threats. They wanted to educate me about what "real" hackers were: themselves. You think a DIY, remote-controlled toaster running on a twenty-five dollar, open-source computer called Raspberry Pi constitutes hacking? Nope, sorry. Or how about programming LED blinky throwies, which you plan on distributing at a rave? Nope again. These may be cool and useful gadgets that require technical proficiency—and they certainly might be blinky—but they are not HACKING. Hacking, they would tell me, is digital trespass: breaking into a system, owning it hard, doing what you want with it. I had recently published my book on free software "hackers," *Coding Freedom: The Ethics and Aesthetics of Hacking*, and it seemed that these InfoSec word warriors thought I had a narrow understanding of the term, one that omitted their world. But, my understanding of the term is much more nuanced than they realized. My definition includes free software programmers, people who make things, and *also* people who compromise systems—but that doesn't mean they have to all be talked about at the same time. My first book was narrowly focused.

Interestingly, while each microcommunity claims the moniker "hacker," some always refute the attempts of other microcommunities to claim the term. So when InfoSec people started yelling at me that free software "hackers" weren't "hackers," I wasn't surprised. I actually appreciated the productive discussions—much more than the veiled threats.

Sometime in 2010 an email arrived in my inbox from a respected hacker encouraging me to attend NYSEC, the informal New York City gathering of security professionals and hackers held monthly at a bar. Or as their Twitter bio describes it, "A drinking meet-up with an information security problem." I figured why not. This was the cordial way of telling me: *get real, start hanging out with real hackers*. Others were less amicable. One of these "hackers" contacted me by email to generously offer me his entire collection of the hacker zine *2600* for my research. I was excited to add the zines to my personal library, and we met at a tiny New York City cafe. Upon broaching the subject of my book, he became agitated, huffing that "configuring Linux is not hacking." This gentleman, who was probably almost forty-five years old, was so upset that he abruptly got up and left. Gentle, compared to the time when a hacker found me online and warned me that he had just witnessed a slew of hackers scheming over IRC to hack into my computer—to teach me a lesson about what real hackers do. Nothing like a show-and-tell hack to make a point. Freaked out, I locked down my systems enough to secure myself and I suspect that the acquaintance who warned me might have convinced the zealous hackers to cool their loins.

Of course, not every security hacker is diametrically opposed to extending the label to free/open-source software developers. Many hackers who deal in matters of security use and write open-source software themselves. One such hacker based in Montreal, David Mirza, has spent countless hours teaching me about the complicated aesthetics and politics of the hacker underground. Formerly in the black hat scene, he now runs an InfoSec company and is an unflagging proponent of open-source software.

But there are differences, important ones. Many of these hackers who work as contractors or on security for governments or corporations constantly face Herculean challenges when securing software applications, operating systems, servers, and networked systems. To truly secure a system means, at a minimum, to occupy the mindset of every possible infiltrator. Often this means engaging in intrusion oneself. This is why many of the best security hackers are former black hats who still might, on occasion, dabble in activity residing in legal gray zones. InfoSec hackers tend to be a touch paranoid, and it is no wonder why. You would be too if you spent most of your waking hours refining your own intrusion capabilities while simultaneously fending off credit card scammers, Russian Business Network associates, Bulgarian virus writers, Chinese state hackers, and the hundreds of other bad actors who actively seek to access valuable systems. Hackers whose ensure security bear the burden of paranoia so the rest of us can sleep a little better at night. (But don't rest too soundly; their advice is often not heeded.)

Anyone who has hung out with hackers knows that when it comes to technology, all types of hackers are unabashed snobs. This stance is not unique to security hackers vs. free software evangelists, nor is it unique to hackers more generally. Vocational arrogance is common to craftspeople—doctors, professors, academics, journalists, and furniture makers. It is simple: the fine art of haughtiness pushes one to do better. However (and for reasons that still mostly elude me), when compared to other activities that might also be considered "hacking," security specialists take elitism to incomparable heights. Praise does not flow easy from the lips of these InfoSec men and woman.

Combining this simplified picture with a recognition of InfoSec's historical derision of Anonymous allows us to more fully appreciate why the security community's adoration of LulzSec is all the more remarkable. The following 2011 Halloween photo might best sum it up:[15]

Dressed as LulzSec, these New York City–based hackers were not only living large and having a grand time—they were also giving mad props to the rebel, misfit hackers. While all the characteristics of the LulzSec mythology are represented, there is one additional element that may not be so obvious: the lack of pants. Many considered LulzSec to be pointing, in badass Internet style, to the fact that the Emperor Has No Clothes. Since forever, security professionals have been yelling from the top of a lonely, wind-swept, barren mountaintop about the dire need for organizations to invest more resources, energy, time, and personnel toward better security. LulzSec, it seemed, had finally found a way to get people to listen.

One may wonder why security is so weak in a sector so large and profitable. After all, cyber (fear) sells.[16] Not only does the industry regularly sell software scams (such as out-of-the-box software solutions that cannot be configured to address the risk profiles unique to an institution), or products intended to replace a dedicated security team that can do more harm than good, but the initial desire for security itself remains a low priority for many firms, even well-funded ones. A New York City–based security hacker explained: "One of the challenges in security is how to get people to take it seriously because at the executive level it just looks like an expense." The fact that Sony—a multinational corporation —could get pillaged with such impunity in 2011 is an indicator of the depth and nature of the problems. Cases like these make hackers who create secure systems completely furious.

LulzSec, more than any other person, report, or group in recent memory, managed to convey a message that many security professionals had been unsuccessfully pitching for over two decades. The effects were similar to the antagonistic antics of L0pht Heavy Industries, a loose association of hackers who regularly met in person. In 1998, during a group conversation, a couple of them coined the term "gray hat" to describe hackers who are ambiguously—and deliberately— situated between the black and white labels that had come to distinguish malicious hackers from more benevolent ones. "Gray hat" hackers are not above acting illegally, but typically they do so only to identify, and publicize, vulnerabilities. L0pht became so successful that in May 1998, seven of its members were invited to testify (in semi-theatrical fashion) to the Committee on Governmental Affairs chaired by Republican Senator Fred Thompson. With his refined, somber, and heavy Tennessee accent, Senator Thompson introduced the "hacker think tank" and explained that "due to the sensitivity of the work done at the L0pht, they will be using their hacker handles: Mudge, Weld, Brian Oblivion, Kingpin, Space Rogue, Tan, and Stefan."[17] Muffled laughter rippled through the chambers, likely because hacker handles were superfluous: C-SPAN recorded the testimony and the hackers were unmasked. Their remarks addressed numerous topics, but the claim that they could take down the entire Internet in thirty minutes jumped out from the rest. This was meant not as a threat. It was a plea to improve the abysmal state of Internet security in 1998.

L0pht's testimony to Congress was deferential; many of the participants wore suits, and an effort was made to present broadly intelligible explanations. LulzSec was not invited to visit Congress—nor could they take down the Internet—but in the course of their errant questing they managed to deliver a similar message. They made people pay attention to the sordid state of Internet security—not by offering a carefully constructed testimonial, but in the mere course of their travels in search of adventure (which happened to include over a dozen high-profile hacks along the way). They did so in the face of US laws, like the CFAA, that were designed to punish any hacker who got caught, regardless of motivation. LulzSec's gutsy hacks against corporate giants and government agencies, now the stuff of legend, were quite effective—maybe even necessary—to get people to wake up.

Many security experts I interviewed directly cited LulzSec's role in making high-level executives heed their messages, at least for a short while (2013 saw a string of massive data breaches: Adobe, Target, Neiman Marcus, LivingSocial, the Washington State Administrative Office of the Courts, Evernote, Drupal.org, the US Federal Reserve, OKCupid ... the list goes on).[18] A 2011 blog post by security researcher and journalist Patrick Gray entitled "Why We Secretly Love LulzSec" was widely read among security professionals and captured their prevailing mood. He explained to me the impact of his piece: "It picked up more buzz than anything I'd ever written, including pieces for ZDNet/CNet, *The Sydney*

Morning Herald, The Age, Wired ... I've written plenty of news stories that went big globally, but this was something entirely different." In the piece, Gray wrote:

> It might be surprising to external observers, but security professionals are also secretly getting a kick out of watching these guys go nuts ... The mainstrem media are having fun criticizing Sony for its poor security, but do we honestly think for a second that the XBox Live network can't be similarly pwnt? (I know the PSN breach hasn't been pinned on LulzSec, but the point stands.) Is there any target out there that can't be "gotten"?[19]

Even if the innumerable security problems plaguing the Internet could not be magically fixed, it was still satisfying to call out the "elephant in the room," as Gray tagged it.

LulzSec's spectacle also revealed the hypocritical charade of many firms, as they performed strange acrobatics to shift blame. A New York City–based security researcher who prefers to remain anonymous explained:

> One thing I think is interesting is that these people [corporations] are getting owned every day, but their info isn't getting splattered all over the Internet. It's usually getting owned by people doing it for profit. The irony is that when people are stealing intellectual property for financial advantage, they won't do anything about it ... I think it's ironic now that LulzSec is making people eat their vegetables.

This position was echoed by Chris Wysopal, one of the original members of L0pht, who now runs a well-respected security firm:

> Corporations take public embarrassment more seriously than stolen intellectual property. The Sony attacks sent chills down the spines of Fortune 100 CISOs and their boards. We

had customers come to us and literally say, "I don't want to be another Sony." They scanned thousands of websites and remediated hundreds of critical vulnerabilities so that didn't happen to them. In this way, LulzSec made the Internet more resilient. In some ways it is like an immunization giving your immune system a taste of the virus that would otherwise kill you and force your immune system to work to build protection.

LulzSec's popularity among security types exceeded its practical role of forcing executives to "eat their vegetables." Its rich but accessible visual vocabulary incarnated the subversive pleasure and magic of hacking, so often left invisible. You may think that making or breaking, exploiting or building, securing and pen-testing cannot involve artistry, creative expression, and pleasure—but this is exactly what these technologists experience: bliss (along with the type of agonizing frustration that only makes the bliss doubly potent in its overcoming). Conveying the nature of this gratification to outsiders is next to impossible, because the technical craft is so esoteric. LulzSec's publicized antics are the most accurate representation I have ever seen of the look, feel, and sensibilities that attend the pleasures of hacking. And each piece of LulzSec's iconography symbolizes the sensual and ideological sides of this world: the boat (standing for the pirate freedom of the high seas), the man with the monocle and suit (snooty l33t hacker), the cat (because if it is related to the Internet, there must be felines), the music (hacking to music is always preferable to doing the deed in silence), manifestos (free expression, dammit!), and law breaking (because rules, fuck them). LulzSec embodied the pleasure of hacking and subversion like no other group. LulzSec also represented a site of longing and fantasy. What the team did so blatantly was something many hackers *wished* they were doing. Some had certainly experienced the same illicit pleasures in days gone by, when the world of computing first opened up to them through exploration and tinkering—but this was typically done without a massive global audience.

Now, not all hackers adored the crew. HTP, the group that loved to pwn Anonymous, extended its loathing to LulzSec. As one LulzSec member who went by the name pwnsauce put it, "HTP saw us as attention-whoring fucknuggets, basically." HTP's viewpoint reflects a long-held ethos in the hacker underground, one that drives some hackers to snub those seeking attention from the mainstream press (attention is anathema to staying out of the "clink"—and LulzSec's failure proved the wisdom of this folk ethos). Even if LulzSec hackers did not do many interviews, they were nevertheless doing everything possible to land major stories by drawing as much attention to themselves as possible. They once did so by attacking the media itself.

Media

Anonymous may not ever have (readily) nominated any individuals to speak on its behalf, but it hosted an IRC channel, #reporter, where dozens of journalists interviewed participants. LulzSec was more secretive, offering no public channel for journalistic access and giving almost no interviews in general (except to Parmy Olson and, occasionally, Steve Ragan). There was no celebrity to showcase, except the group itself. Nevertheless, by the end of June 2011, LulzSec had become something like hacker rock stars. This foray into celebrity territory drew some furrowed eyebrows from the broader Anonymous community, but, for the most part, there was enough distance—LulzSec repeatedly confirmed its autonomy—that even the pseudonymous collective from which LulzSec broke away could enjoy the show without feeling that it affected its own mores and ethical sensibilities.

LulzSec, unlike AnonOps, clawed at the media. Its major hack against the press was directed against PBS in retaliation for its Frontline film on WikiLeaks, *WikiSecrets*. The documentary drew the ire of LulzSec members, notably Sabu, who disliked the film for how it skirted the pressing political issues raised by Cablegate in favor of a sensationalist psychoanalyzing of the "dark" inner life of Chelsea Manning. LulzSec launched a two-pronged campaign. They dumped the personal data of PBS staff and defaced its website, leaving a clever article that could *almost* pass as real (see figure overleaf).

Even if the article was destined (and designed) to be understood as a fake, it worked as a hoax. Perhaps because the scenario was hypothetically plausible, Topiary (its writer) sprinkled the article with giveaways. The proposed source of information—a hand-written diary—was absurdly quaint by today's standards. And the most unbelievable nugget was the suggestion that law enforcement was in on the arrangement—not only because privacy is in short supply for celebrities, but because privacy itself has been nonexistent for a long time. Just in case you were fooled, the story's kicker jolts you back to reality with the nonsensical statement "yank up as a vital obituary" (an anagram of the handles of the LulzSec members who participated in the hack, Topiary, Sabu, Kayla, Avunit), and a reference to the diary-writer's girlfriend, Penny—named after none other than HBGary's president.

While some were disturbed by an attack directed at the media, the Twitter frenzy as the story spread mostly showed adulation. The allure of this act can be explained if we turn to an anthropological definition of defacement provided in Michael Taussig's striking book on the topic: "Defacement works on objects the way jokes work on language, bringing out their inherent magic nowhere more so than when those objects have become routinized."[20] LulzSec laid bare the subject of celebrity by defacing a media object—the journalistic article—with a strong dose of humor.

Every major Western news establishment ran a piece about the bogus article, and most skimmed over the part about the ethically questionable data breach. The political motivation

TUPAC STILL ALIVE IN NEW ZEALAND

Prominent rapper Tupac has been found alive and well in a small resort in New Zealand, locals report. The small town—unnamed due to security risks—allegedly housed Tupac and Biggie Smalls (another rapper) for several years. One local, David File, recently passed away, leaving evidence and reports of Tupac's visit in a diary, which he requested be shipped to his family in the United States.

"We were amazed to see what David left behind," said one of sisters, Jasmine, aged 31. "We thought it best to let the world know as we feel this doesn't deserve to be kept secret."

David, aged 28, was recently the victim of a hit-and-run by local known gangsters. Having suffered several bullet wounds on his way home from work, David was announced dead at the scene. Police found the diary in a bedside drawer.

"Naturally we didn't read the diary," one officer states. "We merely noted the request to have it sent to a US address, which we did to honor the wishes of David."

Officials have closed down routes into the town and will not speculate as to whether Tupac or Biggie have been transported to another region or country. Local townsfolk refuse to comment on exactly how long or why the rappers were being sheltered; one man simply says "we don't talk about that here."

The family of David File have since requested that more action be taken to arrest those responsible for the shooting. "David was a lovely, innocent boy," reported his mother. "When he moved to New Zealand, he'd never been happier."

His brother Jason requested that one part of David's diary be made public in an attempt to decipher it. "Near the end," Jason says, "there's a line that reads 'yank up as a vital obituary', which we've so far been unable to comprehend."

David's girlfriend, Penny, did not wish to make a statement."

MAKE A COMMENT (o)   RETWEET   FACEBOOK   BUZZ   SHARE

behind the hack received only cursory treatment, even though LulzSec published an explicit statement rationalizing its actions. This was a further (and ironic) demonstration of the mainstream media's proclivity for sensationalizing issues—the very behavior exhibited by the WikiLeaks documentary that prompted the operation in the first place.

"We futurescan"

One might think that the corporate response to LulzSec, and by extension Anonymous, was wholly negative. In reality, it was a little more complicated. Starting in the fall of 2011 and peaking in 2012, various individuals and institutions situated in and around the highest echelons of the corporate world began to contact me. I spoke with the founding partner of a venture capitalist firm in New York City, the head of European security for Vodafone, and a senior vice president from TTI/Vanguard (self-described as "a unique forum for senior-level executives that links strategic technology planning to business success"). I gave two talks (one virtual) for an NYU global risk and security group that included chief security officers (CSOs) and other executives from major corporations. Finally I participated at an event run by "World 50," an organization that convenes events for senior executives of mostly Fortune 500 companies.

The list would be incomplete without mentioning my 2012 talk at TEDGlobal in Edinburgh, Scotland. While TED's online videos reach a popular audience of millions, the conference itself is primarily attended by wealthy elites—with the exception of some of the speakers, such as myself, and select attendees who receive financial aid from TED. The privilege of attending TED costs roughly $6,000. Of course, one has to be chosen first (you have to apply). This does not include the costs of travel or accommodations, but it does grant access to some fancy parties featuring copious food and drink, concerts, highly curated TED talks, and the opportunity to converse with some famous and fascinating people (or their assistants, at least). After my talk, Will Smith's personal assistant struck up a conversation with me, making a vigorous attempt to convince me that his boss, who is rumored to be a Scientologist, is actually an avid fan of Anonymous. Was he social-engineering me in an attempt to protect his boss from a potentially career-damaging attack by Anonymous, or did we really just randomly bump into each other?

That was pretty tame compared to another memorable encounter. While sampling the delicious snacks during one of the breaks, a Fortune 500 executive snuck up on me, clutched my arm—rather too tightly, I felt—and, clearly projecting his anxiety onto me, whispered loudly into my ear: "You are *sooooooo* brave to study Anonymous." Just the day before, I had visited a local Anon and his partner. The highlight was touring their garden, where I saw their beehive, followed by a very tasty home-cooked meal of pheasant and sweet potato mash. Afterwards, we watched the documentary *We Are Legion: The Story of the Hacktivists* and his partner was rather floored to learn that there was actually some political substance to Anonymous. All this time, she had thought he had been messing around on his computer engaging in purely juvenile acts. After this gentle experience with a "dreaded" Anon, I found it hard to roll over for this executive's praises of bravery and courage. *I guess I could have been stung by a bee?* I thought to myself.

At one level, these men and women struck me as regular folk. They complained about their spoiled sons and daughters, the exorbitant cost of higher education in the United States, and (some of them, at least—a naturalized Canadian, now that I remember) the lack of universal health care in the United States. Many even engaged in a time-honored workplace pastime: railing against their immediate overseer. Of course, in this milieu, that usually happened to be the CEO of a mega corporation. But make no mistake: during the World

50 event held at the Contemporary Jewish Museum in San Francisco, I heard two twenty-something caterers mutter to each other, not caring that I could plainly overhear, that "it is a different world in there." Take the name tags were were given at the event. These weren't some piece-of-paper-shoved-in-a-plastic-sleeve-with-some-kind-of-branding lanyards. These looked like they came straight out of Restoration Hardware (a high-end American furniture store). Made of metal, the clasp was powered by a magnet. In a pinch, you could probably use one as a ninja throwing star. Sadly, I only used mine to identify myself. After acquiring my name tag and a lunch of seared tuna and other delicacies, we were moved upstairs to an airy, sun-drenched private room decked out with plush chairs for talks, which ranged in subject from massive open online courses (or MOOCs) to Anonymous (mine, of course). In the audience were executives from AstraZeneca, Cargill, Hewlett-Packard, Hilton Worldwide, Huawei Technologies, Hyatt Hotels, Juniper Networks, Monsanto, Rio Tinto, The Coca-Cola Company, and Tiffany & Co. Even though lunch had just been provided, there was an impressive ensemble of snacks and drinks, including beautiful glasses full of M&Ms and ten beverage choices. After the talks, everyone was whisked away to a dinner at a restaurant overlooking the Bay Bridge, which started with an intimate talk by Steve Martin.

Not surprisingly, corporate executives, especially from blue chip companies, wanted nothing more than for someone to wave a wand and make both Anonymous and LulzSec disappear. Executives from technology companies seemed curious and, if nothing else, at least familiar with Anonymous's involvement in a range of political movements. Sometimes they were even interested to learn about Anonymous's role in the Arab Spring. Executives from financial and energy firms tended to be frosty, while those from other industries showed curious mixtures of disgust and fear. One head of communications for a low-cost airline jokingly wished Anonymous would hack her company—the free publicity would be stellar.

What was less expected was a query that I received about Anonymous's potential contribution to the corporate world. TTI/Vanguard approached me to assess whether I could give a talk along these lines to its clients, such as Royal Dutch Shell, Northrop Grumman, Toyota, FedEx, and Expedia. I discovered that TTI/Vanguard was primarily involved in "futurescanning." Apparently, "TTI/Vanguard heightens thinking about technological possibilities. We futurescan. We focus on unanticipated sources of change and evaluate their transformative promise. In dynamic, highly interactive sessions, debate is stimulated and breakthrough ideas flourish."[21]

This is the culture that adopts "disruptive" strategies for the attention economy, for capital gain. Anonymous and LulzSec disrupted in the classical way—without clarification. Sometimes they even fucked shit up. They also demonstrated the importance of art, expression, autonomy, and creation through unalienated labor. Most multinational companies are not compatible with these ideals; they cannot implement these lessons, at least not in a fulfilling and honest way.

TTI/Vanguard's mission statement marked my first exposure to "futurescanning," but then it started popping up everywhere. The most surprising of the bunch came during a phone call with Chris Anderson, the head of TED, prior to the summer event in Edinburgh. He asked whether my talk could include some practical insight for corporate management. Though his request was subtle, it was clear he wanted me to relay a (hyper-inspirational, astonishing, disruptive) lesson from the trenches of Anonymous that could upend conventional wisdom and embolden corporate thinking. Until then, I had worked mostly with TED's other curator, Bruno Giussani. TED vets everything down to the word—he asked me to nix the word "homeland" since it was too politically charged. That said, Giussani was otherwise hands off, offering helpful suggestions that I could adopt or reject. Frankly, I was surprised by Anderson's query. It was clear that if I adopted the corporate lingo, and came up with some whiz-bang way of packaging Anonymous using shallow, amazing-sounding, paradigm-shifting phrases combined with confusing techno-babble, all delivered with breathless enthusiasm, I would have the perfect formula to inspire in these corporate drones the feeling of being in on some mind-blowing insights. And then I could make a lot of money running around bullshitting people until the next paradigm rolled over.

These exchanges gave me a fresh perspective on a contemporary vector of co-optation. Academics who write about the subject have often approached it from the angles of advertising, entertainment, and consumerism—the classic example being Dick Hebdige's seminal analysis of the commodification of punk rock.[22] Countercultural forces of critique, of which punk rock was emblematic, are devitalized when channeled through the corporate advertising apparatus, or turned into commodities through the processing mechanisms of Hollywood or the fashion industry. What I always found interesting about Anonymous was how it had, at least until recently,[23] resisted these forces for one primary reason: most corporations are wary of commodifying Anonymous because they know how direct the repercussions might be. In fact, the case of Anonymous is a curious one in which the opposite process more often occurs; though it is true that Time Warner makes a buck whenever someone buys an official Guy Fawkes mask (Time Warner holds the copyright to the *V for Vendetta* movie), Anonymous has taken a symbol popularized by Hollywood and made it revolutionary. It is a prime example of counter-commodification, a rare occurance.

But if there's one lesson from the corporate execs, it's this: even if they aren't about to claim Anonymous's imagery for their next advertising campaign, it doesn't mean they can't, or won't, find some way to appropriate *something* about Anonymous. If someone can find an uncapitalized, exploitable, futurescanned, innovative, disruptive idea that can flourish in corporate boardrooms, they will. This move, while distinct from more familiar forms of co-optation—since the knowledge transfer may not (necessarily) alter the phenomenon being scrutinized—is still worth understanding a little better. There is a pervasive cottage industry (in the form of think tanks, organizations, and motivational speakers, many from academia, especially pundits who love to inflate the promise of technology) that exists to capture wisdom from every corner of the globe (from gang culture to the Arab Spring) and convert it into a formula for corporate success. This is done so that corporate executives can keep abreast of global challenges, feel great about what they do, strengthen corporate cultural machinery, and make a lot of money off of culture that they don't have to invest in. I suspect in some instances, when corporate executives hone in on a phenomenon like open source, they not only harvest insights for their corporations, but have the power to recalibrate public opinion on the topic. We know very little about the reach of these networks and the possible effects that "futurescanning" might aggregate. It is a subject that would certainly be worth understanding better. Maybe we need to "futurescan" futurescanning ourselves.

"I tell you: one must still have chaos within oneself, to give birth to a dancing star"

LulzSec was not only embraced and celebrated by hackers. It was also widely popular among Internet geeks, political activists, and academics, along with a host of other unmarked spectators. To understand why, it helps to look to the nineteenth-century German philosopher Friedrich Nietzsche, whose investments in questioning truth and morality, elevating pleasure over reason, and embracing cunning and hyperbole can be used (playfully and experimentally) to form the intellectual scaffolding for the work LulzSec and Anonymous did

150 years later. (Indeed, had Nietzsche been teleported into the future and developed a knack for hacking, I suspect he just might have joined LulzSec.)

Nietzsche took the Enlightenment project of critique so much to heart that he turned out to be one of its unremitting critics—helping to inaugurate a more general project of radical philosophy, which would be expanded upon in the twentieth century by a cohort of writers, most famously Gilles Deleuze, Félix Guattari, and Michel Foucault. We might even think of Nietzsche as the Enlightenment's trickster. The objects of his critique were rationality, progress, God, science, and the way that ideas or systems based on absolutist tropes—whether proclaiming truth in science or God—become, in earning wide adoption, more resistant to critique and more capable of binding humans in their grips. For Nietzsche, nothing should be de facto granted or a priori assumed: neither good and evil, nor true and false. Every piece of knowledge that humans conceive of, make, or even discover by looking at the world is, according to Nietzsche, provisional, rooted in judgment, and, though often seeming timeless or natural, understandable only within a specific historical moment.

Nietzsche sought to dismantle the ideological stronghold of truth, rationality, and conventional moral systems for complex reasons. Suffice to say, for our purposes, that he wanted to highlight how the mantle of truth exerts a monopolistic force. Truth implies right, better, and good. Anything sanctioned as truth then works to devalue other domains of creation and experience, like art and myth, which lie outside the orbit of "truth" and are thus slotted in the category of "falsehood." In this ideological binary, art becomes a second-class citizen in the public life of ideas, while fantasy and myth are hardly even allowed to join the party.

Nietzsche was attuned to the vitality of sensuality, myth, and art. Music, poetry, and even the mad laughter of the trickster Dionysus, who he championed, offer an aesthetic life of pleasure.[24] They are pursuits through which humans can overcome their limits and the tragic condition of life: "Not by wrath does one kill but by laughter. Come, let us kill the spirit of gravity!"[25]

More than any other political movement in recent times, Anonymous, and especially its LulzSec offshoot, gives forceful social shape to a number of these Nietzschean philosophical themes. If Nietzsche argued that nothing is sacred, and advocated for a life of enchantment, then LulzSec and Anonymous lived these maxims out. They dared to subvert and break formal law, etiquette, and mores, and experimented with the art of transgression. They reminded us: to make life into art, and art into life, you sometimes need to break rules.

And breaking rules is a difficult task. Back when I taught a course in Communication and Culture, I used to have my undergraduate students violate a norm in public and report back on their experiences. With the exception of one or two eccentrics, who rather enjoyed the assignment (one of them recounted gleefully that her mother walked her by leash and collar, like a dog, on the streets of New York City—and barely anyone batted an eye), it was an extraordinarily hard, even painful, exercise. In fact, a good quarter of the class broke rules in ways that hardly constituted "daring" at all, like asking someone at a cafe whether they could sit at their table.

The pressure to conform to conventions and accept given wisdom is enormous—and often for good reason. Much of Nietzsche's corpus laid bare this tendency and warned of its pernicious effects, which is what the trickster myths address, time and again, albeit in different form. Indeed, one of Nietzsche's most famous characters, Zarathustra, is a trickster-like figure. Living as a hermit for a decade in the mountains, he comes to the realization that one can overcome social mores in favor of self-defined desires and ideas. He descends to share this insight, advocating a process he calls "self-overcoming." Anonymous and LulzSec have existed as instantiations of Zarathustra. LulzSec went a step further than Anonymous, breaking even the rules that had inadvertently taken root in

Anonymous itself, thus posing a challenge to even this emergent order.

It is rare for something actually resembling the trickster myth to come into being in the midst of our contemporary reality, much less with such panache and public presence. These hackers, in their sacrifice (and sacrifice of others), served to remind many of the necessity, pleasure, and danger of subversion.

The awe many felt toward Anonymous and LulzSec can be illuminated by Walter Benjamin's insight regarding the great criminal who, "however repellent his ends may have been, has aroused the secret admiration of the public."[26] This admiration stems from the fact that criminality reveals the limits of the state's monopoly on violence and the force of the law. But LulzSec and Anonymous fundamentally exceeded the frame of criminality—even if they were unable to entirely escape its orbit. LulzSec and Anonymous, in contrast to criminal outfits, were not out for private gain, and in the case of Anonymous, there has been significant social pressure to mute self-interest, personal fame, and recognition. Anonymous performed the broader, Nietzschean lesson embodied in Zarathustra: to act out the secret desire to cast off—at least momentarily—the shackles of normativity and attain greatness—the will to power set to collectivist and altruistic goals rather then self-interested and individualistic desires. Anonymous and LulzSec's artistic chaos, to paraphrase Nietzsche, gave birth to a dancing star. If you think I am overtly romantic about LulzSec and this era of Anonymous, you may be right. But the events that followed ensured this honeymoon phase was shortlived. We can now turn to the death of LulzSec and the rise of AntiSec, and see how this stunning mythos went awry when Anonymous was partially eclipsed by a cult of personality.

CHAPTER 9

AntiSec

One day in February 2011, a twenty-six-year-old Chicago hacker logged onto the AnonOps IRC server and said to himself, "Now here is a productive conversation." Anonymous was in the midst of targeting the notorious Koch brothers, major donors to Wisconsin's Republican governor, Scott Walker. That frigid winter, activists all over the state had marched from the farms and factories into the state's capitol in protest of Governor Walker, who was pushing for a bill that would strip away state employees' rights to collective bargaining. This hacker watched as Anonymous DDoSed the Koch-funded free-market advocacy group Americans for Prosperity.

It was also frigid in Chicago. Whirling around corners and howling down corridors, the powerful winter wind gripped the city. This hacker, Jeremy Hammond, had barely been logged on for twenty minutes before losing his Internet connection. He sighed and pulled his six-foot, lanky body from his chair and shuffled outside. He stood on the back stoop, his fingers numb from the cold, as he desperately tried to adjust the Wi-Fi antenna. His laptop sat connected to the antenna, running "aircrack-ng," which was busy doing its best to break into his neighbor's wireless network. Hammond stood still. He knew that even the most minor movement could affect the wireless signal. It was 3 am, and he was freezing. Going inside wouldn't help; there hadn't been heat in the house for months. With the Internet connection finally reestablished, he returned to IRC, and was bathed in the blue light from his laptop for hours.

As Hammond read everything he could about Anonymous's latest activist jaunts, something tugged at his soul. He identified with Anonymous and he wanted to be a part of it. Hammond was a fiery political activist; without a doubt he was—and remains—one of the most prolific, adamant, unwavering American hacktivists to have ever typed on a keyboard. By his early twenties, direct action had already become a way of life; between the ages of eighteen and twenty-eight, he was arrested eight times during political protests. At the 2004 Republican National Convention, held in New York City, he was scooped up during a drum-banging protest; the following year, he rallied against a neo-Nazi group in Toledo, Ohio, and was arrested for violating an injunction preventing street protests. More recently, in 2010, after burning an Olympic banner to protest Chicago's bid for the 2016 games, he was sentenced to eighteen months' probation and 130 hours of community service. Hammond proudly calls himself an anarchist because he believes passionately in "leaderless collectives based on free association, consensus, mutual aid, self-sufficiency, and harmony with the environment."[1]

By summer 2011, with the snow long gone, he was actively compromising servers and websites for political purposes. It was fateful for him, for a little more than a year later he would be under arrest and headed toward a decade-long sentence in federal prison. Hammond told me about both his previous hacktivism and involvement with Anonymous in September 2013, during our first, and only, face-to-face meeting, at the Metropolitan Correctional Center in New York City where he was locked up awaiting sentencing. After his arrest in March 2012, we had communicated through old-fashioned paper and stamped envelopes (Hammond placed his stamps upside down). When I met him, he was wearing an oversized brown canvas jumpsuit draped over a body that no longer bore the lanky traces of his programming past. His bulging forearms—the most visible indication of the sixty pounds of muscle he had acquired in prison—rested on a brown table in the barren detainee meeting room. A soundtrack was provided by the buzzing and clicking of the fluorescent lights, their glare bouncing off the white cinder blocks. Having already sucked all aesthetic warmth from the room, the administrators found a way to make it even worse—by making it freezing.

In this delightful ambiance, as Hammond told me more and more about his past, it became increasingly clear that his technical skills had been sharpened specifically for their political capabilities.

Growing up with his twin brother and father in the immediate outskirts of Chicago, he was barely out of the crib when he began toying with computer games. By age ten, he graduated to programming his own games in QBasic on a black-and-white 10MHz laptop with MS-DOS6 and Windows 3.1. He got online soon after, setting up an IRC channel for game development. He also discovered and devoured hacker literary genres, like textfiles (also known as philes) and zines. Typically, these texts, "which teach the techniques and ethos of the underground," as Bruce Sterling notes, "are prized reservoirs of forbidden knowledge."[2]

Most exhibit strong anti-authoritarian or edgy overtones, which are patently evident in their titles:

Hacking Bank America CHHACK.ZIP
Chilton Hacking CITIBANK.ZIP
Hackers Digest HACK.ZIP
Phortune 500 Guide to Unix RADHACK.ZIP
Radio Hacking TAOTRASH.DOC
Anarchist Book ANARCHY.ZIP
Barbiturate Formula BLCKPWDR.ZIP
Electronic Terror EXPLOS1.ZIP

Briefcase Locks NAPALM.ZIP
More Pranks to Pull on Idiots! REVENGE.ZIP[3]

Hammond ate this material up and (incorrectly) assumed that most other hackers shared his political sensibilities. It wasn't until high school, when he started to attend the local 2600 meetings, that he experienced a bit of a rude awakening. He remembers most of the participants as "super white hats" whose politics lay nowhere near his nascent anticapitalist sensibilities. But, because he also self-identified as a hacker, he enjoyed attending these meetings. He saw the utility of learning from these people.

And then, as he explained, he was further politicized a little later, when "Bush stole the election, 9/11 happened, and the Patriot Act was passed." At the age of twenty, he cofounded a radical website called *Hack This Site* with a corollary zine called *Hack This Zine*. This titles riff off *Steal This Book,* the 1960s counterculture manual-manifesto written by Abbie Hoffman. (The Yippies published the first hacker/phreak zine, *The Youth International Party Line*, which advocated ripping off AT&T, aka "Ma Bell," as a revolutionary act. Its successor publication, *Technical Assistance Program* (TAP), would shed the overtly leftist political rhetoric.) *Hack This Site* covered computer security but also delved into radical political trends and events from around the globe, like the movement against the war in Afghanistan and the potential threats to democracy posed by computer-based voting machines.

Even if Hammond was an anomaly in the American hacker scene, there were enough kindred souls around the globe to constitute a small, but feisty, band of radical tech warriors. His zine helped breed a cohort of left-leaning hackers. In fact, one of LulzSec's most politically minded hackers, Donncha O'Cearbhaill, aka Palladium, had been a reader before he and Hammond met online. And when Hammond wasn't writing for the zine, he was channeling his technical skills more directly toward his political goals.

In the course of one of his earliest hacks, before he was involved in Anonymous—indeed, before Anonymous even existed as a name to channel activist causes—Hammond left the image of Guy Fawkes on a defaced website. As he briefly touched upon his Guy Fawkes defacement and described his love of the film *V for Vendetta,* his blue eyes sparkled, his otherwise pale face came to life, and the austere room seemed to soften. I prodded him for more details.

It was March 2006, only a year after he started to hack politically. He had teamed up with The BrigadaElectronica, a loose association of radical anonymous hackers. This coalition hacked into the websites of the Philippine National Police, the Malacañang Palace (the official residence of the Philippine president), the Office of the President of the Philippines, and the National Defense College of the Philippines in a show of solidarity with the Sagada 11, a cohort of activists, including a few volunteering with Food Not Bombs who had been detained in the northern Filipino province of Luzon and faced charges of terrorism.[4] (Food Not Bombs is an association of radical collectives serving vegan and vegetarian food to the hungry.)

Hammond wasn't the only budding anarchist fond of the Hollywood blockbuster *V for Vendetta,* released the same month as his hack in support of the Sagada 11. The film's antihero dons a Guy Fawkes mask. Fawkes was once primarily known as a sort of mascot for seventeenth-century British regicide. His failed attempts at regicide are commemorated to this day in the form of a British holiday bearing his name, which celebrates the continuity of the monarchy through the widespread burning of bonfires. British writer Alan Moore adopted the mythologized figure into a dystopian comic book, which became a Hollywood film, which led to the reimagining of Fawkes's visage as that of the quintessential terrorist-turned-icon-of-resistance. Even if all symbols are open to interpretation, some are more elastic than others. While the peace symbol can only signify one single position, this silent smiling man has, over the years, accrued a multi-plicity of meanings before coming to stand as the face of popular dissent.

Soon after his first forays into political hacking, Hammond was arrested and detained in federal prison between 2006 and 2008. He had digitally infiltrated a right-wing organization called "Protest Warrior," whose tag line is "Fighting the Left, Doing it Right"; he pilfered credit card information from their site's database. Since he never used the credit card information, he was only charged for the computer intrusion, escaping the harsher sentence and fines that often attend fraudulent credit card use (the prosecutor was seeking a five-year jail term in addi-tion to a $2.5 million fine, saying, "While Jeremy Hammond tried to make this about politics, we wanted to make this about what actually occurred, that he stole credit cards").[5] Sentenced to twenty-four months in jail and fined $5,358, he was sent to a medium-security prison and served eighteen months.

During our interview he offered a surprising confession. In 2008, as Anonymous began adopting the Guy Fawkes mask he adored, he was initially repelled by the group. He dismissed Anonymous as "script kiddies" (a derogatory term for a tech-nologist lacking real skills) and found the "anything goes" culture of deviant trolling—which crossed the line into racism at times—"alienating." But these were minor reasons compared to his broader rejection of hacktivism more generally. After a few years of political hacking, and two years in jail for the effort, he had asked himself whether "as an environmentalist ... [he] was supporting the industrial beast with technology." For a period he answered "yes," and he backed away.

But with the emergence of WikiLeaks, and the leaks provided by Manning in particular, he saw the potential of technology "to expose crime." At his sentencing, following his hacking stint for Anonymous, he would pay tribute to Manning: "She took an enormous personal risk to leak this information—believing that the public had a right to know and hoping that her disclosures would be a positive step to end these abuses.

It is heart-wrenching to hear about her cruel treatment in military lockup."

Hammond warmed to Anonymous early in 2011. He joined AnonOps during OpWisconsin but remained largely a spectator. As he learned the ropes, he also started to establish connections with others. On June 21, 2011, Hammond finally took the full plunge. He first approached Sabu and wanted to hand over some material but, after failing to connect with him, instead sent a private message to two members of LulzSec, first to Topiary and then to tflow, offering to offload some "candiez" that were in his possession. Hammond had recently gained privileged access to the Arizona Department of Public Safety website and siphoned the data he found there. LulzSec eventually accepted custody of the information and released it in four batches under the title "Chinga La Migra" (Spanish for "Fuck the Immigration Police"). It included email messages, names, phone numbers, home addresses, and passwords belonging to Arizona law enforcement, alongside operational materials such as private intelligence bulletins and training manuals.

The timing was perfect. When Hammond handed over the data, LulzSec was in the midst of a tectonic shift, from Internet trickster-fabulists to revolutionary militants. They had a new agenda and a new flag: "AntiSec," short for Anti-Security. The shift is difficult to explain. Insiders confirmed that even for them, this period was mired in chaos. One Anon told me during an interview: "This was more chaotic in terms of so many subgroups forming, splintering, and redefining themselves … This was the age of LulzSec, AntiSec, TeaMpOisin, the A-Team, CabinCr3w, Buccaneers, Panther Moderns, etc." Mysteries aside, one thing was certain: over the summer of 2011, Anonymous experienced a Cambrian explosion of hacker crews. Where previously a single IRC network (AnonOps) and a breakaway group (LulzSec) dominated the North American and European scene, an archipelago of hacker islands—with AntiSec becoming the most visible and notorious of the bunch—suddenly emerged from the Anonymous waters.

"It's now or never. Come aboard, we're expecting you"

In early June 2011, LulzSec was sailing at a fast clip and leaving behind an extravagant wake for the enjoyment of other Internet denizens. They didn't know at the time, but they were sailing headlong into stormy weather. Seemingly out of the blue, on June 19, 2011, four days before the Chinga La Migra release, LulzSec unfurled "Operation AntiSec." This operation was announced, true to form, via a press release on pastebin.com. But there was one key difference: its language. Featuring only a trace of humor (some bits about lizard blood and a reference to lyrics from the *Love Boat* theme song), its tone was strikingly revolutionary. The release also claimed something that LulzSec had not claimed before—that the operation was an Anonymous project:

> Welcome to Operation Anti-Security (#AntiSec)—we encourage any vessel, large or small, to open fire on any government or agency that crosses their path. We fully endorse the flaunting of the word "AntiSec" on any government website defacement or physical graffiti art.
>
> Whether you're sailing with us or against us, whether you hold past grudges or a burning desire to sink our lone ship, we invite you to join the rebellion. Together we can defend ourselves so that our privacy is not overrun by profiteering gluttons. Your hat can be white, gray or black, your skin and race are not important. If you're aware of the corruption, expose it now, in the name of Anti-Security.
>
> Top priority is to steal and leak any classified government information, including email spools and documentation. Prime targets are banks and other high-ranking establishments. If they try to censor our progress, we will obliterate the censor with cannonfire anointed with lizard blood.
>
> It's now or never. Come aboard, we're expecting you.[6]

Why did Topiary, who wrote the communiqué, push for this revolutionary stance? All evidence points to Sabu. A few weeks prior to the publication of the press release, Sabu had clamored online for the revival of an older AntiSec project.

The anti-security movement had briefly flourished at the turn of the century among some black hat hackers who had contempt for the security industry in general, and for white hat hackers in particular. This was a period when increasingly hackers sought and landed employment in the security industry. Under the mantle of anti-security, a slice of black hat hackers targeted security professionals—doxing them, dumping their mail spools—to protest the increasingly common practice of publicly disclosing exploits and vulnerabilities. Their reasoning, as offered in a founding document, was as follows:

> The purpose of this movement is to encourage a new policy of anti-disclosure among the computer and network security communities. The goal is not to ultimately discourage the publication of all security-related news and developments, but rather, to stop the disclosure of all unknown or non-public exploits and vulnerabilities. In essence, this would put a stop to the publication of all private materials that could allow script kiddies from compromising systems via unknown methods.[7]

While this statement may sound reasonable, the group's actions were aggressively bold. A more recent anti-security manifesto reflects the mayhem these hackers wrought on the security industry (see figure overleaf). As odd as it might seem, part of the motivation behind the original anti-security was cultural preservation, "to take back the scene."

The original anti-security vision was a different animal from the one conceived of by Sabu and Anonymous. While the contemporary Anonymous AntiSec movement held little regard for white hats and was disgusted at what it saw as flagrant greed in the security industry, these were not its main enemies.

---

antisec

/Exposed

- **Fuck full-disclosure**
- **Fuck the security industry**
- **Keep 0days private**
- **Hack everyone you can and then hack some more**

Blend in.
Get trusted.
Trust no one.
Own everyone.
Disclose nothing.
Destroy everything.
Take back the scene.
Never sell out, never surrender.
Get in as anonymous, Leave with no trace.

[Good reads:
Antisec Group Exposed [mirror] [mirror] [mirror] [mirror] [mirror]

[Attachments:
Antisec Group Attachments [mirror] [mirror] [mirror] [mirror] [mirror]

[Check list / Goals:
Take down every public forum, group, or website that helps in promoting exploits and tools or have show-off sections. Publish exploits rigged with /bin/rm to whitehats, let them rm their own boxes for you.
Spread the anti-security movement.
Revive pr0j3ct m4yh3m.

[Rules of Engagement:
Don't get too cocky.
Don't underestimate anyone.

[Contact / Submit paper:

Instead, the AntiSec revival was driven by a more general sense of justice. The point was to own banks, governments, security firms, and other corporations in search of politically damning, leakable information. And, perhaps most crucially of all, the contemporary manifestation of anti-security did not go about its business quietly.

LulzSec's first public mention of AntiSec was on Twitter: "So gather round, this is a new cyber world and we're starting it together. There will be bigger targets, there will be more ownage. #ANTISEC."[8]

Just three days after this message was posted, on June 7, 2011, at 10:15 pm, the FBI visited a towering brick housing project called the Jacob Riis Houses in Manhattan's Lower East Side. They came to this Puerto Rican stronghold to arrest Hector Monsegur, aka Sabu. According to a leaked FBI warrant filed to gain access to Monsegur's Facebook account, a corporation previously hacked by Anonymous culled an IP address that was handed over to law enforcement. The FBI retrieved subscriber information for the IP address, which led to Monsegur's postal and email addresses. The authorities sought access to Monsegur's Facebook account because the "pictures" would allow them "to confirm the identity of the individual who assisted in the unauthorized intrusion" and possibly also land other leads if Monsegur shared any information on the social media platform with his hacker associates. Although only twenty-seven years old, he was the foster parent to his incarcerated aunt's two girls, then both younger than eight. Along with his Anonymous/LulzSec activity, the FBI had evidence linking him to credit card fraud. Facing the prospect of decades in jail and the loss of his two foster children, he flipped.

Just four days before his arrest, the LulzSec crew worried that some of its affiliates had jumped ship. Sabu had claimed he was going to wipe everything:

<Neuron>: Sabu, did we lose people?
<storm>: agreed
<storm>: did we?
<Sabu>: yeah
<storm>: who?
<Sabu>: recursion and devurandom quit respectfully
<Sabu>: saying they are not up for the heat
<Neuron>: im already wiping my enitre desktop
[...]

<Sabu>: yeah
<Sabu>: wipe it all
<Sabu>: im wiping all my shit now

Whatever he did or didn't do then, Sabu went from radical hacktivist to sitting in the FBI's back pocket where he provided a direct portal to LulzSec. The LulzSec team, constantly online, found Sabu's twenty-four-hour absence fishy. To test him upon his return, they asked him to own a server, which he did, quelling any concerns. Of course, the FBI gave him its blessing to proceed so he could maintain his cover.

Soon after his arrest, Sabu jacked up the AntiSec rhetoric previously hinted at in one brief Twitter message. He must have known that Hammond would find it enticing. Hammond would have likely been on the FBI's radar, being one of the only anarchists and hackers in the United States who had already served time in jail. The rhetorical shift marked by AntiSec could just as easily have been a continuation of a sincere commitment. We may never know. But what we do know is that Sabu, just shortly after being flipped, pushed for the AntiSec press release to feature charged political language, and Topiary willingly wrote it. Topiary explained to me via email that

> Sabu was highly interested in my writing of this message, but perhaps more so he was infatuated with LulzSec's at-the-time follower count on twitter and saw it as a platform from which to push this kind of political stance. At the time it seemed no more than misguided angsty teenage performance art, but of course to others it was taken with a far more serious flavour.

The public, journalists, and Anonymous itself were all unaware that the FBI had Sabu on a tight leash. But everyone noticed just how much the press release diverged from LulzSec's style. Media outlets from *AdBusters* to Fox News reported on the press release, with about half a dozen reporters pulling it apart to try and figure out what was going on. Stephen Chapman from ZDNet posed the key question:

> What has existed up to this point as an aimless objective consisting of a series of random, pointless targets, is now coming together as a full-fledged anti-government/anti-establishment movement of potentially epic proportions. Has the digital revolution finally started—something we've been watching Hollywood play out for years now? Perhaps.[9]

Everyone was wondering, including myself, if this was yet another joke or the expression of a true sentiment.

The following day, LulzSec answered. They made good on Operation AntiSec's promise by using Ryan Cleary's botnet to DDoS Britain's Serious Organised Crime Agency. The very next day, on June 21, law enforcement arrested Cleary at his residence in Essex, just outside of London. Newspapers across England were awash with dozens of images of the young man, a core AnonOps hacker and a LulzSec affiliate. As portrayed in the news, he conformed to the stereotype of a dysfunctional, isolated young male. Chubby with milky white skin, he rarely left his bedroom which, while not technically a basement, certainly resembled one, since every window was blocked with homemade silver-foil window blackout. The British tabloids did not miss a beat in sensationalizing every detail.

It was in this frenetic milieu that Hammond reached out to LulzSec with his Arizona material. He had originally wanted to give the data to Sabu, but Sabu was suddenly, and oddly, unresponsive to his queries. Seemingly kindred spirits, Hammond and Sabu had bonded over a shared goal of uniting disparate black hats to rally against injustice and oppression.

So Hammond, operating under the name "Anarchaos," privately messaged Topiary and tflow, emphasizing that he did not want to "touch the torrent seed server with a ten feet pole." tflow happily took the "candiez" and LulzSec immediately pushed the material online, listing it on the Pirate Bay's torrent servers on June 23. Hammond had not earned the trust of the core LulzSec hackers and was not allowed to enter their private chambers. But his hack provided the catalyst through which the AntiSec vision became deed. Hammond wrote the Chinga La Migra press release himself:

> We are releasing hundreds of private intelligence bulletins, training manuals, personal email correspondence, names, phone numbes, addresses and passwords belonging to Arizona law enforcement. We are targeting AZDPS specifically because we are against SB1070 and the racial profiling anti-immigrant police state that is Arizona.
>
> The documents classified as "law enforcement sensitive," "not for public distribution," and "for official use only" are primarily related to border patrol and counter-terrorism operations and describe the use of informants to infiltrate various gangs, cartels, motorcycle clubs, Nazi groups, and protest movements.
>
> [...]
>
> Hackers of the world are uniting and taking direct action against our common oppressors—the government, corporations, police, and militaries of the world. See you again real soon! ;D[10]

Soon after the Chinga La Migra release, Hammond, still on probation for his previous hack, was paid a visit by the Chicago police and FBI for a probation check. He found it odd that for a routine check an FBI agent had joined the probation officer. "When they discovered K2 [synthetic marijuana], they put state charges on me for felony possession of marijuana, charges I beat when the drug results came back," explained Hammond. In jail for a few weeks, Hammond was not around to witness the controversy that his dump stirred among the LulzSec crew. A number of them, such as tflow, pwnsauce, and later Topiary, regretted their decision to release the data.

Although these young men had previously doxed a whole batch of corporate executives and released other, equally sensitive data, targeting police officers felt riskier. This territory, while familiar to Hammond, was unfamiliar to them.

In fact, tflow, who was sixteen years old at the time, encouraged the crew to disband LulzSec. It had only been alive for fifty days, but that is a lifetime on the Internet. Surprisingly, everyone, even Sabu, initially agreed. But then, without warning, Sabu changed his mind. tflow explained it to me: "In the fallout he was just outraged that we all wanted to quit despite him not wanting us to and he generally gets what he wants through manipulation." Ryan Ackroyd (aka Kayla) also recalled one of Sabu's more manipulative—and deeply ironic—tactics: "I remember him saying something like (not word for word) something about him risking his kids coming this far and stuff and that it was unfair to give up."

Despite Sabu's exhortations, tflow's camp ultimately prevailed. LulzSec retired at the end of June 2011. Of course, they couldn't help but go out in style, and so on June 25 they unveiled a final mega-release, including the text of an internal AOL networking manual, half a gigabyte of AT&T internal data, and the emails, usernames, and encrypted user passwords for sites ranging from HackForums.net to NATO's online book shop. Even more interesting than the data itself—at least from the perspective of trickery and myth-making—was LulzSec's final statement, again drafted by Topiary:

For the past 50 days we've been disrupting and exposing corporations, governments, often the general population itself, and quite possibly everything in between, just because we could. All to selflessly entertain others—vanity, fame, recognition, all of these things are shadowed by our desire for that which we all love. The raw, uninterrupted, chaotic thrill of entertainment and anarchy. It's what we all crave, even the seemingly lifeless politicians and emotionless, middle-aged self-titled failures.[11]

The press release passed the LulzSec mantle to the nascent AntiSec movement. These hackers wanted, as tflow put it to me, LulzSec's "legacy of hacks to continue." The final statement continues:

> behind the mask, behind the insanity and mayhem, we truly believe in the AntiSec movement. We believe in it so strongly that we brought it back, much to the dismay of those looking for more anarchic lulz. We hope, wish, even beg, that the movement manifests itself into a revolution that can continue on without us ... Please don't stop. Together, united, we can stomp down our common oppressors and imbue ourselves with the power and freedom we deserve.

In jail, Hammond counted down the days until he could return to his newfound community of uber-political hackers. Upon release, he was, as he put it to me, "ready to rock again." He had no trouble finding willing comrades.

Still, AntiSec's future success was uncertain until three factors converged. First, Sabu, now working full time as an informant, made it his personal mission to keep AntiSec afloat. Second, Hammond functioned as the perfect confederate. A talented hacker who believed in the AntiSec mission, he became its unflagging workhorse, eventually dedicating most of his free time to the project. The third crucial factor was the existence of a broader team. Despite some LulzSec members having bid permanent adieu a number of them joined the new team. The fully constituted AntiSec crew would consist of roughly eight to twelve core participants—larger than LulzSec ever was. Composed of hackers and a few strategists, the team ensconced itself on a secret channel (with the not-so-secret name "#antisec") on a server called "cryto." Many had previously collaborated during the Arab and African Spring ops. I myself knew a number of them from this period, when I hung out on #freedommods, one of the invite-only social channels for the revolutionary ops.

Sabu, so often pegged as the leader of AntiSec, did not actually mastermind the operations or bark orders (in fact, he seemed quite scattered during this period, although later we will see that he went to Hammond with specific hacking requests). The entire AntiSec core team would sometimes work in unison, but more typically they splintered into smaller groups for different operations. For instance, a spin-off channel was created for the hack against the security firm ManTech. Some of the breakaway operations never included Sabu, and his contributions were rarely technical.

Still, Sabu played two vital roles. He was the point man for most exploits and intelligence passed to the team, and he became its public face. Whereas Topiary functioned as a trickster in his handling of PR for LulzSec, Sabu functioned for AntiSec as a seemingly authentic stable representative. Take the following tweet from June 20, a few weeks after his arrest: "Operation Anti-Security: pastebin.com/9KyA0E5v– The Biggest, unified operation amongst hackers in history. All factions welcome. We are one."

A few members of AntiSec also encouraged Sabu to take on a separate, public profile as an individual. Influenced both by AntiSec's prodding and direct pressure from the FBI, that summer Sabu used Twitter with full force, launching a stream of spitfire revolutionary rhetoric. Wielding his charisma, he acquired a cult-like status. With the demise of LulzSec, the mythic tricksters were gone. And while Sabu certainly became mythical, his style of public presentation was by no means that of a trickster. He occupied, instead, the archetypal role of revolutionary hacker outlaw. In the lead-up to this period, I had largely avoided him. But finally, in the middle of the summer, as he rose to prominence, I decided it was about time I reached out.

Sabu

It was American Independence Day: July 4, 2011. Sitting in a boiling room with no air conditioner in San Juan, Puerto Rico—the city where I grew up—I struggled to finish reading an interview with Sabu (the first with this notorious hacker) as beads of sweat trickled down my forehead.[12]

Conducted by Samantha Murphy for the *New Scientist*, the piece offered the first public interview with Sabu. I was feeling lame because I, one of the world's experts on Anonymous, had not even managed a single *conversation* with the kingpin himself. I had kept my distance from him because, to be frank, I found him intimidating. His disposition was not exactly warm and fuzzy. Prior to being flipped, he had kept a much lower online profile, and he exuded a sort of badass revolutionary attitude; he wasn't someone you simply chatted with. Sabu's calls for people to rise up were routinely directed towards his "brothers" and "sisters." During chats on IRC, he would drop the word "nigger" and, unlike the trolls, he seemed to be using it without a hint of irony. Instead of a rich, alienated, white, basement-dwelling teenager, Sabu sounded like a street-hardened brother. Was it possible that his alienation and anger were borne not of middle-class anomie, but instead of poverty, racial marginalization, and torn families?

The interview recounted a 1999 escapade in which Sabu defaced websites in an effort to call for the end of the US military presence on the small Puerto Rican island of Vieques. Done with the piece, I worked up the courage to send him a private message:

> <biella>: hey Sabu just wanted to say props to your work in Vieques
> <biella>: I am from la isla and was quite involved with environmental politics back in the day

I waited for what felt like an eternity for his response. To me, it seemed like the world had stopped, the sweat drops freezing halfway down my back. But in reality, he responded almost immediately:

> <Sabu>: nice

Then:

> <Sabu>: so whats your goal? I see your name associated with being fed/sntich/writing docs on anonymous
> <Sabu>: tell me your true intentions
> <Sabu>: I am interested

My thoughts swirled. In a scene where reputation counts for so much, Sabu's intimation stung. I now understand that his accusation was a smart move; he erected a frame that would make it hard for me to see *him* as a possible snitch. At the time, I could not even fathom that he might be working for the FBI. The question of how I might fend off his accusations eclipsed any other consideration:

> <biella>: Sabu I am just an anthropologist

A millisecond after typing, I realized how stupid that probably sounded. Anyone with a basic knowledge of snitches knows that there is a well-documented history of anthropologists working as covert CIA agents. I tried to regroup:

> <biella>: I fell into Anonymous accidentally back in 2008
> <biella>: via Scientology
> <Sabu>: ok

That did not seem good enough either:

> <biella>: my passion is politics
> <biella>: so I like to study the politics of digital media
> <Sabu>: I understand that

And then I said something that now makes me cringe:

> <biella>: in terms of anon, I am intrigued and am also concerned (FBI, my computer etc)
> <biella>: I take precautions with my data, dont collect certain types of data either, which is frustrating but the only way I see around this
> <sabu>: well whats your point of collecting data?
> <biella>: I am bummed to hear that my name is associated with snitch/FBI but I understand in so far as it is part of the territory
> <Sabu>: historical?
> <Sabu>: social science research?
> <biella>: I would say a combo of both those

I explained that I did not want to uncover "crimes." Rather, I was interested in understanding social dynamics. Although our first conversation went rather poorly, much to my surprise—and relief—our chatting became both more regular and friendlier. I thought that either I'd convinced him of my noble intentions, or he had asked other AntiSec members about me. By this time, I was certain that informants were implanted in AnonOps, but in June and July very few rumors tagged Sabu as a rat, whereas other core Anonymous members were often plagued by accusations. My conversations with Sabu only fueled my paranoia. On July 23 he asked:

> <Sabu>: you're deep into anonymous channels and comms
> <Sabu>: you never get visits from feds?
> <biella>: not yet
> <biella>: i have neither been stopped at the border though i travel without my main computer or no computer, not that i have anything incriminating
> <biella>: i worry about this, i have contacts with the EFF [Electronic Frontier Foundation]

Much like my first conversation with Sabu, when I praised him in the hopes that he would talk to me, he instead began to butter *me* up, even thanking me:

<Sabu>: for all the work you do
<Sabu>: en serio mucho respeto [seriously, much respect]
<Sabu>: at the end of the day this movement can be amazing

He also started dropping hints that the FBI was watching me:

<Sabu>: … just because you're legit doesnt mean they're not follow-
ing you

He was clever: *I* was the potential problem, *not him*. He would point this out repeatedly and then continue on with his revolutionary rhetoric. He made it hard to see him as anything other than a passionate activist, unwaveringly committed to the cause.

The Pleasures of Secrecy

A few weeks after my first conversation with Sabu, I was invited to a secret IRC channel for a one-time conversation among AntiSec members. The participants included a handful of IRC operators from AnonOps and Emmanuel Goldstein, the publisher of hacker zine *2600* and host of a hacker radio show called *Off the Hook*. They convened to gauge whether Goldstein would be interested in lending his support to the AntiSec subproject oriented around propaganda and artistic creation, called "voice." Here I was, invited to the inner sanctum. I watched intensely as the group of roughly twenty participants debated the merits of direct action and the purpose of the voice project.

Sabu set the agenda: "so gentlemen we're going to bring in Emmanuel. He's going to be the voice of anonymous and antisec on the radio and really wants to help push #voice over." As it turned out, Goldstein had made no such promises, and while many seemed open to his participation, others objected immediately. Some accused him of being a snitch. Now, one must understand that rumors of snitching constitute part of the everyday background noise among hackers, and this noise itself becomes one of the main roadblocks against substantiating the claims. During the chat, a critic noted that "2600 has a history of condemning attacks, including when Anonymous ddosed mastercard and others for wikileaks."

Adrian Lamo, the hacker who snitched on Chelsea Manning, had at one point been active in the 2600 scene, with access to an account on 2600's mail/shell server. According to some, Lamo had not been sufficiently purged. Many were upset about these things, as well as about the Hackers on Planet Earth (HOPE) convention, organized by Goldstein and a large team, which featured Lamo on a panel.

I was particularity intrigued by what a figure named Anarchaos was writing in the chat room. He wasn't anyone I had seen online before, and it would still be another few months before I would converse with him for the first time, under a different handle. Goldstein began questioning tactics like DDoSing and street-based black bloc organizing, and Anarchaos staunchly defended their legitimacy. "I've got personal and political reasons for taking direct action against the forces that oppress us. Don't be thinking those that fight with force aren't doing it with brains." Anons on the channel admitted that "we are more than capable of higher sophisticated attacks but regardless, when we are in the trenches firing upon our enemies, we don't need other so-called hackers to be undermining our efforts." Later, someone added that "a diversity of tactics is the most effective way to win campaigns."

What started as a fascinating conversation about diversity of tactics quickly burst into a flame fest. At a certain point, someone asked Goldstein whether he had ever met me (he had not). I used the attention suddenly directed my way to share with him my thoughts on the HOPE panel that included Adrian Lamo. I wrote that it was "mind blowing," and that I was "glad you organized that."

"You wouldn't believe the pressure I was under NOT to do that," replied Goldstein. Some in the chat room took the opportunity to affirm that they were still pissed: "Lamo should not be welcome at any hacker gathering and just another nail in the coffin for many people to write off 2600 as sellouts."

The conversation briefly returned to whether 2600 could contribute to the voice project, before devolving into "lame-ass flaming," as one participant put it. Goldstein decided to exit: "sorry to cause a bitter tone in here so I will split. But we're open to dialogue." The voice project launched soon after on a public IRC channel, without Goldstein's help. Though the mission of the meeting had failed, it did confirm what I had suspected: the AntiSec team contained a number of hackers, like Anarchaos, who were active but hidden. Who were these people? Why had I never seen them before? The core LulzSec participants, like Topiary, tflow, and Sabu, were for the most part well-known figures. It was clear that Anonymous, already so elusive, was blanketed under even more layers of secrecy.

And, increasingly, I was also being swept into this orbit of secrecy. I had tried to keep my distance from channels where illegal activity was organized. When I talked to Anons privately, I frequently requested that they spare incriminating details (knowing that they might be itching to brag about some epic security compromise). I made it clear to everyone that my role as an anthropologist meant that I was often taking notes, saving some portion of logs, and otherwise gathering data. Even though I encrypted my data, I maintained no special privilege that would preclude me from being regarded as an accessory to crime. As a result, I was not invited to secret channels and I (mostly) avoided the boastful stories about illicit hacks. My attitude was also plainly honest, and I think this helped people understand just what it was I was up to—a rarity in a culture of mistrust, suspicion, rumors, and fear. But now things seemed to be changing. I was slipping into deeper, darker recesses of this labyrinth, given fleeting access to private conversations, and becoming increasingly worried that this could devolve into a problem.

Aldous Huxley once wrote: "To associate with other like-minded people in small, purposeful groups is for the great majority of men and women a source of profound psychological satisfaction. Exclusiveness will add to the pleasure of being several, but at one; and secrecy will intensify it almost to ecstasy."[13] For the hackers participating in Anonymous, secrecy was, without a doubt, a major source of what kept them coming back for more. Secrecy provided a sort of sustenance for this underground community. And while "ecstasy" might be too strong a word when applied to my case, I can't deny it: acceptance into this esoteric society gave me a thrilling contact high.

Where Art Thou, Anonymous?

As exciting as it initially was to stand in the shadows with Anonymous, by early August 2011, my mood had soured. The frenetic pace of Anonymous activity had mutated into something new through the sheer militancy of the operations. I began to wonder when the FBI or another government agency was going to nab more Anons, or even pay me a visit. AntiSec, like LulzSec, had settled into a rhythm of near-constant hacking, generating taunting releases that simply begged for a reaction from the state: #FuckFBIFridays, #ShootingSherrifsSaturday, #MilitaryMeltdownMonday.

AntiSec doxed sheriff's offices, defaced and destroyed police organization websites like that of the California Statewide Law Enforcement Association, and leaked the personal information of New York police chiefs. In July alone they attacked the websites of seventy-seven different law enforcement agencies (all hosted on the same server). They dumped a gigabyte of data from Vanguard Defense Industries acquired by hacking the email account of one of its senior vice-presidents. They revealed to the world documents that they had "procured," including a proposal to the FBI from defense contractor IRC Federal for a project called the "Special Identities Modernization (SIM) Project," which aimed to identify people who "might" present a criminal or terrorist risk in the future. They claimed to have infiltrated various internal networks of the US Department of Energy, where they sent messages urging employees to work against the government rather than for it. They hacked the federal contractor ManTech International, publishing over four hundred megabytes of content that detailed its dealings with NATO and the US Army (alongside all its employees' emails). They struck at the mega-security contractor Booz Allen Hamilton; while they were unable to obtain actual documents—though one of Booz Allen Hamilton's employees at the time, Edward Snowden, eventually would—they managed to download ninety thousand military emails from the company's site, which they threw up on the Pirate Bay with a long analysis noting "key facts" about the company, such as its funding breakdown. Things had taken a very serious turn.

During this surge of activity, arrests became more commonplace. By the end of July, fourteen Americans had been arrested for DDoSing PayPal, and British authorities had arrested two members of LulzSec: Topiary in Scotland and tflow in London (tflow's name was not released at the time because he was still a minor). Right before Topiary's arrest, he left behind an adage—it now stands alone on his retired Twitter account: "You cannot arrest an idea."[14]

It was a hot summer. In this climate of menace and threat, I began to suffer weekly nightmares of G-men pounding on my door. I asked myself just what the hell I had gotten myself involved in, and I wasn't the only one. During an interview, one Anon expressed surprise: "None of us knew we'd be here … locked up for decades, on the run, in exile, suicides mental illness ptsd [*sic*] etc etc." Anons increasingly reached out to me with confessions of fear, fueling my own growing unease. On August 1, someone found me and wrote that "shit is getting

EXTREMELY hot atm [at the moment] ... for those who do
AntiSec for instance." The next day, another hacker told me, "I
had helicopter land in a field next to me at 7 am this morning.
My heart rate hit about 200, till I realized it was crop spray-
ing." Between the people freaking out to me in private, the
litany of arrests, my life being put on hold as I poured increasing amounts of time into the research, the highly mediated
text-based pseudonymous interactivity, and the growing tentacles of secrecy, I grew frustrated and burnt out. It was getting
to me. I was worried about the future of Anonymous, about
my future and the lives of those who had been arrested. Some
hackers in AntiSec started to notice that I was down. Some
contacted me privately, encouraging me not to quit. One told
me that if I quit I would miss some really "special things."

I didn't even bother to ask what these things might
be. The leaks and compromises were still going strong,
but they had lost their luster. To me, #FuckFBIFridays
and #MilitaryMeltdownMonday had started to become
#FuckFBIFatigue and #MyMeltdownMondays. I was also
frustrated that, while my access to AntiSec grew, more activity
seemed to be emanating from other, small hacker teams that I
remained largely in the dark about it. The days of large-scale
Anonymous uprisings were being eclipsed. Anonymous had
been exciting to me for a specific reason: it was the largest and
most populist disruptive grassroots movement the Internet
had, up to that time, fomented. But it felt, suddenly, like
AnonOps/Anonymous was slipping into a more familiar state
of hacker-vangaurdism. And it meant, from a purely logistical perspective, that Anonymous was becoming even harder
to study.

In retrospect, there's at least one concrete explanation for
Anonymous's growing fragmentation: direct government
interference. Thanks to Edward Snowden's NSA mega-leaks
in 2013, we know that in the summer of 2011, Britain's
Government Communications Headquarters (GCHQ) targeted AnonOps' communications infrastructure. A GCHQ

special unit called the Joint Threat Research Intelligence Group (JTRIG)—which also engages in COINTELPRO-type meddling—launched DDoS attacks against Anonymous, calling it them "OpWealth" and "Rolling Thunder."[15]

This was the first known instance of a Western government secretly using DDoS—criminalized in the UK and the US—as a tactic against its own citizens. GCHQ claimed that its operation was a success; the leaked slides boast that as a result of its DDoS of AnonOps' IRC, "80% of those messaged where [*sic*] not in the IRC channels 1 month later." By this time, the UK government had already arrested British participants for the same act. One of those arrested, Chris Weatherhead, aka "Nerdo," was a central and much beloved AnonOps operator. Eventually, he would receive an eighteen-month sentence for his role in the DDoS campaign "Avenge Assange/Operation Payback." He was not found guilty of engaging in an actual DDoS itself, but of aiding in the operation by running the IRC server. The British government, on the other hand, has faced no sanction for DDoSing activists. The law, clearly, is not applied equally. As Weatherhead put it on Twitter when he read the news: "My Government used a DDoS attack against servers I owned, and then convicted me of conducted DDoS attacks. Seriously what the fucking fuck?"[16]

This shotgun approach to justice sprays its punishment over thousands of individuals who are engaging in debate and protest, simply because a small handful of people in their midst have committed digital vandalism.

This attempted deterrence may have stalled Anonymous at large, but it did nothing to stop AntiSec. They were on a different IRC network. While some members did get arrested, and others left for a variety of reasons, the consensus was largely that, as one member of AntiSec told me, "there is no turning back."

I had to take a break. I booked a trip to one of the most famous hacker conferences in the world, The Chaos Communication Camp, organized by the Chaos Computer Club every four years in Germany. I reasoned that some offline time spent with hackers I knew, with friends—or at least with people I could actually *look at*—might lessen the vertigo that had set in.

Yet after a string of days and nights at the hacker festival and an early morning flight from Germany, I arrived back in the United States more exhausted than before I had left. The Anonymous spirit, by contrast, seemed to have been refreshed. Making my way through baggage claim, I glimpsed a familiar image on a faraway TV screen—the Guy Fawkes mask. Jolted, I trotted over to the monitor. CNN was showing a tweet calling for "OpBART" ("BART" stands for Bay Area Rapid Transit). From the visual clues provided by CNN, I realized that this operation was not only big. It also seemed to fit the mold of the old-school, tumultuous, large-scale-uprising of the pre-AntiSec Anonymous. The 80 percent of users the GCHQ had supposedly blasted away with its DDoS were back, along with hundreds of newcomers.

OpBART's point of origin can be pinpointed to July 3, 2011, when BART police fatally shot Charles Hill in the San Francisco Civic Center BART station. Though the man had been intoxicated and armed with a knife, killing him struck many as an excessive use of force. It was also a reminder of the general problem of police brutality. In 2009, cops had killed an African-American man, Oscar Grant III, at the Fruitvale BART Station in Oakland. He was shot in the back while they had him pinned to the ground. In response to the shooting of Hill, local organizers coordinated a protest on July 11. Roughly one hundred demonstrators disrupted BART service at the Civic Center BART station. Organizers called for another protest at the Civic Center BART station one month later. BART officials decided to block cellphone reception in stations to thwart the August demonstration. BART spokesperson Linton Johnson explained their rationale to CNN: "We made a gut-wrenching decision that was forced upon us by the protesters ... They [the activists] made us choose between people's ability to use their mobile phones [and] their constitutional right to get from point A to point B."[17]

Last time I checked, the Constitution protects both free speech and freedom of association, but not freedom of transportation. Anonymous geeks, so well acquainted with constitutional rights, naturally got upset. Jackal, the main holder of the @YourAnonNews Twitter account, publicly inaugurated #OPBART with a string of scathing messages. He had over 300,000 followers, and soon after being featured on CNN, the account would amass another 200,000 (which also prompted the FBI to visit Jackal). Anonymous and other concerned citizens relied on the clever hashtag "#muBARTec" to connect this act of censorship to the wide-scale telecom blackout imposed by former Egyptian president Hosni Mubarak just a handful of months earlier, in January 2011.

Jackal was working with a small team. He maintained a semi-private nook, an IRC channel he called "the cabin," that initially included only four individuals. Primarily conceived of as a social space, one of the early members appended the term "cr3w" onto the name, poking light fun at LulzSec and the other self-proclaimed "crews" mushrooming at the time. Operation BART, their very first op, accidentally transformed CabinCr3w from a social channel into a prolific and functioning team. In the coming months they would grow to roughly twenty participants. They would become known as specialists in open-source data mining—muckraking through databases provided by other hackers who would infiltrate servers in search of information (though some hackers from CabinCr3w, like Kahuna [John Anthony Borell III], and w0rmer [Higinio O. Ochoa III] also engaged in digital trespass and were subsequently arrested).

But in mid-August, as OpBART was just beginning, the team remained tiny. And because its labor force was small, participants had to work around the clock for the first three days. Utilizing Facebook, CabinCr3w connected with locals to organize street protests and banded together with the wider Anon community by reaching out to some established organizers. A public #opbart IRC channel on AnonOps' server became a rallying point. Everyone went to work drafting propaganda material to advertise the protest planned for Monday, August 15. In a mode familiar from Operation Avenge Assange, the organizers acted as choreographers—to borrow Paolo Gerbaudo's fitting term—who harnessed and directed a fireball of fury.[18]

Alongside the protest and propaganda, some individuals engaged in some rather dicey, although admittedly lulzy, behavior; it was these acts that attracted mainstream media attention.

For instance, someone claiming the mantle of Anonymous found a racy, semi-nude photo of BART's Linton Johnson on his personal website. This photo was then republished on the "bartlulz" website—to considerable fanfare—along with this brazen rationalization: "if you are going to be a dick to the public, then I'm sure you don't mind showing your dick to the public ... Umad Bro? #Bartlulz."[19]

But more than anything else, it was a string of hacks that attracted national media coverage, from CNN to *Democracy Now!*

First, there was a website defacement on August 14. The interlopers simply defaced myBART.org with an image of Guy Fawkes. This was followed almost immediately by an intrusion that exposed the private data of 2,500 BART customers. A day after the second protest at the Civic Center BART station, organized by Anonymous and local activists, there was another intrusion, on August 17, into a BART police union website. This resulted in the publishing on Pastebin of the home addresses, email addresses, and passwords of 102 BART police officers, among other employees.

The day I returned from Germany, *Democracy Now!* contacted me to inquire whether I could join them the next day to speak about OpBART. I dreaded the prospect of being asked about the blatant privacy violations committed by such hacks, and the gymnastics required to explain the use of such tactics by a collective that ostensibly fought to protect privacy. Thankfully, the next day I was joined on live TV by masked Anon activist Commander X, and it was he who asked to offer a rationale:

> AMY GOODMAN: And your thoughts... on going after the actual passengers themselves, people who might not want that personal information out?
>
> X: ... How else do you get the world to respond and secure your information? How else do you get these companies and these big governments to keep your information, the information you give them voluntarily, safe? I think we got our message across, and I'll bet you one thing: I'll bet you they fix that.[20]

Commander X, who spoke through a voice distorter, was not responsible for the breach, but the alleged perpetrator and a minority of other Anonymous activists shared their rationale. At the time, I had no idea who was behind the hacks, nor how other Anons viewed this breach. But soon after the interview, I returned home to find out.

Although there was tremendous—almost unilateral—support among Anons for protesting BART's act of censorship, the hacking and dumping of private customer data was one of the most internally divisive acts I had yet witnessed. Conversation on the channels, and even publicly over Twitter, was brimming with criticism.

Consider, for instance, what happened when Lamaline_5mg logged in to the public OpBART channel on August 17 and claimed responsibility for the BART police union website hack. She offered a link to the dox:

> <Lamaline_5mg>: Hello y'all
> <CrappyTIres>: Hi Lamaline_5mg
> <Lamaline_5mg>: I have a small contribution.

<Lamaline_5mg>: http://pastebin.com/XX7DJBqw

<Lamaline_5mg>: A leak from http://bartpoa.com/ [BART Police Officers' Association]

<Lamaline_5mg>: Enjoy, and share.

<CrappyTIres>: hmm

*CrappyTIres doesn't like info leaks

<OpNoPro>: were those names ever shared before?

<Lamaline_5mg>: What?

<Lamaline_5mg>: I don't know. I guess not.

<OpNoPro>: You dropped names and passwords

<OpNoPro>: We run a very clean operation here

<OpNoPro>: We are not interested in any thing like that

<OpNoPro>: Please refrain from dropping anybody's private information anywhere on anonymous's behalf... not interested in breaching somebody's privacy... they have a right to it as much as you do

Not everyone agreed with OpNoPro. Others vocally supported the black hat ways of AnonOps:

<sharpie>: that's his dump

<OpNoPro>: Do your jobs privately and nobody needs to know

<sharpie>: stfu

[...]

<Lamaline_5mg>: It's not my fault for their crapy security.

<OpNoPro>: Take it easy sharp pen

<OpNoPro>: This is not a question for debate

<OpNoPro>: This is a question about keeping things separate

<sharpie>: people think this irc is a fucking church knitting group

<OpNoPro>: Please understand the situation

<sharpie>: yeah

<sharpie>: I do

<sharpie>: a lot more than you

<OpNoPro>: There are many portions to the IRC

*CrappyTIres looks for the knitting group

<OpNoPro>: Take it easy sharp pen

<OpNoPro>: Wake up

<OpNoPro>: Keep it separate
[…]
<sharpie>: take your moralfaggotry whitehat shit and shove it
<OpNoPro>: And if you ever see me in a knitting club that will be in
your eyes
<OpNoPro>: You have no idea what my morals are

Sharpie concluded by echoing one of the most common rationales:

<sharpie>: how much publicity do you think "#opbart" would have
had without db dumps?

And then Lamaline_5mg said that she was not even Anonymous—raising the ontological question of just what makes one Anonymous anyway. She showed up on the Anonymous IRC server, proffered some dox, and then proceeded to work with other Anons to craft a message to the press; if that doesn't make one an Anon, then what does? Regardless, the distinction mattered little in relation to the more general ethical questions surrounding hacking and doxing. By now, thanks to AntiSec, these tactics were a common fixture in the Anonymous landscape and would only grow more controversial:

<Lamaline_5mg>: This is not anonymous.
<Lamaline_5mg>: Fuck you.
<w>: OpNoPro, like it or now, fractal chaos and tactics diversity is
what is fueling global revolution
<AlbaandOmegle>: Anon is a shitstarter
<AlbaandOmegle>: because it works
<OpNoPro>: take the dumps somewhere else
<w>: OpNoPro, you cannot prevent people from using an operation
name for doxing, ddosing and hacking
<w>: OpNoPro, even if that was the right choice, you simply can't
<Lamaline_5mg>: I don't use the operation name.

Versions of this conversation would be repeated at least a dozen times elsewhere over the next few days. My reading was that most participants on AnonOps opposed the privacy-violating dumps, but mainly supportive of the other illegal tactics, like the BART website defacement, the email and fax bombing, and the DDoS (regardless of the fact that it failed—BART had implemented good DDoS protection). A minority supported the doxing simply because it served the greater purpose of media attention, or was an example of the "fractal chaos" that partly defined Anonymous.

The doxing also marked the first time that suspicions of a "false flag operation" fully flared within Anonymous. A false flag operation is a secret intervention in which a government agent performs a controversial action on behalf of a political group to seed mistrust and controversy or provide justification for the government's own escalated response.

Two days later, Lamaline_5mg published a statement on Pastebin that seemed to quell rumors of a false flag, though it did little to extinguish the controversy:

> I find it shameful that the media do not condemn taking such drastic actions against a protest after the *killing* of an innocent citizen. He was not proven guilty, or do they actually judge people at their funeral? Implying this guy got a proper funeral.
>
> I also find it disturbingly sad that the San Francisco Bay Area local media is being so supportive of the right to remain anonymous of the BART police personnel, when they didn't give a shit about this man being killed.
>
> Did they condemn the killing of this man?
>
> All I did was give them (the cops) a taste of their own medicine, ie 'Lamaline' which is an (anal) analgesic... (Look it up)
>
> It also means « The cunning », in french.[21]

In a subsequent interview with *SF Weekly*, Lamaline_5mg claimed to be French, female, and a preteen (the last two being unlikely). She said that the BART hack marked her very first intrusion.

In the midst of all this, a pastebin.com message titled "Anonymous is NOT unanimous" was picked up and read by many participants:

> Anonymous has a perception problem. Most people think we're a group of shadowy hackers. This is a fundamental flaw. Anonymous is *groups* of shadowy hackers, and herein lies the problem. Anonymous has done a lot of good in just the past 9 months. It has helped with other groups in providing aid to people on the ground in countries where "democracy" is a bad word.
>
> The mainstream media needs to understand that Anonymous isn't unanimous. I've yet to see wide scale reporting make this distinction. A destructive minority is getting a majority of the press, while those of us who toil in the shadow doing good work for people at home and abroad go unthanked.[22]

This statement captures Anonymous's commitment to difference, plurality, and dissension—similar in form to the type of adversarial politics advocated by radical theorist Chantal Mouffe.[23]

Anons often disagree and engage in a strong war of words. But very little energy is spent on systematically trying to eliminate difference, or carving out some "middle ground" resolution. Instead, differences are loudly voiced, listened to, responded to, and reluctantly accepted; Anons widely acknowledge that nothing drastic or meaningful can be done to eliminate differences, and they carry on with their interventions or, if the disagreements are unbearable, break away to form a new node.

Fuck AntiSec

The OpBART hacking controversy eventually receded. But one controversy remained. As weeks turned into months, criticism of AntiSec's defacements and hacks mounted, even as the group's support base grew. Some Anons saw AntiSec as reckless, and many were suspicious of its motives. Rumors circulated that not only particular actions, but also the entirety of AntiSec might be a false flag operation.

AntiSec, perhaps unsurprisingly, was simultaneously respected, tolerated, and vilified. Many of AntiSec's core members had been essential to past iterations of the Anonymous/AnonOps/LulzSec constellation. Their significance coincided with the partial fading of WikiLeaks, which suffered from internal frictions and legal troubles. AntiSec, it was hoped, might expand to more directly challenge the powers wielded by corporations and governments—not simply by producing momentary spectacles, as is the case with DDoS attacks, but also by whistleblowing—locating and releasing hard evidence of malfeasance.

Despite constant hacks during the late summer and early fall of 2011, very little of real substance was uncovered. (Had Sabu not been an informant, it is likely that AntiSec would have delivered more. The FBI notified some companies of breaches, prompting the fast patching of holes, effectively closing doors that AntiSec had only just opened.) One Anon who had been centrally involved since the fall of 2010 quit in August 2011, largely in disgust over AntiSec. While LulzSec dumped plenty of data—such as usernames, email addresses, passwords, emails, and other documents—much of it was seen to lack political weight. And yet AntiSec managed to remain in the spotlight. People began to resent this. There were many small crews operating, most of them outside of the public eye. The possibility was raised that AntiSec had become counterproductive, funneling attention, labor, and resources into worthless activities. Another hacker who had been a core member of

AnonOps IRC staff explained, "We got pissed off that AntiSec was thrown on us. We had no warning. And they'd been planning it for a while, coopting people from here."

Worse, AntiSec began to raise hackles among some Anons for a time-honoured Anonymous taboo: fame-seeking. One Anon relayed this view on IRC in September 2011 in the course of resigning from the group (pseudonym has been changed):

<ha>: wtf happened to #antisec
<ha>: let me tell you a story
<ha>: gather round kids
<ha>: Once upon a time there was a team of status fag hackers, most of which where okay as people, we all have our flaws. They came to be known as lulzsec
<ha>: These hackers decided it would be a good idea to use there status fag powers to gather anons against the infosec industry.
<ha>: It was then someone decided to give monkies machine guns and taught them the weakness of sql tables. These monkies decided they wanted to look good for lulzsec and hacked every possible thing they could, releasing all the information they plundered reguardless to such things as consequence and public realtions.
<ha>: Private data leaked faster then WikiLeaks brand condom.
<ha>: They continued hacking away hoping to gain a pat on the back from Sabu.
<ha>: Then the summer vacation ended.
<ha>: They found themselves unable to continue there hackery as more pressing matters became apparent, such as who do i sit with during lunch and whats a cooler elective to take, french or band.
<ha>: Thus ends the saga of #antisec

Earlier in the summer, the AnonOps network had grown so critical of Barrett Brown that he decided to quit. He was adamant that he was no longer involved in Anonymous, focusing his energy on "Project PM," a team wiki dedicated to documenting the inner workings of private contractors doing security work for the government. Later, Brown would assume the moniker of Anonymous again—to take on the Mexican drug cartels (a dumb and dangerous bluff). And he would also receive information for ProjectPM from AntiSec, when the group finally procured sensitive data from a security firm called Stratfor. But that was months away. Brown remained, at that time, a reminder that attention-seeking behavior was frowned on.

AntiSec's attention-seeking was more ambivalent and complicated than it had been with Brown. Unlike Brown, AntiSec sought attention under a pseudo-anonymous mantle. And some Anons stood by the crews' actions, holding out hope that their efforts would eventually produce some political, classified, or secret information impossible to procure legally.

A cohort of black hat hackers (unaffiliated with) Anonymous had had enough with AntiSec. A group of underground hackers going by the name BR1CKSQU4D, which they seem to have assumed only temporarily, released a document that included some purported doxes of Anonymous and AntiSec members. They opened by declaring:

! FUCK ANONYMOUS ! FUCK ANTISEC ! FUCK ANONYMOUS ! FUCK ANTISEC[24]

Further along, they did not mince words:

And you wonder why the 90s groups you shout out (with kids and families) won't come out of retirement to help you?

You have accomplished nothing except inflaming 'cyber-war' rhetoric and fueling legislation that will end up with hackers getting 50 years in prison.

The most retarded part is that you dont even realize you are the cause of the very thing you hate;

Every time you DDoS a company Prolexic or DOSarrest sign up a new customer.

Every time you SQL inject some irrelevant site a pentesting company gets a new contract.

Every time you declare cyberwar on the government federal contractors get drowned in grant money.

Other hackers and netizens also began accusing Anonymous of fortifying the cyberwar industrial complex. But it's worth noting that long before Anonymous came to prominence, national governments around the world already aspired to control the Internet and were already developing statutes that eroded individual rights and privacies. Cybersecurity initiatives would be well funded with or without Anonymous. This is not to say that all the group's actions are justified. Still, in the face of such a gargantuan surveillance state, what Anonymous has enabled is a flexible platform for citizens to express their dissent over long-entrenched trends.

But BR1CKSQU4D, wedded foremost to the black hat sensibility, ended the diatribe with a set of threats that harkened right back to the original AntiSec mindset:

> If you support antisec in any way you will be targeted.
>
> Journalists, musicians, laywers, webhosts, VPN providers, political commentators, profiteering businesses, you are all valid targets.
>
> You stepped into OUR world if you don't want to play the game get the fuck off the playing field.
>
> [...]
>
> We have <3 for the scene. Fuck the media.
>
> —BR1CKSQU4D

CHAPTER 10

The Desire of a Secret Is to Be Told

Summer in New York City is oppressive. Soaring temperatures combine with the harsh metropolitan reality to create a dystopian urban hellion. The sun, reflected off the glass skyscrapers, blinds you. Subterranean orifices lead to the city's viscera: the bowels of the stations and the intestines of the subway system, spitting people out. Sweat, sounds, sights, as if these were not enough: you are also enclosed by the mephitic, durian-like rot of the city—smells of deceased rats and human waste, oven-baked by subway stations. So when the cooler fall weather finally settles in, the city sighs with collective relief. The hanging leaves of dazzling burnt yellow, amber, and orange provide a complement to olfactory respite. The swing to fall feels like a new lease on life. Finally, you won't be sweating all night long. Finally, the smell will be washed away. Finally, respite.

On September 17, 2011, I awoke to a bundle of delicate pink, purple, and red flowers protruding from a vase encased in a Guy Fawkes mask. It was my birthday. The timing was perfect: it was a day of protest in New York City. The financial collapse had seared its streak of corruption, oligarchy, and the 1 percent into the minds of an angry generation. Instead of being depressed, oppressed, and immobilized by the combination of the financial situation and the city's heat, the day was crisp and it felt like there was a refreshing optimism that people were ready to act upon. Nobody wanted to call it hope—it was too early to declare such a thing—but the possibility was still on the table.

I grabbed the mask and made my way to Bowling Green, near Wall Street. Approaching the small grassy park, I spied out of the corner of my eye a number of young men with Guy Fawkes masks slung over their shoulders. Upon seeing me, a pair of them nodded. One gave a thumbs up and told me to "Keep up the good work." By early afternoon, protesters had marched to what became the event's target and nerve center, Zuccotti Park (later renamed Liberty Square). Many came and went as the day inched toward twilight and the first General Assembly, but a steady stream of younger activists continually trickled in with camping equipment on their backs and threw their gear down.

Even if Occupy was defined by its rootedness in a place, it was understood that social media could and should play a vital role. Not *the* nor even *a* central agent of revolution, online communication acted more like an adjuvant—it provided an essential boost, facilitated coordination, and allowed those unable to attend bodily to witness and become invested, and entangled, in the events. And so on that first day of Occupy, many of us were hooked to our phones even as we were present at the square. Every half hour or so, I would fetch my phone from my pocket and skim through my Twitter feed. In the afternoon, two back-to-back messages from Sabu vaulted off the screen. A month prior, on August 16, Sabu had vanished from Twitter after enigmatically tweeting, "The greatest trick the devil ever pulled was convincing the world he did not exist. And like that ... he is gone."[1] These new tweets marked his reemergence with a roar:

"ATTN: I never left, I am NOT @AnonSabu or any of those posers. I wasn't owned, arrested, hacked or any of the other rumors. Go get lives."[2] He followed with another: "They tried to snitch me out, troll me, dox every one around me, bait me

into endless arguments but theres one thing they can't do:
STOP ME!"[3]

In an early August chat, Sabu had warned me he was going
dark. "Sabu is a name that doesn't need to exist eventually,"
he wrote.

<biella>: well ok
<biella>: then :-/
<biella>: not saying it does either nor that you should stick around
here, just sayin' dont be a stranger Sabu
<Sabu>: well
<Sabu>: its not like im leaving to be a dick or run away
<Sabu>: its just that the community itself
<Sabu>: needs to look towards itself for motivation
<Sabu>: not me
<Sabu>: I feel too many people follow me
<Sabu>: and im not here to be a leader. yes im a natural born leader
<Sabu>: and yes if I wanted to I can lead this entire movement on my
own if I wanted to live like a dictactor
<Sabu>: but truth is
<Sabu>: I'm not the leader of anything involved with anonymous
<Sabu>: and by me leaving I prove this point

Following his exit from Twitter, and unbeknownst to myself,
Sabu remained active on various secret IRC channels. Also
unknown to me—and, in this case, even to those he worked
so closely with online—the day before our chat, on August
15, he had appeared in court. He had pled guilty to all twelve
charges leveled against him, including conspiracy to commit
bank fraud and aggravated identity theft and three counts of
conspiracy to commit computer hacking. Facing 124 years,
he agreed to work for the government in exchange for the
reduction of his maximum sentence to one hundred years. He
also assented to the "obligation to commit no further crimes
whatsoever."[4]

Unlike his earlier disappearance in June due to his (also

secret) arrest, this time he had notified people that he was going to take some time off. AntiSec members came and went, a factor that further disabled suspicion of Sabu. He also created a permanent connection to IRC using what is typically called an "IRC bouncer," "proxy," or "screen session." When he wished, he could then reattach himself to the permanent connection. This enabled him (and the FBI) to have access to all conversations on the channels, and people could send him messages, even when he was not online. Sabu's method of connecting aroused no mistrust because it is common for hackers, many who are terminal junkies, to rely on such technical proxies.

When he initially left, I took his reasoning at face value. But he was also going dark to deflect some strong accusations that had recently come his way. Just before his public disappearance in August, a hacker named Mike "Virus" Nieves accused Sabu of being a snitch. The logs of this exchange quickly surfaced on Pastebin. It started with Sabu obliquely suggesting that someone in Virus's crew was a rat. Virus bit back hard:

> <Virus>: regarding topiary, you ratted him out
> <Virus>: it's so obvious sabu
> <Sabu>: my nigga
> <Virus>: but I keep my mouth shut
> <Sabu>: you better watch your fucking mouth because I'm not a rat
> <Virus>: I don't get involved
> <Sabu>: and I definitely didnt rat my own boy
> <Virus>: I don't care if "Anonymous" gets pwned
> <Sabu>: I can tell you exactly how he got knocked
> <Virus>: I never liked them, never will
> <Sabu>: and if you actually knew anything you'd know how it went down too
> <Sabu>: for a hot minute there was some troll on twitter that'd hit up atopiary's twitter mentions with
> <Virus>: Anonymous is nothing but a bunch of fat, pimply basement dwelling losers who masturbate 3+ times a day

```
<Sabu>: "jake from shetland"
<Sabu>: he got it from an xbox forums
<Sabu>: topiary was an avid xbox gamer
<Sabu>: was known in the community talked a lot
<Sabu>: one of the forum users doxed him and kept throwing the
info out there
<Sabu>: enough that someone was smart enough to make the
connection
<Virus>: I'm a social engineer, a professional social engineer, actually
<Sabu>: I'm a social engineer too.[5]
```

Sabu tried to defuse the accusation first by showering Virus with compliments, but when that failed, he switched strategies:

```
<Sabu>: you'd know that if I were raided
<Sabu>: I'd take myself down if anything
<Sabu>: I'm the martyr type
<Sabu>: I grew up in the streets
<Virus>: it's a hunch, I'm always right
<Sabu>: this time you're wrong
<Sabu>: I rather go down for my own shit than take down my own
niggas
```

At the time, the accusations seemed plausible, but certainly not definitive. It was just as likely that the spat stemmed from personal conflict—hacker drama—or that Mike Virus was himself a snitch, trying to deflect attention. Virus even admitted that there was little evidence to back up his accusation; he was relying on a hunch. As usual, Sabu was suave *and* fierce in staving off the accusations.

Regardless, his lowered profile signaled that he was being careful. During his hiatus, Anonymous did just fine. The group had gone full throttle with OpBART, and soon after, Occupy engaged its collective attention. Making ops run smoothly requires an increased amount of communication and shared time online, so it is not surprising that in these intensive moments, the rumors exploded like a backdraft—or that they burnt out almost as abruptly as they had flared up. Sabu's return on September 17, the day Occupy started, was a shrewd move that helped nourish his mythos as a bona fide revolutionary. Like a salmon who knows to return thousands of miles upriver to where it was born, Sabu, it seemed, was programmed to show up at an important political happening. His reappearance sent the following message: the allure of a protest overrides everything else. The revolution was what mattered. And accusations that seemed justified by his disappearance quickly looked more like unfounded drama.

Sabu seemed truly excited by Occupy, and as it gained momentum he tweeted about it frequently. Other Anons became similarly preoccupied. The turnout on the first day was so meager that Nathan Schneider, who became one of the most prominent chroniclers of the movement and later wrote a book about it, recalled: "I didn't think it would last. I didn't think it would change anything."[6] But thanks to the persistence of the occupiers, thanks to the social media messages, and thanks to the police (who sparked mass-media attention and public outrage by cracking down against peaceful protesters and marches), in less than two weeks Occupy transformed from smoking embers into a bonfire.

"My days are numbered"

The first week of Occupy, I returned to the camp a few times—and would later join some of the large New York City marches—but as a full-time professor with two classes, a book to finish, and a string of appointments in preparation for an approaching move to a foreign country, it was tough to be there as much as I would have liked. Sometimes other factors kept me away as well. On Tuesday, September 20, my day seemed to be miraculously free, but gazing out my window into the drizzly morning, I was prompted to contemplate all the other valid uses of my time. And call it fate, but had it not been for this lazy reluctance, I might never have met Sabu in the flesh. Of course, reflecting now on the events that transpired, I can only think that it might have been better if I had braved the rain.

Late in the afternoon that day, the rain now gone, I headed to NYSEC, the informal meet-up of security professionals. I ambled toward Swift, a Greenwich Village bar. From a distance, I spotted weev, the famous troll who had headed up Goatse Security and now lived in the Tri-State Area awaiting trial. A cigarette dangled from his mouth and he was talking to two people I did not know.

weev was tipsy and content. You could tell that he was gearing up for a good rant. He sported a pin from Trinity Church, where he regularly attended service—and the sermon he was preparing was on the subject of Occupy. It was unclear whether he supported Occupy or merely saw it as an opportunity to troll. He gave one memorable speech, managing to indict the evil financiers, call out police brutality with a nod to Oscar Grant, and speak to state threats against artisanal cheese makers, all in four minutes. But at other times, weev also held up a sign "ZIONIST PIGS ROB US ALL."[7] weev greeted me. Upon hearing my name, one of the other hackers raised his eyebrows. "So you are Gabriella who studies Anonymous?" he asked. I replied in the affirmative. weev updated us about Occupy and we headed inside. We fetched some drinks and settled into the back room with the twenty or so hackers already there. I figured that the other hacker (let's call him Freddy) likely followed Anonymous from a distance, like many security researchers. But as it turned out, he knew a lot more than I could have imagined. As the evening wore on, Freddy and I found ourselves in a dark corner of the bar. "Are you an FBI agent?" he asked—a question that no longer rattled me the way it might have only a few months previous. I replied, in a somewhat annoyed tone, "No. In fact, I just accepted a position in Canada. Why would the FBI ship me off to a country they largely ignore if I were working for them?"

He clearly knew a great deal about Anonymous, including the secret back-channel IRC groups like #internetfeds. I was informed, also, that he was arranging a meeting between Sabu and Parmy Olson, who was in the midst of writing a book on Anonymous. (Olson says this didn't happen, though she did acknowledge having contact with Freddy.) As our conversation unfolded, it became increasingly clear: he was deep inside Anonymous, and seemed to have known Sabu for quite some time.

Freddy also intimated that Sabu was in New York City. This aligned with hints I had gotten directly from him in our chats. But there were a lot of swirling rumors about Sabu, many maintaining, contrarily, that he lived in Brazil. It seemed equally credible; he worked closely with Brazilian hackers and often spouted off in Portuguese on Twitter.

The information flowed both ways: I spoke about a number of AntiSec and AnonOps IRC backchannels and shared details pertaining to many "black ops." His interest was piqued. And then I mentioned that I was raised in Puerto Rico. Upon hearing this, he offered point blank: "Do you want to meet Sabu?" He could arrange it. I was totally taken aback. I told him, "Meeting him intrigues me, but, to be frank, I am skeptical."

The conversation excited me, less due to the prospect of meeting Sabu—I truly was skeptical—and more for the taste of what many hackers experience all the time: the use of secrets as an valuable object of exchange. Those who write about secrecy commonly recount how an information seeker can, by providing a secret of his or her own, induce further disclosure from his or her interlocutor. Graham Jones, an anthropologist of magicians, describes sharing secrets as "a token of recognition, a gesture of inclusion, a microritual of initiation, and a move in a system of exchange."[8] Sharing secrets can be about revenge or about forging trust. It can be a simple display of status, or a measured revelation in the hopes of prompting a response. But whatever the reasons and whatever the mechanisms, secrets shared often do beget more secrets.

Back in the bar, my mind raced. *Is this guy just a regular guy, or is he working on behalf of the government? We did meet by chance ... didn't we?* Eventually, I decided to leave the bar. At home, exhausted, I transcribed every detail I could remember before passing out fully clothed.

Early the next morning, I made my way to a neighborhood cafe as usual. A couple of hours later, sipping at my second or third coffee, I was lost in work. My IRC client, as was usually the case, was running but ignored. My name flashed on the screen, signaling a private message. Deep in work mode, and allowing no interruptions, I attended to the query after forty minutes had passed. I toggled to the window:

<Sabu>: estas?
<Sabu>: yo
<Sabu>: you there?
<biella>: hi
<biella>: yes
<biella>: am here
[...]
<Sabu>: checkea tu fucking voicemail loca
[...]
<biella>: lol i am wondering here, should i be doing this? :-)
<biella>: giving out my cell to one of the most notorious hackers of all time ?
<biella>: let me listen to the vm first but you know someone you know has it
<biella>: if i went to my office now would you be able to talk? or should i just listen to my VM?
<biella>: i am across the street at a coffee shop
<Sabu>: cono biella just go listen and delete

Back at my office, there was a message and a number. I called and our first phone conversation lasted for an hour. Haughtily declaring himself "the most trusted" hacker, he asked, "What the fuck is up with the snitches?" He then launched into a three-part typology: First, there are the "infiltrators." Second, there are "those that want fame." And third, there are "those that are pinned to the wall and don't want to go to jail." Almost everything he said made me blind to Sabu himself. But just in case I had my doubts, he hammered away with statements like: "Even if the FBI was outside my door and heard what I said, there is no way they could pin the technical act on me … That is why I am not locked up." At the time, this struck me as a perfectly plausible explanation.

The rest of the conversation largely centered on politics, with him ranting and boasting, and me listening. He railed against the NYPD, claiming they were far more corrupt than the FBI—willing to implant false information and break their own rules. He railed against Sony and AT&T, insisting that *they* were the criminals for the shitty state of their security. The conversation turned to WikiLeaks. He proclaimed it a "tragedy" that Assange had squandered an amazing opportunity, but ultimately expressed his love for Manning.

Finally, I had to interrupt and ask, "Why reach out?"

His reply was immediate. "My days are numbered," he reasoned. "This story needs to get out and the media will not do the job." The conversation wound down, leaving me to ponder just what he meant by this.

It wasn't long before we talked again. This time he was on the street, evident from the noise of honking cars and the side conversations between him and his homies. He told me, "Cops are chasing a black kid over a bag of weed." This second conversation centered around his defense of Anonymous's style of hacking. "We are no skids," he insisted, referring to the eternally derided "script kiddies." He described LulzSec as a "proof of concept" which had done more than "any other hacker group in fifteen years." He called AntiSec his brainchild.

I was writing at breakneck speed but, unaccustomed to taking notes longhand, my cramping wrist proved unsuited to the task. Ultimately, none of it was too surprising. Until, that is, the end of the conversation. "I hope I don't sound like a dick," he started. "But I refuse to let my politics die. This is how I feel. I will continue to push for the idea of decentralized organizing." He paused, and then continued, "With decentralization, it is harder to infiltrate." But, "There are snitches." He ended gruffly. He wanted "war. I want total revenge for Recursion. He is just a college student." Just days before, twenty-three-year-old Cody Kretsinger from Phoenix, Arizona, had been arrested by the FBI in connection with hacking Sony Pictures with LulzSec.

During these initial phone conversations, Sabu had intimated that he wanted to meet. I was growing interested in the prospect—but I was determined not to hold my breath. There was much to do in the meantime, as Anonymous's involvement in Occupy escalated. As camps sprang up across North America and Europe, a handful of core Anonymous veterans traded days and nights online for days and nights in the field. A few even found contingents of occupiers who identified as Anons but had never logged into an IRC channel.

On occasion, the two distinct though complementary movements directly crossed streams in a more dramatic fashion. On Sunday, September 25, protesters gathered at Union Square and marched south toward the camp, until police enclosed them behind a length of orange plastic netting. Occupiers chanted, "Shame! Shame! Who are you protecting?! YOU are the 99 percent! You're fighting your own people!" A high-ranking police officer, Anthony Bologna, whipped out his can of pepper spray without provocation and directed the chemical stream at three young women. As the liquid engulfed their faces and stung their eyes, they crumpled to the ground, pleading, "No! Why are you doing that?!"[9] Bologna answered by sauntering away.

Onlookers filmed the entire incident and the video went viral. Anonymous retaliated by swiftly doxing the officer—uploading his name and address to Pastebin. It opened with this message:

As we watched your officers kettle innocent women, we observed you barbarically pepper spray wildly into the group of kettled women. We were shocked and disgusted by your behavior. You know who the innocent women were, now they will have the chance to know who you are. Before you commit atrocities against innocent people, think twice. WE ARE WATCHING!!! Expect Us![10]

Bologna's information was uploaded by a young female college student who "earned her badge" in the CabinCr3w for the effort. During an online interview I conducted with her, she explained the mechanics of her expose: "a lot of rewatching [the video], zooming, trying to get facial features, badge number, and a partial name. It turns out that when I resorted to just a simple google, I found out that he had previously been a problem with abuse, and had a case against him." (There was a pending lawsuit against him brought by a protester at the 2004 Republican National Convention in New York City.)

Since she did not strike me as someone who doxed for doxing's sake, I asked where she drew the line between acceptable exposure and privacy violation: "[the police] work for the public, therefore your life … is public just as a news organisation would hound you." She continued, "morally: I think there is a limit and boundary by which how deep the dox go," claiming she only disclosed information that identified Bologna himself. Other Anons, however, decided to go deeper, doxing members of his family.

The NYPD defended Bologna's actions at first, but soon retracted. An internal police review determined that the officer had indeed violated protocol. As punishment, he lost ten days of vacation and was reassigned to Staten Island (implicitly divulging the NYPD's opinion of the city's smallest borough).[11] There was, at least, a silver lining. The incident helped catapult Occupy onto the national stage. *The Guardian* and other major news outlets reported on the event, quoting directly from Anonymous's Pastebin message and cementing a nascent association between Anonymous and Occupy.[12] From that day on—and especially following the mass arresting of over seven hundred people during a peaceful march across the Brooklyn Bridge—Occupy became a fixture in activist circles and the mainstream media alike.

Meeting Sabu

Thanks to a detailed FAQ published by the New York City Department of Information Technology and Telecommunications, we know roughly how many sidewalk payphones dot the five boroughs: "As of January 2, 2014 there are 9,903 active public pay telephones on or over the City's sidewalks."[13] I, personally, had never even noticed them, until Sabu asked me to use one. He did not want to arrange a meeting online. It felt safer and prudent to use a payphone; key loggers are always a possibility with computers.

Our first rendezvous was scheduled for soon after Bologna's doxing, on October 3 at the Chipotle on St. Mark's Place in the East Village. He assured me that "you will recognize me." The one picture purporting to be Sabu floating around the web was of a wiry, yet muscular, Latino man. I arrived early. The minutes moved slowly, until suddenly, I was aware of a tall commanding figure sauntering toward me. Carrying his large body with aplomb, he seemed to be in his element. It was Sabu. He grabbed my hand and I was afraid it would shatter in his grip. I gathered my things and we went to order food. In the midst of our small talk, Sabu paused, casually nodded to the food prep worker (a tough-looking Latina), and asked, "What's up?"

She replied, "I have not seen you here in a while." As would become increasingly clear, whether in Chipotle, a local diner, or Tompkins Square Park, many locals knew Sabu and treated him with deference—out of respect or fear, I can't say which, but he was clearly a known quantity in the neighborhood.

Before long, he steered the conversation toward his past. "I came from a drug family," he divulged almost immediately, and then continued nonchalantly: "By the time I was thirteen or fourteen, I carried four to five thousand dollars in cash in my wallet." He also explained that he was the "father figure" to his adopted cousins—both younger than seven at the time— though he left the reason for taking on such massive parental responsibilities unstated until later. (When Sabu was thirteen, his aunt and father were sent to jail for dealing heroin. He was raised by his grandmother until she passed away on June 7, 2010, exactly one year before he was apprehended by the FBI. Upon her passing, he assumed parental responsibility for his cousins.)

Sabu said that he worked hard to overcome a "ghetto mentality," an immobilizing mixture of self-hatred and anger. Later, he briefly recounted a few episodes that substantiated his everyday experience with harsh racism. Sabu attended Washington Irving High School, near East Sixteenth Street, alongside many poor students. One day, entering the school, he walked through a metal detector and, carrying a screwdriver, was stopped by a guard. He defended himself: "I am the geek that fixes your system when you forget not to execute 'weird' .exe's." The guard bought none of it and a tiff between the two ensued. Sabu, who felt disrespected, complained to the administration, but found only deaf ears. So he made some noise by penning a strident, and self-described "controversial," missive and circulating it to teachers. The principal deemed it "threatening" and he was temporarily suspended. Sabu, reflecting later upon the incident in a Pastebin document, concluded: "Very well then, it is such a shame that one ... such as myself would have to be deprived of my education because of my writing."[14]

It made immediate sense, then, why Sabu found hacking— with its elevation of ideas and arguments—to be an appealing oasis. This is not to say that the zone of hacking is free of prejudice. Far from it. The white male-dominant scene, with some hackers especially prone to acting out elitist cowboy bravado, is alienating and repellent to many.[15] The barriers are especially pronounced in underground quarters that are composed nearly exclusively of male (and a few transgender) participants. Nevertheless, since ideas are (in theory) exalted over social pedigree, it has functioned as a safe space, at least online, for a class of technical weirdos.[16] The social boundaries erected by hackers also exhibit contradictions: while the gender gap is vast, some identities—such as transgender, queer, or disabled—are more common and accepted. (It took some time, but I eventually figured out that the chatroom #lounge on AnonOps doubled at times as a gay pickup spot.) Sabu's explanation that he "rarely hangs out with hackers in person" hints at the sort of partial freedoms provided by anonymity and technical skills online.

After we said our goodbyes, I could not help but think of Sabu as a cooler and savvier version of Oscar Wao, the lead character in Junot Díaz's electrifying novel on the travails of being a corpulent, ostracized, "hardcore sci-fi and fantasy"– loving nerd of Dominican descent. *The Brief Wondrous Life of Oscar Wao* tells the story of Oscar as he shuttles between New Jersey and the Dominican Republic, bumbling through life while trying to fulfill a cherished rite of passage: getting laid.

Sabu, like Oscar, is a consummate cultural boundary-crosser, flitting easily between vastly distinct cultural spheres. Unlike Oscar, Sabu was no dud, and his machismo was overpowering. He was notorious for hitting on the ladies in #AnonOps and told journalist Quinn Norton in a chat, "I like you quinn, next time you're in new york, you can watch me hack, naked."[17] With me, he was more restrained, alternating between calling me "mi amor" ("my love") and "cupcake."

After our first meeting, now mentally equipped with a picture of Sabu, I resumed my chats with him. *The Guardian* newspaper had asked Sabu to write an op-ed about Occupy. He asked me to give some editorial feedback. Meanwhile, I attempted to convince him to be filmed for Brian Knappenberger's documentary *We Are Legion*:

> \<Sabu\>: also
> \<Sabu\>: if I do this thing with your boy knapp
> \<Sabu\>: you gotta make sure that nigga doesnt leak my identity

More than any other journalist covering Anonymous, Brian Knappenberger had sought out a wide cross section of individuals, pouring his funds and time into a project he was wildly passionate about. I wanted to help him. That Sabu was considering doing it was great news, but I had to reassure him about my ability to be discreet and to impress upon Knappenberger the necessity of further discretion. My protocol was generally one of "silos of interaction." When I chatted on public channels, an observer could get a sense of who I spoke with, but my private chats were largely confidential, following a protocol commonly adopted in Anonymous. Eventually, a small group of the journalist/researcher confederacy—namely Knappenberger and Olson—knew I had met Sabu, but otherwise I kept it to myself.

Our seemingly trivial conversations would sometimes become much more interesting in retrospect. For example, the following conversation, which happened the day after we first met, seemed relatively mundane at the time:

> \<Sabu\>: and ioerror is good people [ioerror = Tor developer Jacob Appelbaum]
> \<Sabu\>: I'm trying to reach out to him
> \<Sabu\>: I know hes been supportive of me in the last year
> \<Sabu\>: I want to support him back
> \<biella\>: yea he has
> \<Sabu\>: during this time
> \<biella\>: i know him well
> \<Sabu\>: they're trying to rail him
> \<biella\>: for over 9 years now

\<Sabu\>: tell him I send my regards then
\<biella\>: i will for sure
\<Sabu\>: if theres anything we can do for him, to pass it through you

At the time, I interpreted this as a reasonable gesture of solidarity. Now, these chats—and his motivations for reaching out to me in the first place—look different. The "we" he referred to was not Sabu and Anonymous. It was Sabu and the FBI—privileged with direct access to all his conversations, including the one above. It would not be the last time he tried to "to reach out to" Applebaum through me.

The Propensity to Sympathize with Others

In late October, as winds shook off the remaining leaves still clinging to branches, Occupy was blossoming. Organizers were branching out; alliances with unions and other civil society groups yielded new rivers of people flowing into Liberty Square on October 15, a planned "day of action." As I marched for hours alongside throngs of strangers, everyone appeared energized and amazed by the vibrant turn Occupy had taken in the short course of a single month. "The Occupy assemblies were opening tremendous space in American political discourse," reflected Nathan Schneider, who also noted that "by mid-October, Occupy Wall Street had an approval rating of more than 50 percent—higher than President Obama or Congress."[18]

Naysayers and pundits would accuse Occupy of being led by lifestyle activists, for fizzling out after being unable to drum up broad-based support—a misguided account made clear by the repressive crackdown that would come, just one month later, to stamp out many of the US camps. Documents procured by the Partnership for Civil Justice Fund through a Freedom of Information Act request reveal that most every law enforcement entity—Department of Homeland Security, the FBI, local police, Fusion Centers, the Joint Terrorism Task Force, the Naval Criminal Investigative Service, and even, oddly, the Federal Reserve—took a keen interest in Occupy.[19] Since the documents are so heavily redacted, it is hard to gauge the specific role played by each organization, but it is clear that, at minimum, they "Cast [a] Wide Net in Monitoring Occupy Protests," as the *New York Times* titled its piece covering the documents.[20] One reason why Anonymous had already thrived for five years was that despite the arrests of members of the collective, its decentralized and online character had made preemption extremely difficult. This would not prove to be the case with Occupy.

I continued to meet Sabu. On some occasions, his two younger brothers accompanied him. The older one was Sabu's sidekick. He admired him and, while not as technically proficient as Sabu, he loved to talk about computers. The younger one, who sported sleek, straight, black-as-night hair and a lot of muscles, was, like many teenagers, absorbed in thought, totally uninterested in the geek talk that consumed the rest of us.

One meeting stands out. On an unusually warm November evening, we hung out in Tompkins Square Park with his brothers again. Then Sabu and I went to the Odessa, a classic New York City diner with a mind-boggling array of dining options. By now, one thing had become clear: Sabu was a talker. Entering the diner, Sabu greeted with a handshake a man whom I presumed to be the owner or the manager. Easing into a booth, we became one with the ageless Naugahyde seats, their well-worn springs clenching us desperately. That day he broached a dizzying number of topics in the course of our conversation: gentrification, the hacker Phiber Optik, Middle East politics, Occupy, his dog (whose name was China, and who had an awful skin condition), the sociology of hacker crews, the Anonymous haters, and dozens of other topics that his mind alighted upon. Among the deluge of details, a few stood out. It was the first time he mentioned a mysterious hacker he worked closely with, whom he called "burn." I now know him as Jeremy Hammond. Sabu boasted that he liked to own security companies while "burn liked to hit the police." And in this conversation, one thing became patently evident: more than anything else, Sabu seemed to genuinely care what others thought of not only himself, but the whole of Anonymous. His contempt for those critical of Anonymous—both journalists and random people on Twitter—was noticeable; he jeered at those who he felt had not treated him, or Anonymous, with respect. Soon after, winding down, he sighed in a weary voice. "I sometimes just want to walk away and quit." He did seem tired, and he had developed a chronic cough since our previous meeting. I knew he had also talked extensively with Olson over Skype, and it struck me suddenly that he had a burning desire for his life story to be put out into the world.

When someone is wearing a mask, there is at least a symbolic reminder that insincerity, duplicity, and play might be at work. Sitting across from Sabu, seeing his face, hearing his voice, and looking into his eyes, I suspended my mistrust, even though I knew that with or without a mask, I really had no access to his true motivations. We can never really access the inner thoughts of other humans; we can only attempt to gauge sincerity or authenticity. Then there's what Hume identified as one of the most enduring qualities of human nature: "No quality of human nature is more remarkable, both in itself and in its consequences, than that propensity we have to sympathize with others."[21]

It's hard to constantly question people's motives. It is precisely the human proclivity to want to sympathize that enables the FBI to perform exploits through its informants. We left The Odessa and, as usual, Sabu lit up a sweet-smelling cigarette. He took a deep puff from the white filter. And then, suddenly, he confessed: "I was indeed a criminal. I used to sell heroin." Then he walked away.

CHAPTER 11

The Sabutage

Although AntiSec had been on a hacking spree, compromising high-profile targets like the FBI, the group was not getting much attention—and the attention it did get was not exactly positive. Certain data dumps, such as those regarding police units (including the International Association of Chiefs of Police, Boston Police Patrolmen's Association, and the Sheriff's Office of Baldwin County, Alabama) struck some Anons as random and incoherent—many people, even within Anonymous, didn't quite see the point. A supporter of information leaks, Anonymous9 felt that AntiSec's ops weren't cutting the mustard. "Just because a lunch menu at Fort Meade might be classified," he told me, "doesn't mean it is interesting much less worth leaking." Then, just in time for "LulzXmas," a mysterious hacker named hyrriiya delivered a gift. On December 13, 2011, a few AntiSec members pulled the journalist Quinn Norton and myself aside into a channel to ask a question:

<Antisec>: will journos cover stuff that's probably
<Antisec>: deeply illegal
<Antisec>: lol
<quinn>: yes, but framing is important
<Antisec2>: Not illegal like ddos or leaking some cops emails. ;)

<biella>: deeply as opposed to surface illegal
<Anon>: we have a table of illegal categories
[...]
***Anon checks the cheatsheet
<biella>: Anon, do you??
<biella>: lolll
***Anon thinks 'fuck we r screwed'
<quinn>: is this like a mandatory minimums kind of chart?
<quinn>: heheh
<Anon>: hahaa
<biella>: OFF THE CHARTS illegal

Soon after this chat, an AntiSec member casually informed me that they possessed credit card data and intended to use it for charitable donations. While he kept the source of the database a secret, it remained one of the few instances where sensitive information was sprung upon me. I publicly maintained my caveat: I could not guarantee the confidentiality of any information given to me. And, as if that wasn't enough to freak me out, Jeremy Hammond (using the name "sup_g") queried me on December 15:

<sup_g>: Not sure if you are down, able, or safe to examine some data pre-release, but there's some mail spools available.
<biella>: not right now, sorry :-(though i look forward to hearing about it

By now, my interactions with Hammond were limited and contained. Most of our conversations were rolled into group chats in the private CabinCr3w channel (where he was "sup_g") and in Barrett Brown's Project PM (where he was "o"). With time, I connected these two nicknames and remained undecided about him. He kept a pretty low profile, except when political discussions would draw him out and suddenly he would flood the chat with his views, in a rather heated fashion. Hammond was hands down the most insurgent of the bunch. Though his dedication was evident, I could not help but at times imagine him to be an agent provocateur.

When he offered me a pre-release of the email spool, my alarms sounded. Is this entrapment? Unlike Brown, whose begging for these very emails fell on deaf AntiSec ears (he was never given them), I desperately tried to avoid receiving this kind of information. And, anyway, why—after all my caveats and all their attempts to remain mum—were they suddenly offering to toss me all this information? It seemed fishy, and it stressed me out.

Thankfully a deeper reservoir of secrets was actually being kept from me. Most significant was that the AntiSec crew, at the onset of December, had become deeply suspicious of Sabu. As one member told me later, various hackers continued appearing, at random, and insisting, mantra-like, that "Sabu is an informant." Hammond too had grown tired of Sabu's reluctance to get his hands dirty, an indicator that something was amiss. At the time, they kept their concerns to themselves.

On Christmas Eve, AntiSec decided to publicly release the details of its most memorable—and unforgiving—hack. In a politically motivated act of corporate sabotage, AntiSec infiltrated the internal network of the global intelligence firm Strategic Forecasting, Inc., better known as Stratfor. AntiSec collected over 50,000 credit card numbers, downloaded almost eight years' worth of company emails—five million in total—and procured countless other records. As a finale, they gutted Stratfor's servers of their data, removing everything they could find (including backups). In what AntiSec described as "an act of loving egalitarian criminality,"[1] they attempted to use 30,000 of the credit cards to donate an estimated $700,000 to "the Bradley Manning Support Organization, the EFF, the ACLU, CARE, American Red Cross, Amnesty International, Greenpeace, some commies, some prisoners, various occupations, and many more unnamed homies."[2] (Only 9,561 of the cards were still valid.) Let's now take a closer look at the events leading up to AntiSec's mothership hack.

Total Mayhem

On December 4, hyrriiya, a member of a small hacker crew called RevoluSec (which worked on infiltrating Syrian government computers, among other projects) reached out to Sabu:

<hyrriiya>: wake up
<hyrriiya>: got funny shit u will love
<Sabu>: im here brother
<Sabu>: whats up
<hyrriiya>: :=
<hyrriiya>: so i hax this intelligence company
<hyrriiya>: by accident

This immediately piqued Sabu's interest:

<Sabu>: we would love to penetrate their users/network for #antisec definitely get me details so I can begin working :)
<hyrriiya>: :p
<hyrriiya>: the network is on hold right now
<hyrriiya>: soon as i extract what i need
<hyrriiya>: i give it to you
<hyrriiya>: but i'd advise to pwn them and sniff for a few months
<hyrriiya>: my own countries secret services use their services :p
<hyrriiya>: cnn uses them
<hyrriiya>: etc
<hyrriiya>: the economist lol

The next day, hyrriiya provided, as Jeremy Hammond later related to me, "the entire [AntiSec] channel a link to Stratfor order databases, including addresses, and credit cards [and] random credit card numbers swiped from the Stratfor database." Sabu created another channel called "#!sec" and hyrriiya delivered the information about the exploit. Hammond described the hack to me in great technical detail (though it's not essential to understanding the story):

No password, oops! which lets you download the entire db dump, from mysql db access, here I am able to insert users into str's [Stratfor's] drupal system, creating an administrator account, then enabling PHP code on drupal articles, and inserting a PHP backdoor into a drupal article allowing remote code execution on str's webserver (they kept different boxes for various services), then rooted the webserver, then was able to log onto their mailserver using an "autobot" user that had access to several of their other internal servers for backup purposes, rooted that too.

As if having no password protection was not negligent enough, Stratfor's credit card information was saved in clear text, instead of behind a digital fortress of encryption, as is standard industry practice. Apparently, while Stratfor sold security briefings to its clients, it did not seem to follow any of its own advice.

AntiSec intended to liberate eight years of emails from Stratfor's servers—more than two hundred gigabytes. Finding a good place to put it, with enough space and bandwidth, was a bit of an issue. Hammond opted to hack some other machines to provide this service. A few other AntiSec members began researching methods toward deeper infiltration into Stratfor's systems, while some who had only wanted to ignite the fire soon departed.

hyrriiya's role was as a messenger alone, and he eventually bailed on the rest of the operation:

<hyrriiya>: also another thing
<hyrriiya>: when i get u the details
<hyrriiya>: please forget that it came from me :)
<hyrriiya>: and that revolusec had anything to do with it :p
<hyrriiya>: as this company is full of crazy feds :p
<hyrriiya>: and we don't need the credit.)
<hyrriiya>: :)
<Sabu>: yup
<Sabu>: #antisec has been to war with feds/nato since june

On Christmas Eve, I received a query from a mysterious user named "ghost__"—another incarnation of Hammond himself, as I later learned. He gave me the most explosive news I would receive in all my time studying Anonymous:

```
<ghost__>: hello
<ghost__>: shit's getting owned on anonops
<biella>: hello
<ghost__>: about to rm -rf a major target
```

I was not sure what he meant by the first statement, but the second was clear. I may be no technology wizard, but I knew what "rm -rf/" was, having been a Linux user for over fourteen years. Once you have root access, this command can delete everything on the system (technically speaking, Hammond conveyed his actions in shorthand because newer UNIX systems have protections built-in, such as requiring the "--no-preserve-root" flag to be passed first, making it harder to delete everything by accidentally typing six characters). I tried to play it cool. I still wasn't sure what he was talking about. He gave a few more details:

```
<ghost__>: it is a major intelligence corporation
<ghost__>: ~30 min
<biella>: hmm ok
<ghost__>: meanwhile, credit cards being used on anonops
```

Soon, my confusion was cleared up by tweets like the following from Sabu: "http://www.stratfor.com - #ANTISEC DISMANTLES A MULTI-MILLION DOLLAR INTELLI-GENCE CORPORATION - watch the video and read the essay. #antisec."[3] I thought to myself, *holy sweet birth of the baby Jesus, this is really happening*!

A handful of people were livid or confused, but most seemed to be riding the wave with trolling/humorous responses on the public channels: "VOTING STILL GOING ON FOR

LULZXMAS DONATION PICK; options are (in order of leading to losing); CANCER, TOR, AIDS, WIKILEAKS, SHELTERS, REDCROSS, ANONOPS."

AntiSec replaced Stratfor's webpage with *The Coming Insurrection*, a revolutionary tract written by the radical, anonymous Invisible Committee. Its ostensibly French authors, seeking to hasten the demise of capitalism, call for new modes of collective association and the rapid deployment of an "effective guerrilla war that restores us to our ungovernability, our primordial unruliness."[4] From Christmas Day through to New Years, the pace of hacking redoubled. Pursuant of a generalized sort of mayhem, AntiSec thought it necessary to thrash more than just a single organization; while news coverage focused almost exclusively on Stratfor, AntiSec had in fact carried out a "coast-to-coast hacking" bonanza, and announced as much proudly in their zine:

> On New Years Eve, while revolutionary comrades brought the noise to the front of jails across the world in support of the incarcerated, we were opening fire on the websites and emails of the 1%, publishing stolen information from police departments in both California and New York. From coast to coast we lulzed as we hit the top police chiefs: skimming their private email and Facebook accounts, blissfully abusing their internal law enforcement portals, and making off quick with their private documents which we then published on tor hidden services and BitTorrent. Finally, we defaced their websites and rm'd their servers, live on IRC and Twitter for the whole world to see.[5]

AntiSec's three additional targets were cslea.com (the California Statewide Law Enforcement Association—self-touted, it is worth noting, as "America's most fascinating law enforcement association"); nychiefs.org (New York State Association of Chiefs of Police); and specialforces.com (a marketplace for, as the name may suggest, gear oriented toward special forces operations). Each site added to the growing AntiSec collection of mail spools, usernames, passwords, emails, phone numbers, and "Law Enforcement Sensitive" documents.

The whole while Sabu remained unflappably brazen and ferocious. In reply to an ex-supporter who blamed AntiSec for being irresponsible, he bit back: "FUCK the intelligence community. the security industry. and everyone in between. We support the people."[6] He painted Stratfor as the criminals: "@STRATFOR has potentially broken the law by storing customer data, unencrypted, on an [sic] publicly accessible insecure server. Question them."[7] The internal accusations and suspicions of Sabu were mitigated by moments like these. But accusations persisted. A few Pastebin announcements surfaced on the subject. One was entitled "Press Release: Stratfor Hack NOT Anonymous" and chided Sabu: "Sabu and his crew are nothing more than opportunistic attention whores who are possibly agent provocateurs."[8]

Just a few weeks prior to LulzXmas, Sabu had finally agreed to meet with Brian Knappenberger to be filmed for his documentary—but only if certain conditions were met. Sabu was to be concealed and his voice distorted, and Knappenberger was to leave no digital trace of his travels or whereabouts. He would have to get to New York City by paying for his airline ticket and hotel in cash—making sure to choose a hotel or place to sleep where ID was not required. I was away for the holidays and returned to New York City (and a relentless downpour) on December 26 expressly to assist Knappenberger and help him connect with Sabu, but Sabu never showed. However, given the major hacks that had just occurred, Sabu's absence seemed more like an indication that he was being careful rather than chickening out.

The next day, and despite the no-show, I decided to make one last effort to see Sabu. I wanted to give him a small gift before I left NYC, the book *Outliers* by Malcolm Gladwell. I went downstairs and called Sabu, asking whether he would come by the next day to pick it up before my partner and I left for Canada. After the wet and miserable failures of the day before, I had serious doubts that he would show up. But Sabu did not disappoint. As my partner and I sat in our car, just minutes before our planned departure time, a huge black pickup truck loaded with guys rolled up, and Sabu hopped out. I went out to meet him. He was in a rush and we were too, so our exchange lasted less than ten minutes. I gave him the book and wished him well. He walked over to our car and my partner rolled down the window. I introduced them (avoiding, as per protocol, any reference to "Sabu" or any other name; he never offered his real one). They shook hands as our scruffy dog looked on. It was the last time I would see Sabu in person.

Back to the Classics

Anonymous activity would soar to new heights over the next three months. AntiSec was still sitting on the full Stratfor email spool, providing nibbles here and there in taunting press releases. Meanwhile, Barrett Brown continued to beg for the emails, and relations between him and the crew became tense. Hammond explained that some AntiSec members at the time "did not like BB [Brown] for many of the same personality-ego-tripping reasons that are already well known." A few were especially upset that he had tweeted about the release before it was made public.

They decided to give the cache to WikiLeaks. Hammond simply went to the WikiLeaks IRC server (largely behind Sabu's back) and the deal was done. "When talking to WikiLeaks," Hammond recounted to me, "they first asked to authenticate the leak by pasting them some samples, which I did, [but] they didn't ask who I was or even really how I got access to it, but I told them voluntarily that I was working with AntiSec and had hacked Stratfor." Soon after, he arranged the handoff. When Sabu found out, he insisted on dealing with Assange personally. After all, he told Hammond, he was already in contact with Assange's trusted assistant "Q." (Later, Wired.com's Kevin Poulsen broke a story about Q, an Icelandic teenager, Sigurdur "Siggi" Thordarson, who voluntarily became an FBI informant in August 2011, handing thousands of WikiLeaks chats and documents over to law enforcement in the process. He did it, reportedly, for "the adventure.")[9] Sabu entered into "conversations with WL about getting some cash for the leaks," according to Hammond, but by that time WikiLeaks already had the documents and were well on their way to processing them for release. In just two months the public would see the emails for themselves.

As the hubbub over the credit card donations simmered down around mid-January, the populist face of Anonymous reemerged in reaction to the Stop Online Piracy Act (SOPA). The far-reaching US copyright bill was unpopular, and not only among civil libertarians. The digerati and Silicon Valley elite also came out against it. SOPA called for, among other things, Google and other search engines to prevent flagged sites like the Pirate Bay from showing up in search results. A massive and elaborate outpouring of dissent ensured the bill's unraveling well before it could pass into law. The linchpin was a "Blackout Day" held on January 18, 2012—a web-based protest of unprecedented scale. A handful of large Internet companies, several public interest groups, and thousands of individuals programmed their websites to display only black, with links urging visitors to write their representatives to express opposition to SOPA. Around seventy-five thousand webpages went dark, including dozens of prominent corporate and nonprofit websites such as Wikipedia, Flickr, Wired, 4chan, and Google.[10] Journalists also wrote a torrent of articles. Less than a week later, SOPA and its Senate counterpart, PIPA, were effectively scrapped—by being tabled indefinitely. In the end, CBS News described the number of participants as "staggering": 4.5 million people signed a petition circulated by Google; 350,000 citizens wrote to their representatives via SopaStrike.com and AmericanCensorship.org; over 2.4

million SOPA-related tweets were written on January 18 alone; and an online White House petition garnered 103,785 names.[11] In response to the petition, the government officially announced the bill's demise: "Moving forward, we will continue to work with Congress on a bipartisan basis on legislation that provides new tools needed in the global fight against piracy and counterfeiting, while vigorously defending an open Internet based on the values of free expression, privacy, security and innovation."[12]

Corporate giants like Google, respected Internet personalities like Wikipedia cofounder Jimmy Wales, and civil liberties organizations like the EFF were all integral to the victory. But the grassroots geek and hacker contingent was also present—including, of course, Anonymous. They churned out videos and propaganda posters, and provided constant updates on several prominent Twitter accounts. When the blackout ended, corporate players quickly receded from the limelight. Anonymous and others, however, continued the seemingly endless fight.

Just the next day, in fact, on January 19, 2012, federal authorities orchestrated the takedown of popular file-sharing site Megaupload. The company's gregarious and controversial founder, Kim Dotcom, was arrested in a dramatic early morning raid in New Zealand. The removal of this popular website was received ominously by Anonymous activists. Although SOPA had nothing to do with Dotcom's arrest, it was a reminder of the enormous regulatory power that copyright industries could wield over web content, with or without formal legal backing: even though no court had yet found Dotcom guilty of piracy, his property was confiscated and his website knocked off the Internet. (While Dotcom's case is still ongoing at the time of writing, the prime minister of New Zealand, John Key, has issued a formal apology for illegal surveillance leading up to the dramatic raid on Dotcom's house, which involved two helicopters and seventy-six officers.[13])

As soon as the news broke, Anonymous retaliated with its largest DDoS campaign to date, downing the homepages of Universal Music, the FBI, the US Copyright Office, the Recording Industry Association of America, and the Motion Picture Association of America, among others—entities, all, which sought to stamp out illegal file sharing. Anonymous and AnonOps changed up their tactics, opting for a different tool than LOIC. This new tool, called PyLoris, was both more cleverly designed and also more powerful; most importantly, it protected the privacy of its user. It worked by making an incomplete connection to the target server and then holding it open for a very long time. Normally, a server has only so many available "slots" for accepting connections. But if the connection is only partially set up, the slot will wait, refusing subsequent connections in the interim. With enough people making and maintaining these incomplete connections, the server's available slots become filled and service is effectively denied.

It all unfolded like the best old-school ops, with the software available to download from a link in the IRC channel topic and the targets announced to the channel for the several thousand people who opted into the attack. Links also pointed to guides on how to better anonymize one's connections using Tor and VPNs.

Just a few weeks later, in Europe, as massive online and offline demonstrations unfolded against the Anti-Counterfeiting Trade Agreement (ACTA), another international copyright agreement, Anonymous again appeared. Following the Polish government's agreement to ratify ACTA, Anonymous took down a slew of their websites and began to heavily publicize the street protests sweeping Krakow. Soon after, Poland's left-leaning Palikot's Movement party donned Guy Fawkes masks during a parliamentary hearing on ACTA—the first, and so far the only, time elected officials adopted the revolutionary symbol. Amid this and many other outcries, the European parliament rejected the proposed law in July 2012.

Afterwards, one of the old-guard Anons, who had been a member of #command as far back as the fall of 2010, reached out to me with the following assessment:

<h>: at the moment it seems as if there is a whole new group of people
<h>: not connected to #antisec [and] working as hard as ever
<h>: which makes me happy and proud of people
<biella>: yea
<biella>: here and a few other places
<biella>: it is good
<h>: and when i saw those polish politicians
<h>: with masks on
<biella>: yea unreal
<h>: I realised that us bunch of motley fools have actually entered the worlds conscious[ness]
<h>: and in some small way are changing things
<h>: :D

As an insider, it's natural that he would seek to puff up Anonymous. But that wasn't all that was going on—his assessment of the group's increasing power seemed accurate. Not long after this exchange, I received a call from a venture capitalist who had helped organize some of the protests against SOPA. He wanted to learn more about how Anonymous operated behind the scenes. The group seemed to pop up unpredictably, he remarked, before musing on the possibility that an outsider contacting and harnessing it toward other fights for Internet freedom. It felt a bit gross—one of Anonymous's core principles is that it will not be anybody's "personal army"—but, if nothing else, his interest demonstrated the accuracy of h's intuition: Anonymous had become an important, recognized, and potent component of the global political mix.

"Admit nothing, deny everything and make counter-accusations"

On February 27, WikiLeaks distributed the Stratfor emails, labeling them "The Global Intelligence Files." Opinions over their political significance varied. A small cohort of journalists,

security specialists, and even some of Stratfor's own customers reacted with a mere "meh." Scant evidence of outrageous
or illegal behavior was contained in the emails, they asserted.
This blasé reaction was colored by the less-than-stellar reputation already enjoyed by Stratfor at the time of the release.
Many viewed the company, frankly, as rip-off artists: "Stratfor
Is a Joke and So Is Wikileaks for Taking It Seriously" was the
insulting headline proffered by Max Fisher in *The Atlantic*.[14]
For an exorbitant fee (up to $40,000 per annum in 2001),
Stratfor subscribers received a newsletter, which Fisher said
contained little more than rehashed news. Of course, the firm's
reputation only plunged further when it was revealed it never
bothered to encrypt its subscribers' credit card information.

Other journalists and members of the public found the emails
to be politically potent, however, providing solid nuggets of
proof that Stratfor profited from morally dubious practices,
such as corporate propaganda dressed as public relations and
the monitoring of activists. The Stratfor emails are indeed
revealing—and occasionally prescient. Take, for instance, the
following excerpt from a lengthier email typed, remarkably,
on an iPhone on December 10, 2010:

> The chaners/anon/b are educated and at the leading edge
> of network based technology, have a nebulous structure of
> loyal people spread through the world with no nationalistic
> foundations bit [*sic*] drawn together under a shared interest
> in chaos (hentai and cats, for fuck sake). There are numer-
> ous examples where they have uncovered identities and
> all personal details of people based on a single photo (of
> a woman putting a cat in a garbage bin for example) and
> bought [*sic*] some serious vigilanty style justice to those they
> disagree with ...
>
> It's going to be very interesting to watch what anon does in
> the 'post-wilileaks' environment. If they move from a bunch
> of tech geeks in mum's basement into a real movement they
> could cause serious trouble and be hard to kill. The coresy

[*sic*] not be the problem but the few unhinged among them could prove to be quite destructive if so inclined.[15]

Journalist Steve Horn sifted through thousands of Stratfor emails and wrote a two-part series examining the tactics deployed by the firm and its predecessors, Mongoven, Biscoe and Duchin (MBD) and Pagan. The founder of MBD, Ronald Duchin—a military man with extensive work experience in public relations—devised the "Duchin formula": "isolate the radicals, 'cultivate' the idealists and 'educate' them into becoming realists. Then co-opt the realists in agreeing with industry." Horn notes that this strategy "is still employed to this day by Stratfor."[16]

The majority of company emails show that "the most important service Stratfor provides is its sociological analysis in service to corporate power and capital, not the dirty on-the-ground work," according to Horn.[17] A smattering of emails also point to more direct involvement in the monitoring of activists. A 1984 explosion at a Union Carbide India Ltd. plant in Bhopal, India—one of the worst industrial disasters of the twentieth century—left thousands dead and over 500,000 exposed to deadly chemicals. Dow Chemical, who purchased Union Carbide, hired Stratfor to keep tabs on various activist groups, such as the Yes Men and Bhopal Medical Appeal, which were publicizing the issue or assisting victims. The documents revealed that Coca-Cola hired Stratfor to watch the environmental group PETA, particularly its operations in Canada in the lead-up to the Vancouver Olympics. And Stratfor sent an employee, self-described in an email as "U/C" (undercover), to infiltrate the local Occupy group in Austin, Texas, with the goal of gathering organizational intelligence—tracking the occupiers' movements and identifying possible ties with environmental activists:

There is a group you may be familiar with called Deep Green Resistance ... Whether anyone in the Fed or elsewhere classifies this group as eco-terror or not, I don't know, but they are nothing but and should be watched ... The local Austin chapter was part of the Occupy Austin crowd at city hall, however, things were not "radical" enough for them since they do not believe in working within the system. When I was working U/C on Nov. 5th, some of my contacts told me that at the General Assembly on Nov. 4th, there was some conflict between regular Occupy people and Deep Green.[18]

These examples harken back to the issues raised in Chapter 7 regarding the HBGary and HBGary Federal e-mails which, among other suggestions both creepy and invasive, contained a proposal to discredit WikiLeaks. Information about corporate espionage, even with these emails, is still scant. Still, between emerging examples of abuse and the difficulty in accessing corporate records, we should, at a minimum, be troubled by cozy ties revealed between private industry and government. If indeed—as one email purports—Stratfor's vice president of intelligence, Fred Burton, lives by the code "Admit nothing, deny everything and make counter-accusations," then we can see the importance of the leaks and whistleblowing activites of Anonymous and its ilk.

Stratfor issued this statement about the authenticity of the leaked emails:

> Some of the emails may be forged or altered to include inaccuracies; some may be authentic. We will not validate either. Nor will we explain the thinking that went into them. Having had our property stolen, we will not be victimized twice by submitting to questioning about them.[19]

Stratfor did, however, comment on two emails that were subsequently widely accepted as frauds: a letter of resignation from Stratfor's founder, CIO, and CEO, George Friedman, which AntiSec wrote, and a fraudulent email purportedly sent to all

Stratfor customers offering a free subscription to the company's newsletter as a peace offering and apology for the breach.

"I needed the truth out there"

Around this time, Sabu became more cocky and defiant in public than ever. In early February, in response to a critic asking about the status of Syrian emails that AntiSec was rumored to have, Sabu barked: "You'll eat your words once we decide to leak what we have. We don't give a fuck about governments. We give a fuck about people."[20] I had not talked to him on the phone since moving to Canada. This wasn't only due to the logistics of moving; calling from an outdoor payphone in the middle of a Montreal winter put one at risk of frostbite. But early in the morning on March 6, Sabu kept harassing me on Twitter. He didn't care how I contacted him, as long as I did it, and as soon as possible. I picked up my home phone and called him.

It was as if he started talking before even picking up the phone: "Fox is going to publish a story about me and the FBI." Sabu explained that the story was slated to go live in just a few minutes. He said that he wanted to explain some things before I read it. Distraught, he said that Fox had "stooped so low" to get at him and his family, but he refused to tell me just what they had done. He said only, "It's not what you think it is." My head spun throughout it all; I grew dizzy. I remember being angry, and having difficulty verbalizing what I was feeling or remembering what he said. And then, somehow, the conversation ended.

As it turned out, there was not one but three stories about Hector Xavier Monsegur, each featuring a giant picture of his face as he sat in front of a computer. There it was: Sabu's cooperation with the FBI. This is what he had been trying to tell me on the phone. I was dumbstruck. The news coincided with a string of indictments also detailed in the articles. In the US, the FBI had just arrested Jeremy Hammond, while in the UK and Ireland, Ryan Ackroyd (Kayla), Donncha O'Cearbhaill (Palladium), and Darren Martyn (pwnsauce) were each indicted on computer conspiracy charges.

The news rolled through the different IRC channels like a shock wave. The CabinCr3w channel hosted a number of people who were very close to Sabu (pseudonyms have been altered):

<round-eyes>: comrade, front page of Foxnews
<round-eyes>: nao
<kama>: k
<round-eyes>: omgomgomg
<flava-flav>: damnnn
<flava-flav>: i didnt know
<flava-flav>: wow
<flava-flav>: fucking sabu
<flava-flav>: guys
<flava-flav>: may i speak
<flava-flav>: for one minute
<Nacho-King>: go
<Mega>: NO
<Mega>: lol jk go on
<comrade>: lol
<flava-flav>: we should frame this as a defining moment
<Nacho-King>: ^
<flava-flav>: like libya after gadaffi
<flava-flav>: we are free of a burden
<flava-flav>: a dead weight
<flava-flav>: clouding everything we where
<flava-flav>: and will be
<Mega>: well he never was a burden to begin with imo
<comrade>: yeah, that's strangely not comforting right now flava-flav
<flava-flav>: and from here on
<Mega>: why not comrade
<flava-flav>: ur missing my point

<flava-flav>: he was a phase
<flava-flav>: and now
<comrade>: lol
<flava-flav>: is a new one
<comrade>: okay
<comrade>: i can go with phase
<comrade>: :D
<flava-flav>: its [an] evolutionary process
<Nacho-King>: right I'm just saying flava-flav a lot of ppl are reacting in a bunch of different ways

Nacho-King was right. While everyone felt the bitter sting of betrayal, a minority still supported Sabu. The Fox News article had, indeed, reported that the FBI dangled a time-honored ultimatum in front of Sabu: he could work for the G-men or have his adopted cousins forcibly removed from his care. Eventually, a number of former Anonymous participants—more hangers-on than hardcore hackers—told me that Sabu had been telling them back in the summer of 2011 "to get the fuck out." It started to become clear why Sabu had been cozying up with the Anons who possessed the hacking skills to enter systems, and not bothering with those who weren't breaking the law. He was targeting those of most interest to the FBI.

A few hours later, a dominant attitude was emerging on the channels, one which echoed the sentiment of an unnamed government official quoted in the Fox report: "You might be a messiah in the hacking community but you're still a rat."

By the end of the day, Sabu's reputation within Anonymous was irrevocably tarnished. And as the news reverberated throughout the Inter-tubes, howls of anger and pangs of betrayal sounded. It took a month before my own anger had receded enough that I could have another conversation with him. He was at his most defiant, opening our conversation with the salvo that he was "disappointed that no one questioned the news report." Then he growled in disbelief at being treated like a "biohazard."

"I protected hundreds of people," he insisted. "I saved a lot of asses. When you have kids, you have to choose. I did the right thing." His only plea for sympathy concerned the fact that he himself faced penalties. He had been arrested, after all, and maintained his liberty only on bail—it remained likely that he would still face ten or fifteen years in prison. Not knowing one's fate is "stressful," he declared. When I asked him how much of what he did and said was directed by the FBI, he barked, "Everything I said on Twitter was my motherfucking point of view." He added later, "I was genuine with my tweets, no one dictated what I wrote." This directly contradicts statements made by one of his handlers as reported by Jana Winter for Fox News. "About 90 percent of what you see online is bulls—,"[21] said the handler, in reference both to posts from Sabu's Twitter account and also "interviews" he gave to the press. Whether this is the truth or an even more elaborate, recursive disinformation campaign, the implication is that Sabu parroted whatever the FBI wanted him to say. There were some tweets—"If god forbid I am arrested, I'll admit to my crimes, and take myself down. I do not believe in bringing others down for my own sins. Thanks"—that we now know were unadulterated nuggets of FBI-influenced BS.[22]

I barely got a word in edgewise, but I did manage to ask Sabu whether he met me at the behest of the FBI. His voice became louder in dismissal. "Jesus Christ! You don't need to ask permission to go to fucking Chipotle and get a burrito!" Unsatisfied, I asked him again why he reached out to me, and I asked a further question about the catalyst of our meeting— the hacker at the NYSEC meet-up. He began brushing this off, before suddenly stopping short. "I needed the truth out there one way or another," he stated clearly. "The more time we spent, the more I felt I could confide in you. It is a shitty situation."

He let loose one final deluge of vitriol: "I expected the nerds to expose my family, but not the media. For the media to post shit on my family!" He added: "There are many informants in Anonymous." Then he wrapped up with some shout-outs, giving props to "Jeremy and Donncha"—two of the most technically savvy and hardworking hackers in Anonymous, who had themselves refused to offer anything to law enforcement (and whose capture had largely been the result of his actions). Then he offered a few parting words: "I still think the idea of Anonymous is beautiful. Decentralization is power."

Law Breaking and Snitches

Around this time, Anonymous participants and some independent journalists like Nigel Parry began raising questions about the official story that had coalesced around the Stratfor hack. On March 25, 2012, Parry penned a detailed blog post titled "Sacrificing Stratfor: How the FBI Waited Three Weeks to Close the Stable Door."[23] He noted how bizarre it was that Stratfor's thorough pwning could occur right under the FBI's nose. After all, the FBI maintained—both in court documents and to the Fox reporter—that Monsegur was on the tightest of leashes the whole time. "The FBI," wrote Jana Winter, "has had an agent watching his online activity twenty-four hours a day, officials said."[24]

Monsegur provided the FBI with direct, real-time access to unfolding developments, and the FBI informed Stratfor of the intrusion almost immediately, in early December. AntiSec only had access to the customer database at this time. It took another ten days for Hammond to infiltrate the rest of the system; Hammond didn't delete the data for another ten days, on Christmas Eve. Stratfor had ample opportunity to step up its security or, if nothing else, back up its data. But it did not. In the aftermath of this hacking blitz, George Friedman, Stratfor's CEO, provided the following vague explanation: "We worked to improve our security infrastructure within the confines of time and the desire to protect the investigation by not letting the attackers know that we knew of their intrusion."[25]

By November 2013, publicly accessible court records had confirmed Hammond's timeline. And yet, for over two years no other journalist had bothered to press Stratfor on its failure to take additional protective measures after the initial intrusion. Nor did they question why the FBI waited until December 24 to deliver Stratfor a second wave of bad tidings—that emails had been downloaded and data was being wiped—when it knew full well that AntiSec had gained wider access days earlier.

The FBI's rationalization for its actions does little to clarify the situation. As Nicole Perlroth of the *New York Times* reported: "The F.B.I. said that it immediately notified Stratfor, but said that at that point it was too late. Over the next several weeks, hackers rummaged through Stratfor's financial information, email correspondence and subscribers' personal and financial information, occasionally deleting its most valuable data—all in full view of F.B.I. agents."[26]

Then, in May 2014, an astonishing bevy of court documents—chat logs, surveillance photos, and government documents from Hammond's court case—were leaked to journalists Dell Cameron and Daniel Stuckey. Armed with them, they were able to corroborate Hammond's timeline at a more granular level. The chat logs in particular go a long way toward confirming, as Cameron wrote, "longstanding accusations that federal investigators allowed an informant to repeatedly break computer-crime laws while in pursuit of Hammond and other Anonymous figures."[27]

Allegations that Sabu aided and abetted illegal activity (recall that it was Sabu who brought the Stratfor vulnerability to Hammond in the first place) were not limited to the Stratfor hack. During Hammond's sentencing hearing in November 2014, he read a statement that included another explosive accusation:

> After Stratfor, I continued to break into other targets, using a powerful "zero day exploit" allowing me administrator

access to systems running the popular Plesk webhosting platform. Sabu asked me many times for access to this exploit,
which I refused to give him. Without his own independent
access, Sabu continued to supply me with lists of vulner-
able targets. I broke into numerous websites he supplied,
uploaded the stolen email accounts and databases onto
Sabu's FBI server, and handed over passwords and backdoors that enabled Sabu (and, by extension, his FBI handlers)
to control these targets. These intrusions, all of which were
suggested by Sabu while cooperating with the FBI, affected
thousands of domain names and consisted largely of foreign
government websites, including Brazil, Turkey, Syria.[28]

As Hammond was about to mention more government targets,
Judge Preska implored him: "Mr. Hammond, we just spoke
about those countries being redacted, I'd appreciate if you
didn't use them." In his statement, Hammond also reminded
the court of the existence of some evidence backing his claims:

All of this happened under the control and supervision of
the FBI and can be easily confirmed by chat logs the government provided to us pursuant to the government's discovery
obligations in the case against me ... Because I pled guilty,
I do not have access to many documents that might have
been provided to me in advance of trial, such as Sabu's communications with the FBI. In addition, the majority of the
documents provided to me are under a "protective order"
which insulates this material from public scrutiny.

Hammond's statement was republished online, with some
websites redacting the names of the countries mentioned and
others including them. Having been told about these hacks
earlier during my first prison visit, I became intrigued about
how much truth might lie behind Hammond's claims. I raised
these questions to some journalists and convinced one to
track them down. Eventually, this culminated in a front-page

New York Times story by Mark Mazzetti in late April 2014, entitled "F.B.I. Informant Is Tied to Cyberattacks Abroad."[29] Then, after the trove of court documents under protective order were leaked, journalists Daniel Stuckey and Blake wrote a detailed play-by-play of Sabu's role in orchestrating hacks against the Brazilian government and various corporate websites. Although many of Sabu's targets were threaded through Hammond, he also offered vulnerabilities to other hackers. In one documented case, he offered a valuable exploit which "opened backdoors to hundreds of Brazilian websites."[30] And all of this was performed under the FBI's careful gaze.

The news that the FBI allowed—or at least abided—Sabu's role in facilitating an illegal hacking spree struck many in Anonymous as a perverse abuse of power. Of course, we don't know—and likely never will—whether Sabu's services were loaned out by the FBI to other three-letter agencies for military ops or intelligence gathering, whether his actions furthered the governments own purposes in some roundabout way, or whether other factors were at work; but when this example is contextualized within the broader American informant system, it becomes clear that the scenario is far from unusual. Law professor Alexandra Natapoff argues that corrupt relations between informants and their handlers are not sporadic, exceptional activities—they are endemic. In her book *Snitching: Criminal Informants and the Erosion of American Justice,* she persuasively illustrates a twisted system that often results in increased cycles of crime and violence. The FBI routinely allows its informants to break the law, Natapoff argues, so long as they are otherwise cooperative. While informants are a necessary tool for the criminal justice system, she concludes that in the program's present configuration, "informant use inflicts significant wounds on the integrity of the criminal process."[31]

Natapoff and other journalists have documented numerous cases of abuse. For instance, in 2005, Yassine Ouassif, a part-time engineering student living in the Bay Area, was escorted off a plane in Paris headed for San Francisco. Despite holding a green card and not being under investigation, he was interrogated for hours in a US Customs and Border Protection facility. Ultimately, an FBI agent offered a choice: become an informant in the Muslim-American community or face deportation to his home country Morocco.[32] A lawsuit filed in April 2014 on behalf of four Muslim men alleges that the FBI placed or kept them on a no-fly list after they refused to spy on Muslim communities in New York, New Jersey, and Nebraska.[33] This sort of bullying aims to intervene directly into a community, changing its very nature without having formally established any wrongdoing.

The majority of cases involving informants never go to trial in the United States, so we only learn about this system— and are able to argue for its reform—thanks to occasional trials and leaks (a reminder of how the Hammond court case leak can serve the democratic process). The fact that Sabu was allowed to facilitate so many hacks under full view of the FBI is testament to the ongoing abuses of the informant system. It also serves as a painful reminder that the state will use methods both legal and illegal to dismantle a movement deemed threatening.

"Trust no one on IRC, ever"

As the news rumbled about Sabu's informant status, it became apparent that while Monsegur's cooperation had made a decisive difference, many participants had neglected to properly secure their information. Anonymous9 expressed it to me this way: "The fact that people got arrested because of him is partially because he was a traitor, and partially because those people were careless. If they hadn't shared personal information with him they would have been fine. Sort of comes back to the whole 'trust no one on IRC, ever' thing."

It may be hard to prove computer crimes after they have

been committed, unless data—such as credit card numbers, emails, or other incriminating information—is found on a suspect's computer. But as computer security researcher Robert Graham put it, chat logs culled by an informant can be used to "convict you of conspiracy, intent, obstruction of justice [and] racketeering."[34] And the prosecution had an enormous hunk of logs from which to build its case. Still, having Sabu around was not enough to nab everyone—some members of AntiSec and LulzSec remain out of reach of the law. Had others been more careful with their operational security, they may have never been caught.

How were mistakes made? Hammond practiced nearly flawless technical operational security, but in chats he revealed personal details. The most significant—which I had seen him mention once in public and once in a private channel—was that he had spent time in federal prison. Given one of his main nicknames, "Anarchaos," his unique status as one of the only bona fide American anarchist hackers to have done time in US prison must have placed him pretty high on the list of candidates. Perhaps the one vital task that Sabu performed for the FBI here was to connect Hammond's potpourri of different nicknames. Below is a snippet of a conversation, filed in the court documents, between Sabu (as "CW-1") and Hammond (as "@sup_g") on Christmas Day:

<CW-1>: hows the news looking?
<@sup_g>: I been going hard all night
<CW-1>: I heard we're all over the news papers
<CW-1>: you mother fuckers are going to get me raied [raided]
<CW-1>: HAHAHAAHA
<@sup_g>: we put out 30k cards, the it.stratfor.com dump, and another statement
<@sup_g>: dude it's big
<CW-1>: if I get raided anarchaos your job is to cause havok in my honor
<CW-1>: <3

```
<CW-1>: sup_g:
<@sup_g>: it shall be so
```

Of course, Sabu proved crucial to the investigations in many other ways: one LulzSec member shared a link to a home-brewed video he hosted on YouTube. With the URL, the authorities sent a subpoena to YouTube for the account's email address, and from there it was trivial to connect his Facebook account. This young hacker had made the grave mistake of uploading incriminating screenshots of a web defacement, which were then shared with another member of LulzSec (oy vey).

Anonymous9's suggestion to "trust no one on IRC" is much easier said than done. The "Sabutage," as one person humorously referred to it, cut so deep because Anonymous, like almost every political movement, was underwritten by friendships and the flourishing of more intimate relation-ships still. Marriages, like the one between the young hacker John Anthony Borell III (Kahuna), from the CabinCr3w, and Sarah Borell, were indebted to chats in the crew's private IRC channel. Topiary shepherded one of his LulzSec mates through a dark period of his life. Even those who never shared per-sonally identifying information were interpolated into strong, lasting bonds. Such connections make it all too tempting, and easy, to be lulled into a state of comfort wherein one betrays their identity by oversharing. Even if one recognizes that this is happening, it is not as simple as simply changing a nickname, scrubbing all markers of the previous identity, and adopting a different style of talk. Parmy Olson highlights this "dilemma" constantly faced by hackers: changing a nick means losing the stable marker of identity and reputation crucial to hacker coworking across time.[35]

A few years later, I asked some Anons why—given creeping suspicions that he was an informant—Sabu was not only toler-ated but actually advanced as AntiSec's public-facing persona. For O'Cearbhaill, one of the other AntiSec Anons, his cha-risma did the trick. Like no one else he was able to rouse public passion with his clarion calls for uprising. Another plausible explanation was advanced by numerous other participants: another figure, Yettie (not his real pseudonym), was himself, for much of the time, a target of copious snitching accusations, which drew attention away from Sabu. At least a dozen core participants had shared with me their fears about Yettie. He had managed to gain access to countless IRC servers and was known for playing with many people's minds—including, I felt, my own. Even Hammond, momentarily operating under the handle "crediblethreat," called him to the mat in an uncommon public display of internal strife in the fall of 2011:

> <crediblethreat>: hey Yettie
> <crediblethreat>: did you tell everybody
> <crediblethreat>: about how and why you were kicked out of antisec core team?
> <crediblethreat>: where were you for all these months?
> [...]
> <crediblethreat>: why the fuck should anyone trust you again, snitch?

To this day no one can definitely say whether Yettie is an informant (or merely creepy). Many others were also accused. Rumors like these are endlessly analyzed in light of what is deemed odd behavior and the scant factual information available to participants. For instance, leaked law-enforcement documents name a "CW-2" (confidential witness 2), implying that there were at least two informants milling around.[36] Many participants also asked why some hackers and participants embedded in the secret channels were never raided or questioned once they decided to go public. These rumors and uncertainties propel the stormy and disorienting atmospherics of paranoia so common in the context of leftist or progressive political movements. Once the fog of fear and confusion settles, it makes it "difficult to sort out paranoia from reality, imaginary enemies from perfectly real ones," in the words of

Ruth Rosen, who chronicled FBI-induced fear in the 1960s women's liberation movement.[37]

Sabu's outing also functioned as a test, pushing Anonymous into a period of introspection. For weeks, as Anons wailed, raged, assessed, reassessed, and freaked out on Twitter and various IRC networks, they wondered what future—if any— remained for Anonymous after such a blow. Would it come to pass, to quote an anonymous government official featured in Winter's Fox News article, that "when people in the hacking community realize their God has actually been cooperation [*sic*] with the government, it'll be sheer terror"?

Knock Knock, We're Here

While the Sabutage fanned the flames of paranoia, it did not spell the end of Anonymous—or even really cultivate a substantial amount of terror. Even if Anonymous could never replicate the high participant levels of its LulzSec/AntiSec days (back when Fox News' description of them as "hackers on steroids" was apt), Anonymous carried along just fine through 2012 and much of 2013, executing major hacks and attacks across the world. Its formidable reputation is best illustrated by an anecdote from the highest echelons of US officialdom.

In 2012, Barack Obama's reelection campaign team assembled a group of programmers, system administrators, mathematicians, and data scientists to fine-tune voter targeting. Journalists praised Obama's star-studded and maverick technology team, detailing its members' hard work, success, and travails, and ultimately heralding the system as a success. These articles, however, failed to report one of the team's big concerns. Throughout the campaign, the technologists had treated Anonymous as a potentially even bigger nuisance than the foreign state hackers who had infiltrated the McCain and Obama campaigns in 2008.[38]

In late November 2012, Asher Wolf, a geek crusader who

acted as a sometimes-informal adviser to Anonymous, noticed that Harper Reed, the chief technologist for Obama's reelection tech team, followed @AnonyOps on Twitter. Much like a trickster, Wolf pointed this out to AnonyOps, suggesting, "let's play with that and see what we can do."[39]

AnonyOps sent Reed a private Twitter message. "Hi. The next few months are big. I thought we should maybe chat." Reed read the message and his "heart sank," as he explained it to me in an interview. He reached out to his boss, the chief information officer, and the head of security for the Obama campaign. They hammered out a variety of possible 140 character replies. Finally, they hit on this bit of genius: "Hey. What's on your mind?" As Harper was about to send the message, the chief information officer, who had been speaking with senior lawyers for the campaign, bolted over to Harper's desk to stop him. They had changed their mind. The best response, they determined, was no response at all. He came seconds too late.

Had Reed known what I did, he would have been spared a day or two of anxiety. AnonyOps was simply interested in initiating a conversation with an influential political figure. Reflecting back on the event during an interview with me, Wolf recalled that

> it was amusing, because we were like kids, playing with boundaries ... with the world's superpower. We'd been through 2010 when the screens poured with rage as the administration went after WikiLeaks and we'd gone through Occupy ... We'd seen people be jailed, disappear ... Maybe, just maybe we were a little fatalistic. And maybe it felt good once, just once to wander up close to the administration that drones small children and flick a cigarette butt in their faces.

As this incident shows, Anonymous had become a specter; its influence had grown so far-reaching that it didn't even have to do anything to have an effect. It is understandable why Obama's reelection team felt perturbed by this ambiguous knock on its digital door. In the two months following Hammond's arrest, Anonymous hacked into hundreds of Chinese government websites; knocked the website for Formula One racing offline after the repressive government of Bahrain, set to host the next Formula One race, had detained and imprisoned protesters; and hacked into the website of the Greek finance ministry, drawing attention to the government's plan to track citizens' bank information in an effort to curtail tax fraud. Over the summer of 2012, Anonymous launched another major hack (again) against the Formula One website, this time coinciding with the Montreal Grand Prix; this was done to protest Bill 78, a controversial measure passed in Quebec to curtail protest activity, which had soared after proposed tuition hikes. Quebec's Human Rights Commission issued a fifty-six page report condemning the bill for its flagrant violation of the province's own human rights charter, notably for the provision that threatened to fine protesters thousands of dollars if they failed to notify authorities at least eight hours in advance of the itinerary of any protest involving fifty or more people.[40] Later that month in India, after a Supreme Court order mandated that local ISPs block torrent websites, file-sharing websites, and even some video-sharing websites, Anonymous retaliated by DDoSing the Indian Supreme Court, the Ministry of Communications and Information Technology, the Department of Telecommunications, the Bharatiya Janata Party, and the Indian National Congress. Like many Anons, AnonOpsIndia took to Twitter to make its views heard: "We will become a #PAIN in the #ASS for the government until they stop #censoring our #INTERNET[.] IT BELONGS TO US!"[41]

Anonymous continued unabated in 2013, remaining committed to ongoing issues, as in #OpLastResort, a series of retributive hacks carried out against the websites of MIT, the US Department of Justice, and the US Sentencing Commission following the suicide of Internet pioneer and activist Aaron Swartz. His family and many admirers felt that his suicide at age twenty-six was a political act borne out of a sense of desperation fueled by his impending trial. Swartz faced thirty-five years in jail and $1 million in fines—simply for downloading a cache of academic journal articles he never released. "Aaron's death ... is the product of a criminal justice system rife with intimidation and prosecutorial overreach," wrote his family and partner.[42] In the video accompanying their hacks and website defacements, Anonymous echoed this assessment:

> Two weeks ago today, a line was crossed. Two weeks ago today, Aaron Swartz was killed. Killed because he faced an impossible choice. Killed because he was forced into playing a game he could not win—a twisted and distorted perversion of justice—a game where the only winning move was not to play.[43]

While initially receiving scant media attention, a trio of North American ops focusing on a recent spate of sexual assault and rape allegations hooked American news-makers. Suddenly, Anonymous was back on center stage. Once again in its preferred position, Anonymous managed to stimulate public debate on an issue too often treated as a mere tantalizing spectacle.

The first case, originating in Steubenville, Ohio, concerned two members of a high school football team facing trial for raping a classmate. The night of the assault, other team members snapped photos of and filmed the unconscious woman, promptly sharing them on social media with sickening celebratory statements. One video, eventually sent to Anonymous, featured a classmate boasting that "they raped her harder than that cop raped Marcellus Wallace in *Pulp Fiction* ... That's how you know she's dead, because someone pissed on her."[44]

In December of 2012, while local Steubenville activist Michelle McKee asserted that a fair trial was impossible in a town that treated the football players as demigods, she reached out to Anonymous and they swooped in. An Anon who had recently taken up the handle "KYAnonymous" (his real name is Deric Lostutter) was at work exposing the identities of posters on revenge porn forums. Reading about the Steubenville case incensed him, and he expressed as much on Twitter. McKee sent him some incriminating material that had circulated with social media accounts of individuals linked to the event. KYAnonymous sprung into action, first releasing an ominous video warning. David Kushner memorably described it for *Rolling Stone*:

> Like a deft poker player, Lostutter amped up his manifesto with a bluff. He claimed that Anonymous had already doxed "everyone involved" with the cover-up and crime—parents, teachers, and kids—and were going to release their private information online "unless all accused parties come forward by New Years Day and issue a public apology to the girl and her family."[45]

By the next day, a hacker named Noah McHugh, who went by "BatCat," allegedly gained access to RollRedRoll.com, the school's sports web portal (named after its buff, red, devil-like stallion mascot), and accessed team emails. KYAnonymous tweeted nonstop while celebrities like Roseanne Barr added their network effect to the cause. Then, on December 29, a cold wintry day, Anonymous's call for a street demonstration in Steubenville was answered by a throng of a thousand demonstrators—with a now-requisite smattering of Guy Fawkes masks. "In a dramatic turn, some of them spoke of their own sexual assaults and rapes, removing their masks to show themselves to the crowd," wrote Kushner.

Anonymous remained hyperactively involved with the Steubenville assault on Twitter, until two teenagers were found guilty of rape in May 2013. One defendant received the minimum sentence: one year in a juvenile correctional facility. The other was sentenced to two years. In November 2013, four Steubenville residents, including the school superintendent, were subsequently charged for covering up evidence of another, earlier rape case, according to the *New York Times*.[46] The FBI raided Lostutter in June 2013, and he is facing indictment under the CFAA; Noah McHugh was allegedly arrested earlier in February. If convicted, they face much longer prison sentences than the rapists.

In April 2013, Anonymous got wind of the case of Rehtaeh Parsons, a straight-A student who had ended her life after what appears to have been a sexual assault at an alcohol-fueled party in Halifax, Canada. The failure to prosecute any of the accused boys, Anonymous charged, was due to inappropriate handling by the Royal Canadian Mounted Police (RCMP). Anons helped raise awareness of the case with a video and a press release demanding Nova Scotia RCMP take immediate legal action against the individuals. Leah Parsons, Rehtaeh's mother, asked for justice to be brought by the authorities, rather than online vigilantes. The Anons behind #OpJustice4Rehtaeh respected this wish by making clear in a subsequent statement that

> We do not approve of vigilante justice as the media claims. That would mean we approve of violent actions against these rapists at the hands of an unruly mob. What we want is justice. And that's your job. So do it. The names of the rapists will be kept until it is apparent you have no intention of providing justice to Retaeh's family. Please be aware that there are other groups of Anons also attempting to uncover this information and they may not to wish to wait at all. Better act fast.[47]

The RCMP reopened the case but downplayed Anonymous's role, insisting the new evidence "did not come from an online source."[48] Anonymous participants, along with some commentators, felt the masked activists had made a decisive difference: "It's entirely clear that the online pressure mattered a great deal in this case,"[49] noted Emily Bazelon of *Slate*. Parsons, initially ambivalent, was eventually thankful Anonymous had intervened. In late August 2013, the RCMP charged the two accused men with making and distributing child pornography (the case is still pending).

The final of the three cases was another incident that never went to trial because the prosecutors deemed there to be insufficient evidence. This case involved a party in Maryville, Missouri, after which seventeen-year-old Matthew Barnett dropped off fourteen-year-old Daisy Coleman outside her home, barely conscious, in a T-shirt and sweatpants, where she passed out in sub-freezing weather. Two in-depth local investigative articles strongly suggested that there was actually more than sufficient evidence to charge Barnett. Comparing the situation to Steubenville, a piece by Peggy Lowe and Monica Sanreckzi for Kansas City Public Media cited the local sheriff: "Did a crime occur? Hell yes, it occurred. Was it a horrible crime? Yes, it was a horrible crime. And did these boys need to be punished for it? Absolutely."[50] When these articles were brought to Anonymous's attention, the group made a lot of noise, in turn bringing the incident to the nation's attention. Eventually, a special prosecutor formally filed a criminal charge against Matthew Barnett—a single count of misdemeanor child endangerment.

Anonymous's interventions in these three cases triggered searing but divided responses. Citizens, journalists, and feminists disagreed over whether Anonymous's interventions had helped or hurt sexual abuse victims. Ariel Levy, in a scathing *New Yorker* article, came down hard against the Anonymous (and other online activists), asserting that the appeal of the group was rooted in the public's naive embrace of a simple archetype: "modern-day Peter Parkers—computer nerds who put on a costume and were transformed into superhero vigilantes."[51] Other responses were more nuanced, going beyond the vigilante argument. During a Huffington Post Live video interview, feminist author Jaclyn Friedman reflected on the "double-edged sword" of Internet activism:

> The victim get victimized once, but they get revictimized when those images and videos are circulated among their peers. But that can in some cases, as we saw with Steubenville—with the help of Anonymous covering those videos—become evidence, so that it is more likely that there will be justice.[52]

Anonymous ignited a desperately needed national conversation about rape culture in the United States and Canada. In an absorbing *New York Times Magazine* article, Bazelon identified a pattern in these three "white-knight ops," a pattern that also applies to a broader sample of Anonymous's political operations, even those that steer clear of vigilantism: when Anonymous jumps into the fray, it is typically due to the group's perception that justice is not being done; in many cases, this turns out to be true.[53] In a follow-up interview the *New York Times* conducted with her about researching Anonymous, Bazelon added,

> I think each operation, or op, needs to be judged individually. Ones that have really responsible people working on them are probably on balance a good thing. I think that is true of Maryville and probably also of the one about Rehtaeh Parsons, although that one is more fraught, because there was an innocent person accused. Others really go off the rails.

Indeed, Steubenville, which sparked the most media attention, was in many respects the most poorly executed of the three ops. Among other problems, the victim herself was doxed by Anons, and locals were harassed. Many Anons were furious at Lostutter for releasing the video (and, once outed, the fury only intensified as he was seen to be behaving in a way deemed as flagrantly self-promotional).

Two qualifications merit addition reflection. If vigilante justice is rightly deemed problematic for skirting the legal process, it arises because existing channels for serving justice are weak or nonexistent. All too often, critics point a finger at the "vigilantes," while ignoring or downplaying the more systemic conditions that in many ways give rise to them. Second, teams are capable of adjustment. I witnessed this dynamic at least a dozen times; after the mistakes made in the Steubenville op, subsequent Anonymous engagements in rape cases were approached with more delicacy, oversight, and care. Of course, such responsiveness is itself fragile—working groups within Anonymous are prone to dissolution. They might function well for three to six months, and then break up following volcanic levels of internal feuding. (Bazelon covers in detail the stormy bickering leading to the dissolution of one such team.) They might then reconstitute later with new members who have not internalized the same hard-learned lessons.

In contrast to other hacker and geek endeavors—like Debian, the largest free software project in the world— Anonymous has no established methodology through which to encode itself as an institution. Only limited—and provisional—protocols exist to perform the roles of adjudication, social reproduction, and mentoring. For instance, IRC channels like #opnewblood, as its name suggests, serve primarily pedagogical purposes. It is a space where newcomers learn the technical and cultural ropes. Certain Twitter accounts, like @YourAnonNews—which at one time boasted over twenty-five contributors who were required to follow a style guide—are a mini-media institution (@YourAnonNews has been criticized by some Anons as micro-imperialist).

Taking stock of the broader Anonymous constellation of practices, we can derive a few fast and loose generalities. Anons tend to forgo rigid regulatory codes in favor of ad hoc, timely, and event-based responses. They even struggle with institutional memory, even when Anons or the media memorialize the ops. To be sure, Anonymous exhibits significant cultural cohesiveness, secured through all the videos, memes, and other cultural lore the group produces; but at the same time, Anonymous either shuns or never implements transposable policies and mechanisms for handling operations. It is not simply that Anons are allergic to formalization. Given that each operation is so distinct, it may prove very difficult to implement best practices in this dynamic milieu, even as we can say that Anonymous does indeed learn from the past.

Of course, if all activist endeavors shunned institutionalization, many broader political goals would suffer. But feminist scholar Larisa Mann identifies the strengths of flexible ad-hoc political endeavors, arguing during an interview, "Anonymous might be ahead of mainstream feminists in fighting small-town rape culture."[54] She elaborated: in contrast to institutionalized actors, Anonymous (along with other fleeting forms of disruptive activism) is free from the shackles of "self-promotion and funding," which are almost universally required for institutional endeavors. These requirements can prevent the sort of nimble and swift response that Anonymous has elevated to a high art.

If there is one conclusion to draw from a cursory review of these cases, it is this: the work of politics and social transformation requires, and can bear, a diverse toolkit—from fine-tuned government interventions to rowdy subversive tactics. We should be wary of christening any particular approach as a magic bullet. If forced to pick between an NGO that works for women's rights and Anonymous's rough-and-tumble, problematic intervention, I would likely pick the former. But this dichotomy is a strawman. The urgent question is how to promote cross-pollination. It becomes prudent for those committed to these political goals to ask how alliances can be fostered, rather than leveling critiques based on tactical differences.

We need compelling stories that dramatize neglected issues, as media scholar and long-time activist Stephen Duncombe has argued; he strongly supports the sort of spectacle provided by Anonymous and so casually dismissed as a juvenile male fantasy by journalists like Levy.[55] Well-funded groups with dedicated teams of lawyers, advocates, and policy strategists, which command the resources for more long-term strategic and sustainable interventions, are sorely needed. We also need (well-paid) investigative journalists who dedicate years to tracking down sources and putting the pieces of difficult puzzles together. But, as we saw in the Maryville case, these strategies, when taken alone and lacking a stirred-up pot of drama, sometimes sadly fail. They simply cannot drum up the sort of attention or collective will necessary to break ingrained attitudes and practices. The real problem lies elsewhere: many people either lack the will or are too cynical to enter the political arena and put up a fight in the first place.

Conclusion: Daybreak

On June 6, 2013, I sat in a frigid New York University auditorium, waiting for my turn to speak at the Personal Democracy Forum (PDF), a yearly event showcasing the Internet's role in nourishing democratic life. I felt myself falling into a vortex of negativity. Writing about those who tunnel and undermine, who desire to be incomprehensible, concealed, and enigmatic (to slightly rephrase Friedrich Nietzsche's opening lines in *Daybreak*), was beginning to seem like an exercise in doom and gloom. Anonymous was still ruffling feathers with political operations, but Barrett Brown and Jeremy Hammond, and numerous others, now sat in prison cells. The Internet had become a giant, sophisticated tracking machine. Private defense firms, corporations like Facebook, and American three letter agencies (alongside their equivalents in other Five Eyes countries) had sunk their claws in deep: collecting our every trace, predicting our every move. Even if each organization and country did so for different purposes and utilized distinct techniques, the net effect was a troubling and pervasive curtailment of rights. Anonymous, I was planning to suggest in my talk, had been "the raucous party at the funeral of online freedom and privacy."

I was not alone in holding this bleak assessment. As one Anon, m0rpeth, had put it to me: "We will be small scattered darknets on the fringes of the Internet after all is lost." Even the organizers of PDF, normally cheery about the power of the Internet to tilt the balance of power in favor of freedom and justice, had admitted at a dinner the evening before that "things have not turned out as we had hoped."

And then, right before being called onto the stage, PDF's co-organizer, Micah Sifry, suddenly and unexpectedly proffered a lifeline. He leaned over, handed his phone to me, and whispered, "There has been a major leak about government surveillance." I skimmed an article on the phone. Written by journalist Glenn Greenwald, it divulged the dragnet collection of metadata phone records by Verizon, on behalf of the NSA. In a few days, Edward Snowden, the whistleblower who had provided the information behind the story, would become a household name. Sifry walked up to the stage to introduce me. Before he did, he broke the news to the audience, and I modified my talk on Anonymous to include this hopeful turn of events.

Snowden's decision to blow the top off the NSA (and, by extension, its British counterpart, the GCHQ) was a risky but carefully plotted act. It substantiated what privacy activists had been warning about for years, providing them with far more solid and extensive facts upon which to base their claims. Laura Poitras, one of the first three journalists to receive the trove of NSA documents, remarked on the novelty of this situation: "The disclosures made by Snowden have lifted a curtain and revealed a vast hidden world where decisions are made and power operates in secret outside of any public oversight or consent. So my vision hasn't really changed, but what I'm able to see has vastly increased."[1] Here is but a fraction of what we we can now see thanks to the mega-leak: the NSA spied upon or directly surveilled thirty-eight embassies and missions; until 2011, the NSA harvested and stored vast swaths of American emails and metadata under a program called Stellar Wind; the NSA compelled tech giants to hand over data using FISA court warrants—while also covertly tapping into fiber-optic cables, like those owned by Google, to secretly siphon even more data; the NSA hacked into Al Jazeera's internal communications systems; the GCHQ led a DDoS attack against Anonymous and hacked Belgacom, a partly state-owned Belgian telecommunications company; and under a program fittingly called Optic Nerve, the GCHQ intercepted and stored webcam images from millions of Yahoo! users. And there was more: a four-month investigation by Barton Gellman and Julie Tate demonstrated that "ordinary Internet users, American and non-American alike, far outnumber legally targeted foreigners in the communications intercepted by the National Security Agency."[2]

Astonishingly, a 2012 NSA report, also included in the leaks, revealed the spy agency's dissatisfaction with all of these accomplishments. The NSA sought to broaden its reach further by deploying an even more aggressive cyberoffensive strategy, allowing them to gather data from "anyone, anytime, anywhere," as reported by Laura Poitras and James Risen for the *New York Times*.[3]

Such aggressive and wide-ranging forms of surveillance preemptively decimate the possibility of a "right to be let alone," to use the famous 1890 phrasing of Samuel Warren and Louis Brandeis, who were among the first to consider the legal basis of privacy.[4] And the style of surveillance employed today strikes not only at the personal, exploratory private sphere deemed valuable in liberal subject formation—it also preempts many forms of association that are essential to democratic life. The radical technology collective and Internet service provider Riseup sums it up well:

> What surveillance really is, at its root, is a highly effective form of social control. The knowledge of always being watched changes our behavior and stifles dissent. The inability to associate secretly means there is no longer any possibility for free association. The inability to whisper means there is no longer any speech that is truly free of coercion, real or

implied. Most profoundly, pervasive surveillance threatens to eliminate the most vital element of both democracy and social movements: the mental space for people to form dissenting and unpopular views.[5]

Intelligence agencies naturally require some secrecy to function effectively in the public interest. But when secrecy is left entirely unchecked—especially when granted to those already afforded extraordinary amounts of power and resources—it becomes a breeding ground for the sorts of abuse we saw emerge under J. Edgar Hoover's helm at the FBI, such as COINTELPRO.

The surveillance apparatus exposed by Snowden is also technologically, and thus historically, distinctive. With enough computer power it becomes frighteningly easy to gather data, especially through complete automation. And as civil liberties lawyer Jennifer Granick points out, "Once you build the mousetrap of surveillance infrastructure, they will come for the data."[6]

The state leans with particular force on collected data and informant reports to actively target niche groups—currently the US and UK spy disproportionately on Muslims, environmental activists, and, increasingly, hacktivists.[7] This is the conclusion reached in *Mapping Muslims: NYPD Spying and Its Impact on American Muslims*, an investigative report about NYPD's tellingly named "Demographics Unit" issued by a trio of nonprofits.[8] Established by a former CIA official soon after 9/11, the program proved so controversial and so ineffective—no actionable intelligence emerged from the collected data—that it was dismantled in April 2014, but only after disrupting and distorting the social fabric of targeted Muslim communities for more than a decade.[9] The program included the use of 15,000 informants and the building of a large dossier through extensive video and photographic surveillance. A Muslim college student featured in the report, Sari, captured the invasiveness in a single sentence: "It's as if the law says: the more Muslim you are, the more trouble you can be, so decrease your Islam."[10] The leaks also confirmed that the NSA monitors "prominent Muslim-Americans," including lawyers, professors, and other professionals even when they have no links to terrorist or criminal activity. After three months of investigative research and extensive interviews with five targets, "all vehemently deny any involvement in terrorism or espionage, and none advocates violent jihad or is known to have been implicated in any crime, despite years of intense scrutiny by the government and the press."[11]

In the United States, Muslim Americans endure the brunt of what the ACLU describes as "suspicionless surveillance."[12] But ubiquitous monitoring has consequences throughout society. As journalist Laurie Penny has persuasively argued, "If you live in a surveillance state for long enough, you create a censor in your head."[13] When video cameras are routine fixtures in urban landscapes; when corporate Internet giants store records of online navigation and communication (and make them frighteningly easy for the NSA to access); and when managers and bosses maintain capabilities to "measure and monitor employees as never before," as reporter Steve Lohr has put it, society at large pays the price.[14] These different vectors of surveillance aggregate, exerting a pressure for us to blend in, to think twice before speaking out, to, in essence, follow a narrow set of prescribed norms. Social conformity encourages quiet resignation and discourages the experimental—and necessarily risky—acts of speaking, thinking, and doing required for healthy democratic dissent.

Will we, with the help of people like the ex-NSA contractor who bore enormous risk in speaking out, manage to compel our governments to curb such abuses and, in so doing, restore our right to associate free of undue surveillance? The hurdles are gargantuan; the sanctioned channels for political change in the United States are frighteningly narrow.[15] The technical architecture of the Internet—wherein centralized, corporate-controlled servers house most of our data—makes capture both trivially easy and ubiquitous; this technical scenario has been described by civil liberties lawyer Eben Moglen as a "recipe for disaster," prompting him and other Internet technologists, like security expert Bruce Schneier, to declare, "We need to figure out how to re-engineer the internet to prevent this kind of wholesale spying."[16] Finally, as ACLU staff technologist Chris Soghoian argues, so long as Internet firms continue to "monetize their users' private data," they can never adopt a truly "pro-user" privacy policy.[17]

And yet, a field which had seemed hopelessly desolate now resembles fertile terrain. The politically engaged geek family continues to grow—in size and political significance. It is constituted by various organizations and activists working with politicians, lawyers, journalists, and artists. Many emerged from the geeky quarters of the Internet. There is Julian Assange, Birgitta Jónsdóttir, Chelsea Manning, the Electronic Frontier Foundation, Sarah Harrison, the Tor developers, Anonymous, Riseup, Edward Snowden, and many more. The last two years have been singular—never before have so many geeks and hackers wielded their keyboards for the sake of political expression, dissent, and direct action.[18]

Increasingly, thanks to their combined actions, we recognize that we stand at a crossroads. Snowden ignited a fiery national conversation over privacy that has continued for over a year—a minor miracle in a mass mediascape that lionizes novelty and eschews long-term, sustained deliberation. There are promising signs of legislative change. In what free speech advocate Trevor Timm described as "a surprising rebuke to the NSA's lawyers and the White House," the US House of Representatives passed a sweeping bill in June 2014 prohibiting warrantless access to Americans' emails and banning intelligence agencies from installing back doors in commercial hardware, with or without vendor complicity.[19] The effects of the leak have in turn reverberated far beyond national borders, as Glenn Greenwald attests:

[Snowden's leak] changed the way people around the world viewed the reliability of any statements made by US officials and transformed relations between countries. It radically altered views about the proper role of journalism in relation to government power. And within the United States, it gave rise to an ideologically diverse, trans-partisan coalition pushing for meaningful reform of the surveillance state.[20]

All this seems even more remarkable when one considers the viciousness with which many government officials, especially within the intelligence community, have reacted to Snowden. One anecdote is emblematic of the attitude: during the 2014 Ottawa Conference on Defense and Security, Melissa Hathaway, former director of the US Joint Interagency Cyber Task Force in the Office of the Director of National Intelligence, recounted to her audience that she learned of Snowden's flight to Russia (to seek political asylum) while in Tel Aviv. "I have to tell you the Israelis have a point of view that I do too. That he should have never been allowed to get on that plane—and then they [the Israelis] took it a little bit further: that the plane would have never landed." As the uproarious laughter died down, Hathaway punctuated the sentiment with a one-liner: "I still might subscribe to their point of view."[21] Yet, even as the American state diminishes Snowden by calling him a mere criminal, his political claims are becoming more salient every day. Hathaway herself acknowledged this in the statement that catalyzed the above anecdote. "Our allies feel betrayed. Their citizens believe that Edward Snowden is a hero."

Snowden has fueled a nascent movement composed of technology collectives, lawyers, journalists, filmmakers, politicians, and NGOs of varying stripes. This movement has lent its voice to the preexisting struggles of groups like the nonprofits Fight for the Future and the Open Technology Institute. The result has been a range of targeted policy and technological campaigns, such as Reset the Net, a grassroots effort to "to spread NSA-resistant privacy tools" so that they might become default features of the Internet.[22] Technologies like The Amnesic Incognito Live System (also known as Tails, an operating system built for anonymity), Open Whisper Systems (an open-source endeavor to develop encryption software for mobile phones), and LEAP (a recursive acronym for the LEAP Encryption Access Project, which modifies existing encryption tools to make them user friendly) are being funded by citizens and organizations like Freedom of the Press Foundation. Snowden himself has endorsed encryption projects as both effective and necessary: "The bottom line is that encryption does work," he told a packed room at South by Southwest in March 2014.[23] These technologies are poised to facilitate some semblance of privacy for future generations of Internet users.

Old World vs. New World

Soon after the first batch of NSA revelations, Ireland saw its first hacking court case. Two members of LulzSec and Anonymous, Donncha O'Cearbhaill and Darren Martyn, were tried in July 2013 for the 2011 defacement of the website of Irish political party Fine Gael. En route to the courthouse in Dublin, I got lost and ended up arriving late. Because I own no personal tracking device (or cell phone, as you will), I did what people have done for centuries: I consulted a paper map and confused myself. It took me another forty-five minutes to reach the correct court, housed in a modern circular glass building. I was sure I had missed the proceedings.

As it turned out, the two cases were sandwiched between more than a dozen petty criminal hearings; it would be another hour before O'Cearbhaill and Martyn stood before the judge. As I waited, sitting next to a local Anon nicknamed Firefly, we had a grand time watching the judge—a sensible and matronly woman in her fifties—gently, but firmly, scold the dozen other defendants. Most of them had been involved in youthful mischief and disorderly conduct. In one case, a twenty-something young lady with stunningly long black hair, an indignant scowl, crossed arms, and an immodest wardrobe was found guilty of beating up a member of the Garda—the local police—while thoroughly inebriated.

The two Anonymous cases clearly stood out from the lineup of brawls and drunken mischief. After hearing both sides in two defacement cases, the judge expressed skepticism about the prosecution's claim that restoring the Fine Gael website was expensive. How, she asked, could it possibly have cost ten thousand euros if nothing was damaged? The prosecution had no answer. The judge concluded that this hack was a "stunt to embarrass a political party rather than to disclose data to the public at large." She did not want to see O'Cearbhaill and Martyn go to jail for the digital equivalent of graffiti. Nor did she think that their acts were laudable. Instead, she admonished both, calling their hack "a terrible abuse of talent." Then she fined them each five thousand euros—payable by October (and with half going to charity)—and ordered them to enroll in a restorative justice program. She did not see what they did as political—had she, the humane punishment might have been even more lenient.

After the case adjourned, O'Cearbhaill and Martyn slipped out with their families. Firefly and I headed out toward the center of town, strolling along Dublin's main canal under the sun—Ireland was experiencing a miraculous two-week heatwave. Together, we did a postmortem of the trial. We agreed that O'Cearbhaill and Martyn got off very light; compared to the Anons tried in the United States, the Irish and British cases were remarkably mild. While the act of defacing a website does not compare to Hammond's actions, the long string of hacks that Ryan "Kayla" Ackroyd, a British national, carried out with LulzSec came a bit closer. In May 2013, after he pled guilty to one charge of hacking the Pentagon and conspiring to hack Sony, Britain's National Health Service, and Rupert Murdoch's News International, the British state sentenced

Ackroyd to thirty months in jail, of which he served ten; notably, he received no fine. In the US cases, even when the prison sentences are relatively short, the fines added on top virtually guarantee years of indentured servitude. At the age of twenty-two, John Anthony Borell III, aka Kahuna of the CabinCr3w, was sentenced to thirty-six months in prison for hacking into multiple police websites and dumping personal data. After serving his time, he will then still have to pay nearly $230,000 in damages.

In addition, many of the charges leveled against hackers in the United States have seemed to come out of left field, as illustrated by the ordeal of Barrett Brown. On March 6, 2012, the same day Fox News outed Sabu and the FBI arrested Hammond, the G-men executed a search warrant for Barrett Brown's residence. Among other things, authorities sought to locate "records relating to HBGary, Infragard, Endgame Systems, Anonymous, LulzSec, IRC Chats, Twitter, wiki.echelon2.org, and pastebin.com."[24] Six months later, in September, the FBI arrested Brown (live on video chat, fittingly) after he—to be entirely frank—set himself up for a raid. He had posted a video online entitled "Why I'm Going to Destroy FBI Agent Robert Smith Part Three Revenge of the Lithe," which featured a hyperbolic tirade against a federal agent who had questioned his mother.[25] As expected, he was then arrested for threatening an FBI agent. An excerpt from Brown's rant might demonstrate more clearly why he was so full of fury—and why the FBI, in turn, was compelled to raid him (rather than simply writing the video off as a piece of performance art):

> Guess what's on my fucking search warrant: fraud! I bring in no money ... a fucking fraud charge for a fucking writer activist, who has no money, who has spent all his money on fucking lawyers for himself and his fucking mother ... Agent Smith posted addresses of [my house and my mother's house] ... He is a criminal, involved in a criminal conspiracy

... Anyway, that's why Smith's life is over. When I say his life is over, I'm not saying I'm going to go kill him, but I am going to ruin his life and look into his fucking kids ... How do you like them apples? As Smith has noted, I'm in danger from the Zetas ... Thanks to that fella [for putting up my address] ... I will assume that since the Zetas often take the guise of Mexican security personnel [and often are] government officials, I'm concerned that the same trick may be played here ... Particularly the FBI ... will be regarded as potential Zeta assassin squads, and as the FBI [knows] ... they know that I'm armed, that I come from a military family, that I was taught to shoot by a Vietnam vet ... and I will shoot all of them and kill them if they come and do anything because they are engaged in a criminal conspiracy and I have reason to fear for my life not just from the Zetas, but the US governments [*sic*] ... I have no choice left but to defend myself, my family ... and frankly, you know, it was pretty obvious I was going to be dead before I was forty, so I wouldn't mind going out with two FBI sidearms like a fucking Egyptian pharaoh. Adios

Alongside charges for these threats, Brown also faced charges related to the Stratfor hack. In his Project PM chat room, he had shared a web link to an externally hosted file containing the leaked Stratfor credit card data. For doing so, he was charged with ten counts of aggravated identify theft and two counts relating to credit card fraud, with a combined total possible sentence of forty-five years (plus the sixty-some years for the other charges). Many other people who had also publicly circulated the link were not charged. Journalist Adrian Chen, who tended to be critical of Anonymous, wrote: "As a journalist who covers hackers and has 'transferred and posted' many links to data stolen by hackers—in order to put them in stories about the hacks—this indictment is frightening because it seems to criminalize linking."[26]

Because Brown was Anonymous's ethical foil, flaunting

himself as the face of a collective seeking to be faceless, he was a divisive figure. Nevertheless, Anons concurred with Kevin Gallagher, the system administrator running Brown's support campaign, when he argued that "it was this journalistic work of digging into areas that powerful people would rather keep in the dark that made him a target."[27] Brown's supporters raised funds, helped secure top-notch lawyers, and worked to publicize his charges.

In a surprising plot twist, the government dropped the linking charges just two days after the defense filed its motion to dismiss. (Dropping the charges avoids bad precedent and allows the government to continue pursuing investigations of the same ilk.) Still facing an extraordinary 105 years in prison, gagged against speaking to the media, and having already spent over a year and a half in custody, Brown accepted a plea bargain. At the time of writing, it remains unclear what the plea bargain will mean for the charges relating to threatening a federal officer.

The takeaway is this: whether one seeks to hack with impunity and anonymity—whether politically motivated or not—or to simply attain the status of a witty and sprightly rabble-rouser, it is best to do so on the European side of the Atlantic (where Anonymous and other forms of geek activism are more common).

Later that evening in Ireland, I was keen to ask O'Cearbhaill his thoughts about the case, but he was nowhere to be found. As it turns out, the Garda had been waiting for him outside of the courthouse, where they again arrested him—not for hacking this time. O'Cearbhaill, a chemistry student, maintained a laboratory at his parent's home. Some of the chemicals could (in theory) be used to make explosives. Although there was not an iota of evidence that he was using, or intended to use, the chemicals for such purposes, he was arrested under Irish antiterrorism legislation.

While the prosecutor later determined that there was insufficient evidence to bring a case, some Anons floated a hypothesis that the Garda was attempting to intimidate O'Cearbhaill into fessing up to his alleged involvement in what had become a legendary hack. Back in early February 2012, AntiSec had released audio of an intercepted conference call among the FBI, Scotland Yard, and the Garda. The subject of the conference call was none other than Anonymous itself. The leaked call was not only a 100 percent lulzly hack, but also an (apparently) lasting embarrassment to the agencies involved, in particular the Garda. It was the email account of one of its own officers that had been compromised to obtain the data needed to "join" the call. (At the time of this writing, no one has been found guilty of this intrusion).

The case may also suggest another reason why law enforcement is hostile toward computer spelunkers. Hackers occasionally make it their mission to "watch the watchers." Two Kevins—Poulsen and Mitnick—had done it before. Media scholar Douglas Thomas, who covered the ordeal of both hackers, noted how "Poulsen hacked into the FBI's systems and discovered a maze of wiretaps and surveillance programs that were monitoring everyone and everything from the restaurant across the street from him to (allegedly) Ferdinand Marcos."[28] AntiSec pulled off the same thing, but even more loudly and publicly.

A few days later, O'Cearbhaill, free again, joined a group of us for a summer picnic on Saint Stephen's Green. I had brought together a range of Anons from different networks and operational iterations, from the ex-Scientologist Pete Griffiths (a keen Anonymous supporter) to David from Chanology, Firefly from AnonOps, and hackers like O'Cearbhaill. He told me more about how he first got into hacktivism at the age of fifteen, and about his father's experiences in the IRA—including the six years he spent in jail and the forty-day hunger strike he carried out. His father, unlike the judge, had naturally understood his son's actions as political. By the summer of 2013, I was confident that most Anonymous participants were politically inclined; they may tunnel and undermine, but they do so in an attempt to dig through to daybreak—to end the dark reign of injustice. Still, something shifts when a person hears stories like the ones O'Cearbhaill shared with me. Fleeting shadows and perceptions become grounded and legible; it becomes so clear that each contributor has a rich life story that has led him or her to Anonymous, and that Anonymous itself functions as a portal to further destinations still.

Indeed, a year later I returned to Dublin and, alongside fifty other audience members, sat in Trinity College's Science Gallery and listened to O'Cearbhaill—now the auditor of the Dublin University Pirate Party—give a talk about Tor, the privacy tool. We were at a meet-up organized by CryptoParty, a grassroots movement that aims to teach cryptography to the general public. The idea was hatched by Asher Wolf and some other geeks in 2012. Just days later, over beers at a pub in London, Mustafa Al-Bassam (tflow) told me about his internship at Privacy International, the leading European NGO fighting for the right to whisper. There are dozens of other examples. Whatever one may think of Anonymous, it clearly acted as a political gateway. Many who left the group will continue, in different ways, to contribute to political life.

Unlike Al-Bassam and many others, Hammond and Monsegur were activists well before they became involved in Anonymous. But their paths diverged radically when their involvement with the collective ended. Soon after news broke about Monsegur's cooperation, he vanished—and nobody had any clue as to where he had gone. As it turns out, he spent seven months in the Metropolitan Correctional Center, the same prison where Hammond was incarcerated before he was moved to Kentucky to serve out his ten-year sentence. An anonymous source had tipped me off—but my pleas to reporters for a detailed investigation as to why he was in prison fell on deaf ears. Only later did I receive confirmation from Hammond himself. It wasn't until May 26, 2014, when Monsegur was finally sentenced after seven delays, that the circumstances leading to Monsegur's rearrest and incarceration were made available to the public. He had violated his bail conditions by penning a blog post and chatting with an Anonymous participant. At the sentencing, Judge Loretta Preska breathlessly trumpeted Monsegur as a model informant and determined that his 2012 stint in jail was punishment enough. He was a free man. Before he strolled out of court, Preska further lauded Monsegur: "The immediacy of Mr. Monsegur's cooperation and its around-the-clock nature was particularly helpful to the government ... That personal characteristic of turning on a dime to doing good, not evil, is the most important factor in this sentencing." Preska's lenient sentence not-so-subtly relayed the following message to future informants: cooperate and you will be treated well.

Although the outcome was far from surprising, Twitter was aflutter with wails of outrage: "Jeremy Hammond is serving a ten-year sentence for hacks that Sabu (working for the feds) told him to do. When will the feds go to prison?"[29] asked @YourAnonNews. "Preska is an absolute disgrace to the concept of justice," offered Firefly during an interview. These laments could do nothing to alter Hammond's situation—but many Anons derived some measure of comfort when, only days later, both *Motherboard* and the *Daily Dot* published accounts which called the government storyline into question —effectively corroborating Hammond's version of the events. Along with cooperating "around-the-clock," the news reports ascertained that Monsegur was given free rein to initiate, coordinate, and carry out dozens of hacks.

Following Monsegur's release, Hammond issued his own statement: "By aggressively prosecuting hackers who play by their own rules, they want to deter others from taking up the cause and hope future arrests will yield more aspiring cooperators. We must continue to reject excuses and justifications that make it acceptable to sell out your friends and become a pawn of cyber-imperialism ... Sabu avoided a prison sentence, but the consequences of his actions will haunt him for the rest of his life. Not even halfway through my time, I would still rather be where I'm at: while they can take away your freedom temporarily, your honor lasts forever."[30] While Hammond's lengthy detention will undoubtedly be trying, his vocal commitment to his principles in spite of his unmasking and incarceration have already proved a beacon of inspiration to many in the activist community.

While it might seem unusual for a researcher to become so entangled with his or her object of study, it has long been par for the course in anthropology. As Danilyn Rutherford writes, anthropological methods "create obligations, obligations that compel those who seek knowledge to put themselves on the line by making truth claims that they know will intervene within the setting and among the people they describe."[31] As part of a letter-writing campaign organized by Hammond's lawyers, I, along with 150 other citizens, wrote to Judge Loretta Preska to ask for leniency; in the letters, we emphasized the political nature of Anonymous. Wherever possible, I have attempted to translate the confusing world of Anonymous for multiple publics. I have also been writing letters to some of the Anons in prison. As part of these obligations, I've thought long and deliberately about the underlying goals motivating this book. Ultimately, I reached the conclusion that I have two clashing objectives: to stamp out misinformation and to embrace enchantment.

First and foremost, in this book I have sought to dispel some of the many misconceptions about Anonymous: many participants like O'Cearbhaill were not primarily driven by a desire to accrue lulz—even if this irreverent spirit still guided social interactions and underwrote strategies. Anonymous has matured into a serious political movement, so much so that many of the trolls from the "Internet Hate Machine" days would "not recognize" the Anonymous of today, as Ryan Ackroyd told me. He is among the tiny fraction of participants who bridged the divide between these now clearly distinctive eras. (Of course this does not mean that the Machine of Hate won't rise again, as an Anonymous activist named "blackplans" tweeted: "Without the trolls, the hackers, the 4chan hordes, how many of you nice, sensitive people would ever have heard of #Anonymous? Remember.")[32]

As part of this first mission, I've sought to avoid extolling Anonymous's every move. Even in its activist incarnations, Anonymous has clearly engaged in morally dubious—and sometimes downright awful—endeavors. The most troubling moments come when innocent people are caught up in the Anonymous cross fire. Some hacks struck me as counterproductive, and not always worth the risks taken by the persons involved. Indeed, parts of Anonymous are riddled with irresolvable contradictions.

And so, when assessing Anonymous, it seems impossible to arrive at a universal—much less neat-and-tidy—maxim regarding the group's effects. Instead, I have tried to relay the lessons of Anonymous by narrating its exploits, failures, and successes. These compiled stories are idiosyncratic and told from the vantage point of my personal travels and travails. There are so many untold and secret tales that, were they publicized, would likely shift our comprehension of Anonymous. While all social life and political movements are complex, even convoluted, displaying endless facets and dimensions, Anonymous's embrace of multiplicity, secrecy, and deception makes it especially difficult to study and comprehend.

This dynamism and multitudinous quality is also one of Anonymous's core strengths. Anonymous is emblematic of a particular geography of resistance. Composed of multiple competing groups, short-term power is achievable for brief durations, while long-term dominance by any single group or person is virtually impossible. In such a dynamic landscape, it may be "easy to co-opt, but impossible to keep co-opted," as Quinn Norton thoughtfully put it during a South by Southwest panel in March 2013. In this way, the multitudinal "nature" of Anonymous precludes its subjection to either aspirational figures working internally, or external figures who would exert influence either through informants, like Sabu, or through exogenous pressure. Anonymous is cryptic, forcing us to work and dance with the scraps and shards it shows us.

That is to say, Anonymous leaves a lot to the imagination. But not everything; it is vital to understand how Anonymous underwent a metamorphosis from underworld trolls into public-facing activists, especially given that nation-states, prosecutors, government officials, and judges would like to cast them all as mere criminals. These powers-that-be are unwilling to acknowledge Anonymous's actions as driven by an activist calling; indeed, it may be the potency and the politically motivated character of the group's actions that prompts the state to so swiftly criminalize them.[33]

And so, while I have aimed to blot out misconceptions, the prospect of fully stripping away the aura of mystery and magic felt somehow unacceptable (were it even possible). Philosopher Jane Bennett urges us "to resist the story of the disenchantment of modernity," and to instead "enhance enchantment."[34] This has been my second aim in collecting riveting tales about Anonymous. This deliberate elevation of enchantment, Bennett argues, is a meaningful political gesture, and one that I am driven to make—for reasons that will become more clear in these last pages.

Given this second goal, it was only natural for me to adopt a mythic frame and invite the trickster along for the ride. The figures in this book embody the contradictions and paradoxes of life, many of which are irresolvable. By telling these characters' stories, lessons emerge, not through dry edicts but, instead, through fascinating, often audacious, tales of exploits. Trickster lore may be patently mythic, but it bears remembering that, at one point, it was spun by human hands. My role has been to nudge forward this process of historical and political myth-making—already evident in the routine functioning of an entity constituted by adept artists, contemporary myth-makers, and concocters of illusion.

Now that we have nearly reached the end of this journey and I have unveiled the objectives guiding my book, it is left to you to judge whether I have displayed the cunning requisite to balance the Apollonian forces of empiricism and logic with the Dionysian forces of enchantment. Whatever your conclusion, please permit me the license to weave some final thoughts through and along the gaps which still remain, and on top of other areas already thick with embroidery. While Anonymous still leaves me frequently bewildered, there are a string of inspiring messages we can glean in its wake.

Anonymous Everywhere

Though it is shifty, and though its organizing structures can never quite be apprehended, Anonymous is composed of people who decide together and separately to take a stand. Who might these people be? A neighbor? A daughter? A secretary? A janitor? A student? A Buddhist? An incognito banker? You? Whatever sort of people are involved today, one thing is certain: what began as a network of trolls has become a wellspring of online insurgency. What started as a narrow reaction to the Church of Scientology now encompasses a global selection of political causes, from fights against censorship in Tunisia, through salvos against North American rape culture, on to condemnations of economic and political injustices in Zuccotti Park and Tahir Square.

Despite an unpredictable—not to mention irreverent and often destructive—attitude toward the law, Anonymous also offers an object lesson in what Frankfurt School philosopher Ernst Bloch calls "the principle of hope." Bloch, having fled Nazi Germany, wrote a three-volume tract on the topic while exiled in the United States. Striving for an "encylopedic" accounting, he unearthed a stunningly diverse number of signs, symbols, and artifacts that channeled hope in different historical eras. The examples gathered range from personal daydreams to time-honoured fairy tales, from the love of music and sports to mystical or philosophical tracts—anything that might spark or communicate a glimmer of hope. Working in the shadow of an overly pessimistic strain of Marxist critique, his opus reminds us that a better world—or at least the understanding of what that world could be—is in our midst. As a sort of philosophical archaeologist, Bloch excavated hidden or forgotten messages of utopia, that they might combat "anxiety" and "fear" in all who encountered them. "The emotion of hope goes out of itself, makes people broad instead of confining them," writes Bloch. "The work of this emotion requires people who throw themselves actively into what is becoming, to which they themselves belong."[35] That a robust activist politics emerged from the depths of one of the seediest places on the Internet—that geeks chose to throw themselves actively into a process of political becoming—strikes me as a perfect enactment of just such a principle of hope.

Bloch indicted "fraudulent hope,"[36] characterized by blind or overt optimism, for its failure to catalyze movement. Instead, his hope is a restless one, sustained by passion, wonder, and even mischief—all qualities embraced by Anonymous. We can see, then, a strong positivity inherent in Anonymous—a striving toward a realistic form of hope that, once manifest, seems suited to impel disruption and change. Of course, these activists hold no monopoly over such affective states of passion and hope. Nevertheless, with the exception of a narrow band of important thinkers like Chantal Mouffe and Jacques Rancière, the emotional character of political life is often relegated to the sidelines—odd, because desire and pleasure are so central to its very being. But there are other reasons, more urgent than simply undoing the omission of such a primary component of activist endeavors, to convey the emotional factors that play an integral role in social change.

In 2008, when the fearsome, Loki-esque band of trolls that then constituted Anonymous took that decisive left turn away from "ultracoordinated motherfuckery" and toward activism, they in essence conquered one of the prevailing sentiments of our times. Media scholar Whitney Phillips convincingly argues that a widespread cynicism pervades our moment—and that in trolls we find one of the most distilled, concentrated, and grotesque extremes of an emotionally dissociative (or politically fetishistic) subculture.[37]

Many theorists and writers from radically distinct traditions, stretching from the American novelist David Foster Wallace to Italian autonomist Franco "Bifo" Berardi, have persuasively argued that cynicism has become a prism through which large swaths of North Americans and Europeans filter and feel the world. Wallace writes about the pervasiveness of "passive unease and cynicism," and calls for "anti-rebels, born oglers" to rise up and "and dare somehow to back away from ironic watching."[38] Bifo, who has written multiple tracts on the topic, turned to poetry to convey the frightening, dead emotional burden of cynicism:

> Before the tsunami hits, you know how it is?
> The sea recedes, leaving a dead desert in which only
> cynicism and dejection remain.
> All you need to do, is to make sure you have the right
> words to say, the right
> clothes to wear, before it finally wipes you away.[39]

Feelings of dejection are not merely figurative shackles. Even when citizens are aware of the forces that fleece the majority, cynicism can disable political change. When this stance becomes prevalent enough, it settles into the sinews of society, further entrenching atomization, preventing social solidarity, and sharply limiting political possibilities.[40] Add anxiety to the mix, and the resulting cocktail becomes the most lethal of poisons. The UK-based radical collective Plan C has penned a perceptive tract entitled "We Are All Very Anxious Now." It connects the dots between dire economic conditions, precarious labor, preemptive crackdowns against activists, a cultural emphasis on self-promotion, and an overpowering technical state of surveillance: "One major part of the social underpinning of anxiety is the multifaceted omnipresent web of surveillance ... But this obvious web is only the outer carapace," they write. "Ostensibly voluntary self-exposure, through social media, visible consumption and choice of positions within the field of opinions, also assumes a performance in the field of the perpetual gaze of virtual others."[41] When this push toward the panopticon is stacked with a litany of broader issues—from growing wealth inequality, waves of global and national recession and unrest, and the looming prospect of climate-induced environmental disaster—it is not difficult to understand how a disabling, pervasive, and frightening uncertainty has come to colonize our states of being.

Cynicism and anxiety may be prevalent, but they are neither omnipotent nor omnipresent; they run up against friction and resistance—every single day. Untold numbers of activists, immigrants, displaced people, refugees, various unknowns, artists, and, remarkably, even some politicians, are all fighting against oppression and pushing against the emotional onslaught that can so easily lead to such existential traps. If we are not careful, we might paint too bleak a picture and reify the very cynicism and anxiety we seek to dismantle. Bloch insisted that we contribute to a living archive of hope, that we take care to listen to and take hold of "something other than the putridly stifling, hollowly nihilistic death-knell."[42]

When we consider that the members of Anonymous know such conditions well, it is either less remarkable, or more remarkable, that they were able to add to this "living archive of hope." I am unable to decide whether Anonymous attracts those with dark, emotional lives, or whether the pseudonymous environment creates a safe space for sharing what are simply universal facets of the human condition. Likely it is some combination of the two. I nevertheless was struck time and again by this pairing of personal pain with the ardent desire for its overcoming.

By sacrificing the public self, by shunning leaders, and especially by refusing to play the game of self-promotion, *Anonymous* ensures mystery; this in itself is a radical political act, given a social order based on ubiquitous monitoring and the celebration of runaway individualism and selfishness. *Anonymous's* iconography—masks and headless suits—visually displays the importance of opacity. *The collective* may not be the hive it often purports and is purported to be—and it may be marked by internal strife—but *Anonymous* still manages to leave us with a striking vision of solidarity—*e pluribus unum*.

"A small fire demands constant tending. A bonfire can be let alone. A conflagration spreads"—so said Anonymous activist papersplx. By embracing the mask, which sociologist Richard Sennett rightly notes is "one of culture's oldest stage props connecting stage and street," Anonymous took the dynamics of theatrical trickery and transferred them from the Internet to the everyday life of resistance.[43] Anonymous became a generalized symbol for dissent, a medium to channel deep disenchantment with a dictator, with a law, with the economy, with the culture of rape—basically, with anything. Anonymous, always the risk-taker, liked to play with fire— and many participants despised or shunned safety measures; it is not surprising that the group itself, as a whole, eventually caught fire, blazing a path for others. Some got burned—both participants and targets alike. Or as Firefly put it in the film *We Are Legion*: "It's like a phoenix. It might occasionally catch fire and burn to the ground but it'll just be reborn from the ashes. It'll be reborn stronger." Pushing hard against rules and boundaries may often lead to entrapment or demise, but the entity's core animating idea—Anonymous if free for anyone to embody—positions it well for resurrection and reinvention.

Anonymous has appeared many times like a vision, confounding us as we watch the bright flashes of its delightful (and offensive and confusing) dreams. It is this quality of straddling, on the one hand, mythic space, and on the other, the reality of activists taking risks and taking action, that makes the group so enticing. Taken at a distance, it's like observing the northern lights, a quiet but mythic battle of gods and tricksters in the night sky, a sky all the more enchanting because it is everyone's to watch. The power of Anonymous's eponymous anonymity is that we are all free to choose whether or not to don the mask.

Acknowledgements

E ven if a single concept is destined to fail at adequately conveying the vast and intricate geography fabricated by Anonymous activists, in writing this book I found myself consistently returning to one particular governing trope: the maze. Every attempt to traverse, understand, or describe a given state necessarily corrupted it, adding further entropic inputs which ensured a different experience for any who would participate within it or even simply watch. So, as it turns out, researching and writing about Anonymous was a thrilling but taxing enterprise. I spent years collecting too much material, attempting to build my own labyrinth that would allow me to chart a course through theirs. But when I set out to unravel the tangled threads, to find my way out of the collected stories, rumors, conversations, and secrets into some coherent and lucid narrative, I realized in horror that the gossamer material was disintegrating in my hands. I was lost in the nether regions between mazes, with no bearings and no way out. Thankfully, a host of friends, colleagues, strangers, and Anons helped me find my way, nudging me along on my journey and contributing to its ultimate manifestation as a book.

This project was long in the making. Its beginnings can be traced to a Killam Postdoctoral Research Fellowship I held at the University of Alberta in 2006–7, and a fortunate introduction to Dr. Stephen A. Kent, who, in his work as professor of sociology, curates the largest academic Scientology archive in the world. In the midst of a frighteningly frigid winter, I dove into the archive with hopes of emerging with a short historical side project describing a case known among geeks as "Scientology vs. the Internet." Being more accustomed to interviewing people than making sense of heaps of (in this case, very strange) documents, Kent thankfully and graciously walked me through the confusing, fascinating, and at times disturbing innards of an organization so many geeks love to loathe.

In January 2008, my historical project leaped into the present when, in the course of targeting the Church of Scientology, Anonymous underwent a broader and surprising metamorphosis from fearsome pranksters to fervent protesters. I was hooked. It seemed only natural to follow these mad hatters and see if anything would come of their bold and unexpected foray into protest culture—and clearly something did. By that time I had relocated to New York City and discovered a physical portal into Anonymous through the rambunctious local cell that welcomed me to its monthly protests. In turn, I welcomed members of the cell into my classroom, where my students and I benefited from both their eloquent lectures on the political significance of Anonymous and their theatrical antics demonstrating the lulz. Little Sister, Sethdood, and Matthew "PokeAnon" Danziger met with me on numerous occasions and proved lively interlocutors. The latter two even sat for formal interviews. I also experienced the delight of close acquaintance with Chanology Dublin and other Irish Anons; they were some of my most intrepid teachers. I crossed the ocean to draw upon this valuable resource on numerous occasions, and by my third trip in a three-year span, it was clear that a few of them, notably Pete, David, Firefly, and Donncha, had become more than sources—they had become friends. I look forward to future exchanges.

In 2010, when Anonymous broke into public consciousness with its direct-action digital campaign protesting the banking blockade leveled against WikiLeaks, I was fortuitously on sabbatical at a sanctuary—the Institute for Advanced Study at Princeton. The punishing pace of activity that subsequently cascaded from the AnonOps network would have been nearly impossible to follow were it not for the glut of time I was afforded. Conversations with two colleagues in my cohort, Manu Goswami and Tanya Erzen, helped shape my thinking on the topic. Anthropologist Didier Fassin proved an inspirational mentor, whose boundless willingness to share feedback was confirmed again after I presented on Anonymous at a recent workshop on public ethnography held at the IAS.

As 2010 turned into 2011, I lost myself full time in the ever-shifting maze of Anonymous. At times ambling with no direction or purpose, and at other times ardently driven to fulfill a mission, I spoke with dozens upon dozens of participants, benefiting from their time, experiences, insights, and critiques. I thank every one of you and I am sorry for my inability to remember and list all of your names—whether real, fake, or pseudonymous. A few folks necessitate special mention, going beyond the call of duty in their willingness to guide me. Early on, Trivette, meddle, and n0pants each spoke to me one-on-one and opened various doors in so doing. I found welcome homes in #reporter, #freedommods, and eventually #cabincr3w, where conversations ran into the hours and were always lively and illuminating. Over time, a handful of other folks put me on different paths of thinking. Anonymous9— teeming with energy—was inexhaustibly helpful. This book, at least in this form, would simply not be possible without him. m0rpeth was probably the first of a handful of insiders to implore me to stop drinking the Kool-Aid; his trenchant critiques of emergent power structures made it easier for me to intuit them and, in so doing, apprehend the many strains of internal critique existent in Anonymous. blackplans, a consistent presence spanning different eras and scenes, was boundlessly erudite and witty about Anonymous and hackers (not to mention life in general). Andrew Auerhenheimer, certainly far from being anonymous, or a fan of Anonymous, taught me a lot about trolling, often through his trollish arguments and statements, but thankfully never trolled me. Many others spent quite a bit of time chatting with me, including c0s, AnonyOps, Barrett Brown, evilworks, q, mr_a, sharpie, kantanon, shitstorm, owen, Avunit, emmi, Jackal, p0ke, crypt0anonymous, Nicole Powers, Nixie, Commander X, JMC, papersplx, Lauri Love, and others who will remain anonymous.

Over time (and due to a string of arrests), the circumstances of my research changed in equal measure with the public perception of its subjects. Many Anons have endured difficult legal battles and time in prison. Given just how complicated their lives became, I am all the more grateful that they made time for me. The book could simply not have been completed without the generosity and the acumen of Jeremy Hammond, Mustafa Al-Bassam, Donncha O'Cearbhaill, Darren Martyn, and Mercedes Haefer, each of whom poured hours into answering endless strings of sometimes repetitive questions. Chris Weatherhead and Jake Davis also met with me in person to share many of their experiences; Ryan Ackroyd, who I only started to interact with recently, commented thoughtfully on the "Internet Hate Machine" and informants.

During research I could be found chatting with a number of journalists and filmmakers who, like me, spent an enormous about of time toiling away trying to crack the Anonymous puzzle. Their presence was welcome—talking shop and trading some research notes proved to be both comically relieving and professionally invaluable. Conversations with Quinn Norton, Asher Wolf, Steve Ragan, and Brian Knappenberger were instrumental to my thinking on Anonymous. Steve Ragan also deserves special mention for sharing so freely—most journalists are far more guarded about their possessions. Knappenberger's film and Parmy Olson's engrossing account of Anonymous and LulzSec proved to be valuable resources for this project.

In 2013, a slew of colleagues read a couple of early chapters and dispensed thoughtful commentary: Danielle Citron, Nathan Schneider, Jonathan Sterne, Darin Barney, Christine Ross, Carrie Rentschler, Sandra Hyde, Michael Ralph, Whitney Phillips, and Chris Kelty. Over the years, I have lectured extensively on Anonymous, and it would be impossible to take stock of all the bountiful feedback I received; however, comments from Paul Eiss, Angela Zito, Faye Ginsburg, Haidy Geismar, Daniel Miller, Alberto Sanchez, and Bob Rutledge are of particular note.

At McGill University, I am fortunate to hold a position designed to enable my engagement in both outreach and writing; I am deeply grateful to the generous donor who provides its funding. The environment at McGill has proved stimulating, and I am especially thankful to all the Bits, Bots and Bytes participants for contributing to a research forum and scholarly exchange that has become one of the highlights of my month. Two of its members, Scott Kushner and Elena Razlogova, read and commented incisively on additional material shared outside of the meet-up. My undergraduate student and unflagging research assistant Maya Richmond has successfully hunted down every last bit of material I asked her to procure while also providing sharp insights regarding hackers and tricksters. Caroline Habluetzel, who received a PhD from our department, also provided invaluable and meticulous research assistance, all while battling cancer. She passed away in May 2013 and will be missed. My graduate class, "Technological Underworlds," was given an early draft of the first five chapters to read, resulting in fascinating questions and the identification of various problems. Darcie DeAngelo went beyond the call of duty to provide extensive commentary. Molly Sauter was completing her own book— *The Coming Swarm: DDOS Actions, Hacktivism, and Civil Disobedience on the Internet*—throughout the same period, and reading the manuscript proved both essential and fascinating as I worked through the ethics of digital direct action.

Writing a book for a popular audience while remaining faithful to complex, esoteric, technical, and legal details is a formidable challenge. I sought the advice of a host of experts to ensure that I was not misrepresenting these nuances. Orin Kerr, Marcia Hoffman, Ahmed Ghappour, and Andres Guadamuz read through the legal sections. Many technologists and hackers always delivered answers to my many questions: David Mirza, Chris Soghoian, Dino A. Dai Zovi, Chris Wysopal, Space Rouge, James Atkinson, Patrick Gray, Dan Guido, Morgan Marquis-Boire, and Brian Martin. Meanwhile, journalists Kim Zetter and Ted Bridis clarified some uncertainties I held about hackers and FBI policies toward informants. Any inaccuracies that remain stem from my inability to follow the excellent guidance of these consultants.

Family members should be thanked for enduring the negative consequences of book writing—and the Andersons were patient and gracious as the last three holiday seasons saw me not quite as present as everyone else. My father, an unflagging supporter of my work, ensured that his friends, most of them retired, learned something important about Anonymous. My dog Roscoe, with his cute snaggletooth, was daily able to woo me from my desk, ensuring that I took necessary breaks from writing.

Finally, there are three people whose imprint is everywhere in this book and who have read it start to finish, two of them more than once. My partner Micah Anderson, who spends his days (and too often nights) running a privacy-friendly ISP, is a talented writer. He read the first few chapters, took me aside, and clued me in to the fact that I needed to be far more lively and descriptive if this was to be a nonacademic/popular book. His subsequent readings of every chapter always generated useful comments or edits. He certainly doused with gasoline all my attempts at humor, before throwing a match and fueling the fire with jokes of his own. Some were just too wild and imaginative and I had to stamp the fire out, but in the aftermath, things were typically much improved. I am extremely thankful that he is willing to be part of the creative process, and that he put up with me as I wrote two books back to back—something I will never, ever do again.

In part because of Micah's advice—and in part due to my own proclivity to explain everything—I went completely overboard with writing. Two people were poised to contain me, call out my inconsistencies, help me whittle the manuscript down to an appropriate size, and generally do everything in their power to make this a better book.

First, my research assistant Matt Goerzen, who is also my MA student and a quirky and talented artist specializing in, among other topics, anonymity, was a first line editor. Trained as a journalist, he is also a dexterous writer gifted in adding a touch of grace and clarity to any prose that comes his way. Since he has deeply pondered and completed so much research on the cultures of online anonymity, his comments were sharp and discerning. This book is much stronger because of his unstinting willingness to impart his wisdom. I will be forever grateful that he took on the role of my most trusted guide and interlocutor, and I only hope I can return the debt as his MA thesis supervisor.

When entertaining possible publishers, I wanted one that would help me reach the right balance between analysis and accessibility; Verso immediately presented itself as the number-one candidate and it has been a pleasure working with the entire team, including Mark Martin, Colin Beckett, Jennifer Tighe, and Jacob Stevens. I am especially grateful to have worked with Andrew Hsiao. When my book ballooned to an unacceptable size, I will confess that I dreaded the stringent measures he might enact to trim the manuscript. As I feared the worst, his advice ultimately proved both stellar and specific, making the pruning process far less painful than could have been. He went through the manuscript with a fine-tooth comb; he was persnickety about the small details of phrasing, he entertained the value of my arguments, and he zoomed out to identify the sections, sentences, and even chapters where shaving and cutting were necessary. There were moments when, if it were possible to hug someone through email, I would have hugged him, multiple times. I have also thoroughly enjoyed our conversations about publishing and politics and look forward to many more in the future.

Finally, I would like to thank all of the masked activists and pranksters for staging this wildly epic play and giving me the opportunity to write about it.

A Note on Sources

In presenting a popular ethnography of Anonymous, this book leans heavily on journalistic convention and sourcing methodologies. Many readers will wonder how the information contained herein can be verified, given that lies, guile, and fabrication are the tools of the trade—often wielded with pride—by those operating under the mantle of Anonymous. But while some of the anecdotes recorded remain unverifiable, or simply accompanied by chat logs, they complement a factual narrative largely made possible by legal records. Indeed, this book could not have been written were it not for the unmasking of many participants upon their arrest and prosecution—and the troves of careful (and sometimes problematic) information made public by law enforcement toward this end. Additionally, while anonymity by nature enables individuals to speak out against and challenge powerful institutions, upon capture and sentencing many participants are suddenly afforded a different sort of freedom: the ability to speak honestly about their personal identities and experiences as individuals, distanced from a collective or protective pseudonym. Access to chat logs and especially court documents has further enabled me to authenticate many claims made by Anons and their colleagues prior to arrest (in the great majority of instances what I had been told turned out to be true).

The extensive chat logs cited in the book come from numerous sources: from public IRC channels, from published logs put online by Anonymous, from private logs given to me, and finally from logs submitted as court evidence and leaked to reporters. In instances where no documents existed, I have attempted to interview multiple participants and relied, where possible, on accounts published by respected media figures. It is a sad reality that many fascinating tales and participants, unable to be substantiated beyond rumor, were not included in these pages. Since many of the figures covered in this book are now well known to the public—and have been written about extensively—I have not changed their names or their pseudonyms, except in instances where doing so might pose a threat to the individual in question.

This book should be read as a collection of personal experiences and reflections. While I address major events and historical turning points, and attempt to be inclusive of multiple (even, at times, conflicting) perspectives, there is much more at work within Anonymous than what is in these pages.

Notes

Introduction: "And Now You Have Got Our Attention"

1. "Dear Fox New," YouTube video, posted by dearfoxnews, July 29, 2007, last accessed July 8, 2014, available at http://www.youtube.com/watch?v=RFjU8bZR19A.
2. This quote comes from a class lecture.
3. "Message to Scientology," YouTube video, posted by ChurchOf Scientology, Jan. 21, 2008, last accessed July 4, 2014, available at http://www.youtube.com/watch?v=JCbKv9yiLiQ.
4. Siobhan Gorman, "Power Outage Seen as a Potential Aim of Hacking Group," online.wsj.com, Feb. 21, 2012.
5. Sam Biddle, "No, Idiots, Anonymous Isn't Going to Destroy the Power Grid," gizmodo.com, Feb. 21, 2012.

1. On Trolls, Tricksters, and the Lulz

1. Danielle Keats Citron, *Hate 3.0: The Rise of Discriminatory Online Harassment and How to Stop It* (Cambridge, MA: Harvard University Press, forthcoming); Danielle Keats Citron, "Cyber Civil Rights," *Boston University Law Review*, vol. 91 (2009).
2. For a detailed critique of the CFAA and recommendations for reform see http://www.eff.org/issues/cfaa.
3. Tom McCarthy, "Andrew Auernheimer's Conviction over Computer Fraud Thrown Out," *theguardian.com*, April 1, 2014.
4. Joseph Carey, Twitter post, July 22, 2013, 10:22 am, http://twitter.com/JDCareyMusic/status/359362756568285184.
5. weev, "I am weev. I may be going to prison under the Computer Fraud and Abuse Act tomorrow at my sentencing. AMA.," reddit, March 17, 2013, last accessed May 21, 2014, available at

http://www.reddit.com/r/IAmA/comments/1ahkgc/i_am_weev_i_
may_be_going_to_prison_under_the/c8xgqq9.

6. Daniel Bates, "Standing by Her Man: Strauss-Kahn's Wife Puts Her
   Mansion Up as Collateral to Get Him out of Jail and She's Paying the
   Rent at His 'Golden Cage,'" *dailymail.co.uk*, May 21, 2011.

7. "Lulz," Encyclopedia Dramatica, last accessed May 23, 2012, available at http://encyclopediadramatica.es/Lulz

8. For early references to "lulz" on Jameth's LiveJournal site, see http://
   web.archive.org/web/20021102004836/http://www.livejournal.com/
   users/jameth (last accessed May 22, 2014).

9. Whitney Phillips, "LOLing at Tragedy: Facebook Trolls, Memorial
   Pages and Resistance to Grief Online," *First Monday* vol. 16, no. 12
   (2011).

10. Many of these insights are delectably explored in Lewis Hyde's majes-
    tic account *Trickster Makes This World: Mischief, Myth, and Art*
    (New York: Farrar, Straus and Giroux, 1998).

11. Ibid., p. 9

12. Alex Galloway and Eugene Thacker, *The Exploit: A Theory of
    Networks* (Minneapolis, MN: University of Minnesota Press, 2007).

13. Phil Lapsley, *Exploding the Phone: The Untold Story of the Teenagers
    and Outlaws Who Hacked Ma Bell* (New York: Grove Press, 2013),
    226.

14. Steven Levy, *Hackers: Heroes of the Computer Revolution—25th
    Anniversary Edition* (Sebastapol, CA: O'Reilly Media, 2010).

15. Adam L. Penenberg, "A Private Little Cyberwar," forbes.com, Feb. 21,
    2000.

16. "Biography of u4ea," soldierx.com, last accessed May 21, 2014, avail-
    able at https://www.soldierx.com/hdb/u4ea.

17. Marco Deseriis, "'Lots of Money Because I Am Many': The Luther
    Blissett Project and the Multiple-Use Name Strategy," in *Cultural
    Activism: Practices, Dilemmas and Possibilities* (Amsterdam: Rodopi,
    2011), 65–93.

18. Trond Lossius, "/55\[Fwd: [max-msp] it's over]," /55\ mailing list,
    Jan. 15, 2001, last accessed May 21, 2014, available at http://www.
    bek.no/pipermail/55/2001-January/000102.html. A good example
    of Nezvanova's art can be found at http://www.nettime.org/Lists-
    Archives/nettime-bold-0009/msg00073.html (last accessed May 21,
    2014).

19. Lee Knuttila, "Users Unknown: 4chan, Anonymity and Contingency,"
    First Monday, vol. 16, no. 10 (Oct. 2011).

20. "Internet Hate Machine" was a phrase used by a local Fox News
    program in Los Angeles in 2007 to describe Anonymous. The group
    promptly turned the phrase into a popular meme.

21. Phillips, "LOLing at Tragedy."

22. David Graeber, "Manners, Deference, and Private Property in Early

Modern Europe," *Comparative Studies in Society and History*, vol. 39 (October 1997): 694–728.

23. Christopher Kelty, *Two Bits: The Cultural Significance of Free Software* (Durham, NC: Duke University Press, 2008).

2. Project Chanology—I Came for the Lulz but Stayed for the Outrage

1. Anonymous, "The Story Behind the Tom Cruise Video Link," Why We Protest, July 27, 2013, last accessed May 23, 2014, available at http://whyweprotest.net/community/threads/the-story-behind-the-tom-cruise-video-leak.93170/page-4.

2. "The Cruise Indoctrination Video Scientology Tried to Suppress," gawker.com, January 15, 2008, last accessed July 11, 2014.

3. L. Ron Hubbard, "Scientology Technology," *The Auditor*, no. 41 (1968).

4. XENU TV, "The Story Behind the Tom Cruise Video Link," Why We Protest, Sept. 7, 2011, last accessed May 23, 2014, available at http://whyweprotest.net/community/threads/the-story-behind-the-tom-cruise-video-leak.93170/page-3#post-1875660.

5. "Code of Conduct," YouTube video, posted by ChurchOfScientology, Feb. 1, 2008, last accessed May 23, 2014, available at http://www.youtube.com/watch?v=-063clxiB8I.

6. Cain, "Hal Tuner Raid Planned for Tomorrow," The PFLD, April 20, 2007, last accessed May 23, 2014, available at http://episkoposcain.blogspot.ca/2007/04/hal-turner-raid-planned-for-tomorrow.html.

7. Asterix, "August Theme: Anonymous Takes Back Chanology," Why We Protest, July 14, 2008, last accessed May 23, 2014, available at http://whyweprotest.net/community/threads/august-theme-anonymous-takes-back-chanology.18139/page-2.

8. Why We Protest, http://whyweprotest.net/community/threads/false-press-we-need-to-deal-with-this-immediately.80242

9. "Operation Slickpubes," Motherfuckery, Jan. 10, 2009, last accessed May 23, 2014, available at http://motherfuckery.org/this-is-how-a-post-looks.

10. "In 2009, NYPD Issued 'Surveillance Request' to 'Identify' Anonymous Members During Their Anti-Scientology Rally," techdirt.com, Sept. 4, 2013, last accessed July 11, 2014.

11. Eric Hobsbawm, "Subculture and Primitive Rebels" in the *Cultural Resistance Reader* (London and New York: Verso, 2002), 136.

12. Ibid., 147

13. Tony Ortega, "Meet the Man Behind WWP, the Web Home of Anonymous and Project Chanology," The Underground Bunker, June 22,

2013, last accessed May 23, 2014, available at http://tonyortega.org/2013/06/22/meet-the-man-behind-wwp-the-web-home-of-anonymous.

14. Online interview with author.

15. Anonymous, "What the Dicks Is Marblecake and What Do They Do?" Why We Protest, July 23, 2008, last accessed July 4, 2014, available at http://whyweprotest.net/community/threads/what-the-dicks-is-marblecake-and-what-do-they-do.16012/page-13.

16. Paolo Gerbaudo, *Tweets and the Streets: Social Media and Contemporary Activism* (London: Pluto Press, 2012).

17. Jo Freeman, "The Tyranny of Structurelessness," *The Second Wave*, vol. 2, no. 1 (1972).

18. "Operation Clambake Present: The Scientology Fair Game Policy," Operation Clambake: Undressing the Church of Scientology, last accessed May 23, 2014, available at http://www.xenu.net/fairgame-e.html.

3. Weapons of the Geek

1. David Leigh, "Guardian Gagged from Reporting Parliament," the guardian.com, Oct. 12, 2009.

2. Christian Christensen, "Collateral Murder and the After-Life of Activist Imagery," medium.com, April 14, 2014.

3. Evan Hansen, "Manning-Lamo Chat Logs Revealed," wired.com, July 13, 2011.

4. Lamo has claimed that, since he has published some articles, he is a journalist. He has also said that he is a minister for the Universal Life Church. See Luis Martinez, "Bradley Manning Accuser Adrian Lamo Takes the Stand," Dec. 20, 2011, abcnews.go.com.

5. Ed Pilkington, "Bradley Manning's Treatment Was Cruel and Inhuman, UN Torture Chief Rules," theguardian.com, March 12, 2012.

6. Raffi Khatchadourian, "No Secrets," newyorker.com, June 7, 2010.

7. The connection can be drawn even further, as the young Julian Assange had his own foray into fighting Scientology as well. Back in Australia, he ran a free speech Internet service provider, Suburbia, which hosted anti-Scientology material. He also organized an anti-Scientology protest in Melbourne in 1996.

8. Wilford's Dog, "AMA Request Sabu from LuLSec this would be amazing," reddit, Sept. 23, 2011, last accessed May 29, 2014, available at http://www.reddit.com/r/IAmA/comments/kpfsp/ama_request_sabu_from_lulsec_this_would_be_amazing/

9. Guest, "Untitled," July 5, 2010, last accessed May 29, 2014, available at http://pastebin.com/ytZ7N1x7.

10. For reasons of privacy, this is not a real IP address.

11. For more on botnets, see Finn Brunton's excellent *Spam: A Shadow History of the Internet* (Cambridge, MA: MIT Press, 2013).
12. "Activists Target Recording Industry Websites," bbc.com, Sept. 20, 2010.
13. Ernesto, "Anti-Piracy Outfit Tries to Erase History," torrentfreak.com, Oct. 15, 2011.
14. David Kravets, "Wired Exclusive: I Was a Hacker for the MPAA," abcnews.go.com, Oct. 22, 2007.
15. Enigmax, "Anti-Piracy Outfit Threatens to DoS Uncooperative Torrent Sites," torrentfreak.com, Sept. 5, 2010.
16. Enigmax, "4chan DDoS Takes Down MPAA and Anti-Piracy Websites," torrentfreak.com, Sept. 18, 2010.
17. "Hackers Hit Hollywood's Piracy Watchdog," reuters.com, Sept. 19, 2010.
18. Christopher Williams, "Piracy Threats Lawyer Mocks 4chan DDoS Attack," theregister.co.uk, Sept. 22, 2010.
19. Nate Anderson, "'Straightforward Legal Blackmail': A Tale of P2P Lawyering," arstechnica.com, June 6, 2010.
20. "Lords Hansard text for 26 Jan 201026 Jan 2010 (pt 0003)," parliament.uk, last accessed May 29, 2014, available at http://www.parliament.the-stationery-office.co.uk/pa/ld200910/ldhansrd/text/100126-0003.htm.
21. Nate Anderson, "The 'Legal Blackmail' Business: Inside a P2P Settlement Factory," arstechnica.com, Sept. 28, 2010.
22. Enigmax, "ACS:Law (Gay) Porn Letters Target Pensioners, Married Men," torrentfreak.com, Sept. 25, 2010.
23. Charles Arthur, "ACS:Law and MediaCAT Close Their Doors, Ending Filesharing Claims," theguardian.com, Feb. 4, 2011.
24. "ACS:Law Solicitor Andrew Crossley Suspended by SRA," bbc.com, Jan. 18, 2012.
25. Josh Halliday, "ACS:Law Solicitor at Centre of Internet Piracy Row Suspended," theguardian.com, Jan. 18, 2012.
26. Ernesto, "Behind the Scenes at Anonymous' Operation Payback," torrentfreak.com, Nov. 15, 2010.
27. "Anonymous Is Not Unanimous," last accessed May 29, 2014, available at http://pastebin.com/4vprKdXH.
28. "PPi Ask Anonymous to Stop Payback," The pp.international.general, Nov. 2010, last accessed May 29, 2014, available at http://lists.pirateweb.net/pipermail/pp.international.general/2010-November/thread.html#8046.
29. Pirate Parties of the UK and US, "Pirate Party Op," Nov. 19, 2010, last accessed May 29, 2014, available at http://www.scribd.com/doc/43400303/Pirate-Party-OP.
30. Ernesto, "Behind the Scenes at Anonymous' Operation Payback."
31. Online interview with author.

32. Ibid.
33. For an example, see "Untitled," Feb. 24, 2011, last accessed May 29, 2014, available at http://pastebin.com/0Y5CkrF9.
34. Online interview with author.
35. Online interview with author.
36. gster, "DDoS Attacks on Pro-Copyright Groups: Pirate Parties and 'Operation Payback,'" Play Station Universe, Nov. 25, 2010, last accessed May 29, 2014, available at psu.com.

4. The Shot Heard Round the World

1. Art Keller, "Dozens (Yes, Dozens) Show Up for Anonymous' Million-Mask March," newsweek.com, Nov. 7, 2013.
2. Justin Elliot, "The 10 Most Important Wikileaks Revelations," salon.com, Nov. 29, 2010.
3. Martin Beckford, "Sarah Palin: Hunt WikiLeaks Founder Like al-Qaeda and Taliban Leaders," telegraph.co.uk, Nov. 30, 2010.
4. Kathryn Jean Lopez, "On This Sunday Outrage," nationalreview.com, Nov. 28, 2010.
5. At the time, statistics were available at http://irc.netsplit.de/networks/top10.php and http://searchirc.com/channel-stats.
6. Richard Stallman, "The Anonymous WikiLeaks Protests Are a Mass Demo Against Control," theguardian.com, Dec. 17, 2010.
7. For precise figures, see Molly Sauter, *The Coming Swarm: DDOS Actions, Hacktivism, and Civil Disobedience on the Internet* (London: Bloomsbury Academic, 2014).
8. Noam Cohen, "Web Attackers Find a Cause in WikiLeaks," nytimes.com, Dec. 9, 2010.
9. Parmy Olson, *We Are Anonymous: Inside the Hacker World of LulzSec, Anonymous, and the Global Cyber Insurgency* (New York: Back Bay Books, 2013), 109.
10. Sean-Paul Correll, " 'Tis the Season of DDoS—WikiLeaks Edition," PandaLabs Blog, last accessed June 3, 2014, available at http://pandalabs.pandasecurity.com/tis-the-season-of-ddos-wikileaks-editio.
11. Sean-Paul Correll, "Operation:Payback Broadens to 'Operation Avenge Assange,'" PandaLabs Blog, last accessed June 3, 2014, available at http://pandalabs.pandasecurity.com/operationpayback-broadens-to-operation-avenge-assange.
12. Nick Davies, "10 Days in Sweden: The Full Allegations Against Julian Assange," theguardian.com, Dec. 17, 2010.
13. Michel de Certeau, *The Practice of Everyday Life*, trans. Steven Rendall (Berkeley: University of California Press, 2011), xix.
14. Jon Snow, Twitter post, Dec. 9, 2010, 5:22 am, https://twitter.com/jonsnowC4/status/12814239458656256.

15. Zeynep Tufekci, "WikiLeaks Exposes Internet's Dissent Tax, Not Nerd Supremacy," theatlantic.com, Dec. 22, 2010.

16 Online interview with the author.

17. Mikhail Bakhtin, *The Dialogic Imagination: Four Essays* (Austin, TX: University of Texas Press Slavic Series, 1981).

18. Ethan Case, "The Dark Side of Anonymous: Everything You Never Knew About the Hacktivist Group," policymic.com, Jan. 3, 2012.

19. "Untitled," Dec. 10, 2010, last accessed June 3, 2014, available at http://pastebin.com/WzzJ1Jp3.

20. Joel Johnson, "What Is LOIC?" gizmodo.com, Dec. 8, 2010.

21. Gerry Smith, "Feds Charge 13 Members of Anonymous in 'Operation Payback' Attacks," huffingtonpost.com, Oct. 3, 2010.

22. For the definitive account of early hactivism, see Tim Jordan and Paul Taylor, *Hactivism and Cyberwars: Rebels with a Cause?* (New York: Routledge, 2004).

23. Molly Sauter, "'LOIC Will Tear Us Apart,'" *American Behavioral Scientist*, 998, vol. 57 (2013): 983–100.

24. Frances Fox Piven, *Who's Afraid of Frances Fox Piven?: The Essential Writings of the Professor Glenn Beck Loves to Hate* (New York: New Press, 2011).

25. Sauter, "LOIC Will Tear Us Apart."

26. Elinor Mills, "Old-time Hacktivists: Anonymous, You've Crossed the Line," cnet.com, March 30, 2012.

27. Tod Gemuese, Facebook comment on page of Cult of the Dead Cow, Jan. 10, 2013, last accessed June 5, 2014, available at http://www.facebook.com/groups/28828338908/permalink/10151344658883909.

28. For an extended and illuminating discussion on the DDoS campaign as an intervention that furthers speech objectives but also qualifies as conduct, see Sauter, *The Coming Swarm*.

29. Ethan Zuckerman, Hal Roberts, Ryan McGrady, Jillian York, and John Palfrey, *2010 Report on Distributed Denial of Service (DDoS) Attacks*, Berkman Center for Internet and Security, Dec. 20, 2010, available at http://cyber.law.harvard.edu/publications/2010/DDoS_Independent_Media_Human_Rights.

30. For example, in March 2013, the *Los Angeles Times* issued a correction after erroneously stating in a post that an indictment charged Anonymous with what amounted to hacking. See Matt Pearce, "Wisconsin Man Indicted in Anonymous Attack of Koch Industries," latimes.com, March 27, 2013. The correction appears near the end of the article.

31. Lee Mathews, "Man Fined $183,000 for Helping Anonymous Ddos a Site for One Minute," geek.com, Dec. 10, 2013. Ryan J. Reilly, "Loading Koch Industries Website Too Many Times in 1 Minute Just Cost this Truck Driver $183,000," huffingtonpost.com, Dec. 3, 2013.

32. Sandra Laville, "Student Convicted over Anonymous Cyber-Attacks," theguardian.com, Dec. 6, 2012.
33. Joe Kloc, "Anonymous's PayPal 14 Enter Pleas, Most May Skirt Jail," dailydot.com, Dec. 5, 2013.
34. Anu Passary, "Anonymous Members Plead Guilty in Paypal DDoS Attack Case," techtimes.com, Dec. 8, 2013.
35. Somini Sengupta, "British Police Make Arrest in Net Attacks," nytimes. com, July 27, 2011.

5. Anonymous Everywhere

1. Eduard Kovacs, "Anonymous Hackers Leak Documents on Governor of Italy's Lombardy Region," softpedia.com, Nov. 25, 2013.
2. See Carola Frediani, *Inside Anonymous: A Journey into the World of Cyberactivism* (Informant, 2013).
3. Lina Ben Mhenni, "Tunisia: Censorship Continues as WikiLeaks Cables Make the Rounds," globalvoicesonline.org, Dec. 7, 2010.
4. Quinn Norton, "2011: The Year Anonymous Took On Cops, Dictators and Existential Dread," wired.com, Jan. 11, 2012.
5. Ibrahim Saleh, "WikiLeaks and the Arab Spring: The Twists and Turns of Media, Culture, and Power," *Beyond WikiLeaks: Implications for the Future of Communications, Journalism and Society* (New York: Palgrave Macmillan, 2013), 237.
6. WikiLeaks, "Cable: 09TUNIS516-a," wikileaks.org, last accessed June 5, 2014, available at https://www.wikileaks.org/plusd/cables/09TUNIS516_a.html.
7. John Pollock, "How Egyptian and Tunisian Youth Hacked the Arab Spring," technologyreview.com, Aug. 23, 2011.
8. See twitter.com/TAKRIZ, last accessed June 5, 2014.
9. "Tunisia Suicide Protester Mohamed Bouazizi Dies," bbc.com, Jan. 5, 2011.
10. "Thousands of Tunisia Lawyers Strike," aljazeera.com, Jan. 6, 2011.
11. Tarek Amara, "Tunisian Government Says Two Killed in Clashes," reuters.com, Jan. 9, 2011.
12. See anonnews.org/press/item/135, last accessed June 16, 2014.
13. For a few representative articles claiming Sabu as the leader see: Charles Arthur, "The Darkness at the Heart of Anonymous," theguardian.com, Aug. 23, 2011; Josh Halliday, "LulzSec Mastermind Sabu: An Elite Hacker and Star FBI Informant," theguardian.com, March 6, 2012; Andy Greenberg, "LulzSec Leader and Informant 'Sabu' Let Off with Time Served," wired.com, May 27, 2014. For articles claiming Topiary as the leader, see: Adrian Chen, "Meet the LulzSec Leader Arrested by British Police Today," gawker.com, July 27, 2011; Peter

Finocchiaro, "LulzSec Leader 'Topiary' Arrested in Britain," salon. com, July 27, 2011.

14. John Cook and Adrian Chen, "Inside Anonymous' Secret War Room," gawker.com, March 18, 2011.

15. Arthur, "The Darkness at the Heart of Anonymous."

16. Joseph Menn, "SPECIAL REPORT—U.S. Cyberwar Strategy Stokes Fear of Blowback," reuters.com, May 10, 2013.

17. Ibid.

18. Although I have access to most of the subsequent log, there was no other mention about why the zero-day did not pan out, and when I asked some participants, no one could remember why. It is not unusual for an issue or possibility that is raised and explored to not pan out and never be discussed again.

19. Tom Jagatic, Nathaniel Johnson, Markus Jakobsson, Filippo Menczer, "Social Phishing," *Communications of the ACM*, (Fall 2007): 94–100.

20. "St. Jude Memorial and Virtual Wake," *The Well*, August 1, 2003, last accessed July 6, 2014, available at http://www.well.com/conf/inkwell. vue/topics/190/St-Jude-Memorial-and-Virtual-Wak-page01.html.

21. Spencer Ackerman, "Former NSA Chief Warns of Cyber-Terror Attacks if Snowden Apprehended," theguardian.com, Aug. 6, 2013.

22. Ryan J. Reily, "Stephen Heymann, Aaron Swartz Prosecutor, Compared Internet Activist to Rapist: MIT Report," huffingtonpost.com, July 31, 2013.

23. Hal Abelson, "The Lessons of Aaron Swartz," technologyreview.com, October 4, 2013.

24. Gabriella Coleman, "Gabriella Coleman's Favorite News Stories of the Week," techdirt.com, Oct. 12, 2013.

25. Miller McPherson, Lynn Smith-Lovin, and James M. Cook, "Birds of a Feather: Homophily in Social Networks," *Annual Review of Sociology*, Vol. 27 (2001): 415–44.

26. Roli Varma, "Why So Few Women Enroll in Computing? Gender and Ethnic Differences in Students' Perception," *Computer Science Education* vol. 20, no. 4 (2010): 301–16.

27. For more precise figures, see Christina Dunbar Hester and Gabriella Coleman, "Engendering Change? Gender Advocacy in Open Source," June 26, 2012, last accessed July 9, 2014, available at http://culture digitally.org/2012/06/engendering-change-gender-advocacy-in-open-source/.

28. Ibid.

29. See Douglas Thomas, *Hacker Culture* (Minneapolis, MN: University of Minnesota Press, 2003).

6. "Moralfaggotry" Everywhere

1. Barret Brown, Twitter post, Nov. 9, 2011, 9:56 pm, https://twitter.com/BarrettBrownLOL/status/134464512064626689.
2. Barret Brown, "Why the Hacks Hate Michael Hastings," vanityfair.com, June 23, 2010.
3. Ian Shapira, "'Anonymous' Movement Views Web Hijinks as Public Good, but Legality Is Opaque," washingtonpost.com, Jan. 25, 2011.
4. Richard Borshay Lee, "Eating Christmas in the Kalahari," naturalhistorymag.com (originally published in Dec. 1969).
5. "US Urges Restraint in Egypt, Says Government Stable," reuters.com, Jan. 25, 2011.
6. Although some Anons certainly dabble in credit card fraud, they are not in the business of large-scale carding and identity theft. One of the most notorious carding rings—Shadowcrew—was busted in November 2006 in what journalist Kevin Poulsen has described as "the biggest crackdown on identify thieves in American history." Poulsen, *Kingpin: How One Hacker Took Over the Billion-Dollar Cybercrime Underground* (New York: Broadway Books, 2012), 113.
7. For the definitive account of Operation Sundevil, see Bruce Sterling's *The Hacker Crackdown: Law and Disorder on the Electronic Frontier* (1992), available at http://www.mit.edu/hacker/hacker.html.
8. "Document Management in the FBI," ch. 2 in *An Investigation of the Belated Production of Documents in the Oklahoma City Bombing Case*," US Justice Department, March 19, 2002, last accessed June 16, 2014, available at http://www.justice.gov/oig/special/0203/chapter2.htm.
9. Since the FD-302 provides a summary of an interview instead of a transcript, activists and lawyers have long criticized it for its bias. Civil liberties lawyer Harvey Silverglate encapsulated its problems in an op-ed: "Frightened and confused interviewees, who, if they deny they said what any 302 report claims they uttered, can then be indicted for making false statements" (Silvergate, "Unrecorded Testimony," bostonglobe.com, May 11, 2013). In May 2014, the FBI reversed its policy and will now mandate recording for most interviews with federal suspects. (Andrew Grossman, "FBI to Record Most Interrogations of Suspects in Federal Custody," online.wsj.com, May 21, 2014.)

7. Revenge of the Lulz

1. Jules Boykoff, *The Suppression of Dissent: How the State and Mass Media Squelch USAmerican Social Movements* (New York: Routledge, 2006), 121.

2. Ibid., 115–17.
3. Ibid., 118.
4. US Senate Committee to Study Governmental Operations with Respect to Intelligence Activities, "COINTELPRO: The FBI's Covert Action Programs Against American Citizens," April 23, 1976, last accessed June 18, 2014, available at http://terrasol.home.igc.org/HooverPlan.htm.
5. Quoted in "The FBI, COINTELPRO, and the Most Important Robbery You've Never Heard Of," Privacy SOS, April 3, 2013, last accessed June 18, 2014, available at https://www.privacysos.org/node/1015.
6. Mark Mazzetti, "Burglars Who Took on F.B.I. Abandon Shadows," nytimes.com, Jan. 7, 2014.
7. Glenn Greenwald, "The Leaked Campaign to Attack Wikileaks and Its Supporters," salon.com, Feb. 11, 2011.
8. Nelson D. Schwartz, "Facing Threat from WikiLeaks, Bank Plays Defense," nytimes.com, Jan. 2, 2011.
9. See Eric Lipton and Charlie Savage, "Hackers Reveal Offers to Spy on Corporate Rivals," nytimes.com, Feb. 11, 2011.
10. Marcus Kabel, "Ark. Court Says Wal-Mart Can Copy Data of Fired Worker," utsandiego.com, April 13, 2007.
11. Gary Ruskin, "Spooky Business: Corporate Espionage Against Nonprofit Organization", Center for Corporate Policy, 23. Available at http://www.corporatepolicy.org/spookybusiness.pdf.
12. Ibid. Emphasis my own.
13. Peter Bright, Nate Anderson, and Jacqui Chang, *Unmasked* (Amazon Digital Services, 2011), 54
14. Nicole Perlroth and David E. Sanger, "Nations Buying as Hackers Sell Flaws in Computer Code," nytimes.com, July 13, 2013.
15. Ryan Gallagher, "Cyberwar's Gray Market," slate.com, Jan. 16, 2013.
16. Nate Anderson, "Black Ops: How Hbgary Wrote Backdoors for the Government," arctechnica.com, Feb. 21, 2011.
17. Ruskin, *Spooky Business*, 3.
18. Available at http://pastebin.com/raw.php?i=u4mtivNN, last accessed June 17, 2014.
19. Mike Masnick, "Play by Play of How HBGary Federal Tried to Expose Anonymous … And Got Hacked Instead," techdirt.com, Feb. 11, 2011.
20. Joseph Menn, "Cyberactivists Warned of Arrest," ft.com, Feb. 5, 2011.
21. Emails sent in the fall of 2010 discussed closing down HBGary Federal for not being profitable, and suggested that Aaraon Barr's "CEO job was under threat." (See page 28 in *Unmasked* for emails detailing the company's financial position.)
22. Peter Bright, "Anonymous Speaks: The Inside Story of the Albany Hack," arstechnica.com, Feb. 15, 2011.

23. Aphorism by Karl Wilhelm Friedrich Schlegel, nineteenth-century Romantic (and super oddball!).

24. Available at http://archive.today/lMuqh#selection-207.17-207.32, last accessed June 18, 2014.

25. John Cook and Adrian Chen, "Inside Anonymous' Secret War Room," gawker.com, March 18, 2011.

26. Dan Kaplan, "Anonymous Takes Over Security Firm in Vengeful Hack," scmagazine.com, Feb. 7, 2011.

27. "Hacker of Sacramento Company HBGary Pleads Guilty," FBI press release, March 6, 2012, last accessed June 18, 2014, available at http://www.fbi.gov/sacramento/press-releases/2012/hacker-of-sacramento-company-hbgary-pleads-guilty.

28. Parmy Olson, "Victim of Anonymous Attack Speaks Out," forbes.com, Feb. 7, 2011.

29. According to the plan, Palantir would provide its expensive link analysis software running on a hosted server, while Berico would "prime the contract supplying the project management, development resources, and process/methodology development." HBGary Federal would come alongside to provide "digital intelligence collection" and "social media exploitation." Nate Anderson, "Spy Games: Inside the Convoluted Plot to Bring Down WikiLeaks," arstechnica.com, Feb. 14, 2011.

30. Parmy Olson, "Congressman Probing HBGary Scandal Fears 'Domestic Surveillance,'" forbes.com, March 23, 2011.

31. Barrett Brown, "The Cyber-Intelligence Complex and Its Useful Idiots," theguardian.com, July 1, 2013.

32. Tim Shorrock, "US Intelligence & Oursourcing," last accessed June 17, 2014, available at http://timshorrock.com/?page_id=141.

33. Tim Shorrock, "Put the Spies Back Under One Roof," nytimes.com, June 17, 2013.

8. LulzSec

1. Steve Ragan of the *Tech Herald* also communicated with LulzSec members while reporting on a technical accounting of the hacks.

2. 2600, Twitter post, July 22, 2013, 10:22 am, http://twitter.com/2600/status/76931363755925504.

3. "A Little FAQ About Me vs. Anonymous," Asherah Research Group, May 24, 2012, last accessed June 24, 2014, available at http://www.backtrace-security.com/blog/844473-a-little-faq-about-me-vs-anonymous.

4. "Anonymous Message to Sony about Taking Down Playstation Network," YouTube video, posted by Johnny John, April 22, 2011, last accessed June 24, 2014, available at http://www.youtube.com/watch?v=aTbLA_1nkgU.

5. "The Light It Up Contest—Geohot," YouTube video, posted by geohot, Feb. 12, 2011, last accessed July 7, 2014, available at http://www.youtube.com/watch?v=9iUvuaChDEg.

6. Cory Doctorow, "Embattled PS3 Hacker Raises Big Bank to Fight Sony," boingboing.net, Feb. 22, 2011.

7. Quoted in Jason Mick, "Anonymous Engages in Sony DDoS Attacks over GeoHot PS3 Lawsuit," dailytech.com, April 4, 2011.

8. Patrick Seybold, "Update on PlayStation Network and Qriocity," PlayStation.com, Apr. 26, 2011, last accessed, July 11, 2014.

9. Colin Milburn, "Long Live Play: The PlayStation Network and Technogenic Life," in *Attractive Objects: The Furniture of the Technoscientific World*, edited by Bernadette Bensaude-Vincent, Sacha Loeve, Alfred Nordmann, and Astrid Schwartz (Pittsburgh: PA, University of Pittsburgh Press, forthcoming).

10. Owen Good, "Welcome Back PSN: The Winners," kotaku.com, May 21, 2011.

11. Paul Tassi, "Sony Pegs PSN Attack Costs at $170 Million, $3.1B Total Loss for 2011," forbes.com, May 23, 2011.

12. "Sony Fined £250,000 After Millions of UK Gamers' Details Compromised," Information Commissioner's Office, Jan. 24, 2013, last accessed June 24, 2014, available at http://www.ico.org.uk/news/latest_news/2013/ico-news-release-2013.

13. "Outro," *HTP Zine 5* (2013), last accessed June 24, 2014, available at http://www.exploit-db.com/papers/25306.

14. LulzSec, Twitter post, May 10, 2011, 7:52 am, http://twitter.com/LulzSec/status/68116303004708864.

15. Picture taken by Alexander Sotirov. Republished with permission.

16. For an excellent account covering the many threats plaguing Internet security, see Ron Deibert, *Black Code: Surveillance, Privacy, and the Dark Side of the Internet* (Toronto: Signal, 2013).

17. "Hackers Testifying at the United States Senate, May 19, 1998 (L0pht Heavy Industries)," YouTube video, posted by Joe Grand, March 14, 2011, last accessed June 24, 2014, available at http://www.youtube.com/watch?v=VVJldn_MmMY.

18. In fact, in 2013, one security report estimated that there was a 30 percent increase in the total number of infiltrations compared to 2012. These numbers are not bulletproof, but they do give a sense of the depth and extent of infiltrations for a given year. See "ITRC 2013 Breach List Tops 600 in 2013," Identity Theft Resource Center, Feb. 20, 2014, last accessed June 24, 2014, available at http://www.idtheftcenter.org/ITRC-Surveys-Studies/2013-data-breaches.html.

19. Patrick Gray, "Why We Secretly Love LulzSec," Risky Business, June 8, 2011, last accessed June 24, 2014, available at http://risky.biz/lulzsec.

20. Michael Taussig, *Defacement: Public Secrecy and the Labor of the Negative* (Stanford: Stanford University Press, 1999), 5.

21. See the TTI/Vanguard homepage at http://www.ttivanguard.com. Last accessed June 24, 2014.
22. Dick Hebdige, *Subculture: The Meaning of Style* (London: Routledge, 1979).
23. A major Hollywood producer has recently purchased the film rights to a *Rolling Stone* story covering Operation Steubenville, an Anonymous operation concerning a rape case in Ohio. Until the movie is released, it is impossible to say whether the film will distort and tame Anonymous' countercultural message.
24. For a detailed discussion about the role aesthetics and hyperbole play in Nietzsche's thought and writing, see Alexander Nehamas, *Nietzsche: Life as Literature* (Cambridge, MA: Harvard University Press, 1987).
25. Friedrich Nietzsche, "Thus Spoke Zarathustra" (1891), available at http://philosophy.eserver.org/nietzsche-zarathustra.txt (last accessed July 7, 2014).
26. Walter Benjamin, *Selected Writings, Volume 1: 1913–1926*, eds. Marcus Bullock and Michael W. Jennings (Cambridge, MA: Harvard University Press, 1996), 239.

9. AntiSec

1. Chris Hedges, "The Revolutionaries in Our Midst," truthdig.com, Nov. 10, 2013.
2. Sterling, *The Hacker Crackdown*.
3. Ibid. The list of philes is a partial rendition of a longer one in Sterling's account.
4. hacktivists of the world, unite, "Philippine Hackers Target National Police, Demanding the Release of the Sagada 11!," Indybay, March 22, 2006, last accessed June 25, 2014, available at http://www.indybay.org/newsitems/2006/03/22/18099531.php. See also "Electronic Civil Disobedience Journal," *Hack This* Site, 2007, last accessed July 9, 2014, available at http://mirror.hackthissite.org/hackthiszine/hackthis zine5.txt
5. Stuart Luman, "The Hacktivist," chicagomag.com, June 25, 2007.
6. "Operation Anti-Security," June 19, 2011, last accessed June 25, 2014, available at http://pastebin.com/9KyA0E5v.
7. "Anti-Security: Save a Bug, Save a Life," last accessed June 25, 2014, available at http://web.archive.org/web/20010301215117/http://anti.security.is.
8. The Lulz Boat, Twitter post, June 4, 2011, 5:34 am, http://twitter.com/LulzSec/status/76960035145650177.
9. Stephen Chapman, "Operation Anti-Security: LulzSec and Anonymous Target Banks and Governments," zdnet.com, June 20, 2011.

10. "Chinga La Migra Bulletin #1," June 6 23, 2011, last accessed July 9, 2104, available at http://thepiratebay.se/torrent/6490796/Chinga_La_Migra.
11. "50 Days of Lulz," June 25, 2011, last accessed June 25, 2014, available at http://pastebin.com/1znEGmHa.
12. Samantha Murphy, "Exclusive First Interview with Key LulzSec Hacker," *New Scientist*, no. 2820 (July 9, 2011). Available at http://www.newscientist.com/article/dn20649-exclusive-first-interview-with-key-lulzsec-hacker.html#.U6bPdB_7Gi0. (Last accessed June 26, 2014.)
13. Aldous Huxley, *Complete Essays*, (Chicago: Dee, 2000 [1934]), 526.
14. Topiary, Twitter post, July 21, 2011, 9:02 pm, https://twitter.com/atopiary/status/94225773896015872.
15. Mark Schone et al., "Exclusive: Snowden Docs Show UK Spies Attacked Anonymous, Hackers," nbcnews.com, Feb. 4, 2014.
16. Chris Weatherhead, Twitter post, Feb. 5, 2014, 8:39 am, http://twitter.com/CJFWeatherhead/status/431059633071878144.
17. Transcript, *CNN Newsroom*, Aug. 15, 2011, last accessed June 25, 2014, available at http://quiz.cnn.com/TRANSCRIPTS/1108/15/cnr.08.html.
18. See Paolo Gerbaudo, *Tweets and the Streets: Social Media and Contemporary Activism* (London: Pluto Press, 2012).
19. Available at http://bartlulz.weebly.com. (Last accessed June 25, 2014.)
20. "Disguised Member of Hacktivist Group 'Anonymous' Defends Retaliatory Action Against BART," democracynow.org, Aug. 16, 2011.
21. "Untitled," Aug. 19, 2011, last accessed June 25, 2014, available at http://pastebin.com/zug52JVA.
22. "Anonymous Is Not Unanimous," Aug. 17, 2011, last accessed June 25, 2014, available at http://pastebin.com/4vprKdXH.
23. See Chantal Mouffe, "Deliberative Democracy or Agonistic Pluralism?" *Social Research*, vol. 66, no. 3 (Fall 1999): 745–58.
24. *Brick Squad*, vol. 1, last accessed June 25, 2014, available at http://download.adamas.ai/dlbase/ezines/Br1ck_Squ4d/br1ck_squ4d_vol.1.txt.

10. The Desire of a Secret Is to Be Told

1. The Real Sabu, Twitter post, Aug. 17, 2011, 4:43 am, http://twitter.com/anonymouSabu/status/103763961064865792.
2. The Real Sabu, Twitter post, Sep. 17, 2011, 1:43 pm, http://twitter.com/anonymousabu/status/115133670213435393.
3. The Real Sabu, Twitter post, Sep. 17, 2011, 1:52 pm, http://twitter.com/anonymousabu/status/115136117925347328.
4. "USA v. Hector 'Sabu' Monsegur Transcript August 15, 2011," last

accessed June 27, 2014, available at http://cryptome.org/2013/02/usa-v-monsegur-11-0815.htm.

5. Available at http://pastie.org/private/om3mrqvbdbmg8esddkcmw# 2-3,347,353,365,376. (Last accessed June 27, 2014.)

6. Nathan Schneider, *Thank You, Anarchy: Notes from the Occupy Apocalypse* (Berkeley: University of California Press, 2013), 28.

7. Drew Grant, "Hacker Hero 'Weev' Stops by Occupy Wall Street [Video]," observer.com, Oct. 21, 2011.

8. Graham Jones, *Tricks of the Trade: Inside the Magician's Craft* (Berkeley: University of California Press, 2011), 94.

9. Jeanne Mansfield, "Why I Was Maced at the Wall Street Protests," Sept. 26, 2011, last accessed June 27, 2014, available at http://pastebin.com/Wkckd9bR.

10. "BadCop d0x," Sept. 26, 2011, last accessed June 27, 2014, available at http://pastebin.com/nC4f5uca.

11. "Anthony Bologna, Pepper Spray NYPD Officer, Transferred to Work in Staten Island," huffingtonpost.com, Oct. 26, 2011.

12. Karen McVeigh, "Occupy Wall Street: 'Pepper-Spray' Officer Named in Bush Protest Claim," theguardian.com, Sept. 27, 2011.

13. "DoITT – Frequently Asked Questions – Public Pay Telephones," NYC.gov, last accessed June 27, 2014, available at http://www.nyc.gov/html/doitt/html/faq/payphone.shtml.

14. "Sabu / LulzSec leader," June 7, 2011, last accessed June 27, 2014, available at http://pastebin.com/TVnGwSmG. Some of the details of this event also came from Steve Fishman's fascinating profile of Sabu, "'Hello, I Am Sabu…,'" nymag.com, June 3, 2012.

15. For thoughtful critiques of gender dynamics in geek communities, see geekfeminism.org.

16. The role of weirdness is thoughtfully explored by hacker Meredith Patterson in her essay "When Nerds Collide," medium.com, March 23, 2014.

17. Quinn Norton, "How Antisec Died," medium.com, Nov. 21, 2013.

18. Schneider, *Thank You, Anarchy*, 76.

19. "FBI Documents Reveal Secret Nationwide Occupy Monitoring," Partnership for Civil Justice Fund, Dec. 22, 2012, last accessed June 27, 2014, available at http://www.justiceonline.org/commentary/fbi-files-ows.html.

20. Colin Moynihan, "Officials Cast Wide Net in Monitoring Occupy Protests," nytimes.com, May 23, 2014.

21. David Hume, *A Treatise of Human Nature*, eds. David Fate Norton and Mary J. Norton (Oxford: Oxford University Press, 2000), 204.

11. The Sabutage

1. http://ulrikbrask.dk/operation-m4yh3m, last accessed July 5, 2014.
2. Ibid.
3. The Real Sabu, Twitter post, Dec. 24, 2011, 2:49 pm, http://twitter.com/anonymouSabu/status/150664330763964416.
4. The Invisible Committee, *The Coming Insurrection* (2007), last accessed July 9, 2014, available at http://tarnac9.wordpress.com/texts/the-coming-insurrection/.
5. "Operation m4yh3m," last accessed July 9, 2104, available at http://ulrikbrask.dk/operation-m4yh3m.
6. Ibid., Dec. 25, 2011, 3:54 pm, http://twitter.com/anonymouSabu/status/151043065501593601.
7. Ibid., Dec. 25, 2011, 4:57 pm, http://twitter.com/anonymouSabu/status/151059108353683456.
8. "Press Release: Stratfor Hack NOT Anonymous," Dec. 25, 2011, last accessed June 30, 2014, available at http://pastebin.com/8yrwyNkt.
9. Kevin Poulsen, "WikiLeaks Volunteer Was a Paid Informant for the FBI," wired.com, June 27, 2013.
10. For a full list of participating sites see sopastrike.com.
11. Chenda Ngak, "SOPA and PIPA Internet Blackout Aftermath, Staggering Numbers," cbsnews.com, Dec. 19, 2012.
12. Victoria Espinel, Aneesh Chopra, and Howard Schmidt, "Combating Online Piracy While Protecting an Open and Innovative Internet," We the People: Your Voice in Our Government, last accessed July 1, 2014, available at http://petitions.whitehouse.gov/response/combating-online-piracy-while-protecting-open-and-innovative-internet.
13. Greg Sandoval, "New Zealand PM Apologizes to Kim Dotcom; Case Unraveling," cnet.com, Sept. 27, 2012.
14. Max Fisher, "Stratfor Is a Joke and So Is Wikileaks for Taking It Seriously," theatlantic.com, Feb. 27, 2012.
15. "Re: Wiki Hackers Talk to *The Economist*," Global Intelligence Files, March 28, 2013, last accessed July 1, 2014, available at http://wikileaks.org/gifiles/docs/10/1075390_re-wiki-hackers-talk-to-the-economist-.html.
16. Steve Horn, "How to Win the Media War Against Grassroots Activists: Stratfor's Strategies," mintpressnews.com, July 29, 2013.
17. Email communication with the author.
18. Gary Ruskin, *Spooky Business: Corporate Espionage Against Nonprofit Organizations*, Center for Corporate Policy, 34. Available at http://www.corporatepolicy.org/spookybusiness.pdf.
19. "Stratfor Statement on Wikileaks," digitaljournal.com, Feb. 27, 2012.
20. The Real Sabu, Twitter post, Feb. 3, 2012, 10:22 pm, http://twitter.com/anonymouSabu/status/165636278770077697.

21. Jana Winter, "EXCLUSIVE: Inside LulzSec, a Mastermind Turns on His Minions," foxnews.com, March 6, 2012.
22. The Real Sabu, Twitter post, Aug. 16, 2011, 8:22 am, http://twitter.com/anonymousabu/status/103456479964700672.
23. Nigel Parry, "Sacrificing Stratfor: How the FBI Waited Three Weeks to Close the Stable Door," NigelParry.com, March 25, 2012, last accessed July 2, 2014, available at http://www.nigelparry.com/news/sacrificing-stratfor.shtml.
24. Jana Winter, "EXCLUSIVE: Inside LulzSec, a Mastermind Turns on His Minions."
25. George Friedman, "The Hack on Stratfor," Stratfor.com, Jan. 11, 2012, last accessed July 1, 2014, available at http://www.stratfor.com/weekly/hack-stratfor.
26. Nicole Perlroth, "Inside the Stratfor Attack," nytimes.com, March 12, 2012.
27. Dell Cameron, "How an FBI Informant Orchestrated the Stratfor Hack," dailydot.com, June 5, 2014.
28. "Sentenced to 10 Years in Prison, Jeremy Hammond Uses Allocution to Give Consequential Statement Highlighting Global Criminal Exploits by FBI Handlers," sparrowmedia.net, Nov. 15, 2013.
29. Mark Mazzetti, "F.B.I. Informant Is Tied to Cyberattacks Abroad," nytimes, April 23, 2014.
30. Daniel Stuckey and Andrew Blake, "Exclusive: How FBI Informant Sabu Helped Anonymous Hack Brazil," motherboard.vice.com, June 5, 2014.
31. Alexandra Natapoff, *Snitching: Criminal Informants and the Erosion of American Justice* (New York: NYU Press, 2011), 44.
32. Lee Romney, "Pressured to Name Names," latimes.com, Aug. 7, 2006.
33. Adam Goldman, "Lawsuit Alleges FBI Is Using No-Fly List to Force Muslims to Become Informants," washingtonpost.com, April 22, 2014.
34. "Notes on Sabu Arrest," Errata Security, March 6, 2013, last accessed July 1, 2014, available at http://blog.erratasec.com/2012/03/notes-on-sabu-arrest.html#.U64Kjx_7Gb8.
35. Parmy Olson, *We Are Anonymous: Inside the Hacker World of LulzSec, Anonymous, and the Global Cyber Insurgency* (New York: Back Bay Books, 2013), 400.
36. John Leyden, "Sabu Wasn't the Only FBI Mole in LulzSec, Suggest Leaked Docs," theregister.co.uk, Jan. 10, 2014.
37. Ruth Rosen, *The World Split Open: How the Modern Women's Movement Changed America*, Revised Edition (New York: Penguin, 2006), 281.
38. Brian Todd and Kevin Bohn, "Computers of Obama, McCain Campaigns Hacked," cnn.com, Nov. 6, 2008.
39. Online interview with the author.

40. "Quebec Human Rights Commission Slams Bill 78," cbc.ca, July 19, 2012, last accessed July 2, 2014, available at cbc.ca, July 19, 2012.
41. AnonOpsIndia, Twitter post, May 17, 2012, 6:08 am, http://twitter.com/opindia_revenge/status/203079500983050240.
42. "Official Statement from Family and Partner of Aaron Swartz," RememberAaronSw.com, Jan. 12, 2013, last accessed July 2, 2014, available at rememberaaronsw.com/memories.
43. "Anonymous Operation Last Resort," YouTube video, posted by Aarons ArkAngel, Jan. 26, 2013, last accessed July 7, 2014, available at http://www.youtube.com/watch?v=WaPni5O2YyI&feature=youtu.be.
44. Jason Howerton, "Disturbing Video Leaked of Ohio High School Students Joking About Alleged Gang Rape," theblaze.com, Jan. 2, 2013.
45. David Kushner, "Anonymous vs. Steubenville," rollingstone.com, Nov. 27, 2013.
46. Trip Gabriel, "Inquiry in Cover-Up of Ohio Rape Yields Indictment of Four Adults," nytimes.com, Nov. 25, 2013.
47. "#OpJustice4Rehtaeh," YouTube video, posted by Anonymous Canada, last accessed July 9, 2014, available at http://www.youtube.com/watch?v=7_D_zvizzKA.
48. Cited in Emily Bazelon, "Non-Consensual Sexting Leads to Child Pornography Charges for Two Men in Rehtaeh Parsons Case," salon.com, Aug. 8, 2013.
49. Ibid.
50. Peggy Lowe and Monica Sandreczki, "Why Was the Maryville Rape Case Dropped?" kcur.org, July 11, 2013.
51. Ariel Levy, "Trial by Twitter," newyorker.com, Aug. 5, 2013.
52. "Is Maryville the Next Steubenville?" Huffington Post Live, Oct. 16, 2013, last accessed July 1, 2014, available at http://live.huffingtonpost.com/r/segment/is-maryville-the-next-steubenville/525d71012b8c2a4a3d0000d2.
53. Emily Bazelon, "The Online Avengers," nytimes.com, Jan. 15, 2014.
54. The discussion was prompted by Larisa Mann's published commentary on a similar topic. Mann, "What Can Feminism Learn from New Media?," *Communication and Critical/Cultural Studies* (Summer, 2014): 1–5.
55. Stephen Duncombe, *Dream: Re-imagining Progressive Politics in an Age of Fantasy* (New York: New Press, 2007).

Conclusion: Daybreak

1. Lauren Cornell, "Primary Documents" (interview with Laura Poitras), *Mouse Magazine*, Issue 40, last accessed July 7, 2014, available at http://www.moussemagazine.it/articolo.mm?id=1020.
2. Barton Gellman and Julie Tate, "In NSA-Intercepted Data, Those Not Targeted Far Outnumber the Foreigners Who Are," washingtonpost.com, July 5, 2014.
3. James Risen and Laura Poitras, "N.S.A. Report Outlined Goals for More Power," nytimes.com, Nov. 22, 2013.
4. Samuel Warren and Louis Brandeis, "The Right to Privacy," *Harvard Law Review*, vol. IV, no. 5 (Dec. 15, 1890). Last accessed July 2, 2014, available at http://groups.csail.mit.edu/mac/classes/6.805/articles/privacy/Privacy_brand_warr2.html.
5. https://help.riseup.net/en/about-us/newsletter/2013/08.
6. Jennifer Granick, "My Dinner with NSA Director Keith Alexander," forbes.com, Aug. 22, 2013.
7. See especially Will Potter, *Green Is the New Red: An Insider's Account of a Social Movement Under Siege* (San Francisco: City Lights Publishers, 2011), and Arun Kundnani, *The Muslims Are Coming!: Islamophobia, Extremism, and the Domestic War on Terror* (New York: Verso, 2014).
8. Muslim American Civil Liberties Coalition, Creating Law Enforcement Accountability & Responsibility (CLEAR), and Asian American Legal Defense and Education Fund (AALDEF), *Mapping Muslims: NYPD Spying and Its Impact on American Muslims* (2013). Last accessed July 2, 2014, available at http://aaldef.org/press-releases/press-release/new-report-launched-nypd-spyings-impact-on-american-muslims.html.
9. Tim Cushing, "Former FBI Agent: NYPD's Muslim-Spying Demographics Unit Was Almost Completely Useless," techdirt.com, April 28, 2014.
10. *Mapping Muslims*, 55.
11. Glenn Greenwald and Murtaza Hussain, "Under Surveillance," theintercept.com, July 9, 2014.
12. "Factsheet: The NYPD Muslim Surveillance Program," ACLU, last accessed July 2, 2014, available at https://www.aclu.org/national-security/factsheet-nypd-muslim-surveillance-program.
13. Laurie Penny, "If You Live in a Surveillance State for Long Enough, You Create a Censor in Your Head," newstatesman.com, June 17, 2013.
14. Steve Lohr, "Unblinking Eyes Track Employees," nytimes.com, June 21, 2014.
15. Recently, two professors from Northwestern and Princeton examined

nearly two thousand policy changes in light of extensive data on lobbyists, the American elite, and the preferences of ordinary Americans. They concluded what many already suspected to be the case: "Economic elites and organized groups representing business interests have substantial independent impacts on US government policy, while mass-based interest groups and average citizens have little or no independent influence." Martin Gilens and Benjamin Page, "Testing Theories of American Politics: Elites, Interest Groups, and Average Citizens," *Perspective on Politics*, forthcoming.

16. Eben Moglen, "Freedom in the Cloud: Software Freedom, Privacy, and Security for Web 2.0 and Cloud Computing," speech given at meeting of the New York branch of the Internet Society, Feb. 5, 2010. Available at http://www.softwarefreedom.org/events/2010/isoc-ny/FreedomInTheCloud-transcript.html (last accessed July 2, 2014). Bruce Schneier, "The US Government Has Betrayed the Internet. We Need to Take it Back," theguardian.com, Sept. 5, 2013.

17. Christopher Soghoian, "Protecting Privacy Can Conflict with Free Business Models," Section 7.1 in *The Spies We Trust: Third Party Service Providers and Law Enforcement Surveillance*, PhD Dissertation, August 2012.

18. For two recent books on geek politics see Jessica L. Bayer, *Expect Us: Online Communities and Political Mobilization* (Oxford: Oxford University Press, 2014), and Patrick Burkhart, *Pirate Politics: The New Information Policy Contests* (Cambridge, MA: MIT Press, 2014).

19. Trevor Timm, "Congress Wants NSA Reform After All. Obama and the Senate Need to Pass It," theguardian.com, June 20, 2014.

20. Glenn Greenwald, *No Place to Hide: Edward Snowden, the NSA, and the U.S. Surveillance State* (New York: Metropolitan Books, 2014).

21. "Cyber Security in the Post-Snowden Era," panel at 2014 Ottawa Conference on Defence and Security. Video available at http://www.cpac.ca/en/programs/public-record/episodes/31366144 (last accessed July 2, 2014).

22. See the website of Reset the Net at resetthenet.org.

23. Quoted in Derek Mead, "'The Bottom Line Is That Encryption Does Work': Edward Snowden at SXSW," motherboard.vice.com, March 10, 2014.

24. "On the FBI Raid," March 7, 2012, last accessed July 8, 2014, http://pastebin.com/vZEteA3C.

25. "Why I'm Going to Destroy FBI Agent Robert Smith Part Three Revenge of the Lithe," YouTube video, posted by Grenalio Kristian Perdana Siahaan, Nov. 25, 2012, last accessed July 3, 2014, available at http://www.youtube.com/watch?v=VcMHdfvnEk4.

26. Adrian Chen, "Former Anonymous Spokesman Barrett Brown Indicted for Sharing a Link to Stolen Credit Card Data," gawker.com, Dec. 7, 2012.

27. Kevin M. Gallagher, "Barrett Brown, Political Prisoner of the Information Revolution," theguardian.com, July 13, 2013.

28. Douglas Thomas, *Hacker Culture* (Minneapolis, MN: University of Minnesota Press, 2003), 241.

29. Your Anonymous News, Twitter post, May 27, 2014, 10:53 am, https://twitter.com/YourAnonNews/status/471318266255011840

30. Jeremy Hammond, "Jeremy Hammond Reacts to Hector Monsegur's 'Sentencing': Rejects the NSA White Hat Sabu Ideology," posted June 2, 2014, last accessed July 9, 2014.

31. Danilyn Rutherford, "Kinky Empiricism," *Cultural Anthropology*, vol. 27, issue 3 (Aug. 2012): 465–79.

32. Anonymous, Twitter post, May 12, 2014, 11:52 am, http://twitter.com/blackplans/status/465897377468260352.

33. I would like to thank Scott Kushner for pointing out the subtle but important difference between unwillingness to acknowledge action as political versus delegitimization conducted precisely because the action is seen as politically potent.

34. Jane Bennett, *The Enchantment of Modern Life: Attachments, Crossings, and Ethics* (Princeton, NJ: Princeton University Press, 2001), 4.

35. Ernst Bloch, *The Principle of Hope*, Vol. 1, (Cambridge MA: MIT Press, 1995), 3.

36. Ibid., 5.

37. Whitney Phillips, *This Is Why We Can't Have Nice Things: Mapping the Relationship between Online Trolling and Mainstream Culture* (Cambridge, MA: MIT Press, forthcoming 2015).

38. David Foster Wallace, "E Unibus Pluram: Television and U.S. Fiction," *Review of Contemporary Fiction*, vol. 13, no. 2: 151–94.

39. "Waiting for the Tsunami - Bifo," YouTube video, posted by alterazionivideo alterazionivideo, August. 29, 2007, last accessed July 8, 2014, available at http://www.youtube.com/watch?v=5eojG4Hom3A#t=10.

40. Of course, due to the enormous plurality exhibited in contemporary industrial societies, it is naive and dangerous to boil something as complex as political sentiments to single "structures of feeling," to borrow Raymond Williams's useful phrase. It would be equally naive to entirely discard an analysis of dominant trends—whether economic or affective—such as the turn to cyncism. Raymond Williams, *Marxism and Literature* (Oxford: Oxford University Paperback, 1978).

41. Plan C/The Institute for Precarious Consciousness, "We Are All Very Anxious," last accessed July 9, 2014, available at http://www.weareplanc.org/we-are-all-very-anxious.

42. Bloch, *The Principle of Hope*, Vol. 1, 5.

43. Richard Sennet, *Together: The Rituals, Pleasures and Politics of Cooperation* (New Haven, CT: Yale University Press, 2012), 242.

Index

A

A-Team, 283

Abelson, Hal, 172

Abene, Mark (Phiber Optik), 86, 87

Ackroyd, Ryan (Kayla), 173, 174, 215, 265, 291, 353, 385, 392

ACS:Law, 99, 100–5

ACTA (Anti-Counterfeiting Trade Agreement), 89–92, 95, 96, 97, 98, 112, 348

Adbusters, 288

Adams, Henry, 118

Admin/Operator (AOP) list, 117

Adnon, 144, 145–8, 154, 165, 166, 170, 171, 173

Adobe, 261

afk (away from the keyboard), 146

Aiplex, 97, 98, 99, 101, 111

aircrack-ng, 277

Al-Bassam, Mustafa (tflow), 114, 171, 172, 173, 390

Al Jazeera, 153

Alexander, Keith, 6

"All About Barrett Brown. Add your comments guise," 229

Amamou, Slim, 144, 145, 166

Amazon, 119, 120, 127, 139

AmericanCensorship.org, 346

Americans for Prosperity, 277

The Amnesic Incognito Live System (Tails), 383

Anansi (trickster), 33

Anarchaos (Jeremy Hammond), 289, 298, 299, 362

see also Hammond, Jeremy

Anarchist Book, 279

Anderson, Chris, 270, 271

Anderson, Nate, 101, 211, 234

AnonLeaks, 228

#anonleaks channel, 231

#anonnews channel, 147

AnonOps, 3, 88, 89, 99, 101, 105–9, 111, 112, 116, 118, 120–3, 125, 126, 128, 133, 134, 139, 143, 147, 162, 166, 170, 181, 182, 201, 240, 243–7, 253, 283, 296

#AnonOps channel, 331

AnonOpsIndia, 367

AnonSnapple, 184–8, 190, 191, 192, 201, 232

anontunisia (anont), 167, 168–9

anonymity, 3, 38, 41, 44, 45, 65, 144, 151, 203, 206, 230, 331, 383, 388, 399

Anonymous:

as becoming harder to study, 302

best-known piece of art, 61

commitment of to difference,
    plurality, and dissension, 311
commitment of to politically
    engaged style of hacking, 72
complexity of, 49
as conduit for confrontational
    activism, 130
confusion about, 3
described, 1
as difficult to describe and
    resistant to being slotted, 115
as difficult to study/comprehend,
    393
diversity within, 174, 175
dynamism and multitudinous
    quality of, 393
as encompassing abundance of
    relationships, structures, and
    moral positions, 114
as ensuring mystery, 398
flexibility of, 17
on-the-fly decision making as
    staple of, 126
as having no established
    methodology through which
    to encode itself as institution,
    373
as having no universal mandate
    as collective, 131
heterogeneity of participants in,
    173, 174
as hydra, 48, 75
iconography of, 399
as jujitsu-like force of trickery,
    50
as leaving a lot to the
    imagination, 394
as living out maxim for life of
    enchantment, 274
meaning of official in, 92
membership in as self-defined,
    174
as multitudinous, 16
as no boss pointing to a fixed
    destination, 156

as not your personal army, 145,
    349
as not unanimous, 106, 311
as often reactive rather than
    proactive, 127
ontological question of just
    what makes one Anonymous,
    309
as open to chance, chaos,
    mutation, 118
opinions of hackers on, 256
organizational structure of,
    8–9
origins of, 4–9
as platform for citizens to
    express dissent, 315
as prolific, 16
relationship of with court of
    public opinion, 7
as serious political movement,
    392
as specter, 366
as symbol of dissent, 399
as unpredictable, 16, 17
Anonymous9, 177–8, 193–4, 337,
    361, 363
AnonyOps, 127–8, 365–6
anthropology, methods of, 392
#antiactaplanning, 90
anti-brand brand, 16
anti-celebrity ethic, 17, 47, 49
Anti-Counterfeiting Trade
    Agreement (ACTA), 89–92, 95,
    96, 97, 98, 112, 348
AntiSec (Anti-Security), 48, 236,
    275, 283, 286, 291, 292,
    312–15, 326, 337, 339, 362
#antisec channel, 292, 313, 340,
    341, 342, 349
anti-security movement, 285, 286
AOL, 237, 291
Appelbaum, Jacob, 84, 85, 333
Arab and African Spring, 17, 149,
    192, 269, 272, 292
argot, 31, 45

Arizona Department of Public Safety, 237, 283
Armstrong, Gerry, 77
ARPANET, 38
arrests, 9, 16, 38, 50, 71, 88, 91, 111, 134, 135, 140, 141, 145, 156, 169, 170, 173, 183, 190, 191, 193, 194, 197, 215, 237, 255, 278–9, 282, 287, 288, 289, 293, 301, 302, 303, 305, 320, 327, 334, 353, 355, 361, 366, 369–70, 384, 386, 388, 390, 391
Ars Technica, 210, 216, 234
Arthur, Charles, 156
ASCII art, 248
Assange, Julian, 82, 84, 85, 88, 106, 120, 126, 127, 194, 198, 199, 208, 326, 345–6, 382, 414n7
Associated Press (AP), 152
AT&T, 23–4, 26, 32, 36, 237, 248, 280, 291, 326
The Atlantic, 350
Auernheimer, Andrew (weev), 19–20
    see also weev
Avunit, 215, 243, 265

B
Backtrace Security, 240, 241, 242, 243
Bahrain, 143, 367
Bakhtin, Mikhail, 131
Bank of America, 193, 208
banning/banishment, 40, 188, 190, 192, 253
Bantown, 19
Barbiturate Formula, 279
Barlow, John Perry, 121
Barnett, Matthew, 371
Barr, Aaron, 212–17, 219–21, 224–6, 233, 235, 237, 240
Barr, Roseanne, 369
bartlulz website, 7, 306

BatCat (Noah McHugh), 369
Bazelon, Emily, 370, 372, 373
BBC, 96, 228, 244
Bethesda Softworks, 237
Ben Ali, 145, 147, 149–53, 166
Benjamin, Walter, 275
Bennett, Henry, 209
Bennett, Jane, 394
Berardi, Franco (Bifo), 397
Berico Technologies, 208, 234
best practices, 374
Bharatiya Janata Party, 367
black bloc organizing, 298
black hat attitude/hackers/scene, 237, 238, 239, 258, 285, 289, 308, 314, 315, 344
black ops, 324
Blackout Day, 346
Blake, Andrew, 359
Bloch, Ernst, 395–6, 398
bodybuilding.com, 44
Boing Boing, 135
Bologna, Anthony, 327–8
Boogie Nights (film), 21
Booz Allen Hamilton, 301
Borell, Emily, 362
Borell III, John Anthony (Kahuna), 305, 362, 386
Boston Police Patrolmen's Association, 337
botnets, 60, 92–5, 98, 102, 121, 125, 127, 133, 134, 135, 137, 139, 253, 254, 289
Bouazizi, Mohamed, 148, 151
BR1CKSQU4D, 314, 315
Brandeis, Louis, 379
Brazil, 143, 324, 359, 360
Brian Oblivion, 261
Briefcase Locks, 280
The Brief Wondrous Life of Oscar Wao (Diaz), 331
BrigadaElektronica, 281
Bright, Peter, 215
British Metropolitan Police, 169

BRoTHeRHooD oF WaReZ
(BoW) (hacker group), 37
Brown, Barrett, 182–4, 189, 218,
219–20, 221, 223, 225, 228,
229–32, 234, 235, 313–14, 338,
339, 345, 377, 386–8
/b/tard, 41, 45, 66
Buccaneers, 283
bulletin board system, 37, 194
#bump chat room, 96
Bunker, Mark, 54, 63
Brunton, Fred, 352

C
C&C (command-and-control)
channel, 93, 94
CabinCr3w, 283, 305, 306, 328,
338, 354, 363, 386
Cablegate, 119, 265
California Statewide Law
Enforcement Association, 300,
343
Cameron, Dell, 358
Canadian Security Intelligence
Service (CSIS), 10–16
Carnegie Mellon, 36
CBS News, 346
CDNs (Content Delivery
Networks), 139
Center for Corporate Policy, 209
CFAA (Computer Fraud and Abuse
Act), 24, 25, 140, 244, 261, 369
Chanology/Project Chanology, 2,
56, 57, 60, 66–74, 76, 81, 89,
90, 95, 106, 116, 154, 178, 181,
182, 241, 389
The Chaos Communication Camp,
304
Chaos Computer Club, 304
Chapman, Stephen, 288
Chen, Adrian, 155, 230, 387
Chilton Hacking, 279
"Chinga La Migra," 283, 284, 289,
290
choreographers, 75, 306

Christensen, Christian, 82
Christman, Tory, 78
Church of Scientology, 2, 5–6, 11,
53–66, 70, 73, 76, 77–9, 81,
241, 414n7
CIA, 169, 171, 295, 380
The Citizens' Commission to
Investigate the FBI, 203, 206,
211
civil disobedience, 107, 112, 129,
190
Cleary, Ryan, 253, 254, 255, 289
Clinton, Hillary, 119, 191
cloaking, 43, 134, 173, 206, 253
cslea.com (California Statewide
Law Enforcement Association),
343
CMS (content management
system), 215
CNET, 138
CNN, 121, 182, 304, 305, 306,
340
Code of Conduct (video), 64
*Coding Freedom: The Ethics
and Aesthetics of Hacking*
(Coleman), 257
CogAnon (Aaron Barr), 212, 217,
223, 225–7
COINTELPRO, 203, 205–9, 211,
236, 303, 380
Colbert, Stephen, 214
Coleman, Daisy, 371
"Collateral Murder" (video), 82–3,
84
collective identity, individual
identity subsumption of into,
46
collectivism, divide between
individualism and collectivism,
49–50
Communist Party USA, 203
The Coming Insurrection (Invisible
Committee), 343
#command channel, 102, 108, 109,
110, 116, 118, 121, 122, 123,

124, 126, 133, 134, 154, 165, 348

command-and-control (C&C) channel, 93, 94

Commander X (Christopher Doyon), 182, 307

Committee for Congressional Affairs, 260

Computer Fraud and Abuse Act (CFAA), 24, 25, 140, 244, 261, 369

Content Delivery Networks (CDNs), 139

Cook, John, 230

co-optation, 271, 272, 351, 393

copyright industry/lobby/trade associations, 98, 99, 101, 116, 347

Corley, Eric (Emmanuel Goldstein), 85, 86, 87, 195, 297, 298–9

corporate espionage/sabotage, 209, 210, 211

correct technology, 59

Coyote (trickster), 33

CPU, 68–9

crediblethreat (Jeremy Hammond), 364

Crossley, Andrew, 100, 101, 105

Cruise, Tom, 2, 53–4, 56, 61

CryptoParty, 390

cryto (server), 292

CSIS (Canadian Security Intelligence Service), 10–16

C-SPAN, 261

Cult of the Dead Cow (hacker group), 138, 240

cultural cohesiveness, 373

cyberwarfare, 6

c0s (Gregg Housh), 62, 182, 223, 225, 226, 231

D

Daily Dot, 391

darr, 73, 74, 174

data, slurping of, 24

David (from Chanology), 389

Davis, Jake (Topiary): *see* Topiary

DDoS (distributed denial of service): ethics, 129–32, 135–42, 198

history, 5, 90–3, 95–8, 105, 106, 107, 109, 110–12, 116, 118, 120, 121, 124–6, 128, 134, 153, 154, 158, 160, 192, 193, 198, 200, 243, 246, 253, 277, 289, 301, 303, 304, 310, 347–8, 367, 379

as illegal, 6, 63

LOIC, 101, 133

see also Low Orbit Ion Cannon (LOIC) methods, 2, 134, 312

#ddos channel, 92

DDoS protection, 100, 102, 103, 139, 310

de Certeau, Michel, 126

DEF CON, 195

DeGrippo, Sherrod, 30

Debian, 373

Deleuze, Gilles, 273

Democracy Now! 306

Department of Telecommunications (India), 367

Der Spiegel, 118

Deseriis, Marco, 39

DeWolf, Jamie, 77

Dianetics, 5, 58, 60

Díaz, Junot, 331

Digg, 67

digital civil disobedience, 107

digital direct action campaign, 120

digital protest tactics, 139–41

digital trespass, 256, 305

Dionysus (trickster), 33, 70, 274, 395

direct action blockade, 138

direct action political tactics, 88

direct government interference, 302–3

dirk diggler, 21–2

disruptive tactics/activism, 136, 137, 256

distributed denial of service (DDoS): *see* DDoS (distributed denial of service)

Doctorow, Cory, 245

do-ocracy, 75

Dotcom, Kim, 347

double standards in operation, 111

doxing, 7, 9, 14, 73, 235, 241, 242, 246, 254, 285, 300, 309, 310

Doyon, Christopher (Commander X), 182, 307

Dyson, Jay, 37

Drupal.org, 261

Dublin Chanology cell, 76

Dublin Offlines, 76–8

Duchin, Roland, 351

Duchin formula, 351

duckie, 162

Duncombe, Stephen, 374

E

Ebner, Mark, 54

ED (Encyclopedia Dramatica), 30, 32, 35

egalitarianism, ideal of, tactics for enforcing, 189

Egypt, 143, 191–2, 200, 305

Ekeland, Tor, 24, 25

El País, 118

Électricité de France, 209

Electronic Disturbance Theater (EDT), 135–6

Electronic Frontier Foundation (EFF), 89, 296, 347, 382

Electronic Terror, 280

elephant in the room, Internet security problems as, 262

Emick, Jennifer, 241, 242

enchantment, politics of 394

encryption, 73, 216, 222, 341, 384

Encyclopedia Dramatica (ED), 30, 32, 35

Enturbulation, 67

Epic Fail Guy, 64

epic wins, 44, 46, 66

epilepsy forum attack, 69

Eshu (trickster), 33, 63, 96, 241

ethical leaking vs. unethical leaking, 251

European prosecution of hackers, compared to US prosecution of hackers, 388

Evernote, 261

EveryDNS, 126

F

Facebook, 153, 213, 241, 287, 306, 343, 363, 377

fail0verflow, 244

Falcon (Jake Davis), 249–54

Falkvinge, Richard, 108

false flag operation, 310, 312

fame-seeking, 46, 47, 48, 313

Fawkes, Guy, 271, 281–2, 306

FBI, 9, 84, 88, 134, 135, 193, 195, 196–7, 199, 203–4, 206, 214, 220, 233, 237, 287, 288, 293, 297, 300, 301, 305, 312, 320, 327, 333, 335, 348, 353, 355, 356, 357, 358, 360, 361, 386

FD-302, 196, 420n8

federal prosecution, 172

femanon hackers, 174

fifth estate, 84

Fight for the Future, 383

file sharing, 96, 97, 98, 116, 125, 146, 148, 347, 348, 367

Financial Times, 213, 214, 215, 220

Fine Gael, 384, 385

fines, 171, 386

Firefly, 384, 385, 389, 391, 399

Fisher, Max, 350

Five Eyes countries, 377

Flickr, 153, 346

flooding, 3, 238

Food Not Bombs, 281

Forbes, 181, 233, 250
forbes.com, 238
Ford, Henry, 209
Formula One website, 366, 367
Foucault, Michel, 273
4chan, 32, 41–6, 47, 48, 49, 51,
    60, 64, 101, 197, 248
4chan's random bulletin board /b/,
    4, 41, 43, 49, 56
fourth estate, 84
Fox News, 1, 2, 65, 66, 237, 240,
    248, 254, 288, 353, 355, 356,
    357, 365, 386
fox.com, 247
fraudulent hope, 396
Fred, 92, 122, 123–4
Freddy, 323, 324
free flow of information, 3
Free Software Foundation, 89
free speech/freedom of speech, 16,
    40–1, 58, 71, 72, 108, 129, 131,
    132, 138, 148, 153, 163, 164,
    199, 200, 245, 305, 382
Freedom of Information Act, 83,
    205, 333
Freedom of the Press Foundation,
    384
#freedommods channel, 292
Friedman, George, 352, 357
Friedman, Jaclyn, 371
Frontline, 265
#FuckFBIFridays hashtag, 300,
    302
Fusion Centers, 333
Futaba Channel, 41
futurescanning, 270, 272

G
Gallagher, Kevin, 387
Gallagher, Ryan, 210
Gawker, 26, 54, 55, 230
Gay Nigger Association of America
    (GNAA), 20, 24, 26, 45
Gayniggers from Outer Space
    (film), 20

GCHQ (Government
    Communications Headquarters)
    (UK), 302–3, 304, 378, 379
Geek Distraction Disorder (GDD),
    156
Gemuese, Tod, 138
geohot (Hotz, George), 243–5
Gerbaudo, Paolo, 75, 306
ghost__ (Jeremy Hammond), 342
gibnut, 157–9, 161, 165
Gilens, Martin, 430–1n15
Giussani, Bruno, 270–1
Gizmodo, 134, 135
"The Global Intelligence Files,"
    349
Globe and Mail, 152
GNAA (Gay Nigger Association of
    America), 20, 24, 26, 45
GNU/Linux, 244, 255
Goatse Security, 23, 24, 25, 32,
    248, 250, 323
Gobo, 109, 110, 111
Goldstein, Emmanuel (Eric
    Corley), 85, 86, 87, 195, 297,
    298–9
Rave, 90–1, 95, 96, 98, 106, 111
Google, 168, 346, 347, 378
goon, 45
government, working for,
    Anonymous participants
    agreeing to, 319, 353
    see also informants
Government Communications
    Headquarters (GCHQ) (UK),
    302–3, 304, 378, 379
Graeber, David, 47
Graham, Robert, 361
Granick, Jennifer, 380
Grant, Oscar, III, 304, 323
gray hat hackers, 260
Gray, Patrick, 261–2
Greenpeace, 38, 209, 339
Greenwald, Glenn, 207, 208, 378,
    382
Greenway, Patricia, 54

Griffiths, Pete, 77, 389
Guardian, 25, 82, 118, 120, 156,
    328, 331
Guattari, Félix, 273
Guy Fawkes Day, 95
Guy Fawkes mask, 4, 44, 64, 65,
    67, 72–3, 75, 77, 271, 281, 282,
    304, 317, 318, 348, 369

H
h, 349
Habbo Hotel raids, 4–5, 45, 46
Hack the Planet (HTP) (hacker
    group), 253–4, 264
Hack This Site, 280
Hack This Zine, 280
hacker groups: BRoTHeRHooD
    oF WaReZ (BoW), 37
    Cult of the Dead Cow, 138,
    240
    Hack The Planet (HTP), 253–4,
    264
hacker handles, 261
hacker literary genres, 279
hacker underground: *see*
    underground hackers/hacker
    underground
hacker wars, 38, 254
hackers: arrogance of, 258–9
    black hat attitude/hackers/scene,
        see black hat attitude/hackers/
        scene elitism, 38, 162, 192,
        259
    free and open source software,
        174, 256, 258, 305
    gender, 174, 175, 331
    general, 59–60, 167, 192,
        256–7, 259, 263, 298, 320,
        330
    gray hat hackers, 260
    hired by copyright industry, 98
    history, 9, 23, 24, 25–6, 48, 50,
        72, 85, 106–7, 156, 158, 160,
        194, 254, 256
    left-leaning hackers, 280

    security hackers, 237, 256, 258,
        260, 323
    stereotype of, 166, 173, 175,
        289
    taking political matters into
        own hands, 106, 107
    uber-political hackers, 292
    white hat hackers, 37, 215, 280,
        285
Hackers Against Geeks in
    Snowsuits (Hagis), 37, 38
Hackers Digest, 279
Hackers on Planet Earth (HOPE),
    81, 84, 85, 88, 89, 195, 298
hackers on steroids, 2, 237, 365
HackForums.net, 291
hacking: Anonymous's
    commitment to politically
    engaged style of, 72
    artful hack, 167
    described, 60
    as described by hackers, 256–7
    jailbreaking as specialty, 243–4
Hacking Bank America, 279
hacktivism, 135, 156, 192, 194,
    233, 268, 278, 282, 288, 380,
    389
Haefer, Mercedes, 174, 194–9
Hammond, Jeremy, 156, 277–83,
    288–90, 292, 293, 334, 338–42,
    345, 346, 353, 356–9, 361–3,
    377, 385, 390–2
handle (nick), 116
hardened lulz-seekers, 68
Harrison, Sarah, 382
Hastings, Michael, 184
Hathaway, Melissa, 383
Haydn, Michael, 171
HBGary Federal/HBGary, 207,
    208, 210–16, 218, 220, 224,
    228, 230–7
Hebdige, Dick, 271
Hermes (trickster), 33
Heymann, Stephen, 172
Hill, Charles, 7, 304

Hispano-Anons, 143
hive, 55, 102, 110, 120, 134, 165, 220, 399
Hive Mind mode, 136
Hobsbawm, Eric, 71
Hoffman, Abbie, 280
Hoffman, Marcia, 24
Hoglund, Greg, 211, 212, 214, 222, 223, 224, 225, 228, 233
Hoover, J. Edgar, 203, 204, 380
HOPE (Hackers on Planet Earth), 81, 84, 85, 88, 89, 195, 298
hope, principle of, 395, 396
Horn, Steve, 351
Hotz, George (geohot), 243–5
Housh, Gregg (c0s), 62, 182, 223, 225, 226, 231
"How to Protest Intelligently," 199–201
HQ, 231
HTP (Hack the Planet), 253–4, 264
Hubbard, L. Ron, 77
Huffington Post Live, 371
Hume, David, 335
humor, 2, 31
   see also lulz
Hunton and Williams law firm, 208, 209, 214
Huxley, Aldous, 300
Hyde, Lewis, 34
hyrriiya, 337, 340, 341

I
IFM (Internet Freedom Movement), 89–90, 95
illegal tactics, 7, 13, 63, 88, 90, 92, 98, 108, 111, 209, 299, 310
image management, 182
imprisonment, 156, 171, 242, 278, 279, 282, 356, 359, 362, 377, 386, 388, 390, 391, 392
Indian National Congress, 367
Indian Supreme Court, 367
indictments, 353, 369, 387

individual identity, subsumption of into collective identity, 46
individualism: divide between individualism and collectivism, 49–50
possessive individualism, 47
informants, 8, 14, 199, 242, 290, 292, 296, 312, 335, 339, 346, 356, 358, 359–61, 363, 364, 380, 391
Information Commissioner's Office, 105, 247
Information Ministry, 145
InfoSec community, 256, 257, 258
"Inside Anonymous's Secret War Room," 230
institutional memory, 373
institutionalization, 17, 374
International Association of Chiefs of Police, 337
International Federation of the Phonographic Industry, 99
International Subversives, 85
Internet: as privatized zone, 127
as tracking machine, 377
Internet activism, double-edged sword of, 371
Internet demonstration, Anonymous as first large-scale effort, 130–1
Internet Freedom Movement (IFM), 89–90, 95
Internet Hate Machine, 1, 5, 46, 65, 67, 228, 392, 412n20
Internet Motherfuckery, 4
Internet Relay Chat (IRC):
   #anonleaks channel, 231
   #anonnews channel, 147
   #AnonOps channel, 331
   #antisec channel, 292, 313, 340, 341, 342, 349
   C&C (command-and-control) channel, 93, 94
   channel founder/channel operator, 116–17

#command channel, 102, 108, 109, 110, 116, 118, 121, 122, 123, 124, 126, 133, 134, 154, 165, 348
#ddos channel, 92
denotation of channels, 116
#freedommods channel, 292
as important communication application for Anonymous, 8, 17
#internetfeds channel, 109, 110, 148, 154, 157, 162, 166, 173, 247, 324
#kittencore channel, 114
#lounge channel, 130, 185, 191, 215, 331
#marblecake channel, 61, 62, 64, 72–6, 154, 182, 201
#opbart channel, 305, 306, 307, 309
#opdeface channel, 157, 162, 163
#OpEgypt channel, 191, 192
#operationpayback channel, 101, 109, 120, 126, 130, 131, 133
#ophbgary channel, 216, 217, 218, 228
#opnewblood channel, 373
#OpTunisia channel, 147–58
#press channel, 60, 73
private channels
see private channels (IRC)
#propaganda channel, 130, 165, 192
public channels
see public channels (IRC) #pure-elite channel, 156
#reporter channel, 169, 178, 181, 182, 184, 185, 193, 215, 264
#savetpd (Save the Pirate Bay) channel, 101
#savetpbmods channel, 102
#!sec channel, 340

secret cabals and channels
see secret cabals and channels #upperdeck channel, 114
#website channel, 72
Internet security: pathetic state of, 238, 256, 261
problems with as elephant in the room, 262
Internet tricksterdom, 35–46
Internet trolling: *see* trolling (of Internet)
#internetfeds channel, 109, 110, 148, 154, 157, 162, 166, 173, 247, 324
interrogations, 199–200
Invisible Committee, 343
iPad 3G Account Slurper, 24
iPhone, 243, 244
IRC (Internet Relay Chat): *see* Internet Relay Chat (IRC)
IRC bouncer, 320
IRC Federal (defense contractor), 301
IRCops, 117
Ireland, 66, 143, 353, 384, 385, 388
Italy, 143, 213

J
Jackal, 305
JacksonBrown (Spitler, Daniel), 24
jailbreaking (hacking specialty), 243–4, 245
Jameth, 19, 30, 31
joepie, 147
Johnson, Hank, 234
Johnson, Linton, 7, 304, 306
Joint Terrorism Task Force, 333
Joint Threat Research Intelligence Group, 303
Jones, Graham, 324
Jónsdóttir, Birgitta, 382
JSTOR, 171, 172
Juicy Fruit, 210

K

Kahuna (John Anthony Borell):
   see Borell, John Anthony
   (Kahuna)
Kansas City Public Media, 371
Kayla (Ackroyd, Ryan), 173, 174,
   215, 265, 291, 353, 385, 392
Keeping Scientology Working, 59
Keller, Art, 113
Kelty, Chris, 48
Kent, Stephen, 58
kernel, 161
Kerr, Orin, 24
Key, John, 347
King, Martin Luther, Jr., 204
Kingpin, 261
#kittencore channel, 114
`k, 222, 224, 231, 232
Knappenberger, Brian, 181, 331,
   332, 344
Knappenberger and Olson, 332
Knuttila, Lee, 43
Koch brothers, 277
Koch Industries website, 140
K-rad, 155, 157–62, 164, 166
Kretsinger, Cody (Recursion), 327
Ku Klux Klan, 127
!Kung, 189–90
Kushner, David, 369
KYAnonymous (Deric Lostutter),
   368, 369, 372

L

L0pht Heavy Industries, 260–2
La Quadrature du Net, 89
Lamaline_5mg, 307–8, 309, 310,
   311
Lamo, Adrian, 83–4, 85, 86–7,
   298, 414n4
Lapsley, Phil, 36
lark, 125
Laurelai, 218, 241
law-abiding tactics, 108
   see also legal tactics
Le Monde, 118

leaderfagging/leaderfags, 62, 110,
   230
leadership: Anonymous as
   leaderless, 109, 113, 156, 165,
   398
   choreographers, 75, 306
   Internet search for Anonymous
      leader, 155–6
   leaderfagging/leaderfags, 62,
      110, 230
   soft leadership, 76
LEAP (LEAP Encryption Access
   Project), 384
Leavy, Penny, 214, 218, 219, 221,
   222
legal tactics, 7, 13, 63
   see also law-abiding tactics
legally gray tactics, 7
legislative change, 382
legitimacy vs. legality, 111–12
Levy, Ariel, 371, 374
Levy, Steven, 36
Liberty Square, 318, 333
Libya, 143
Lieberman, Joe, 120, 126
LiveJournal, 30, 67
Living Social, 261
Lohr, Steve, 381
LOIC: *see* Low Orbit Ion Cannon
   (LOIC)
#loic hive, 110
Loki (trickster), 16, 34, 37, 396
Lola, 92, 95
Lolcats, 44, 155
Lolcats memes, 41
Lostutter, Deric (KYAnonymous),
   368, 369, 372
Louise, 239
#lounge channel, 130, 185, 191,
   215, 331
Low, Peggy, 371
Low Orbit Ion Cannon (LOIC),
   101, 120, 130, 131, 133, 134,
   135, 136, 137, 158, 198
Lucas, Lord, 101

lulz, 2, 4, 7, 8, 9, 11, 16, 19, 25,
    30, 31–3, 46, 67, 70, 71, 181,
    201, 203–36
lulz-driven action vs. moral goals,
    66
LulzLeaks, 250, 251
LulzSec, 48, 114, 156, 173, 174,
    181, 236, 237–40, 247–50,
    252–6, 259, 261, 263, 264–72,
    274, 275, 283, 284, 291, 362
LulzXmas, 337, 343, 344
Lyon, Amber, 182

M
Macpherson, C. B., 47
Malakanyang Palace, 281
Mann, Larissa, 374
Manning, Chelsea, 82, 83–4, 88,
    106, 148, 223, 265, 282, 298,
    326, 339, 382
ManTech International, 233, 293,
    301
*Mapping Muslims: NYPD Spying
    and Its Impact on American
    Muslims*, 380
#marblecake channel, 61, 62, 64,
    72–6, 154, 182, 201
Martyn, Darren (pwnsauce),
    248–9, 250–1, 264, 290, 353,
    384–5
Maryville, Missouri case, 371, 375
MasterCard, 3, 119, 126, 127, 141,
    185, 193, 198
Mays, Benjamin Elijah, 113
Mazzetti, Mark, 359
MBD (Mongoven, Biscoe &
    Duchin), 351
McGill University, 40
McHugh, Noah (JustBatCat), 369
McKee, Michelle, 368–9
McKinnon, Gary, 194
media: Anonymous as duping of,
    99
    attention for Operation BART,
    306

author as media mouthpiece for
    Anonymous, 181
as compelled to cover
    Anonymous, 50
consensus never to attack, 200
coverage of AntiSec press
    release, 288
as driven batty by Anonymous,
    50
as not getting enough of LulzSec
    antics, 238
role in making Anonymous
    what it is, 14, 16, 46, 49
validation from as solidifying
    Anonymous, 106
*see also specific media outlets
    and publications*
MegaUpload, 347
Mele, Nicco, 121
Menn, Joseph, 158, 213
Middle East, 201, 334
Milburn, Colin, 246
Milhon, Jude (St. Jude), 167
militant tactics, 9
#MilitaryMeltdownModay, 300,
    302
Ministry of Communications and
    Information Technology, 367
Mirza, David, 237, 258
MIT, 36, 171, 172, 367
Mitnick, Kevin, 38, 86, 194, 389
Moglen, Eben, 381
Moher, Patty, 54
Mongoven, Biscoe and Duchin
    (MBD), 351
Monsegur, Hector Xavier (Sabu):
    see Sabu (Hector Xavier
    Monsegur)
Moore, Alan, 281
moral goals vs. lulz-driven action,
    66
moral leveling, 190
moralfaggotry/moralfags, 62, 67,
    68, 69, 147, 201, 240, 309
More Pranks to Pull on Idiots! 280

Motherboard, 391
motherfuckery.org, 70
Motion Picture Association of
America (MPAA), 96, 97, 99,
100, 102, 103, 138, 348
Mouffe, Chantal, 311, 396
mpaa.org, 139
Mubarak, Hosani, 191, 305
#muBARTec hashtag, 305
Mudge, 261
multiple use name, 39
Murphy, Samantha, 294
Muslims, 380–1
myBART.org, 306
Myspace, 67
m0rpeth, 377

N
namefagging/namefags, 46, 185,
189
Namshub, 241, 242, 243
Natapoff, Alexandra, 360
National Lawyers Guild, 194
NATO, 291, 301
Naval Criminal Investigative
Service, 333
Nawaat/Nawaat.org 148—149,
151
NBC, 54, 205
Neiman Marcus, 261
nerd scare, 194–9
New York State Association of
Chiefs of Police (nychiefs.org),
343
New York Times, 82, 84, 118, 121,
152, 208, 210, 228, 334, 358,
359, 369, 372, 379
New York Times Magazine, 372
New Yorker, 371
newfags, 42, 68
#newor chat room, 96
News International, 169, 385
Newsweek, 113
Nezvanova, Netochka, 39–40, 46
NIC, 158–9, 320–1

nick, 116, 362
Nietzsche, Friedrich, 272–4, 275,
377
Nieves, Mike: *see* Virus
Ninjasec, 251
n00bs, 42
Northrop Grumman, 210, 224,
270
Norton, Quinn, 147, 181, 331,
337, 393
NSA: *see* US National Security
Agency (NSA)
Nyan Cat, 239
nychiefs.org (New York State
Association of Chiefs of Police),
343
NYPD, 71, 326, 328
NYSEC, 257, 259, 323, 356

O
Obama, Barack, 365
Obama Administration, 119
OccultusTerra (IRC server), 90
Occupy movement, 2, 49, 50, 181,
318, 321, 322, 323, 327–9, 331,
333–4, 351–2, 366
O'Cearbhaill, Donncha
(Palladium), 280, 353, 356, 363,
384–5, 388, 389, 390, 392
Ochoa III, Higinio O. (w0rmer),
305
Off the Hook (radio show), 297
Office of the President of the
Philippines, 281
Office of the US Trade
Representative (USTR), 90, 96
offline protesting tactics,
punishment for as compared
to punishment for digital
protesting tactics, 140
OKCupid, 261
oldfags, 73
Olson, Parmy, 121, 181, 233, 238,
250, 264, 324, 332, 335, 363
O'Neill, Gráinne, 194

#opbart channel, 305, 306, 307, 309
#opdeface channel, 157, 162, 163
#OpEgypt channel, 191, 192
Open Technology Institute, 383
Open Whisper Systems, 383–4
Operation Anti-Security (#AntiSec), 284, 289, 293
Operation Avenge Assange, 3, 121, 135, 137, 138, 141, 143, 147, 154, 303, 306
Operation BART (OpBART), 7–8, 304, 305–10, 312, 321
Operation Leakspin, 143
Operation Payback (o:p), 96, 99, 100, 108, 110, 112, 121, 122, 125, 128, 135, 146, 154, 193, 303
Operation Psychout, 73
Operation Slickpubes (OpSlickPubes), 70, 71
Operation Sony (OpSony), 243–7, 248
Operation Steubenville, 424n23
Operation Sundevil, 194
Operation Thunder, 303
Operation Titstorm, 89
Operation Tunisia (OpTunisia), 143–8, 154, 157, 165, 166, 177, 182, 192, 418n13
operations security (OpSec), 255, 362
#operationpayback channel, 101, 109, 120, 126, 130, 131, 133
#ophbgary channel, 216, 217, 218, 228
OpJustice4Rehtaeh, 370
OpLastResort, 367
#opnewblood channel, 373
OpNoPro, 308–9
#OpTunisia channel, 147–58
OpWisconsin, 283
Ouassif, Yassine, 360
owen/Owen, 185–9, 190, 213, 214, 227

owning process, 160
Oxblood Ruffin, 138

P
Pagan, 351
Page, Benjamin, 430–1n15
Palantir Technologies, 207, 208, 234, 422n29
Palin, Sarah, 120, 126
Palladium (Donncha O'Cearbhaill): *see* O'Cearbhaill, Donncha (Palladium)
PandaLabs security blog, 121, 122
Panther Moderns, 283
papersplx, 399, 404
Parry, Nigel, 357
Parsons, Leah, 370
Parsons, Rehtaeh, 370, 372
Partnership for Civil Justice Fund, 333
Partyvan Network (IRC), 57
Pastebin, 238, 284, 310, 311, 320, 327, 328, 386
Patriotic Nigras, 19
PayPal, 3, 119, 121, 123–7, 138, 141, 185, 198, 301
PBS, 237, 265
Penny, Laurie, 381
Perlroth, Nicole, 358
Personal Democracy Forum (PDF), 377, 378
Phiber Optik (Mark Abene), 86, 87
philes (textfiles), 279
Philippine National Police, 281
Phillip, Whitney, 32, 396
phishing, 93, 166, 167, 168, 169
Phortune 500 Guide to Unix, 279
phreaking, 35–6, 85
Pinkertons, 209
PIPA (Protect IP Act), 346
Pirate Bay, 97, 98, 100, 101, 106, 107, 111, 216, 289, 301, 346
Pirate Party, 107–8, 110, 112, 154, 390

PKE, 227–8
Plan C, 397
PlayStation Network (PSN), 243, 246, 247, 262
Poitras, Laura, 378, 379
policies/mechanisms for handling operations, 373
political life, emotional character of, 396
political ops, 2
Polish Palikot's Movement Party, 348
polyphony, 131
Poole, Chris (moot), 43
Poulsen, Kevin, 346, 389
pranking, 2, 31, 35, 36, 37, 60
Preska, Loretta, 359, 391, 392
#press channel, 60, 73
primary ideal, of Anonymous, 47
Primitive Rebels (Hobsbawm), 71
Privacy International, 390
private channels (IRC), 10, 102, 116, 155, 157, 240, 253, 332, 362
private intelligence contracting, 234–5
private message (PM), 148, 227, 283, 294, 325
Project Chanology: *see* Chanology/ Project Chanology
Project PM (PPM), 234, 313–14, 338, 387
#propaganda channel, 130, 165, 192
Protest Warrior, 282
proxy, 320
prvt.org, 241
pseudonymous environment, 173, 398
PSN (PlayStation Network), 243, 246, 247, 262
public channels (IRC), 101, 102, 109, 110, 116, 117, 130, 154, 191, 253, 264, 299, 332, 342
Public Knowledge, 89

publicity videos, 6, 11
Puck (trickster), 33–4, 96
#pure-elite channel, 156
pwning, 215, 264, 357
pwnsauce (Darren Martyn), 248–9, 250–1, 264, 290, 353, 384–5
PyLoris, 348

Q
q-lined, 179
Q/q, 213–214
q, 179–80, 185–8, 213–14, 217, 222
Q (Sigurdur "Siggi" Thordarson), 346

R
Radar, 54
Radio Hacking, 279
Radwaddie, 123, 124, 125, 126
Ragan, Steve, 181, 264
rage comic, 239
Rancière, Jacques, 396
random dice day, 88, 90, 95, 96, 98
Random forum, 41
    see also 4chan's random bulletin board /b/
rape culture, 372, 374, 395, 399
Ravel (Sue), 72
Raven (Trickster), 33
Recording Industry Association of America (RIAA), 96, 99, 102, 104, 348
Recursion (Cody Kretsinger), 287, 327
reddit, 26, 44
RedHack, 156
Reed, Harper, 365, 366
Religious Technology Center, 54, 59
#reporter channel, 169, 178, 181, 182, 184, 185, 193, 215, 264
Reporters Without Borders' Press Index, 144
repulsive order of the financiers, 22

Reset the Net, 383
resistance, everyday tactics of, 126
Reuters, 99
RevoluSec, 340, 341
Risen, James, 84, 379
Riseup, 379, 382
rofled, 70
Rolling Stone, 369, 424n23
RollRedRoll.com, 369
root (full administrator), 160
Rosen, Ruth, 364
Rosol, Eric J., 140
Royal Canadian Mounted Police
    (RCMP), 370
RSA Security Inc., 233
rubik, 155, 157, 159, 160, 161–4
ruin life campaigns, 21
Rule #17, 64
Rustle League, 19
Rutherford, Danilyn, 392

S
S., Bernie, 85–6
Sabu (Hector Xavier Monsegur),
    87–8, 155, 156, 181, 215, 218,
    219, 233, 237, 241–2, 248, 251,
    253, 254, 255, 265, 283, 285,
    287–8, 289, 291, 292–3, 294–7,
    299, 312, 318–22, 324, 325–35,
    339, 340, 344–6, 353–62, 390,
    391
Sabutage, 363, 365
Sagada 11, 281
Saleh, Ibrahim, 150
San Francisco BART (Bay Area
    Rapid Transit), 7
    see also Operation BART
    (OpBART)
Sanreckzi, Monica, 371
Santayana, George, 118
Sauter, Molly, 136
#savetpd (Save the Pirate Bay)
    channel, 101
#savetpbmods channel, 102
Schneider, Nathan, 322, 333

Schneier, Bruce, 382
Scientology, Church of: *see* Church
    of Scientology
Scientology-oriented activism
    (4chan thread on), 55
Scientology vs. the Internet, 58
Scott, James, 107
screen session, 320
script kiddies, 158, 282, 285, 326
Sea Org, 77
#!sec channel, 340
secrecy, as sustenance for
    Anonymous participants, 300
secret cabals and channels, 74,
    102, 109, 112, 114, 130, 154,
    248, 250, 292, 297, 299, 319,
    324, 364
secrets, sharing of, 324
security, challenges in, 260
security industry: black hat hackers
    as having contempt for, 285,
    344
    reliance of on hackers and
    researchers, 25
Sennett, Richard, 399
Serious Organised Crime Agency
    (UK), 169, 237, 289
SETI@home, 94
711chan, 55, 57
SF Weekly, 311
Shadowcrew, 420n5
Shapira, Ian, 184
Sharpie, 308–9
shell access, 160
Sheriff's Office of Baldwin County,
    Alabama, 337
shitstorm, 185–8, 190, 193
#ShootingSherrifsSaturday, 300
Shorrock, Tim, 235
Sidi Bouzid, 151
Sifry, Micah, 378
Silverglate, Harvey, 420n8
the sir, 239
skiddies, 158
Skype, 21, 47, 183, 255, 335

Slab City, 22, 23
Slate, 370
Slaughter, Jessi, 44–5, 240
Slim, 144, 173
    see also Amamou, Slim
Smith, Lamar, 234
*Snitching: Criminal Informants
    and the Erosion of American
    Justice* (Natapoff), 360
snitching/snitches, 85–6, 87, 88,
    195, 295, 296, 297–8, 318, 320,
    321, 325, 327, 357, 363, 364
snooty 133t hacker, 263
Snowden, Edward, 171, 301, 302,
    378, 380, 382, 383, 384
social bandits, 71
Social Security numbers, 7, 21, 32,
    216
Soghoian, Chris, 382
Solicitors Disciplinary Tribunal,
    105
Something Awful, 32, 45
Sony, 237, 244, 245, 246, 247,
    260, 262, 263, 327
SonyRecon, 246
SOPA (Stop Online Piracy Act),
    346, 347, 349
SopaStrike.com, 346
Space Rogue, 261
spam bombing, 93, 94
"Special Identities Modernization
    (SIM) Project," 301
specialforces.com, 343
Spitler, Daniel (JacksonBrown), 24
Spooky Business (Center for
    Corporate Policy), 209, 211
St. Jude (Milhon, Jude), 167
Stallman, Richard, 120
Stanford, 36
Steal this Book (Hoffman), 280
Stefan, 261
STEM (Science, Technology,
    Engineering, and Math) fields,
    174
Sterling, Bruce, 279

Stern, Carl, 205
Steubenville, Ohio football case,
    368–73
StickyDrama, 44
Stop Online Piracy Act (SOPA),
    346, 347, 349
Stratfor, 314, 339–45, 349–52,
    357–8, 362, 387
Strauss-Kahn, Dominique, 29
Streisand, Barbara, 53
Streisand Effect, 53
structurelessness, tyranny of, 76
structures of feeling, 432n40
Stuckey, Daniel, 358, 359
Sullivan, William Cornelius, 204
superaltern, 48
surveillance, current style of, 209,
    379–81
Swartz, Aaron, 171, 172, 367–8
Swedish prosecutor, 126
Syria, 143, 359

T
tactics: digital protest, 139–41
    direct action political, 88
    disruptive, 136, 137, 256
    for enforcing ideal of
        egalitarianism, 189
    illegal, 7, 13, 63, 88, 90, 92, 98,
        108, 111, 209, 299, 310
    law-abiding, 108
    legal, 7, 13, 63
    legally gray, 7
    militant, 9
    punishment for offline
        protesting tactics as
        compared to punishment for
        digital protesting tactics, 140
    of resistance, 126
Tails (The Amnesic Incognito Live
    System), 383
Takriz, 151
Tan, 261
Target, 261
Taussig, Michael, 265

TeaMp0isoN, 283
Team Roomba, 19
Team Themis, 208, 209, 228, 234
TeamViewer, 167
Tech Herald, 181
Technical Assistance Program
  (TAP), 280
techno-tricksterism, 35
TED, 267–8, 270
TEDGlobal, 273
Telecomix, 192, 200, 201
textfiles (philes), 279
tflow, 166–73, 215, 241, 248–51,
  252, 283, 289, 290, 291, 299,
  301
Thomas, Douglas, 389
Thompson, Fred, 260
Thordarson, Sigurdur (Siggi) (Q),
  346
tieve.tk, 96
Timm, Trevor, 382
Time magazine, 204
Time Warner, 271
Tinychat, 183
Tits or gtfo (get the fuck out), 195
Topiary, 16, 155, 179–80, 181,
  182–3, 215, 217, 238, 249, 250,
  252, 253, 255, 265, 283, 285,
  288, 289, 290, 291, 293, 299,
  301, 320–1, 363
  see also Davis, Jake (Topiary)
top-level domain (TLD), 159
Tor, 332, 348, 382, 390
TorrentFreak, 98, 106, 108
TorrentSpy, 97
traffic floods, 139
transparency, 36, 75, 76, 84, 182,
  199
tricksters, 33–5, 96, 182, 240, 273,
  274–5, 293, 394
Trogo, 122–3, 124, 125, 126
trolling, 4, 6, 8, 19, 19–46, 32, 35,
  38, 39, 41, 45, 50, 62, 182, 282
Truman, Harry, 203
TTI/Vanguard, 267, 270

Tufekci, Zeynep, 127
TuniLeaks, 149
Tunisia, 2, 142, 143–5, 147–55,
  157–60, 162, 163, 164, 166,
  167, 182, 191, 395
  see also OpTunisia
Tupac article (bogus), 266
Turner, Hal, 65–6
20th Century Fox, 169
2600, 86, 239, 257, 280, 297, 298,
  299
Twitter, 127, 128, 130, 151, 182,
  183, 212, 238, 241, 248, 254,
  257, 265, 286, 293, 307, 318,
  342, 353, 356
Twitter Revolution, 201
2chan.org, 41

U
u4ea, 37, 38
ultracoordinated motherfuckery, 6,
  58, 60, 81, 396
unauthorized access, 24
underground hackers/hacker
  underground, 35, 36, 37, 85,
  174, 194, 253, 258, 264, 314
Universal Music, 348
#upperdeck channel, 114
Urban Dictionary, 45
US Army, 301
US Copyright Office, 348
US Department of Energy, 301
US Department of Homeland
  Security, 333
US Department of Justice, 367
US Federal Reserve, 261, 333
US government: on cyberwarfare
  class of activities, 6
  going after online political
    protesters, 135
  as leading client in market in
    zero-days, 210
  on WikiLeaks most extensive
    leak, 118
US National Security Agency

(NSA), 6, 7, 13, 14, 23, 84, 171, 302, 378–9, 384
US prosecution of hackers, compared to European prosecution of hackers, 388
US Senate, as target of LulzSec, 237
US Sentencing Commission, 367
Usenet, 38–9, 40, 41
USTR (Office of the US Trade Representative), 90, 96

V
V for Vendetta (film), 64, 271, 281
Vanguard Industries, 300–1
Vanity Fair, 184
Venezuela, 143
Vera, Ted, 212, 214, 220, 224
Verizon, 378
Violentacrez, 19
Virtual Private Networks (VPNs), 144, 348
virtual sit-ins, 129, 135–6, 162, 253
Virus (Mike Nieves), 320–1
Visa, 126, 127, 141, 185, 193, 198
Vonnegut, Kurt, 122

W
Wales, Jimmy, 347
Walker, Scott, 277
Wall Street Journal, 6
Wallace, David Foster, 397
Walmart, 209
Wao, Oscar (character), 331
War Resisters League, 203
warez groups, 37
warrants, 190, 193, 194, 215, 287, 386
Warren, Samuel, 379
Washington Post, 184
Washington State Administrative Office of the Courts, 261
"We Are All Very Anxious Now" (Plan C), 397

We Are Anonymous (Olson), 121
We Are Legion (documentary), 331
weapons of the geek vs. weapons of the weak, 107
Weapons of the Weak (Scott), 107
Weatherhead, Chris (Nerdo), 140, 303
#website channel, 72
weev, 20–9, 31, 32, 35, 36, 45, 46, 195, 248, 323
see also Auernheimer, Andrew (weev)
Weld, 261
"What Is LOIC?" (Gizmodo), 134
white hat hackers, 37, 215, 280, 285
white-knight ops, 372
WhyWeProtest, 63, 67, 72, 74, 76
WikiLeaks, 3, 81–5, 87, 88, 118–22, 123–4, 126, 127, 128, 130, 132, 138, 143, 147, 148, 149, 153, 157, 159, 185, 193, 206, 207–8, 213, 234, 265, 267, 282, 298, 312, 313, 326, 343, 345, 346, 349, 352, 366, 382
"The WikiLeaks Threat," 207, 208, 210
Wikipedia, 346, 347
WikiSecrets (film), 265
Williams, Raymond, 432n40
WIN Magazine, 203
Winter, Jana, 356, 357, 365
Wired, 84, 147
Wired.com, 97, 181, 346
Wise Beard Man, 63, 71
Wolf, Asher, 181, 365, 366, 390
Wysopal, Chris, 262
w0rmer (Higinio O. Ochoa III), 305

X
Xetron, 210
The X Factor (TV show), 248, 252

Y
Yahoo! 67, 379
Yettie, 363–4
Yippies, 280
Your Anonymous News/@
    YourAnonNews, 305, 373,
    391
youthful idealism, 173
*The Youth International Party
    Line*, 280
YouTube, 1, 26, 244, 245, 363

Z
Zarathustra (character), 274–5
ZDNet, 288
zero-day/oh day, 158, 159, 210,
    286
zines, 239, 254, 257, 279, 280,
    297, 343
z-lined, 179
zombie flash mob, 70
Zuccotti Park (Liberty Square),
    318, 333
Zuckerman, Ethan, 139

On the Typeface

This book is set in Sabon, a narrow Garamond-style book face designed in 1968 by the German typographer Jan Tschichold. Tschichold had been a leading voice of sans-serif modernist typography, particularly after the publication of his *Die neue Typographie* in 1928. As a result, the Nazis charged him with "cultural Bolshevism" and forced him to flee Germany for Switzerland.

Tschichold soon renounced modernism—comparing its stringent tenets to the "teachings of National Socialism and fascism"—and extolled the qualities of classical typography, exemplified in his design for Sabon, which he based on the Romain S. Augustin de Garamond in the 1592 Egenolff-Berner specimen sheet.

Sabon is named after the sixteenth-century French type-founder Jacques Sabon, a pupil of Claude Garamond and proprietor of the Egenolff foundry.